Select Reviews . . . .

"Having read the astonishing … it reflects my own journey in … the active priesthood. I was private secretary to two diocesan bishops, until in the end my final appointment literally crushed me emotionally even physically and almost spiritually. [I was ill with a virtual nervous breakdown for a year] . . . . Looking back I think my efficiency and dedication to the magisterium showed (the second bishop's) modernist side up so he had to push me out . . . . I would be interested to know when this brave man's book will be published and available.'"

—Edmund, a laicized Catholic priest in a European diocese.

[*Betrayed* . . . is] "exceedingly forthright, charming, humorous in places, poignant in other places and very insightful . . . very nice flow, which lends itself to an easy read."

—Name withheld on request

"I think anyone who reads [*Betrayed by the U.S. Bishops*] would be prompted to do some soul-searching on whether they have done as much as they could to keep the Catholic Church true to Christ's teaching."

—Anonymous

"(T)his book is about your life as a young man from the farm who decided to become a priest, worked in the major apostolate of the Papal Volunteers and engaged in the many global battles therein; retired from the sacred ministry to pursue another type of real ministry and along that way built a beautiful family; this volume . . . is also enhanced with much needed catechesis."

—A Catholic Colleague

"I like the flow and the bits of drama, which add buttress support to your overall presentation. I like the inserts of catechesis.

"Yes, the other heresy that is widely present in the seminaries is a new evolution of Arianism. I got in deep trouble for speaking out against this heresy. The 20th/21st century form of Arianism denies the Consciousness of Christ (i.e. He didn't know He was God—Ed.) Modernists want to posit that He grew in awareness of Himself . . . . It is a demonic subtler form of Arianism . . . ."

—Former Seminarian

BETRAYED:

AN AMERICAN CATHOLIC PRIEST SPEAKS OUT

MODERN HERESIES EXPOSED

The Memoirs of a laicized, married, Roman Catholic Priest

By

Raymond A. Kevane, S.T.L., J.C.D.

authorHOUSE®

AuthorHouse™
1663 Liberty Drive
Bloomington, IN 47403
www.authorhouse.com
Phone: 1-800-839-8640

© 2012 by Raymond A. Kevane. All rights reserved.

No part of this book may be reproduced, stored in a retrieval system, or transmitted by any means without the written permission of the author.

Published by AuthorHouse 07/20/2012

ISBN: 978-1-4685-9432-4 (sc)
ISBN: 978-1-4685-9433-1 (e)

Library of Congress Control Number: 2012907221

Any people depicted in stock imagery provided by Thinkstock are models, and such images are being used for illustrative purposes only.
Certain stock imagery © Thinkstock.

Because of the dynamic nature of the Internet, any web addresses or links contained in this book may have changed since publication and may no longer be valid. The views expressed in this work are solely those of the author and do not necessarily reflect the views of the publisher, and the publisher hereby disclaims any responsibility for them.

Contents

APPENDICES

AN ACT OF CONSCIENCE

On July 1, 1969, I presented my controversial report to the subcommittee of bishops to whom I reported as National Director of the Papal Volunteers for Latin America. From that point on I became conscious that I had someone following me wherever I went for the next five or six ***years***—in Washington, D.C., in Sioux City, Iowa, when I returned there, and finally for a few years after I moved to the west coast. And I received one veiled death threat.

I was followed in such a way that I could not fail to notice that it was happening. In other words, whoever was behind it almost certainly wanted me to know. It was, therefore, an effort to convey a message to me—at least so I hoped. In the midst of all this, while I was waiting for a reaction from the bishops to my report, my telephone was tapped, and, although I reported my concern to the telephone company, they would neither confirm nor deny the tapping. The faint noises which had become a part of every phone conversation, after a few days, stopped entirely—which proved, to me at least, that my phone had indeed been tapped. A truly frightening incident occurred just a few days after my report to the bishops' committee. A very friendly person approached, clearly presenting himself as having my best interests at heart. I had known him for simply a matter of days—not more than a week or so. After a lengthy discussion of my situation, he gave me what was ostensibly a friendly warning: I needed to be very careful, because I could be assassinated; for example, he said, I could end up as an accident on a lonely country road.

Harry Truman, when he was president, said "If you want a friend in Washington, get a dog."

I did not know then and I do not know to this day whether these things (being followed, tapping of my telephone, the death warning) were done by friends or foes. Friends, i.e. good churchmen, might have been trying to dissuade me from going public with the things I knew. If that were true, it would be a matter of 'good' people stooping to actions in which the 'end justifies the means.' If they were 'good,' would they not have simply talked to me about it?

If they were my enemies, their actions served as a warning to me to stay away from the press or any kind of public exposé; if they had seen me visiting a reporter, it is easy to imagine what they might have done to me.

Regardless of any fears anyone might have had along that line, I had no intention of "going public" with any of my knowledge, because I was taken up with the "misguided loyalty" which was prevalent at the time. To me such an action on my part would have put the Church in a bad light, and might have developed into widespread negative publicity.

I am now in my eighties. The ambience is vastly different now than it was then when I was in my early thirties. I had been appointed to the international responsibilities of the PAVLA program at a very young age—about twelve years ordained—because of the three remarkable volunteers who went to the Amazon in Brazil in less than a year after I was appointed Diocesan Director of the Papal Volunteers for Latin America in Sioux City, Iowa. At that time, bishops were rarely criticized. In the forty years during which I have watched the Catholic Church wax and wane, the pedophile priest scandal hit our society and even a certain number of bishops were caught in pedophile activities. But the bishops were criticized the way they handled, or failed to handle, the priests who were caught in those activities.

These days, things have changed dramatically: it is rare that one does not find a pejorative story about some bishop in some magazine or newspaper about once a week (my guess). What I have written, therefore, does not seem at all out of line in this day and age.

Moreover, the newly codified Code of Canon Law of the Catholic Church is much more direct than the previous one in the way it encourages the members of the Church to make public important criticisms they have of the way the authority in the Church is handling their responsibilities, particularly someone like myself with advanced degrees and extraordinary experience. The pertinent Canon is quoted in the first pages of this book.

However, my primary reason for writing this book is to respond to the dictates of my conscience. After these many years I know now that the evil I saw is not restricted to the relatively few people I dealt with in those days. Since I have seen first hand so many things which bring attention to how two principal heresies—Modernism and Americanism—have made enormous inroads into the faith of far too many members of the Catholic Church—Cardinals, Bishops, Clergy, Religious and Laity—bringing ***change*** to the eternal, unchanging doctrine which Jesus Christ left with His Church. This must be stopped or many Catholics will lose their souls.

THE TITLE OF THIS BOOK

The heresy of Americanism is so deeply entrenched among the U.S. Bishops that they allowed a lay apostolate program initiated by a Pope to die because they failed to give it the support it needed and deserved. This will become clear as this book unfolds. Hence, the title ***"Betrayed."***

DEDICATION

It is a great honor and privilege for me to dedicate this book to those on this earth whom I admire much more than most: ***The Papal Volunteers for Latin America***—those who served before, during and after my tenure as National Director of the program. There were hundreds of them in nineteen countries during the five years when I was in charge. I don't know how many there were during the year or two before I arrived, and I don't know how many in the year the program lasted after I resigned. I believe all of them came into the program with a spirit of adventure, but, knowing a great many of them as I did, I am certain that all of them joined the program because of their deep faith and their intense desire to be involved in the work of the Church.

I wish also to dedicate this book to the many **Diocesan PAVLA Directors** who were working hard to recruit volunteers and develop the means of supporting them during their service in Latin America. By the time I resigned, more than 100 had been appointed. And the dedication extends also to those bishops who saw the program as truly a work of the Church.

A special mention, very important to me, goes to the **Lay Advisory Board in Sioux City**, two attorneys and an insurance agent—all chosen because they had the special recommendation of their pastors—who worked with me as we planned the diocesan program. They worked with me without compensation, and I do not recall that they even received expenses. They were a dedicated group. Probably none of the four of us will ever forget how we felt when, after a well-attended presentation in Fort Dodge, Iowa, three who were to be our first volunteers—two men and a woman, a teacher, an electrician and a nurse—worked their way through the crowd to the stage to tell us they wanted to join. After a few months of preparation, they were assigned to the Archdiocese of Manaus on the Amazon River in northern Brazil. Their service was exemplary. That initial success led me to be chosen as the National Director.

In that same context, I know that **other diocesan directors had advisory boards** who deserve special mention, and I myself, after a year or so, had a **twelve member National Planning Board**, including one of those who had worked with me in Sioux City. This latter group—comprised of returned Papal Volunteers, diocesan directors, members of local diocesan advisory boards, Latin American laity and priests, and one carefully chosen bishop—also served without compensation, but, as I recall, they did receive expenses.

The Papal Volunteers for Latin America visibly captured the imaginations of untold numbers of people who wanted to see it flourish. The program therefore was a danger to those, who, for their own nefarious reasons, did not want to see the power of the lay apostolate unleashed in support of the Church and her growth. Since these lay volunteers were supported by the bishop in whose diocese they originated, and since they were received and supported by the bishop of the diocese in the country to which they were assigned, they became a powerful force to preserve the structure of the Catholic Church as it has existed for many centuries. Foreseeing this, those forces in the U.S. and Latin America who wanted to topple and ***replace*** the structure of the Church in the western hemisphere saw fit to destroy the Papal Volunteer program. There will be much more on this subject as the book progresses.

ACKNOWLEDGMENTS

There is an almost endless list of those who gave me unflagging support throughout my twenty years in the active priesthood. Above all else, of course, I owe everything that I am and that I have to my parents whose devotion to the Church and to their faith was total, even in the midst of and throughout the depth of the Great Depression and the worst of its aftermath.

Two of my brothers have always been outstanding role models. They are Monsignor Eugene Kevane, my oldest brother, who died in 1996, and my second oldest brother, Philip Kevane, who is remarkably active at the age of 93, ten years older than I. I am the youngest of six.

My wife Lillian and I—for me there is no doubt—were destined for each other from all eternity. Through a series of events which only God could have engineered, we were available to each other after the dreadful events in Washington, D.C. and after Pope Paul VI granted my request for laicization with permission to marry. With her help I was able to accept the suffering I had to bear, to forgive and to pray for all those at whose hands I had suffered.

John Cardinal Cody, Archbishop of Chicago, in charge of one of the largest dioceses in the world, always took time to talk with me, and, toward the end, used his authority to have the PAVLA program taken away from the Latin America Bureau and established in an independent Lay Apostolate agency. Unfortunately he failed. He was pitted against Cardinal Dearden, Archbishop of Detroit and President of the U.S. Conference of Bishops at the time, who had chosen Bishop Joseph Bernardin, Director of the USCC, who in turn supported Father Colonnese, Director of the Latin America Bureau of which PAVLA was a part. The day finally came when Cardinal Cody called me and told me, "We've lost. You had just as well return to your diocese." As the reader will see, I did as he suggested.

Not too much later, Cardinal Cody died in agony, excoriated and lied about because he was devoted to the Pope and to traditional doctrine. After his death, because of his extensive suffering, he was described as a modern day martyr, and someone said about him: "God certainly knows how to put the finishing touches on a special soul."

Monsignor Claire Dwyer, PAVLA diocesan director in the Archdiocese of Baltimore, was a good friend of mine. After the presentation of my report to the bishops' subcommittee, (see Part IV, Chapter 35) I visited him. For the first time since my move to Washington D.C., I told him the whole story including the report to the bishops. He whistled and said, "You've pushed at the power tower." He meant that I couldn't possibly win, and of course he was right.

The Archbishop of Mexico City in 1964-1969 gave me every support I requested, including personally dedicating the *Hogar Interamericano*, our own language training center for the volunteers on the way to their assignments. His own personal representative was Father Hector Samperio, a prince of a priest who was responsible for most of the successes of PAVLA in Mexico.

The Archbishop of Salvador, in northeast Brazil, was a saintly bishop among generally holy bishops. Once I slept on a (very uncomfortable) couch in his residence; another time, when he was gone on a trip, he invited me to sleep in his (very comfortable) bed. Most Latin American bishops offered me their guest rooms, but in most instances I had already been offered lodging where the volunteers were stationed. An interesting comparison: I was never invited to stay in the residence of a U.S. bishop.

The contributions of John Muldoon and Madeline Creason—both former Papal Volunteers who gave additional time in PAVLA's National Office—are described in Part IV, Ch. 48 of this book.

I deeply respect the Office of Bishop and bishops themselves as successors to the Apostles.

CHAPTER 1

Introduction

Dying Man on a Street in Portland, Oregon

On an occasion that I will never forget (1973/74), a year or so after my wife and I were married before the Chancellor of the Archdiocese of Portland in Oregon, I was walking on a street in downtown Portland one afternoon, when I saw a man who had collapsed on the street about 30 feet or so ahead of me. His eyes were visibly fixed on me and followed me as I walked. The crowd around him seemed to part appropriately so he could watch me—or so that I could watch him. I was very conscious of what I had learned in my years of study in Theology and Canon Law: Even though I was laicized, I had the authority and the obligation to give a dying person the last rites and to give at least conditional absolution to him or her. Convinced that this man was dying, I pronounced the words of conditional absolution as I moved toward him. When I finished, he smiled, continued to look at me, and died; I saw the vacant look come into his eyes. I am convinced as he lay dying he was given the knowledge that I was a priest and knew that I was giving him absolution.

I hope and believe it is true that I helped this man save his soul. I take deep and personal satisfaction knowing that I was able to do the same on other occasions for another ten or twelve dying people.

This all began nearly 60 years ago when I was ordained a Catholic priest in Rome, Italy, on December 19, 1953, in the course of four years of study of Theology. Twenty years later, in 1972, at my own request, I was laicized by Pope Paul VI with permission to marry. The reasons for my request will be disclosed later in this book.

Everything written in this book is intended to edify, not to denigrate. It is written in the spirit of deepest respect and love for the Church as the Mystical Body of Christ. This includes the Pope, the bishops and clergy, the religious, and the broad base of the faithful, and including those whose consciences are such that if they knew the true intent of Christ, they would become Catholics.

This book may be well characterized as my ***memoirs***, but also as an ***exposé***. With fifty nine years, as I write, since I was ordained a Catholic priest, fifty eight years since I earned my Licentiate in Theology and fifty five years since I was awarded my Doctorate in Canon Law, I have seen a great deal and, while I have seen so many, many good people, religious, priests, bishops and cardinals, I believe I can say without hesitation, "I have seen it all (almost)." At any rate, I would never have attempted to write this book unless I felt I could shed some light on the state of the Catholic Church in the United States in the last half of the 20th century and the early 21st century. In doing so, I hope to help strengthen those whose faith may be shaken by current events. I hope that what I write can to some degree reverse the harm that has befallen the Catholic Church from the time that I was a little boy until now when I am in the twilight of my life.

As the reader moves through the book, he or she will find that my background includes the elements which the Code of Canon Law requires for the Christian faithful to express their opinions on Church matters to the authorities:

> According to the knowledge, competence, and prestige which they possess, [the Christian faithful] have the right and even at times the duty to manifest to the sacred pastors their opinion on matters which pertain to the good of the

> Church and to make their opinion known to the rest of the Christian faithful, without prejudice to the integrity of faith and morals, with reverence toward their pastors, and attentive to common advantage and the dignity of persons. (Canon 212, §3)

During my more than eighty years, I've had a breadth and depth of education and experience which many do not have. I would never trade it for something else, although, as is clearly portrayed, my life had a balance of difficult occurrences as well as miraculously positive ones.

In the theology of the Catholic Church, a priest is ordained forever, (in the liturgy of ordination, the ordaining bishop says to each candidate, "Thou art a priest forever, according to the order of Melchisedech") and that priesthood cannot be taken away. This sacrament, like others, imprints an indelible mark on the soul which in heaven will lead to greater glorification, and in hell to greater degradation. I therefore explicitly retain the power to confect and administer the sacraments. As a matter of obedience, however, I am generally restricted from doing so.

Since the day of my ordination to the priesthood, I had embedded into me and have carried within me that specific Sanctifying Grace which is unique to the Sacrament of Orders.

* * *

I'd like to proceed chronologically through five different segments of my life from early life on a farm in Iowa, through college and seminary education. I'll describe my life as a priest, including my additional experiences in Europe, my duties in diocesan offices, followed by national and international responsibilities. Later, my life as a laicized married priest, starting when I was forty two years of age, added a new perspective to my many years of experience with the Church.

Parts I to V deal with five segments of my life. Parts VI-&VII are conclusions which I hope the reader will find enlightening and useful. Part IV has a special prominence in that it deals with the Papal Volunteers for Latin America, one of the very most important programs of the Lay Apostolate in the history of the Church, brought into being by a Pope and gaining a special prominence. And it was my honor to be appointed the director of that international lay apostolate program and my duty to defend against its enemies.

In the course of my local, national and international duties, I encountered two principal heresies which are in the process of trying to modify the unchangeable doctrine of the Church. They are the Heresies of Americanism and of Modernism. I will expose these as we come across them. The Papal Encyclicals which first identified these heresies are given in full in Appendix B and Appendix C of this book. They merit our study so that we will be better prepared to support the doctrines which Christ left with His Church.

* * *

I love the Catholic Church. And as my far-from-perfect spiritual life becomes—as I sincerely hope—stronger and I become closer to Christ, the Trinity, and the Blessed Mother, my love of the Church as the Mystical Body of Christ grows stronger with the passing years. Now, in the later years of my life, I feel the obligation in conscience to point out to my brothers and sisters in Christ—bishops, clergy, religious and laity—how the Catholic Church in the United States, through the actions and inaction of its imperfect representatives of Christ, has drifted grievously from the directives which Christ Himself imposed and which the Popes in Rome have faithfully preserved and expounded over the centuries. I believe I have the right to do so and the obligation to do so because of my education, because of what I have become, and because of what I have seen and experienced, as will be recounted.

"Your Brother was Absolutely Right. We Should Have Listened to Him."

These words were spoken by Cardinal Umberto Madeiros, Archbishop of Boston, to my brother, Rev. Msgr. Eugene Kevane, within two years after I resigned my position as national director of the Papal Volunteers for Latin America. On July 1,1969 when I presented my report to the committee of bishops who oversaw the Papal Volunteer program, before he was a Cardinal, Bishop Madeiros, Bishop of Brownsville, was a member of that committee. As my brother explained it, "The Cardinal ate humble pie," in saying that the bishops should have listened to me.

When I learned at the time of the meeting in 1969 that Bishop Medeiros could not attend, my heart sank, because he was a strong bishop and unquestionably loyal both to the Pope and to Church Doctrine. His absence was to have a massive effect on the outcome. This is one of the many factors which caused me to entitle this book ***"Betrayed***", because in spite of his belated insight (and, I assume, the insight of an unknown number of others), the Papal Volunteer program was allowed to fade from history.

After I resigned my position as National Director of the Papal Volunteers for Latin America and returned to my own Diocese of Sioux City, Bishop Joseph M. Mueller supported me fully, appointed me Chancellor of the diocese, and he assured me at the time the priests of the diocese also supported me. A few months later, I found this to be absolutely true. As Chancellor of the diocese, I was in the middle of a meeting of priests. I don't recall the purpose of the meeting, but at some point one of the priests brought up a sidebar and asked me a few questions about the PAVLA fiasco I had undergone in Washington, D.C. He concluded by saying (I'll never forget his words), "The bishops really hung you out to dry." The rest of the priests in that group clearly agreed with him. What that priest said suggested the title of this book. Rightly or wrongly, by that time, because of the way they handled the pedophile priest crisis, the bishops had gained a reputation as not being completely loyal to or supportive of their priests, but, "to save their own skins" were willing to play politics and condemn the priests who were charged without giving them much of a hearing. The bishops were criticized by the Vatican for the way they handled it, and were reprimanded by the conference of Religious Superiors for mishandling the problem.

A practical way to describe the Heresy of Americanism is to say that, in the eyes of such a heretic, the Constitution of the United States is at least equal to, if not superior to, the doctrines which Jesus Christ established with the Apostles to safeguard for all time in His Church. This translates, in a burst of political correctness, into the thought that alleged pedophile priests are to be condemned without any presumption of innocence (the concept of *'zero tolerance')*.

The title ***"Betrayed"*** is more than appropriate because the events surrounding the demise of the Papal Volunteer program—which was an example of the lay apostolate at the highest level—represents ***betrayal*** at several levels.

First of all, Christ Himself called for the involvement of the laity in the work of the Church—in their families, in the holiness of their lives within society, and they worked shoulder to shoulder with the Apostles, the first bishops and clergy in the Early Church. The laity were called by Christ, not by the hierarchy as is commonly supposed. Therefore, the (in)action of the bishops in letting the Papal Volunteer program die was a betrayal of Christ Himself.

Second, since the Church is in fact the Mystical Body of Christ and carries within it at all times all the commands of Christ, there is the on-going requirement for the laity to infuse their personal holiness into their families, their work-day world and their social life. The bishops' action in allowing the Papal Volunteer program to be terminated was a betrayal of the Church.

Third, the Papal Volunteer program was initiated by Pope Paul VI, the Vicar of Christ, whose actions were of compelling importance. I'm sure the bishops gave no thought to this fact as they failed to support perhaps the most important activity of the Lay Apostolate of all time—described as such by the Apostolic Delegate at the time that the PAVLA headquarters was in Chicago (1964-1966). It is speculation on my part, but I am as sure as I can be that, in professional solidarity, the conference of bishops conformed to the wishes of a fellow bishop, Joseph Bernardin, who is sufficiently described in the text of this book as an anti-Church pedophile. In so doing, they betrayed their own Pope.

Fourth, the bishops betrayed Vatican Council II, some of whom were perhaps present during some of its sessions. The Council presents the Lay Apostolate as a most important element in the overall work of the Church in leading God's people to holiness.

Fifth, hundreds of Papal Volunteers individually spent three years in an assigned diocese in nineteen countries of Latin America. I have no idea of their individual holiness, but I am sure, from my own personal observation, that many (most) of them were daily communicants, giving the finest kind of example to the teachers, electicians, doctors, nurses, etc. among whom they worked. The bishops of Latin America in whose dioceses the volunteers worked uniformly gave them high praise. Representative of many Latin American bishops, the President of the Chilean Conference of Bishops, put his praise into writing and sent it to me at the PAVLA National Office. Clearly, the U.S. bishops betrayed those wondrous volunteers who did such marvelous work.

Sixth, it is obvious that the Catholic Church in Latin America has been betrayed by our bishops, in that the Catholics of Latin America—bishops, clergy, religious, laity—were looking forward to an entirely new and different relationship between the religious people of the two cultures.

Seventh, I must confess that for years I, as the National Director of the PAVLA program, have felt betrayed by the bishops when they failed to support me and the program, ignoring all the evidence I had provided to them, taking two years, after PAVLA was disbanded, to acknowledge that I ". . . had been absolutely right, and they should have listened to him." That helped, of course, but it did not take away the fact that they had failed to support me in a most important undertaking and allowed the work the Volunteers and I had done to fade into obscurity.

What I Hope This Book Can Accomplish

In the following pages, I will present in chronological order my lifetime of experiences, beginning with the 160 acre farm where my five siblings and I were born and raised in Northwest Iowa, through twenty three years of formal schooling which ended with a doctorate in Rome, Italy, three years after I was ordained a priest.

You will read about the many simultaneous responsibilities I was given after my return to my diocese. They were not an overload (as some have said) but were a personal pleasure and, relatively minor in terms of responsibility and work when compared, in their totality, with what I consider the culmination of my priestly career: National Director of the Papal Volunteers for Latin America, chronicled in Part IV of this book. This responsibility provided me the intensely pleasurable and spiritually uplifting experience of working with many sincerely devout men and women of this country and sending them to work among and for the sincerely devout bishops, religious and laity of the Catholic Church in as many as nineteen countries of Latin America. At that same time, I wrestled with evil. I saw and worked among bishops and priests who were completely enslaved by the Heresies of Americanism and Modernism—and worse, as the reader will see. And I wrestled with specific bishops, priests and laity who bent every effort to destroying the Papal Volunteer program, because they feared it would interfere with their own intention to implant a Marxist philosophy into the Church in all countries of Latin America.

There are a number of things which I hope the publishing of this book can accomplish:

1. **The hundreds of Papal Volunteers who gave three years of their lives in service to the Church in Latin America deserve to emerge from the obscurity into which the lack of support by the bishops has thrust them.** Not long ago, in speaking to a very prominent convert to Catholicism, I mentioned the "Papal Volunteers for Latin America," and he said, "What's that?" Since the PAVLA program was what it was, it seems to me it should be mentioned in every convert training program as a prime example of the Apostolate of the Laity. I urge every bishop who may read this book to promote awareness of the Papal Volunteers and of what they accomplished. Their incredible accomplishment is described in Part VI of this book.
2. **Hopefully this book can help those U.S. Bishops who lean toward the Heresies of Americanism and Modernism to recognize the error of their ways and return to complete loyalty to the Vicar of Christ in the Vatican.**
3. **Many Catholics have lost their way** (see studies in Part VII, Chapters 52, 53, and 54). They have lost their belief in the Real Presence, fail to attend Mass as required, support abortion and artificial contraception, believe they can validly divorce and remarry, and many other aberrations. I pray that this book may provide some of the grace required to help them overcome the Modernist, Americanist forces which pull them away from the Eternal Truths which the Catholic Church gives them and bring them back to the practice of the True Faith.
4. **There are non-Catholics who are openly seeking the Truth. I hope that this book can help some of them to make the final decision of conversion to the Catholic Church.**
5. **Pope Benedict XVI recently established an office in the Vatican called the "*New Evangelization*" which is intended to re-kindle the practice of the Catholic Faith in every**

country of the world. The success of the Papal Volunteer program as described in Part IV of this book can serve as an example of how the Pope's ***New Evangelization*** program can be achieved.

PART I

BIRTH TO COLLEGE GRADUATION: 1928 TO 1946

CHAPTER 2

My Family Tree

My grandfather—my father's father—some said, was a genius. An Irish immigrant from Dingle, Ireland, Tom Kevane came through Ellis Island as a young man, worked his way to Northwest Iowa, got married, started his family, and acquired many hundreds of acres of land which no one wanted. He chose all low land, given to flooding, leaving large ponds after heavy rains. He foresaw what no one else did: That the land could be tiled so that the flooded land would quickly drain, leaving behind some of the most fertile fields in that part of Iowa.

I remember him for the first time when he was thought to be in his nineties. But he didn't know exactly how old he was. I remember nothing of his wife—she was 'bald as an egg' someone said. I don't remember anything of my other two grandparents on my mother's side. I know only that they immigrated from Germany from the small farming town of Steinefrenz, less than 100 miles north of Frankfurt and perhaps100 miles east of the city of Cologne.

When my Irish grandfather came through Ellis Island, he neither spoke nor wrote English. When he gave his name in the original Irish, someone wrote it as 'Tom Kevane,' a name that usually came into English as Cavanaugh or Kavanagh. But as it was written then and as it is written now, it is pronounced within the family as ***Kuh-ván.*** We think that is the original Gaelic pronunciation.

My parents, Michael Kevane (no middle name) and Sarah Agnes Distel were both born in northwest Iowa within a few months of each other in 1886, he a second generation Irish-American, she a second generation German-American. When they were married, an Irish/German union was looked upon with great disfavor, but they weathered that and became an outstanding and respected couple in the communities they related to: 1) Storm Lake, the Buena Vista County seat and home to St Mary's Parish to which they belonged; 2) Rembrandt, a very small town about five miles NE from the farm; and 3) Truesdale, an even smaller town about two to three miles SSE of the farm. Storm Lake is10 miles south from the farm and was a long journey every week to Sunday Mass, first by horse and buggy (which I don't remember), then by Model T Ford, then by Model A Ford . . . and so on. My parents were both devout Catholics by family tradition and birth and they did their best to pass that on to all six of their children. They succeeded, apparently totally. My mother had an eighth grade education, my father not quite that much. They taught us by their personal example which was no less than outstanding, and by ensuring that we studied and memorized the Baltimore Catechism.

[When many years later in Chicago I told a Modernist, Feminist nun that after four years of Theology and three years of Canon Law, all in Rome, my faith remained precisely the same as they had taught me as a child. She was very skeptical. The full training I had received in Rome simply expanded on all they had taught me and gave me the Scriptural, Traditional, Theological, Philosophical and Rational basis for those truths. She retorted, rather testily, "That's impossible. The Church has changed." Which meant, of course, if she was talking about doctrine, that she herself was into heresy. It's generally accepted doctrine that Divine Revelation to mankind was closed with the death of the last Apostle, and that body of revealed truth was given to the Church to guard. It was this that prompted St. Paul to entreat Timothy, "O Timothy, guard the Deposit entrusted to you." (1 Timothy 6:20)]

The Farm

Shortly after my parents' wedding, my grandfather sold one of his parcels of land to them. Later, because of the Depression my parents couldn't make the payments and he simply deeded it over to them, as a gift. It was a farm of 160 acres with a house, barn, and several other outbuildings. My mother was 42 years of age when I was born on Dec. 18, 1928, something of an afterthought, she often said.

Education

All of my siblings and I attended Scott Center Grade and Junior High School, about 1½ miles from our house. We walked, therefore, three miles every school day. I remember one day when there had been a foot or more of snow when my father walked ahead to break a trail for the youngest three of us.

The first five years of my education were spent in this one-room school house, which consisted in one classroom for eight grades of students, and a one-room apartment for the teacher. She was on premises for five days each week and stayed the weekend or went home depending on circumstances. The school building was centered on one acre of land, had two outhouses, no internal facilities; I have no memory at all about availability of water. The school closed in 1939 at the end of my fifth year, although it still stands as a voting precinct.

To summarize: My formal education began in a one room school house in Scott Township, Buena Vista County, Iowa, and ended with a Licentiate in Sacred Theology from the Gregorian University in Rome, Italy, staffed by the leading Jesuits of the time, and a doctorate in Canon Law from the Lateran University in Rome, Italy, staffed by professors selected from the Vatican City State. These were two of the most prestigious universities in the world, and if I'm not mistaken after all these years, they still are. My formal education spanned twenty three years. Scott Center school produced three doctoral students. Oddly enough, the other two were my oldest brother Eugene, and my third youngest brother Clement.

My Vocation

I began my four years of high school in the fall of 1942 at Rembrandt High School. We used to say facetiously that there were 100 people in Rembrandt when we happened to be in town. Actually it probably had a few hundred residents, as it does to this day.

We were the only Catholic family for miles around. It was a heavily Lutheran community and, as I recall, we were treated as a family with great respect and friendship without exception. Until my senior year in high school, I had not a single Catholic school mate. There were two Catholic students in my senior year.

I believe I developed my determination to study for the priesthood sometime during my grade school years, perhaps initially triggered by the fact that my oldest brother, Eugene, was sent to Rome to study for the priesthood when I was five years old. I was nine when he came home, and he was a complete stranger to me at that time. The intention of becoming a priest stayed quietly and consciously in my mind throughout grade school and high school, during all the work on the farm.

It didn't occur to me to discuss my plans with any of my family until my Junior or Senior year when the question came up about what I would do after graduation. We then talked to my brother the priest, then to our pastor at St. Mary's parish in Storm Lake, and finally to the bishop. I never wavered in my plans.

CHAPTER 3

Life on the Farm

There was/is no better place to grow up than on a farm. After all these years, I am convinced that this is true. It was a great blessing for me. We were isolated enough to simply live by our own moral values, even as we had friendly and respectful neighbors with whom we could, and did, interact.

"Early to bed and early to rise, makes one healthy, wealthy and wise." There is a grain of truth in that old saying, but it needs to be qualified a bit in our case.

Fairly early to bed and really early to rise (the cows always needed to be milked so they wouldn't start bawling because of the pressure on their mammary glands), working hard all day from dawn to dusk (except Sunday, of course), led all or most of us to good health. We were, however, living proof that it did not lead to any kind of wealth—except an interior, spiritual kind—and living off the land did engender a kind of practicality and common sense that stays with a person for the rest of his life, throughout all facets of his life, with an understandable number of mistakes.

After growing up on a farm, one learns to work, how to work, and learns everything from carpentry to field work. One of my classmates, Dwight, was endlessly competing with me in everything, from school (he was a 'C' student, I was pretty much on a straight

'A' track; he was a poor athlete while I was the star of the school, etc., etc.) One day when we were shelling our corn in preparation for selling it, he came to our farm with his father who was a trucker. I was shoveling ear corn into the trench in the middle of the corn crib onto a conveyor which took the corn into the shelling machine. He took my shovel and began to shovel the corn fast and furious to demonstrate how much better he was than I. If my memory is accurate, he lasted no more than five minutes, certainly not even ten. While he was big and strong, he was raised in town, and therefore never had to do hard work, nor had he learned how; this incident occurred about 3:00 p.m. I had been working since 8 or 9 in the morning and probably went on for another couple of hours. When one does hard work day after day for 8 or 10 hours, it is essential to learn how to pace oneself. And that has many ramifications into the rest of one's life.

Life on the farm was an unending series of long working days, a variety of work experiences, working with hand tools, building, dealing with the birth (and sometimes death) of pigs and cattle—a learning experience which I would say is second to none. One snowy, blustery day in the middle of winter, I was sent to follow one of our sows which was about to have piglets for the first time. My father and mother somehow knew that this mother pig would have a problem. I found about eight or ten little newly born pigs along three fence lines of our pasture (about a ten acre field), put them each in a gunny sack as I found them, took them back to the house where my mother put them in the oven of our kitchen stove until they were warmed up enough to be taken back to the barn and attached to their mother.

One day I was walking with my mother across our yard and saw a rooster attacking a hen. I asked my mother, "Why do they do that?" She responded, somewhat testily, "Oh, figure it out for yourself." That was the extent of my sex education at home, except much later for a small book which my older brother received from a priest friend of his. What my mother said was enough. She knew that I already understood. It doesn't take much time on a farm to observe how cows, pigs and horses propagate themselves, and it doesn't take long to transfer that to an understanding of how human children come to be born.

CHAPTER 4

My College Years

As I said earlier, during my junior and senior years of high school, I made it known that I wanted to study for the priesthood. It was decided that I would attend Trinity College in Sioux City, Iowa. I started as a Freshman there beginning the fall of 1946, shortly after World War II ended. It was an intimidating experience for me, to move from a completely rural life to a large city and a college with many more students than attended our small high school. I was a country boy, and all of my school mates, as I recall, were born and raised in the city. There were probably some exceptions, but I didn't know it at the time.

My First Temptation to Change My Career

During my high school years, I believe I had the reputation as an outstanding pitcher. Although our baseball team, as a team, was no more than second rate, we won almost all of our games, primarily because I would usually allow only two to three hits per game (our problem was in our fielding errors), and I would have eighteen to twenty one strikeouts per seven inning game. In spite of how good I was as a pitcher and generally as a baseball player, I gave no thought at that time to any career other than the priesthood.

On the same campus as Trinity College was Trinity High School, a boys school, with students from the entire Sioux City, Iowa area. The high school had an excellent baseball team. Their coach somehow found out about my ability as a pitcher and asked me to pitch to his team during batting practice. Their coach asked me to do two things: 1) pitch to them in such a way as to let them hit, and in another segment, 2) do my best to strike them out. During the second phase of batting practice, I was able to strike most of them out, or they would pop up, or hit easy grounders.

They were a good enough team that major league scouts visited them occasionally. One day during one of the batting practices, a New York Yankee scout stood behind me to watch them bat. When the session was over, he volunteered to me that I could almost certainly pitch in the major leagues, but he also advised me that it would be a hard life. (Maybe he was a Catholic and knew I was studying for the priesthood.) At any rate, his opinion of my pitching ability hit me hard and it constituted a temptation to revise my career plans. But I decided against making a change, partly because of his warning of how hard a life it would be. Always a baseball fan, and following the lives of many of the major league players, it didn't take me long to set aside all regret that I had decided not to pursue a baseball career. And I have been grateful to that Yankee scout that he had been so direct and honest with me about the kind of life that baseball players had to live.

Homosexuality—My First (but not last) Encounter

I never saw homosexuality in the animal world. Once in a great while, I saw a cow somewhat half-heartedly and for a few seconds mount another cow, but it never occurred to me to think anything good or bad about the act. When I saw a bull mount a cow and stay with it for an extended period of time, that had enormous significance for the growth of our herd and the livelihood of our family.

When, about half way through my first year of college, I encountered true homosexuality, I was totally unprepared, and, in my naiveté, had no idea what was happening nor how to handle it.

On this particular afternoon, one of my classmates came to my room, engaged in general conversation, and then locked my door, came to me, put his arms around me and kissed me on the lips. It made me terribly uncomfortable, and I thought he would notice that and stop. But he kept at me until finally I was more than uncomfortable—which he noticed and misinterpreted. He said "Get a towel." He himself got my towel and when he came back to me, I told him "I've never done anything like this before." He immediately stopped, left my room, and two days later left the seminary. This incident came entirely out of the blue. If there were any prior warning signs that this classmate was building up to this encounter, I simply didn't see them.

For reasons I do not know, homosexuals over the years seem to have been attracted to me. There were many encounters in the course of my younger life—through my twenties and thirties. These incidents, which will come up as I proceed with these reminiscences, have taught me a number of things about the homosexual personality and ways to deal with them firmly but with charity and patience. I'll come to those perceptions later in this work. For example, during my Theology studies in Rome, Father Edwin Healey, S.J. spent a great deal of time in teaching us how to deal with the homosexual in the confessional.

CHAPTER 5

Loras College—
Sophomore to Senior Years

Trinity College and High School closed at the end of the 1946-1947 school year, primarily I believe because my brother Father Eugene Kevane had organized and built the 13 parish central Catholic High School in Sioux City, Iowa, named after an earlier bishop, Heelan Catholic High School.

Therefore, in the fall of 1947, I entered my Sophomore year all the way across the state at Loras College in Dubuque, Iowa. In one sense, it was a high quality college, having a preponderance of very good professors, with a few who were frankly terrible. We had the expected courses in literature, three years of Latin, one course in Greek which taught me the alphabet, some phrases that were later useful, but I certainly did not learn how to speak it. The same was true of Latin, but later in Theology I learned how to speak, write and converse in Latin. It was a good rounded education. I graduated with a 3.9 average (out of 4.0)—among the few leaders in the class.

As I look back on it, the most important courses for me at the time and applicable in later studies, were the various courses in Philosophy. It was very important to me, both at the time and later in the study of Theology, to learn how the mind works and to develop an understanding of the material and spiritual sides of our lives. It was important to know—for example—as we see a tree that a picture forms in our mind in some abstract form what a tree is, so that if later we see a tree we have never encountered before, we instantly recognize it as a tree. In a similar fashion, we form a mental image of a cat, and thereafter will immediately recognize a cat, be it large or small.

It was also important to learn that all things, whether material or spiritual, are composed of two elements: *essence* and *existence*. A cat and a tree both have *existence*; but it is their *essence* that makes them to be what they are. In a similar fashion, all things have *substance* and *accidents*. It is the accidents which differentiate each from the other. So the essence and accidents of, *e.g.*, a tree are roots, trunk, branches and leaves and immobility. The essence and accidents of cats are mobility, agility, a mind which is limited, etc.

We will consider later on how these concepts apply to Theology, *e.g.* how we can demonstrate that the limited knowledge we have of God is rationally possible even as we do not understand the things we know, and how, through the infinite power of God, there can be such a thing as His Real Presence in what appears to be bread and wine. The accidents (appearance) of bread can remain, but the substance—by the unlimited power of God—is changed into Christ Himself.

After three years at Loras College I graduated *summa cum laude* in 1950, and the next important phase of my life began that fall.

PART II

FOUR YEARS OF STUDY OF THEOLOGY IN ROME AND TRAVEL IN EUROPE: 1950 TO 1954

CHAPTER 6

The Trip to Rome, Italy

Toward the end of my senior year at Loras College, Most Rev. Jos. M. Mueller, Bishop of Sioux City, informed me that I would be sent to the North American College in Rome, Italy, for four years of study of Theology and ultimately to be ordained to the priesthood. A classmate of mine, Dean Walz, another Iowan, was also being sent to Rome by the Archdiocese of Dubuque. We began to make plans for the trip, finally deciding to travel from New York on a relatively small Greek ship called the *Nea Helas* (New Greece) which was to have one stop-over in Lisbon, Portugal and finally land at Naples, Italy, with a final roughly two hour train trip to Rome. The only truly terrible experience on that trip was my own seasickness

The House on Humility Street

We were met in Naples, Italy, by George McFadden, a seminarian from Sioux City who had been sent to Rome the year before. He accompanied us by train to Rome and took us to the North American College in roughly the center of Rome on *Via dell'Umiltá* 30 (Humility Street #30). There I met Monsignor Richard Burns, the Vice Rector, who assigned me a room and gave the small group of us who had arrived that day our initial orientation. It was considerably later that we met Most Rev. Martin J. O'Connor, the Rector, with whom we had only occasional contact because he was extremely busy with the construction of the new North American College on the Gianiculum Hill, which was a short distance from Vatican City and St. Peter's Basilica. We didn't know this at the time, but, after three years at the Casa (which we called the House—Casa—on Humility Street), we were to move into the new North American College in 1953, where my class was to spend our fourth and final year—1953-1954—in the study of Theology.

My first year in Rome was particularly difficult. The transition from years of living and working on a farm and attending a small college, and then adjusting to an entirely different culture was a major challenge. To learn a new language—Italian—and to attend classes given in a language in which I was not yet proficient—Latin—was both unsettling and intimidating. I don't know if I took longer than others to make the adjustment, but I do know it continued as a personal problem for several months. But there was a particularly difficult insight which I wrestled with during that first year.

Study and Life as a Seminarian

And thus began seven years of study and travel in Europe—seven years which reshaped my life and gave me an experience for which I have been grateful all my life. My school mates numbered about 150—my memory is very faulty and I'm guessing—representing probably 30 or more states and more or less 100 out of 194 dioceses in the U.S.

A bit later on, I will explain the theological insights which I had during those years, and the doctrines of the Church which have always had special meaning for me.

CHAPTER 7

My First Real Understanding of Evil in the World

During my first and second year as a seminarian at the North American College in Rome, I had an experience which shaped my perspective for the rest of my life, one to which I should have paid more conscious attention in later years than I did. At that time, the communist party was making a major effort to win the national elections in Italy. The struggle was headline news, as I remember it, for weeks and months. The possibility that the communist party would win was so strong that Pope Pius XII not only urged the people of Italy to vote against the communist party, but he also opened all the religious houses and urged all the strictly cloistered religious men and women who normally never emerge from their monasteries to leave their cloisters and to cast their votes on the appointed day. Tensions were high. The two major parties were using every weapon at their command to win voters.

There was a Jesuit priest at the time who was a very charismatic, dynamic speaker. He was described as "the golden voice of the Catholic Church in Italy." Whenever and wherever he was scheduled to speak, people thronged to the site by the hundreds and the thousands. I myself attended a couple of his presentations and was greatly impressed, not so much by what he said, because my Italian was not yet very good, but by the way he handled himself and by the response of the crowd. He was one of the most powerful influences in Italy at that time.

Two or three days before the elections, this charismatic priest delivered a bombshell. He revealed that he was a life-long communist, and that he had joined the party at the age of 12. It was announced in the press, or at least generally speculated, that he was chosen by the communist party at that young age, indoctrinated in the communist philosophy and later became a '*plant*' in a Jesuit seminary. He obviously followed all the rules, acquitted himself on his best behavior and was a model seminarian. He was ultimately ordained, built a reputation, and waited for the proper moment when his superiors decided he should reveal himself. His entire life was a lie. There have been examples of that throughout history, up to the present and in our own country. More on that later.

The ploy backfired. The communist party lost the elections by a wide margin. The Italian people, whose faith is deep and strong and whose love of the Church and the Pope is profound and firm, were angered by the trickery and turned on the communist priest and his party.

Since that time, I have known from personal experience that the Catholic Church has bitter enemies. Before that experience I knew in a somewhat sterile fashion that this was true, for example, from reading certain scriptural admonitions (e.g., the epistle of St. Peter: "Diabolus sicut leo rugiens circuit, quaerens quem devoret."—1 Peter 5, 8. ("The devil, like a roaring lion, circles, seeking whom he may devour"—I give the Latin text, because I first read that text in a Latin New Testament and it has always been in my mind in that form.). Unfortunately, for the rest of my life, I still remained naïve enough not to recognize evil and evil intentions when they were staring me in the face. The reader will learn of a number of such instances as this text moves along.

I learned much later on in my life that the Vatican has plenty of people—even Cardinals—who are bent on the destruction of the Church as the Mystical Body of Christ, where the Pope, as the successor to St. Peter, is the greatest force for good in the world. I believe it is a given that, where the forces of good prevail, there will also be congregated the greatest forces for evil and destruction.

CHAPTER 8

The North American College

Life as a student in Rome offered an endless array of experiences which one could glean from the City of Rome itself, from all of Italy with its almost numberless points of great interest, and all the countries west of the Iron Curtain: Austria, Germany, Holland, Belgium, England, Ireland, France, Spain, Portugal, Switzerland. It was my good fortune to take extensive trips through all of those except Spain. And my visit to Portugal was very brief.

The North American College in Rome, Italy, was established and is supported by the Bishops of the United States as a place of residence for seminarians and priests who are sent to Rome for higher studies principally in Theology, Canon Law, and Scripture.

In 1950 when I started my four years of Theology studies, the North American College was in one location, sometimes called the 'House on Humility Street'—so called from its address in Italian: *Via dell'Umiltá 30*. My first three years of Theology study were spent in that residence.

During those three years (and probably long before), the new North American College was being built on the Gianicolum Hill, an easy five to ten minute walk to St. Peter's Basilica. My class, the class of 1954, was the first to 'graduate' from the new college. All of us were ordained to the priesthood in the chapel of the new college on December 19, 1953, by Bishop Martin J. O'Connor, the Rector of the college.

When we moved to the new college from the House on Humility Street, the latter became the 'graduate house' where I spent 1954 to 1957 as a priest in the study of Canon Law, where I received a doctorate.

The Daily Routine

Every day for four years began, of course, with Mass for the entire student body at an early hour: My memory is hazy but I believe it was 6:30 a.m. Mass was a bit later on Saturday and Sunday because there were no classes on the weekend. Mass was followed immediately by breakfast in the refectory. Except on *very* rare occasions, breakfast consisted invariably of hard rolls, some flavor of jam or jelly (the most unpleasant, for me, and the most frequent, was orange marmalade), and, of course, coffee. The coffee in Italy was so good that when I finally returned to the U.S., it took me a year to begin once again to drink coffee, because coffee in this country didn't measure up to what I had gotten addicted to in Italy.

Classes were held at the Jesuit Gregorian University beginning at 8:00 a.m., each lasting one hour. The front entrance of the Gregorian University was no more than one minute's walk from the rear entrance of the 'Casa' which we called our residence. We were back in our residence for lunch and then a daily one-hour siesta, followed by an hour for study. The daily walk (see next section) began at 4:00. Dinner was always a formal affair, and the first part of the meal was eaten in silence as one of us read a scriptural reading from a pulpit over the entrance to the refectory. After dinner there were communal prayers in the chapel, which was followed by a quiet period for study and lights out at 10:00 p.m.

The house was divided into groups of students called '*camaratas*', from the Italian word 'camara' meaning 'room.' Each of us had a private room and each group of eight or 10 had an upperclassman who was designated as a 'prefect' and a classmate who was designated a 'beadle'.

The prefect had little authority and the beadle even less. There perhaps was some kind of communications purpose in the set-up, but I believe the primary purpose of the camarata was to allow for the daily 'walks in Rome' to take place in an organized way.

Walks in Rome

It was a stroke of genius to have the entire student body of the North American College leave the premises every day for an hour to visit important and historic sites in Rome. In those days—the 1950's—every seminarian and every priest wore a cassock, not a suit and collar. And each national grouping wore a distinctive one. Each *camarata* walked as a group (8, 9 or 10 individuals) with a specific target chosen informally by voice recommendations, or, I was told, in some cases, by decree of the Prefect.

The genius of the tradition was that it put about 20 groups of American seminarians for an hour every day on the Streets of Rome. It provided for some much needed exercise for the seminarians who spent many hours in prayer, in class, and in intense study, and it provided for a living history lesson as we visited the incredibly numerous historical sites of Rome: The major basilicas such as St. Peter's (the Pope's Chapel), the Sistine Chapel with Michaelangelo's famous ceiling and walls, St. John Lateran (the Pope's Archdiocesan Cathedral), St. Mary Major, St. Paul Outside the Walls, the Moses by Michelangelo—to name less than one percent of the wonders of Rome. Beyond that, of course, are the remnants of the Roman Empire-buildings, bridges and other structures which stand to this day.

A recent (1999) visit to Rome with my wife revealed that much has changed. The cassock is no longer the required dress for a priest (seminarian) on the streets of Rome. They now wear a black suit and collar, as it has been in the U.S. for all of my life. Whether they have their daily walks, I do not know. I hope they have at least some substitute for that tradition. I didn't think to inquire whether the seminarians still attend the Gregorian University for Theology or the Lateran University for Canon Law studies. One thing that has certainly changed is the use by the seminarians of the elevators which are available in the new North American College. Before we moved into the new North American College in my final year in Theology (1953), the Vice Rector, Msgr. Richard Burns, gave as one of the facts of life in the new 5 story college: "There are elevators for the staff and shafts for the students." I'm sure that part of the rationale for that policy is that climbing stairs would be beneficial for the physical health of the seminarians.

The 'Black' Permission

Once a month in our first year, twice a month the second year, three times monthly in our third year, and, in our fourth year, as often as we pleased, we could don a black cassock with no distinctive features and go where we pleased in Rome for personal shopping, to visit sites of particular interest, and simply to walk the streets in complete anonymity, simply a cleric among the hundreds of clerics who infested the streets of Rome. My favorite personal visit, of course, was to St. Peter's basilica and the Sistine Chapel. There were a number of other favorites: St. Mary Major, St. John Lateran, St. Paul Outside the Walls, the Roman Forum, the Moses, the Trevi Fountain (of 'Three Coins in the Fountain' fame), the Spanish Stairs, the Holy Stairs across the street from St. John Lateran (transported from Jerusalem by St. Helen—the stairs on which Jesus walked while on His way to His crucifixion)—to name just a few of thousands of items of surpassing interest.

St. Peter's Basilica and the Sistine Chapel were and are a treasure trove all by themselves. The tradition in Rome and the rest of the Catholic world told us that the main altar in St. Peter's stands and has stood for centuries directly over the tomb of St. Peter, the first Pope. Tradition also tells us that this immense church was built over a cemetery which was located on a sloping hill—a very difficult construction challenge. Tradition in Rome also taught us that the head of St. Peter is maintained as a relic at the main altar of St. Mary Major, across town.

St. Peter's was a show case for hundreds of masterpiece oil paintings (including not a few Caravaggio's) and of statuary, whose most important example was the ***Pietá*** standing to the right of the Basilica as one comes in the main entrance doors.

It was my great privilege during my Theology studies to be selected—I don't know why—to join a small group who would be taken on a tour of the excavations which were on-going under St. Peter's basilica. The director of those archeological excavations was a Jesuit priest who was also an architect, engineer and archeologist. He gave us a presentation of the findings from the work that he and his group and their predecessors had done over the years, and then led us on a tour of the area under the basilica. Among many other things, he showed us a huge foundation stone which hung out in mid-air above our heads with obviously nothing to support it and told us they had encountered many other similar instances. His implication, though he didn't say so directly, was that the untold tons of materials above which constituted the basilica proper were being somehow maintained in some unknown (miraculous?) fashion which could not be explained by standard modern construction techniques.

As he took us through the cemetery under the basilica, the tombs became increasingly ornate until we reached the most ornate of all, which was directly under the main altar of St. Peter's, and which contained the body of a headless man. All of the tests they had done demonstrated that these were the bones of St. Peter, and, when they applied modern testing techniques, they found that the head at St. Mary Major matched the bones in the headless body in St. Peter's tomb.

As we stood at the tomb of St. Peter, we looked through an ornately carved window and saw the steps that led from the main floor of the basilica down into the crypt under the main altar, through which a person could look from outside into the very spot on which we stood within the tomb. It was an unforgettable experience.

Aside from visiting historical and modern day sites, it was a major pleasure of mine to simply sit at a sidewalk café with a cup of coffee, and watch the citizens of Rome as they went about their daily lives, to talk to some of them with my ever-increasing ability in the Italian language. I became accustomed to a culture which is entirely different from our U.S. culture and one which I came to love and admire and feel entirely at home in. Parenthetically, I became equally at home in the cultures of Germany, Switzerland and Austria. (Have I mentioned that my mother was second generation German and my father was second generation Irish?) Learning those languages and adjusting to those cultures was an excellent preparation for my future duties as National Director of the Papal Volunteers for Latin America. In that position I was able to feel almost instantly comfortable in the nineteen countries of Latin America in which we had Volunteers stationed. I'll have much more to say on that subject later.

CHAPTER 9

First Year Tour of Europe— Summer of 1951

It seems almost impossible and feels like it was a dream that I experienced four years of life and study in Rome, plus another three years as a priest during the study of Canon Law. Perhaps even more dreamlike is the memory of travels throughout Italy and all the countries of Western Europe.

The arrangement between my parents and the Bishop of Sioux City, was that the diocese would pay the tuition and other expenses of attending the North American College, and my parents would provide me with personal expense money including whatever travel I undertook during my studies. My parents, farmers at the end of World War II, were, to put it mildly, not well off. So, in terms of personal expenditures, I spent as little as possible. It was true that after the war, their situation began to improve, but it took a number of years for them to recover. Therefore, I decided that my first two years of summer travel (two months each summer) would be by bicycle, using the train as little as possible. I purchased an Italian touring bicycle, with five gears (this was the summer of 1950) and relatively inexpensive. I traveled each summer with one or two companions. This allowed us to travel somewhat anonymously without the stigma of being perceived as rich, occupying Americans. This gave us a major advantage. The train system offered inexpensive fares, and also allowed for bicyclists to buy tickets to a given destination, and, for a small additional fee, to put their own bicycles on a baggage car and remove them at the destination and simply pedal away. Since Europe was in poor economical shape after the war, bicycles were in abundant use.

My classmate, Don Hellmann, and I, during the summer of 1951 pedaled away from our summer villa near Castelgandolfo, located down the hill about a half mile from the Pope's summer villa, and headed north toward Assisi where we visited the basilica of St. Francis and the convent where St. Clare is entombed. St. Clare's body is entombed in a glass coffin under the main altar in the convent church. Dating from the early 13th century, there was still flesh on her body, e.g. her lips were visible as her body lay there.

In the valley below Assisi is a church dedicated to Mary, the Mother of God, and in the church is the *Portiuncula*, a small chapel within the church which was the original chapel which St. Francis established for his order. During our visit, there was a story circulating among the people of Assisi and its surroundings about an incident involving the mayor of Assisi. This man was a dedicated Communist who was bitterly anti-Catholic and outspokenly opposed to devotion to the Blessed Mother. Within the year before our coming, the mayor stood on the steps of that church in the valley, delivering a vicious speech against the Blessed Virgin. He died on the spot, of a heart attack it was said, and since that time the statue of Our Lady at the peak of the façade of the church with a halo of lights around her head, was seen to move. On every occasion, a large part of the crowd saw the movements, others did not. The movements were more commonly seen at night, but were also observed during the daylight hours. I myself saw the movements of the statue, but only at night. There were those who said that the circle of lights over the statue's head created an optical illusion. This may have been true, but there were always large numbers who maintained they saw no movement at all, even at night when the 'optical illusion' was supposedly operative.

The entire visit to Assisi was a standout experience for me in all my travels. But there were many others.

We bicycled from Assisi north to Venice. Although we had heard and read much about Venice, a city built on water with no streets, no cars, but only water canals for streets and boats being its only vehicles, the reality of Venice was completely unexpected. The road ended at a huge parking lot at the edge of the water. We parked, locked our bikes, and walked across a long bridge, carrying our saddle bags and found a very inexpensive hotel. And we began three days in what in my own mind I have always referred to as 'the magic city.' The weather was perfect and the city was ***quiet***. The only noise in the city was the fluttering of pigeon's wings in St. Mark's square, and, always in the distance, was the muffled sound of motor boats (water taxis, police boats, water buses). St. Mark's Basilica was awesome, prompting hours of contemplation. St. Mark's square was surrounded by outdoor restaurants, coffee shops and other retail stores. Gondolas were everywhere, long, canoe-like boats propelled by a single gondolier standing in the rear with his oar. Our evenings were taken up in coffee shops talking to the residents of Venice, using a combination of our still poor Italian and their halting English. Like all Italians, they were a very friendly people. We visited a glass-blowing factory and were much more than simply impressed with the level of artisanship we saw. We each were given (or bought?) some delicate artifact, each so skillfully packed that they survived the next four years and arrived in the spring of 1954 as gifts for my family.

As we proceeded on our bicycle tour, moving northward, we now faced the Italian Alps which stood between us and the country of Austria. This was the first of two times during our 1000 mile tour of Italy, Austria, Germany and Switzerland that we gave in and used the train for the next leg of our journey.

Austria

After only two or three hours on the train we went from sea level in Venice to several thousand feet up in the Alps at the Brenner Pass, on the northern border of Italy, and the southern border of Austria. We retrieved our bicycles and headed toward the customs area.

On the Italian side was a small *albergo*, a hotel, and we thought its prices were reasonable. However, across the border in Austria, fifty to one hundred feet away was an Austrian *Gasthof*, which we were to come to know was a typical small hotel in the three German-speaking countries we were to visit. We asked the Italian border guard if we could leave our bicycles and check out the price at the Austrian hotel. He pleasantly agreed. To our great surprise (I don't remember the exact figures), the Italian hotel charged roughly $25.00 per night, while the Austrian one charged less than $10.00! It was obviously an easy decision—we moved into Austria that afternoon.

That evening, still at the Brenner Pass, we had an excellent meal at a very good restaurant for an astonishingly low cost. During the meal, I had a never-ending thirst, probably a combination of the few miles we traveled by bicycle and the much higher altitude. I discovered a delicious drink called Apfelsaft, served cold, which my one year of college German taught me meant apple juice. So for simply a few pennies per glass I had perhaps six or seven glasses, one after another. My 6 ft. 4 in. traveling companion, Don Hellmann, apparently didn't believe I knew any German at all, so he was nervously expecting me to get drunk. By that stage in my life, I generally could recognize the taste of alcohol, and, besides, I knew that the German word for fermented apple juice was *Apfelwein* (literally, 'apple wine'). It was a minor incident, but in sixty years I have never forgotten the heady feeling of that first evening at dinner in a new country, nor have I forgotten how worried he was about what I was doing.

The next morning, we strapped our saddle bags onto our bicycles and headed north, down the other side of the mountain, heading for the city of Innsbruck which is located deep in a valley between the

Brenner Pass and the Austrian Alps to the north. It didn't take long, and it was a glorious ride; it was very easy because we coasted all the way, and the closer we came to Innsbruck, the more the Alps on the other (north) side of Innsbruck loomed larger and larger and higher and higher. It was a breathtaking sight. We had packed a picnic lunch and stopped to eat about halfway down, not only to eat, but to spend some time drinking in the beauty that lay all around us. The city of Innsbruck was now fully visible to us, the mountains North of Innsbruck hung over the city; we could see the mountain behind us where we came from; to the West, looming large, were the Austrian/Swiss Alps, and to the East was the continuation of the valley in which Innsbruck was located and which we would traverse in the next day or so to the city of Salzburg.

That night and the next day in Innsbruck was my first taste of the Germanic culture, which was vastly different from the Italian culture in which I had now spent a year, and both were vastly different from the culture of the United States, and, as we were to learn, Austria was greatly different from the cultures of Germany and Switzerland, even as within each of those countries there were conspicuous subcultures.

After perhaps one day in Innsbruck, we headed East toward Salzburg. It was a relatively easy trip, because the two cities were generally at the same altitude in the same valley within the Austrian Alps. I don't recall that Innsbruck was famous for anything special, but Salzburg at that time was considered a major music center in all of Europe. Only Vienna, as far as I know, had a superior reputation for music, but we had no access to Vienna since it was behind the Iron Curtain. During two or three days in Salzburg, we attended two orchestral presentations, and came across several impromptu instrumental recitals on the streets in the afternoons and early evening.

Salzburg is a beautiful city. Its people were different than those of Innsbruck in a way that I have learned never to try to describe. After becoming more than passingly acquainted with more than twenty five different cultures (much more on that later), I know that while people are people the world over, they are nevertheless *their own kind of people* in every country, in every region of those same countries, and from city to city.

West Germany

From Salzburg we moved northward into another culture change, into postwar Germany. Our next major and longer stop was the city of Munich, the central city of the region of Bavaria in Germany. The entire region was heavily Catholic and could well have been established as a separate Germanic culture. As an example, the *platdeutsch* (German dialect) spoken in Munich was completely incomprehensible (so I was told) to someone who spoke the dialect of, *e.g.*, Frankfurt in northern Germany.

While the city of Munich was (and I presume still is) beautiful, its people were closely knit, and unusually friendly to visitors. The principal memory I have of the city, and perhaps its most known landmark, is the Hofbraühaus which is basically a beer factory with a very large bar. By prearrangement we met three of our classmates who were also on their summer travels. Probably on our second day in Munich we visited that incredible bar.

In some fashion, the unforgettable experience of an evening in the Hofbraühaus symbolized for me the friendliness, the community-mindedness and the general comfortable and welcoming nature of the Bavarian people.

Frankfurt am Main

From Munich we bicycled north and west to Frankfurt which, as its full name makes clear, is located on the Main River. We visited several small German towns along the way. While they were all interesting, just one stands out. I have no idea in what town this occurred, but we stopped for the night at a small *Gasthoff* whose owner quoted us his price for the night, based, I'm sure, on his appraisal of us as bicyclists. In a year of life in Europe, we had learned the benefits of negotiation; so we made him a counter-offer and ended up with a considerable saving. He then asked us our nationality. We were obviously not German, and we spoke some Italian among ourselves to add to our negotiating strength.

Ultimately, since he was a licensed inn-keeper, we were required to surrender our passports to him during our stay. When he saw our passports, he was obviously angry because he didn't charge us enough. He said, "You can't be Americans. Americans don't travel by bicycle, they travel around in big limousines." Nevertheless, when the time came for us to pay him, he did take the money.

Our first sight of Frankfurt as we came over a rise, looking at the city from East to West was a shock. The city was in total ruins. Except for a few small buildings which were obviously newly constructed since the end of the war, the only building left standing was the Frankfurt Cathedral which was intact, including its very tall spire. This illustrated the astonishing accuracy of the U.S. bombings. Using the technology of the 1940's, they hit what they wanted and avoided targets they wanted to save. We saw this same pattern in every major German city we visited: the churches and Cathedrals were saved; everything else was flattened. The most flamboyant example was the city of Stuttgart where the U.S. Command established its headquarters after the war: the buildings they used for the purpose received hardly a scratch during the bombing.

In their efforts to survive, the citizens of Frankfurt used every means available. One of these was, I believe, the precursor to the Fast Food industry in the U.S. On the sidewalks at many of the intersections in Frankfurt, enterprising individuals had set up small tables or booths where they had bratwurst on sale, with a bun and mustard. It was a delicious combination, and it was my first introduction to real German sausage.

Sometime during the first scholastic year, I had made contact with relatives in Germany on my mother's side of the family. I knew they originated in the small farming community of Steinefrenz, to the north and east of Frankfurt. Their family name was Bendel, three brothers and three sisters. I was at least a second cousin to them. Two of the brothers were priests, one of the sisters was a religious nun. The older brother was the pastor in a small parish in the town of Mammolshain, located twenty or thirty miles north of Frankfurt where his youngest sister was married and his second oldest sister was his housekeeper.

After a few days in Frankfurt amid the devastation, we bicycled north into the Taunus Mountains, a fruit producing area of Germany, and where the small town of Mammolshain was located.

Arriving in Mammolshain, we found the church and the rectory and were greeted with boundless enthusiasm by Father Bernhard Bendel, the pastor, and by his sister/housekeeper. I was still using my not-much-more-than-college-German and I addressed them as I had everyone in Austria and Germany using the formal forms. For example, *Sie Sind* means 'you are' when speaking to a stranger or shopkeeper; *du bist* also means 'you are' when speaking to someone who is more than an acquaintance, such as a relative. So Father Bendel gave me a strong lecture that, since we were related, I must address him and his sister in the informal form of address. It was hard for me to adjust to, since I had never used it except to study it in class.

As I got to know my German relatives, I was deeply impressed. They had survived the very hard times of World War II. Father Bendel himself was a strong Catholic figure in Germany, and had been throughout the war, in opposition to the Nazis and the Gestapo. He was called in by the Gestapo many times and threatened with arrest if he didn't stop his activities. As he told me, he kept on doing what he had been doing, always with his heart in his throat with the fear of arrest hanging over him. He told me that his younger brother, Berthold (also a priest) had been conscripted by the Hitler Youth and was in danger of succumbing to the Hitler brainwashing. When his younger brother came home on furlough, occasionally, Bernhard said he several times held him down on the kitchen table and drove some sense into his head.

During the five times when I visited Father Bernhard Bendel during the summers I was in school, he told me of many, many priests and other Catholics who were arrested, imprisoned and finally executed during the Holocaust. I'll come back to the subject, but I have since wondered why the Jews have spent so much time complaining about the deaths of their fellow Jews without mention of how many other people were persecuted and how Pope Pius XII quietly offered conversion to the Jews so that they could proclaim that they were not Jews—which saved many lives. Pius XII also gave safe haven to hundreds of Jews in the Papal villa in Castelgandolfo. Father Bendel personally knew priests who were executed in Dachau because of their activities against the regime. He told me about an incident, considered to be absolutely true, that as a priest stood before a firing squad, they suddenly saw the figure of Christ on the Cross. The executioners couldn't bring themselves to fire, and as a result that priest was saved.

Father Bendel took me to a special seminary in his Diocese of Limburg, where the future priests were being trained to enter the German and Russian societies as 'undercover' priests who would in secret celebrate Mass and administer the sacraments clandestinely. The Catholic Church, throughout World War II in the most difficult of circumstances, was very strong and was doing everything in its power to take care of her people.

In the 1960's I had a client in Oregon whose parents and his siblings were Jews in Germany during World War II. They took the opportunity to convert to Catholicism, were able to save their lives, and later emigrated to the U.S. They had high praise for Pope Pius XII for all the things he did in a clandestine way. All the years I was in Rome (1950 to 1957) Pope Pius XII was hailed as a heroic figure for the way he held the good Italian Catholics together under Mussolini and brought support to everyone who was living under Hitler. It pains me, knowing these things, to have so many Jews criticizing the Pope who was their great supporter, and to have so many Jews complaining so vehemently about their sufferings during the Holocaust (which was in truth an unimaginable horror), but not acknowledging the incredible pains of so many others. There will be more on this subject later on.

Those several days with my relatives in post-war West Germany, using my very imperfect German and Fathers Bernhard and Berthold Bendels' halting English—and a couple of visits by a former small-town mayor, who did his University studies in England, whose British English therefore was nearly perfect—led me to a far deeper understanding of the pre- and post-war attitudes of at least the West German culture. I saw deep pain: Father Bernhard's sister said, with tears in her eyes, "Raymond, we are a conquered nation." I heard tortured memories: The former small-town mayor described some of the things he was forced to do under the Nazi regime, because, he said, they held his daughter and threatened her with torture and execution if he didn't follow their instructions. I also saw deep relief that the Nazi regime was no longer and they could look forward to a return to near normal life. And I saw hope: They trusted the Americans as much as they could trust anyone any more. An example they gave: "The American soldiers are so good to our children, and generally are compassionate toward all Germans."

South Along the Rhein

As we started the last half of our bicycle tour, I was conscious of a greater understanding of the people with whom we spoke, mostly because of the deep communication with my relatives and their friends, but also because I was rapidly improving in my use of the German language.

We got started back to Rome on the wrong foot. We took our bicycles onto the Autobahn, which is a system similar to our Interstate Highway network—one of a few good things, we were told a few times, which Hitler accomplished, but which, everyone emphasized, in no way made up for the horrors of his regime.

After a mile or two on the Autobahn, we were stopped by two German policemen who told us with great politeness and circumspection that bicycles were forbidden on the Autobahn and we would have to take another route. Which, of course, we did.

Heading south, every city we visited had its own "personality", and yet they were all pretty much the same: Darmstadt, Heidelberg, Oberammergau—all showed the aftermath of the war with their flattened buildings, the valiant struggle to build anew, and now, after the in-depth conversations with my relatives, I was able more easily to detect the underlying hope, determination and relief among the people I talked to.

With one exception, every visit was a positive experience. The exception, quite naturally, was Dachau. We saw the ovens where people were cremated by the thousands—by the thousands we were told, perhaps more. And I'll never forget the very large sign outside of those ovens which proclaimed ***Nie Wieder!*** (***Never Again!***) It is as a result of those atrocities that the German culture remains wounded to this day. While no one attributes those horrors to the Germans living today, there is the realization within the German culture that it was ***their people*** who elected Hitler, and allowed him to remain in power. While in some form of denial it has been driven deeply into the German psyche, it is nevertheless there and has continual outcroppings. One major example: It is a felony punishable by time in jail for a person in Germany to deny the holocaust. By what right does a civil authority tell its citizens what they must believe relative to historical events?

In my opinion, something similar has occurred with the Jews whose ancestors put Jesus Christ, the Messiah, to death in a most horrible way. It was their people who performed this atrocity**: *They put the Son of God to death!*** And they live in denial of that; they live with that guilt in their psyches. (See a discussion of this phenomenon in Part V, Chapter 44).

Darmstadt was, and I assume still is, a beautiful city. But hanging more clearly in my memory is the city of Heidelberg. Even Germans seem to have a love affair with the city. A song about the city was written long ago, and I believe I heard it sung in the Hofbräuhaus in Munich: *"Ich Hab' Mein Herz in Heidelberg Verloren"*—I lost my heart in Heidelberg. This city was for the most part spared during the bombings of World War II. This is wine country—as is true perhaps down the length of the Rhein River. In the basement (if that's the right word) of Heidelberg's ancient castle is what was described as the world's largest wine cask, with a dance floor built on top of it. I have no idea how many gallons the cask would hold, and I do not know if it was in use at the time. I was impressed with the size of the cask, but the so-called 'dance floor' was very small; perhaps two or three couples could use it simultaneously, with not much room to maneuver.

Oberammergau, famous for its production once every ten years of the Passion Play, was an unforgettable visit, mostly because it stood as a symbol of the depth of faith among the German people in that sector. It was an off year, so we didn't have the chance to see the Passion Play. We also visited the Convent of Siessen where Maria Innocentia Hummel at the age of 20 became a Nun. Having a major flair for art, she had attended Munich's Academy of Applied Arts where she befriended two Franciscan Sisters from a teaching order that emphasized the arts. She entered the convent of Siessen, and at the age of 23 took the name of Maria Innocentia. The members of the convent encouraged the Sister to pursue her artwork. Soon, small German publishers began printing her artwork in the form of postcards. These charming cards came to the attention of Franz Goebel, the head of the Goebel porcelain company. She began producing the figurines of young boys and girls which have become famous the world over as 'Hummels'. During that visit, I purchased one of those figurines—a little girl sitting on a fence—which I have to this day.

Switzerland

We continued what was a relatively easy bike ride along the Rhein River, south toward Switzerland. As we proceeded, the Swiss Alps began to loom majestically into the sky as we approached. When we crossed the Swiss border, the bicycling continued to be relatively easy until we reached the foothills. For perhaps fifty miles, the road snaked in and out among what were smaller mountains. It was a sensational ride. As we proceeded, the mountains grew larger and larger, until we reached the point where we simply could not go on. I cannot remember the name of the town where we finally gave up, boarded a train, and proceeded to a higher altitude where once again the highway would be relatively level. The Alps in Switzerland rise to 12,000 to 14,000+ feet, with the highest peak, Mount Blanc, at 15,774 feet, standing at the south end of Switzerland along the border with Italy.

An unforgettable sight after boarding the train with our bicycles stowed in the baggage car, was of a striking church with a tall spire. We saw it initially at the same level as the town where we boarded the train. As the train climbed on a corkscrew path up into the mountains through a series of tunnels, the church appeared four additional times. We would emerge from a tunnel and see that same church, appearing smaller as we climbed and emerged at a higher level. Finally, after achieving the altitude of the major tunnel which traversed Switzerland North to South, we saw the church no more; actually we saw very little of anything as the train proceeded through mile after mile of what I believe must be one of the very longest tunnels in the world. We were told that along that length, a train encountered a very lengthy East-West tunnel, and that during the war two trains had collided at that point. When we reached the altitude we had ascertained was the proper place for us, we disembarked, took our bicycles and began a general descent toward Italy. In terms of sheer natural beauty, that last bike ride through southern Switzerland, for a person who knows that the world and the universe was *created* by God, represented a protracted and powerful meditation. (Many years later, I was to discover that the State of Washington in the U.S. has mountain scenery every bit as breath-taking as those I saw in Switzerland; all one has to do is drive East on Federal Highway 20 from Interstate 5 in the Northwest corner of the State.)

Back to Italy

We crossed the border back into Italy at the Italian town of Chiasso. Our destination for that day was the large industrial city of Milan, most famous for its operas and its opera house known as ***La Scala***, believed to have been the largest in the world, and famed for its unusual architecture. We decided that we would attend an opera that evening. The theater was more than impressive. It had more than 3,000 seats organized into 678 pit-stalls, arranged in six tiers of boxes. We were in one of the two upper tiers with a perfect (as was likely true of every seat in the house) view of the stage. The stage is one of the largest in Italy.

The trip back to Rome was relatively uneventful. We bicycled along the west coast of Italy, with the Mediterranean to our right. We passed by (not visited) the five small towns (*Cinque Terre*—literally, five lands), with Corneglia being the first town south of Milan. We did not visit that town at that time (my wife and I stayed there for a few days in 1999) because it was high in the mountains, as were three of the rest. At the southern town of the group, La Spezia, we put our bicycles on a train and took the final leg of the journey to Rome.

CHAPTER 10

Second-, Third-, and Fourth-Year Studies in Theology

As I began my second year of studies of theology (1951-1952), I realized that a great deal had changed for me personally. I was much more comfortable with living in Italy and being so far from home. While I was not yet at all fluent in Italian, I could comprehend the spoken word much more completely than during the previous year, and, of course, the written word (e.g. newspapers and magazines) was much more comfortable for me and was improving steadily.

During the previous year, the classes, all of which were presented in Latin, were for the most part incomprehensible. This was not because I couldn't *understand* Latin. After all, I had four years of college classes in Latin and therefore had a reasonably strong vocabulary and a real understanding of the structure of the language. My problem—and every American seminarian had to weather this initial barrier—was that the classes were presented in a wide variety of accents. My professors ranged from German, Italian, Swiss, Austrian, French, Dutch, Spanish, Portuguese, Polish, Basque (a region of France and the single most difficult to understand)—to name most of the countries of origin of the faculty. In my second year this problem was considerably improved for me. And of course in my third and fourth years of classes, I didn't look on it as a problem, with the exception of a Basque professor who remained almost completely incomprehensible. I wonder to this day whether he had a speech impediment.

The second scholastic year (and the third and the fourth) was, in terms of the daily schedule, essentially a carbon copy of the first: Morning prayers and Mass, breakfast, walk to classes, walk back from classes, lunch, siesta, study, daily walks, dinner, evening prayers, study, night prayers, lights out.

The differences, of course, were substantial. The subjects presented during the classes were new and different each year. It seemed to me that they became increasingly important and more deeply significant, but perhaps it was simply that I could understand how the new subjects melded with those of the previous year(s) so that my comprehension of the overall Deposit of Faith which Christ left with His Church became successively more complete. In the process of attending those four years of Theology classes, it occurred to me that my faith remained exactly as I had learned it from my parents. The only difference was (is) that my faith is stronger because it is now based on evidence from reason, scripture, infallible pronouncements by the Pope and Church, the Fathers, and the undeviating Tradition of the Church through the ages.

In all remaining years of classes in Theology I had an increasing understanding of the powerful role of the Pope and the Vatican in world events, and, of course, in my fourth year (Dec. 19, 1953) I was ordained a priest in the new North American College.

Two or three important realizations developed for me beginning in my second year of Theology and has grown stronger for me throughout my remaining studies in Theology and Canon Law in Rome, and has been with me ever since.

That awareness had to do primarily with the commanding figure of the Pope and his stature, not only in Rome and Italy, but also in the rest of the world. When I arrived in 1950 Pope Pius XII had been Pope since 1939 and he remained as Pope until his death in 1958, a year after I returned to my diocese from the last of my studies in

Rome. When he was succeeded by Pope John XXIII, it was difficult for me to adjust to the realization that a different person was now the Vicar of Christ on earth.

It was Pope Pius XII who, on November 1, 1950, infallibly declared the dogma of the Assumption of the Blessed Virgin, body and soul, into heavenly glory. After arriving in Rome only three or four months before, it was my great privilege to attend that formal declaration among the tens of thousands of the faithful who were present for the event.

While I was attending classes during my second or third year, Pope Pius XII declared formally that the transubstantiation of the bread and wine into the Living Christ occurred precisely with the priest's pronunciation of the words "This is my Body," and "This is the Chalice of my Blood." This made its way into our classrooms almost immediately because it was touted by the Vatican as a major and most important pronouncement.

I believe it was in my second year of Theology that the Communist Party entered into an all-out drive to win the national elections, and Pope Pius XII countered with all his powers, as presented earlier in Chapter Seven.

As I said, Pope Pius XII was a commanding figure in Rome, in Italy and in all the world. The stories circulating about his interventions were continuous. Whenever he presided at a function in St. Peter's, he was initially carried on the shoulders of eight men—four on each side—through the shouting throngs of the faithful gathered in St. Peter's to see him and to attend the function. As each ceremony was getting started, the Pope just inside the main entrance to the Basilica sat upon the ***Sedia Gestatoria*** (loosely translated: a *portable throne*)—essentially a chair mounted on a platform—and was lifted above the crowd by eight men, four on each side, and carried through the basilica to the main altar. As the Pope was lifted at the start of each ceremony, there was a predictable rising cheer and applause from the crowd. Pope Pius XII was a very popular figure. The *Sedia Gestatoria* was discontinued and replaced (probably during the pontificate of Pope John Paul II) by what is called the ***Popemobile***—a jeep-like white electrical vehicle which was driven inside and outside the basilica. After Pope John Paul II was nearly assassinated, it was enclosed in bullet-proof glass.

Pope Pius XII during the Holocaust accomplished two things which were still very much on the minds of people in Rome and Italy. He decreed that the Jews in Germany and wherever the Nazis were in power could be baptized and converted to Catholicism to lessen the likelihood that they be tortured and killed. It was generally believed, as far as I could tell, that this action by Pope Pius XII saved many hundreds of Jews from torture and death.

In the course of four years of study of Theology (1950-1954) at the Gregorian University in Rome, Italy, I became so comfortable in the Italian culture that it became something of a second home for me. But I had much to go through yet. After my second year of Theology was my tour of France and a visit to the Shrine of Our Lady of Lourdes.

In the time remaining in my study of Theology, I completed my second, third and fourth year of classes, toured France by bicycle, visited England and Scotland, was ordained a priest in my fourth year, finished my studies and was awarded a Licentiate in Theology, and returned to my diocese for the summer. The events of those remaining years are highlighted in the following chapters.

CHAPTER 11

Bicycle Tour Through France—Summer 1952

After traveling about a thousand miles through Austria, Germany and Switzerland during my first summer vacation, I decided I would try for about the same mileage through France. I convinced two classmates to join me (or they recruited me): Charlie Von Euw (pronounced 'you') and Ray Gelting. We agreed to meet at a given city in northeastern France (I don't recall exactly where), so I put my bicycle on a train to Frankfurt, Germany and having once again visited my relatives in Mammolshain and Steinefrenz for about a week, headed for France on a train with my bicycle. (Each year for several years, this visit to my relatives was an enlightening experience because I learned much more about the German culture and became increasingly adept in speaking the German language.)

My two companions and I immediately headed for the Normandy section of France, along the north coast. Three things stand out on that part of the trip: 1) The people of Normandy were very nice, friendly and helpful. We were to discover that this was not entirely true in most of the rest of France. 2) We visited the American cemetery in Normandy with its nearly 10,000 crosses memorializing the incredible number of American soldiers who died during the initial invasion of Europe during World War II.

This always raised the question in our minds why most of the French treated us with what appeared to be hostility, arrogance and condescension. We thought—and I still think—that there should have been some expression of gratitude toward us since it was our own countrymen who died so that they were now speaking French rather than German, and that they might have respected our efforts to speak French and not deride us for speaking it poorly. 3) *Mont San Michele* is a striking phenomenon, considered to be an island, about two miles off the north coast of Normandy in France. It is approximately 500 feet high, said to be a solid granite outcropping, is shaped like a round pyramid with a very broad base, has a shopping area and a residential area and a restaurant or two, with a raised, paved road leading to it from the mainland. When the tide is in, it is an island; when the tide is out (more than two miles) it is simply part of the mainland. Since the sheep in the area graze on seaweed when the tide is out, it is famous for the unique taste of its mutton. Since mutton has never been one of my favorite foods, I can't make a judgment whether the flavor was better, or even different than all other samples.

St. Bernard of Clairvaux

From the Normandy coast we bicycled to the city of Clairvaux and its Abbey founded by St. Bernard. Since we wanted to attend Mass and receive Communion at the Abbey, we got up early and bicycled from sea level to a much higher altitude. It was exhausting, exacerbated because we were fasting from midnight. (For those not old enough to remember, in the 1950's it was required that a person fast from midnight—no food or water—in order to receive communion.) So when we arrived in Clairvaux, we were much more exhausted than usual. After Mass, we purchased an enormous picnic breakfast, ate it in a park, and were astonished at how much of our energy was restored. We went on another one hundred miles that day and slept in Paris that night.

Paris was in so many ways a beautiful city and a deep disappointment. We were truly impressed with the glorious architecture and art work which has distinguished that city for centuries. The Basilica of Notre Dame, the Eiffel Tower, the Moulin Rouge, the Mona Lisa and the Venus de Milo—these and all the other sites which most people can name, even if they have never visited the city.

My overall impression of the city of Paris is that it was—and I presume still is—archeologically and artistically magnificent. I have fourteen decorative plates hanging on the walls of our home, representations of the fourteen outstanding sites in Paris, the art work all done by Louis Dali. They bring back clear memories of that time when I visited all of them in person.

My appreciation of this enormous beauty was tempered by a great deal of disappointment and sadness emanating from two sources. One disappointment was the hostility, unfriendliness and clear anti-Americanism we encountered among the French in Paris. The latter was particularly irritating in the light of the nearly 10,000 American servicemen graves we had just visited. Without those soldiers' sacrifices, France would never have been allowed to return to what it had been.

The second source of disappointment in Paris (and, I believe, in France in general) was the obvious loss of faith. On Sunday, we attended Mass at Notre Dame cathedral, and, a week later, at another large Parisian church. Each was designed to seat two thousand to four thousand people. In each case, the churches were magnificent, but each had about twenty people in attendance. The celebrant of each Mass, when it came time for his sermon, climbed circular stairs to a magnificent pulpit high over the congregation, and then delivered what appeared to be a passionate exhortation to this nearly non-existent congregation. Very appropriately it was about this time that the book *France Pagan* was published. It could not have been more obvious that many of the people of France, somewhere along the line, had lost their Faith.

The next leg of our journey was a sojourn into the past along the *Loire* river valley south of Paris. We visited the many castles along the river, dating from medieval times. After a few days of visiting those castles we circled back to a final weekend in Paris.

CHAPTER 12

The Shrine of Our Lady of Lourdes

Our next destination was the city of Lourdes in the southwestern corner of France, a long way from Paris. Therefore we put our bicycles on a train and traveled overnight to Lourdes, arriving I believe around 9:00 a.m. Our entire attitude changed, or at least mine did, from a more sight-seeing frame of mind to making a pilgrimage to a holy site.

After finding rooms for the two or three nights we intended to stay, we walked to the Shrine. We found that whoever had designed the area had used a great deal of common sense. The church or basilica which had been built over the Shrine was located squarely in the middle of a four or five acre plot which was fully enclosed within a high wall. No commercialism of any kind was permitted inside those walls.

As we entered the main entrance of this compound, the huge basilica was facing us. The Shrine where the Blessed Virgin had appeared so many times to St. Bernadette was left as an open cave under the right side of the church, with a statue of the Blessed Virgin standing on an outcropping several feet off the ground, in the exact place, we were told, where the Blessed Virgin herself had stood as she appeared to Bernadette.

The spring which Bernadette had uncovered, digging with her hands where the Blessed Virgin had told her to, was and is still flowing, although I don't believe anyone has ever found a natural source for the water. As we arrived, there was a very long line of the lame, sick, people on stretchers, waiting to get to the waters where they could be immersed in a tub of water, wash themselves, or drink the water. Off to the left of the Shrine itself was a huge pile of crutches, canes, walkers, wheel chairs—thousands of them!—all of which had obviously been left behind by previous visitors who had been cured of whatever malady had plagued them. It was a sight never to be forgotten.

Since 1858 when the Blessed Virgin appeared to Bernadette, there has been a continuing series of individual miracles at Lourdes—people who never walked before got up and walked, missing flesh was restored; the list is unending. However, another on-going miracle is the hundreds and thousands of people who attend Mass and receive Communion every day at the Shrine, unlike in Paris where it seems hardly anyone attends Mass and receives the Sacraments. Most of the individual miracles, we were told, occur at Benediction of the Blessed Sacrament every day at 4:00 p.m., as if, as at the wedding feast at Cana, the Blessed Virgin entreated her Divine Son to perform miracles.

Each purported miracle at Lourdes is examined by a commission of scientists, doctors, ranging from Catholics and Protestants to professed atheists. Having heard this, I have often wondered how an atheist who proclaims that a given cure was unexplainable by natural causes can remain an atheist. The answer, of course, is two-fold: As St. Paul says there is no such thing as an atheist, just people who convince themselves that there is no God, and secondly, the Faith is a gift of God and only He can provide the grace which allows a person to accept Him.

CHAPTER 13

End of the Tour and Back to Class—3rd Year of Theology

Having immersed ourselves for a few days in the incredible aura of the Shrine of Our Lady of Lourdes, we once again took to our bicycles and traveled east along the south coast of France, along the Riviera. Aside from the beauties of the Mediterranean to our right, the mountains of south France on our left, something of a mixed experience was a visit to the chapel in the town of Vence where Picasso had decorated the chapel in a small convent of nuns. Since the town of Vence is only a few miles north of the south coast of France, and since Picasso was a famous artist, we felt a visit was obligatory.

I had now lived in Italy for two full years and had continued my daily walks in Rome, I had become familiar with quite a number of famous artists and works of art: Michelangelo (the Sistine Chapel, the Pietá, Moses, the David in Florence, etc.); Bernini; Caravaggio; and many others which were in so many ways equally impressive.

So I was astonished to see what the art work in the chapel in Vance turned out to be. To my admittedly inexpert eye, they were nothing but a series of *stick figures,* all of them consisting of an oval for a face with no features, straight lines for arms and legs, fingers and toes. The one or two nuns we talked to seemed to hold these 'works of art' in something I can describe as *awed reverence* and appeared to venerate those images at least as much as the Blessed Sacrament in their own tabernacle. A member of their congregation was quoted as saying that it was wonderful to be able to simply use one's imagination as to what the faces of Christ and His Mother really look like. The crowning absurdity came when the nun took us back to the sacristy and showed us a thick stack of the preliminary sketches which Picasso had prepared as 'practice' for the final art work. All the 'practice' sketches, like the finished 'works' on the walls of the chapel, were *stick figures* in all sorts of different poses.

Proceeding eastward along the French Riviera after the visit to Vence, we stopped in Monaco, where, not long before, Grace Kelly had married Prince Rainier. While my companions gambled a bit, I just watched because I didn't dare lose anything since I had just enough money, I hoped, to get back to Rome. After a couple more days on the bicycles, we returned to the North American College. Later on that school year when there was a rumor that Grace Kelly was pregnant, one of my classmates made the remarkable weather forecast (he called it) that there's going to be "a little Rainier in Monaco." He didn't get much of a rise out of anyone.

CHAPTER 14

Preparation For Work as a Priest

While my memory plays tricks on me as I grow older, I believe it was this particular school year that I took extended classes taught by Father Edwin Healy, S.J., an internationally renowned Moral Theologian in the 1950's. Of course, other professors that year taught a number of advanced courses in Theology. The general purpose of Father Healy's classes was to cover the vast array of human actions—thoughts and activities—ranging from good and virtuous actions such as the Beatitudes and the elements in Christ's Sermon on the Mount—in other words, how to develop a more perfect Spiritual Life—and the darker side of human activities: *imperfections* through *venial sins* to *mortal sins.* Since one of our most important duties as priests was to hear confessions and grant absolution to penitents, it was essential that we learn what constitutes each of those three latter concepts and help people understand the difference.

Perhaps my greatest satisfaction as a priest was to be able to give solace to a guilt-ridden young woman, who, as a girl, had been raped by a priest. I was able to convince her that she had committed no sin at all, not even a venial sin. And I couldn't even suggest to her that she was entirely too trusting, because it was an era when matters of sex were not taught even (especially?) in a Catholic school, nor by parents. Priests were held in very high esteem.

At the time I first heard her confession, I didn't know who she was. A great benefit of most confessionals is that the priest cannot see through the screen that is placed between him and the penitent, and it's impossible to recognize a voice since sins are presented in what amounts to a loud whisper.

Back to the earlier subject: An ***Imperfection*** is simply something we could improve in order to enhance our spiritual lives. An example could be distraction in saying our prayers, unintended irritability, being less sympathetic and understanding than a given situation requires, and many things along that line. A ***Venial Sin*** is an action (or omission) regarding a subject matter contained in the Ten Commandments or the Precepts of the Church which is not grave but which is performed (or omitted) consciously with reflection and consent of the will. Examples might be showing irritability and impatience regarding a matter important to another person; another example: taking the name of God in vain mostly as a matter of habit without much thought or reflection. A ***Mortal Sin*** (so named because it 'kills' the supernatural life of grace in the soul) has three elements: serious matter, sufficient reflection, and full consent of the will. And of course much was said in my class in Rome about what 'serious matter' is, what constitutes 'sufficient reflection,' and what does 'full consent of the will' really mean. If a person does not know what these things are, it would be well to discuss them with a priest in the confessional (or outside the confessional).

The Seal of Confession

The concept of the Seal of Confession is so important that Father Healy spent a great deal of time on the subject. It simply means that whatever a penitent may divulge in confession may *never* be revealed by a priest, not even under oath. If a priest is asked a question whose answer he knows from the confessional, he can legitimately say "I don't know" because, as Father Healy put it, he doesn't know with any *communicable* knowledge. It is knowledge he is *forbidden* to reveal under pain of serious sin. It is one of the elements of the Sacrament of Penance which has made it so beneficial to Catholics since its founding by Christ Himself. They know that once a sin has been confessed and the priest has given absolution, that it can never be revealed by the priest, and the penitents are once again restored to the supernatural life as sons of God, with the indwelling of the Holy Spirit and of the Trinity. In the two thousand year history of the Catholic Church, there is no record of an occasion when a priest has broken the Seal of Confession.

A priest can and should take steps to ensure his future protection. He can always avoid looking at the penitent, and he should never try to determine the identity of him or her. It is permissible for a priest to *indirectly* divulge knowledge from the confessional. After all, Father Healy himself was using his years of hearing confessions to develop his class presentations on the subject. I heard a priest reasonably and licitly draw a conclusion that American Catholics apparently no longer believe that artificial contraception is sinful, because, he said, no one ever confesses it any more.

Scrupulosity

One of the more difficult penitents to deal with, as Father Healy told us—and I found it to be true in twenty years of hearing confessions almost weekly—is the ***scrupulous*** person. The most scrupulous person (there are different degrees of scrupulosity) will feel that almost everything he/she thinks or does is sinful (usually mortally) and lives in a constant state of guilt. The most common 'specialization' of the scrupulous penitent revolves around the sixth commandment. For such a person, the simple act of looking at, or touching, a crucifix (e.g. saying the rosary) is a grave sin because the crucifix has the nearly naked figure of Christ hanging on it. The simple act of gazing briefly on an attractive member of the opposite sex for such a person is thought to be gravely sinful.

Scrupulous penitents live in internal anguish and agony. Their tormented and tortured souls (I personally believe that many of them are under direct attack by the devil) cause them to be profoundly vulnerable and super sensitive to criticism, and to perceive criticism when none is intended. Therefore, the priest/confessor must approach them with a tender, empathetic loving care which will help them to begin to understand that their state of mind is not normal and they must fight against it because it holds them back in the development of their spiritual lives. So I always did my best to help such penitents to understand scrupulosity and to encourage them to recognize it. I have said many, many times, "Unless you can swear on a stack of bibles that what you did or thought was sinful, then you must ignore it. If it is indeed sinful, then it will fall back on me and you will not be guilty of it. Whenever you go to confession, come back to me personally. If that is impossible, explain the problem to another priest and tell him how I told you to deal with it. And pray constantly that this burden be taken away from you."

It was a great satisfaction to me over the years to see many (hopefully all?) scrupulous penitents gradually overcome the problem.

And it was important always as a confessor to be sensitive to the penitent who might develop scrupulosity about a given sin or series of sins in the past. Whenever the priest detects, for example, a tendency to repeat the confession of a given sin, it is important to tell the penitent emphatically that, now that you have confessed this sin, you should never repeat it in confession again.

Homosexuality

Father Healy emphasized that homosexuals must be treated with great care, love and understanding, because they have a very difficult problem to deal with. Whether their unnatural proclivity was with them from conception and birth, or whether it was instilled later in life through their own action or the actions of others, they have a special burden to bear. The priest must insist with them that they are given the grace sufficient to deal with the burden, and, if they are to be truly children of God, they *must* deal with it. Since the Sixth Commandment allows only the married person to engage in the pleasures of sex, the homosexual must face the absolute need to abstain from sex on a lifelong basis. Difficult? Of course it is. Since the homosexual ***knows*** that he or she is not like most people, there can be and often is a deeply buried anger that makes them deny the problem and insist that they can love like anyone else. As a result, they are under constant temptation to engage in sexual activities. They must accept the fact that God has reserved the Sacrament of Matrimony for a man and a woman, and that there can never be such a thing as same-sex marriage, no matter how many civil governments try to legislate it into existence.

The only reasonable stand of the priest is to recognize the difficulties homosexuals face, consistently and gently encouraging them to offer up to God the sacrifice of abstaining from any sexual activities—which will build up grace and a spiritual strength they could never otherwise have. Over a period of time, a priest can help them accept their situation and live their lives accordingly. And I personally have seen this happen.

As I encountered homosexuality for the first time during my first year in Trinity College, I encountered it again during my years in Rome. My guess in retrospect is that something less than 5% of all the seminarians there were homosexual. One of my classmates was easily recognizable as a homosexual. All of us knew that and simply accepted it in him. Many years later, he became a bishop, opened his cathedral to homosexuals and publicly celebrated a Mass specifically dedicated to them.

I learned over the years that, for whatever reason, homosexuals were attracted to me. An upperclassman in Rome used to visit me in my room almost every day after lunch, simply to talk. I knew, however that he was homosexual, but I also knew that he himself had not yet recognized this in himself. Later on, I came to know another priest who, at the age of about 35, told me that he had always known that somehow he was different than most, and had only recently discovered that he was homosexual. He had lived, and continued to live, a celibate life. Those are the only two examples I ever encountered who were unaware of their own sexual proclivity.

As I progressed in the priesthood and in life, as the reader will see, I encountered homosexuality quite a number of times and was forced, at least on one occasion, to deal with it rather harshly.

Spiritual Direction

As we continued with our Moral Theology classes, Father Healy emphasized Spiritual Direction as an important role of the priest in confession. A penitent, while confessing his or her sins, is especially open to advice from the priest. He strongly advocated taking whatever time the penitent seemed to need and want in discussing ways to improve his/her spiritual life, and give no thought to a line of penitents waiting their turn.

I determined that I would always follow that advice, particularly when dealing with the scrupulous penitent, homosexuals, those returning to the Church, the first confession of converts, those who had not been to confession in many years, and those who seemed especially guilt-ridden because of the specific sins they had committed. When I came back to the United States, I encountered a completely different attitude, pretty much what I have called an 'assembly line' approach: hear their confession, give them absolution and a penance and send them on their way—waste no time. This was apparently taught in all or most U.S. seminaries. I could never subscribe to that, and I always had a long line of penitents waiting for me. While a few American priests quite directly criticized me for spending the time, I never changed my approach, because with Baptism, Communion and Confirmation, the Sacrament of Penance is at the core of the Catholic Faith. Actually it must be said that all seven Sacraments are at the core of the Catholic Faith. Beyond that, of course, as has already been said, the Sacrament of the Eucharist, the Real Presence and the Mass stand as the source and the center of the grace of all the other Sacraments.

A study made years ago and now mostly forgotten and/or ignored suggested that Catholics who regularly confessed their sins had significantly fewer mental and emotional issues than those who had no such access. The acknowledgment by Catholics of the reality of sin, both mortal and venial, their admission that they commit at least venial sins, and the act of confessing those sins to a representative of God Himself, allows for the absolution of those sins, the deletion of the temporal punishment due for those sins, and it increases the virtue of humility in the penitent. It is a profoundly beneficial Sacrament. After living in seven different parts of the United States and now more than eighty years of age, I have observed that Catholics do not go to confession in the great numbers I saw in my grade and high school years. While it is still a precept of the Church that we go to confession and receive communion at least once during the Easter Season—and I hope that Catholics in general observe at least that minimum—I believe when I was young that the majority of Catholics went to confession every two weeks to once a month. When we visited Rome a few years ago, we saw people going to confession in large numbers in every church and basilica. Unfortunately, it appears that much has been lost among the Catholics in the United States. We will have much more to say on this subject as we move along.

Absolution

The main reason for going to confession is to take advantage of the authority every priest has to forgive our sins. Christ Himself said to His Apostles (and through them to all their successors), "Whose sins you forgive, they are forgiven them; whose sins you retain, they are retained." (John 20:23)

Therefore, after a penitent has confessed his/her sins, the priest will suggest that he or she recite the act of contrition, and then he will say, as he makes the sign of the cross, "Therefore I absolve you from all your censures and sins in the name of the Father and of the Son and of the Holy Spirit."

Penance

After giving absolution, the priest will say "For your penance . . . . ," as a means of substituting for the temporal punishment due for our sins. ('Temporal' punishment, of course, means the pain and suffering we should undergo in this life to make recompense for that sin, or the time in Purgatory for the same reason.) As Father Healy taught us in his Moral Theology class, the priest has that authority, and whatever he establishes will replace that punishment. He suggested that it be something the penitent can easily remember and easily accomplish, such as the recitation of Hail Mary's and Our Father's, perhaps five decades of the rosary for more serious sins confessed. One of my classmates in college told me that he was given a penance of getting down on his knees in his room and kissing the floor three times. While the priest undoubtedly had a good intention of enhancing humility, it seemed to me that this particular penitent was confused and unsettled by the penance.

To reassure those who had no time immediately to say their penance, or forgot to do or say their penance from a previous confession and don't remember what it was, they can simply mention that in the next confession and the next priest can simply designate a penance to replace the forgotten one.

CHAPTER 15

Travel to Britain—Summer of 1953

In the summer of 1953, I changed my *modus operandi.* I had sold my bicycle, traveled by train to Mammolshain, Germany to visit my relatives, and then proceeded by plane to London, England, where I spent a month visiting the principal sites of importance in England. I was as impressed as anyone with the many historically and currently important sites in London. I won't go into them, because far better descriptions than I could present are available in innumerable historical and tourism books. I would refer the reader to those many sources.

The most important event for me that summer was to make contact with two people who were at that time to provide me with a place to stay and who were to become close friends. Shortly after I landed in London, I was introduced to Mrs. Joan McKenzie who offered me a room in her large boarding house. Having met her, I went with her by bus to her house. Later that day, I met her husband, David, who was an accountant. To make ends meet, in addition to his income as an accountant, they rented out rooms to six or seven boarders, and she managed the boarding house. An interesting couple, he was a Scotsman, small in stature, perhaps 5'5", and she was an English woman, a bit taller than he. There was something of an easy-going cultural tension between them. For example, he contended that in order to make a proper cup of tea, the cream must first be poured into the cup, followed by the tea itself. The English way, as she insisted, was to pour the tea first and then add the cream. When they asked my opinion, they were crestfallen that I had to honestly say that I detected not the slightest difference in taste between the two methods. That was explained away eventually because as an American I had little or no experience with tea.

An interesting sidebar: The English had tea in the morning for breakfast, tea in the middle of the morning, once again for lunch at noon, 'high' tea in the afternoon about 4:00, and finally tea for dinner at 8:00 p.m. or so. For a bedtime snack, they served coffee. When I asked them why the late evening change to coffee, their answer was "Tea keeps us awake."

I visited the McKenzie's every summer after that first meeting, later on I stayed with them when I was working on my doctoral dissertation and used the Library of London as my research source. They visited me once in Rome and once in the United States probably 20 years later.

In varying degrees I learned to adjust to and respect the cultures of the countries I visited and traveled through: Germany, Austria, Switzerland, France, England and Italy. For some unknown reason, I never visited Spain. In Germany, especially in those areas in which my relatives lived, I was received by them, of course, and by their friends and acquaintances with the finest kind of openness. And I was received well in other parts of Germany because I spoke German with a reasonable degree of fluency, to the point that I was usually taken to be Dutch, not American—I spoke well but had some kind of an accent. The same was true in Austria and Switzerland. In France, it was quite clear that they simply 'put up' with us. The animosity toward Americans was blatant—except in Lourdes and Normandy where the virtue of charity was boundless.

The reception in England was decidedly mixed; we were looked upon something like 'estranged cousins.' Whatever hostility

I encountered in England was tempered, of course, by the close friendship which developed between Joan and David McKenzie and myself.

Italy, on the other hand, was and is unique. Italians are open and friendly; they welcome visitors from any part of the world. The Vice Rector of the North American College spoke to us about this, noting that tourism in Europe was at its strongest in Rome, where the atmosphere of welcome and friendliness was well beyond the norm. Four of my own experiences underlined this: When I was completely lost, looking for a specific place to visit, twice in Rome, once in Florence, and once in Venice, I stopped a passerby and asked for directions. In each case, they not only gave me directions, but then stopped whatever they were doing and actually ***led*** me to the site I wanted, finally stopping when we could see where I wanted to go and pointed to it before leaving me.

The epitome of all such incidents occurred during the visit to Italy by Joan and David McKenzie when we were in Venice. On a very hot day, we had visited the beach and, as we walked along the beach between the city and the waterfront, Joan collapsed and her husband and I were able to help her to sit on a bench in front of a statue. An elderly Italian woman instantly understood that Joan was suffering from heat prostration, called on someone to use a parasol to protect her and ordered a young man to go to the nearest pharmacy and bring back a certain medicine. After Joan had recovered, I tried to offer some money to the elderly woman and the young man who had purchased the medicine, and they both firmly refused. The McKenzie's, of course, were deeply grateful and astonished, because they had never known how invariably charitable the Italians were, both internally with their own kind, and with foreigners.

In 1999 my wife and I visited the town of Fiesole, known for its exotic gardens and water fountains, got completely lost and couldn't find our way back to the train station to return to Rome. A young man we asked for directions, walked with us until we could see the train station a block or so away.

Returning for a moment to my years in Rome as a student, I recall that it was a great pleasure after seven years to return to my own country, but I have ever since been conscious of the values I lived with in Italy which we do not have in the United States.

CHAPTER 16

My Ordination to the Priesthood—December 19, 1953

In the spring of 1953, Msgr. Richard Burns, the Vice Rector, announced that construction of the new North American College on the Gianicolum hill near Vatican City would be completed in the next few months and we would move *en masse* into it for the next school term. It was a massive structure—five stories high—much larger than the House on Humility Street which we had occupied for the past three years.

The date of the ordination to the priesthood for my class was announced at about that time. The event was so significant that four members of my family decided to attend: My parents, both in their sixties, my oldest brother, Eugene, a priest about fifteen years older than I, and my second oldest brother, Philip, ten years my elder. It was a major sacrifice for them. They had to close down the farm, selling the cattle and the large flock of chickens and simply leave it behind for what I believe to have been two to three weeks. The ordination ceremony was held in the beautiful chapel of the New North American College.

The ordaining celebrant was Bishop Martin J. O'Connor, Rector of the North American College. That was a memorable occasion, but then so were the next seven to ten days when I celebrated my very first Masses at sites I had chosen long before. My very first Mass the next morning I celebrated at the tomb of St. Peter, an altar in the crypt under the main altar in St. Peter's Basilica. My second Mass I celebrated at the Altar of the Chair which was located at the far end of the Basilica in the apse, which had above it the chair which according to Tradition St. Peter himself had used. I celebrated Mass every day thereafter, accompanied by my family, at St. Mary Major's, at St. John Lateran, the Mother of all Churches throughout the world, at St. Paul's Outside the Walls, and at a number of other places which were important to me after my years in Rome.

CHAPTER 17

Completion of Theology Studies—Spring 1954

The final drive toward qualifying for the Licentiate in Theology (considered to be a year or more beyond the Master's degree) was nothing less than frightening. "Frightening' is the only word I can think of which adequately describes the experience. Beyond frightening, it was among the worst ordeals I have ever undergone.

It was nerve-wracking for a number of reasons. First, the tests we were to undergo were oral—we were to be questioned by a number of our professors. Second, the tests covered all four years of material which, in the minds of all of us, required cramming every day for two or three months. Third, we were given one hundred 'theses' or subjects relating to dogmatic, moral and scriptural subjects, any one or several of which the examiner could choose, and which we were then required to explain, describe and prove in the time (fifteen minutes) allotted with each of four professors. Fourth, the letter of the alphabet which was chosen that year (1954) was the letter, 'L' meaning that students whose names began with 'L' were the first to undergo the examinations, which meant, of course, that my letter 'K' was among the last to be examined. It was very difficult, over a period of a month or more, to see my classmates undergo their examinations, come back relieved, pack up and happily start their trip back to the

United States, while a few of my classmates and I had to wait until the bitter end. As I recall, the day of my examination was the very last day for the entire University with students from all over the world. And the Fifth and final fright was that as four of us waited outside the last classroom where the examinations were held, one of my classmates brought up a specific thesis which he didn't understand and asked for help. When I went into the examining room, that particular thesis was on my mind. When the examining professor chose a different thesis, I unconsciously began to recite what we had just talked about in the hall. The professor was very kind, seemed to understand what was happening and simply asked me questions which demonstrated that I did in fact know the subject he asked me about. After fifteen minutes, a bell rang, and I went to another corner, and so on through four fifteen-minute examinations.

Later that same day, I learned I had a passing grade (actually I was given 9 out of 10 points) so I was granted my Licentiate and became a recognized Theologian. I made my final preparations and started my journey back to the Sioux City Diocese.

The Death of My Father

My father died in the early months of 1954, in his seventies. I gave no thought to attending his funeral primarily because I thought the authorities at the North American College would not permit it, but I was also convinced that no one had the money required for such a trip. Certainly I didn't have it and funeral expenses would probably make it impossible for my family to help with it. Since my parents had been so close for so many years, my mother, I was told, was completely grief-stricken.

It was a matter of diocesan tradition that I should celebrate a 'first Mass' at St. Mary's, my home parish in Storm Lake, Iowa, not long after I returned home. Therefore, a couple of months after my father's death, I asked my sister and two brothers who were close to my mother's situation whether I should ask her to make arrangements for that occasion. They all agreed that it could be good for her. It became clear that we had made a good decision because she once again took full charge of her life, and she turned the celebration into a complete success.

The Bishop assigned me to parish work in Sioux City for the rest of the summer until it was time for me to return to Rome to pursue my doctorate in Canon Law.

Since I was at that time an ordained priest, I consider the next three years of study in Rome to belong to Part III, next, which, together with Part IV, describes the many and varied responsibilities that were mine during my twenty years in the active priesthood. Before getting into that, I want to conclude Part II by summarizing, in the next chapter, the principal theological doctrines which I studied at the North American College, 1950 to 1954.

CHAPTER 18

Full Preparation for the Priesthood

During the four years of study at the North American College in Rome, I studied an enormous range of subjects: dogmatic and moral theology, the doctrines of the Church which have been formally defined, doctrines which have been held in Tradition for the life of the Church, doctrines which are definable, Scripture and its inspired nature, the nature of Tradition. . . . etc . . . etc.

At this point, I will simply list those subjects which were at the time particularly significant for me and which remain so to this day. A deeper discussion of them will be found in Part VII, Chapter 57 where they are presented both for study and as a means of combating the errors and weaknesses which have worked their way into the U.S. Church.

The Existence of God

It is the discipline of Philosophy (see Part I, Chapter 5) which demonstrates the proofs for the existence of God. St. Thomas Aquinas, who in the eyes of many was the ultimate philosopher, presented five proofs for the existence of God, each of which in its own way is entirely persuasive, some of them, perhaps depending on the nature of the person, more so than the others. This subject will be presented more in depth in Part VII, Chapter 57.

Original Sin

Adam and Eve were created by God as our proto-parents. The doctrine of Original Sin as committed by Adam and Eve in the Garden of Eden carries with it incredible ramifications for the human race down through the centuries and millennia.

The Trinity

The Trinity is one of the greatest mysteries among the revelations we have received from God.

The Blessed Virgin Mary

It was a great honor for me, an event stamped in my memory, when on November 1, 1950, having been in Rome only a few months during my first year in the study of Theology, that I attended the solemn infallible declaration by Pope Pius XII of the dogma of the Assumption of the Blessed Virgin Mary, body and soul into heaven without undergoing death.

Four Principal Dogmas Regarding the Blessed Virgin

Over the centuries, many doctrines regarding the Blessed Virgin have been proclaimed by the infallible pronunciations of a succession of Popes. The four principal dogmas are:

- Her title as Mother of God
- Her Immaculate Conception
- Her Perpetual Virginity
- Her Assumption into Heaven

The Incarnation

The following thesis is of principal importance to the People of God: ***"Only in the hypothesis that God demanded condign justice in atonement for the sin of Adam and Eve was the Incarnation necessary"*** (my translation from the Latin.)

Thus, as I said before, the Catholic Church in her Holy Saturday liturgy can see a major benefit in the terrible sin of Adam and Eve: "O happy fault which merited such a great and incomprehensible Redeemer." (Translation from my memory of the Latin text.)

The Eucharist and Real Presence— The Core of the Catholic Faith

The Catholic Church is the only religion on earth which professes the Real Presence of Jesus Christ on her altars, during the celebration of the Mass, and Who lives in her tabernacles—and Who lives in each of her members.

The Seven Sacraments

The help God provides to His people is grace. He provides two kinds of grace: 1) Actual grace and 2) Sanctifying grace. ***Actual graces*** are daily occurrences given to us by God, such as special people who providentially come into our lives, the moments of awe when we are struck, for example, by a remarkable view of mountains, of the stars, and meditate upon the magnificence and omnipotence of our Creator. ***Sanctifying grace*** is that which is created by God and infused into our souls by means of the Sacraments so that we can have the Indwelling of the Holy Spirit, the Trinity residing within us, our sins forgiven, and live our supernaturalized lives as Children of God.

The Sacraments were instituted by Christ Himself first of all to elevate each of us into a supernaturalized life as Children of God, then to maintain or regain that supernatural life, and to enable it to grow within us in the course of our lives.

Baptism

All of us are born with Original Sin on our souls. Christ Himself initiated the Sacrament of Baptism so that we could be cleansed of that sin, receiving Sanctifying Grace for the first time, and thus become 'children of God', elevated into a supernatural way of life. The baptized person can legitimately say with St. Paul, "I live now, not I, but Christ lives in me." (Gal. 2, 20).

The Eucharist—First Communion

Jesus said "I am the living bread that came down from heaven. Whoever eats of this bread will live forever; and the bread that I will give for the life of the world is my flesh.' (Jn 6:51). We should begin receiving communion at the youngest possible age. It is the major means of increasing the Sanctifying Grace we have in our souls after Baptism.

The Mystical Body of Christ

That the Roman Catholic Church constitutes the mystical presence of Jesus Christ on earth has been the tradition of the Church since the time of Christ. In fact, Christ Himself refers to His Church in that way—"Abide in me, and I in you. As the branch cannot bear fruit of itself unless it remain on the vine, so neither can you unless you abide in me" (Jn 15:4)

In one of the final sections of this book, I will have much more to say about what it means to be a Catholic, and about the different ways in which a person can be a member of the Mystical Body of Christ. There is no more important event in our lives than to belong to the Church—the Mystical Body of Christ—the way Christ Himself wants us to be.

The Sacrifice of the Mass

The very first Mass of the newly forming Catholic Church was celebrated by Christ Himself when, at the Last Supper, the night before He knew He was to die, He took bread in His hands, blessed it, broke it and gave it to his Apostles, saying "Take and eat, all of you: This is my body which will be offered up for you;" and again taking the chalice of wine He said, "Take this all of you and drink from it. This is the chalice of my blood which will be shed for you . . . . Do this in commemoration of me."

The Sacrament of Penance

The power to forgive sin was instituted by Christ Himself—as all seven Sacraments were—so that anyone who commits sin can be absolved by His priests. Christ entrusted this authority over sin to all the Twelve (Mt. 18:18) after first having given it personally to Peter.

Confirmation

Baptism, the Eucharist, and the Sacrament of Confirmation together constitute the sacraments of Christian initiation. For by the sacrament of Confirmation, the baptized receive a specialized form of Sanctifying Grace whereby they become, as I learned many, many years ago from the Baltimore Catechism, "soldiers of Christ."

The Sacrament of Matrimony

God created man and woman so that together they could participate in His creative powers. Since Adam and Eve, every man and woman, have been empowered to bring together the created materials which can initiate a new life, into which God Himself implants a soul which He has newly created.

The Sacrament of Sacred Orders—The Priesthood

During the ceremony of the ordination of a priest, the ordaining bishop declares "Thou art a priest forever, according to the order of Melchisedech." As the High Priest of his time, Melchisedech offered his Old Testament sacrifice, using bread and wine.

The Sacrament of Extreme Unction

Now known quite commonly as the Sacrament of the Sick, this Sacrament was instituted by Christ Himself (as is true of all seven) to provide the grace needed as a person passes from this life to the next, and therefore to provide the support the dying person needs as the devil endeavors to inflict the final temptations which would take the soul away from God into Hell. And while this has always been the primary purpose of this sacrament, it has frequently restored good health to a dying person.

Systems of Government

Another somewhat vacuous class had to do with different systems of government, ranging from Communism, through Socialism, Dictatorships, Capitalism, all in an effort to present to us students what forms of civil government were acceptable to the Catholic Church. As I recall, there was also an effort by the professor to present a *philosophy* of civil society which would be acceptable to the Catholic Church. In my mind, he failed miserably to come up with even remotely acceptable conclusions.

Perhaps the most important of these atypical classes was one whose subject was the nature and purpose of government. Even though the study of government was not at all satisfying, a very important concept came out of it: The so-called ***Perfect Society***, which is so called because it contains within it all the tools it requires to achieve its goals. There are two: the civil society and the divine society. It was this concept which allowed Jesus to respond to those who were testing him:

> So Jesus said to them, "Repay to Caesar what belongs to Caesar and to God what belongs to God." They were utterly amazed at him. (Mark 12:17 and Luke 20:25)

There are as many civil societies in the world as there are sovereign countries. There is one Divine Society—The Church founded by Christ Himself. It is unfortunate that the Heresy of Americanism has apparently led the Church in the United States to join the civil society rather than maintain its independence. An example: In at least one U.S. diocese (the evidence would suggest many of them) a couple seeking a declaration of nullity of their marriage must first obtain a civil divorce before the ecclesiastical tribunal will begin proceedings toward declaring a prior marriage bond null and permitting the couple to validly enter into a true marriage. In actual fact, the Church alone has jurisdiction over a Sacramental Marriage Bond; a civil society has no authority to declare such a marriage contract null and void for any of the reasons given in Canon Law.

However, after the Church declares the nullity of a marriage, the person so freed must seek a civil divorce in order to avoid a charge of bigamy.

PART III

20 YEARS IN THE ACTIVE PRIESTHOOD

CHAPTER 19

Canon Law Studies—1954-1957

My first three years as a priest were devoted to the study of Canon Law. Therefore, in the fall of 1954, I returned to Rome. My residence was a comfortable one, in that I had spent three of my years in the study of Theology in the old North American College before moving for the fourth year into the newly constructed College on the Gianicolum Hill near the Vatican. Now I resided in the newly designated and remodeled North American College Graduate House, still known as the "House on Humility Street."

The move from undergraduate to graduate life was a dramatic change for me. I now lived in a two-room suite—a study and a bedroom: the reconstruction of the living area was extensive. Now as a priest and no longer a seminarian, I was free to come and go as I pleased—except for daily classes. Most (all?) of us celebrated our own early morning Mass on the side altars of the chapel. All of our meals were available at scheduled times.

One major change was the University I attended. For the next three years I would attend classes at the Lateran University, following four years of Theology at the Jesuit-run Gregorian University. The Lateran University was attached to St. John Lateran Basilica—about a five minute bus ride from our residence. St. John Lateran Basilica is designated as the "Mother of all churches worldwide"—a loose translation chiseled in Latin in marble near its main doors. The basilica is the Cathedral of the Pope in his capacity as the Bishop of the Diocese of Rome. The University, therefore, has a very special standing in the educational program of the Catholic Church. The professors were—and I assume still are—Canon Law experts whose specialties coincided with the various *dicasteria* (bureaus) of Vatican City to which they were assigned.

A General Overview of Canon Law

The Law of the Church covers a very broad range of subjects, and it is also very technical. In some fashion or other, it ranges through all Dogmatic and Moral Theology, much of Scripture, and how the Church is structured to accomplish her goals which are to lead her members to salvation. Its purpose is to follow the command of Christ to His Apostles who represented all of us, "Go and preach the gospel to all nations, baptizing them in the Name of the Father and of the Son, and of the Holy Spirit." (See Mark 16:15 & Matthew 18:19) The Canon Law deals with all the Sacraments, in addition to Theology and the Scriptures, and covers the Precepts of the Church (Christ told St. Peter, His first Pope, "Whatever you bind on earth, it will be bound in heaven, and what you loose on earth, it will be loosed in heaven."—Mt 18; 18.)

The Precepts of the Church will be presented in their entirety in Part VI.

Activities in Europe as a Priest and Canon Law Student

While I don't recall the specific courses I took during my first year of Canon Law study (actually, my fifth year as a student in Rome), I see no reason to look them up. The general extent of all three years of Canon Law are summarized above.

Now, as a priest, I could and did offer assistance to parishes and Catholic institutions around Rome at some of the busiest times, e.g.

Holy Week services, and to military chaplains when they had a special need, e.g. at Christmas time or Holy Week and Easter Services, or to replace them when they took their vacations.

Yet Another Encounter with Homosexuality

During Christmas vacation in 1954, I was invited to the Army base in Nurnberg, Germany, when there was a greater demand for confessions and extra Masses. When I arrived at the base, I found a Jesuit priest also there to assist the Catholic chaplain. He and I had dinner together that evening to discuss the 'division of labor' among the things we had been asked to do. To my intense dismay, there was another item on his agenda which I vaguely foresaw but was to be made painfully aware of during the night.

I had been given a room in the BOQ (Bachelor Officers' Quarters), and I assume he also was staying there. At about 1:00 A.M. or 1:30, he knocked and scratched at my door and called out to me in a stage whisper. At dinner, since by now I had experienced a number of encounters with homosexuals—starting in the seminary during first year college—I thought I recognized the signs. So I was gravely suspicious of his motives for knocking at my door in the middle of the night. Fortunately, as I had been advised, I had locked my door. So I asked him through the door what he wanted. He said "Just let me in." I told him to go back to bed and let me sleep. He continued to knock and scratch at my door for a half hour. He finally left. Actually, it seemed much more than a half hour. Needless to say, I didn't sleep very well that night.

The next morning at breakfast, I asked him, "Are you a homosexual and is that what you had in mind last night?" And he said yes. The situation gave me an opportunity I never before had—to explore the state of mind of such a person. I asked him many questions. For example, "Are you an active homosexual?" meaning do you engage frequently in sexual activities with men? The answer, of course, was yes. Do you have and do you seek to have sexual activities with many different men? Again yes. During the course of this conversation he seemed completely unabashed, and at one point stood and asked me to go to bed with him.

My intention was to treat this priest as I had been taught in Moral Theology: with kindness, sympathy and with direct honesty. I told him, of course, as firmly as I could that he was in serious trouble, both with the Sixth Commandment and with his vow of chastity, and that he should bend every effort to changing his life. He agreed he should change his life style, but it seemed to him to be very difficult, and I got the impression that he felt it would be impossible to do so. I told him that his Theology should tell him that he had a free will and with a good deal of prayer and well-planned action he could certainly succeed. There was no doubt, as has been true of every homosexual with whom I have had some kind of confrontation, that he was deeply and unconsciously bitter that he had this condition, but in almost every case, the homosexual was in extreme denial that anything was wrong. "After all," I heard time after time—and also from him—"God is love and these are acts of love, so there is nothing really wrong about it." I have no idea what happened with him. I never heard from him again. In case the reader is wondering, I was never in the slightest degree attracted to such a person. To me, what they suggested was distasteful and unnatural, and it was difficult for me to maintain an empathetic relationship with them during the discussions which I had initiated.

Summer Vacation—1955

During my first year of Canon Law study, it was required that I choose the subject for my doctoral dissertation. My two great interests beyond the Mass and the Real Presence were, theologically and canonically 1) the Sacrament of Matrimony, and 2) the Lay Apostolate. I chose the Sacrament of Matrimony at least partly because it embodies both concepts. Marriage, so my thinking went, is the source of the Lay Apostolate, in that the primary purpose of marriage is the begetting of children and raising them to be good Catholics—the basic form of the Lay Apostolate which was strongly emphasized throughout the history of the Church and would be very directly addressed by Vatican Council II.

Largely because of my friendship with Joan and David McKenzie, I had a basic understanding of how the Church of England came to be, so I undertook a study whose title was later to become *"Matrimonial Procedure in the law of the Church of England and in the Code of Canon Law: A Comparative Analysis."*

Henry VIII in his earlier years had been given the title "Defender of the Faith," and apparently was a devout Catholic. His first marriage, however, to his great disappointment, produced no male issue. He therefore petitioned the Holy See for an annulment of his marriage so he could marry again. This was in the early 1500's. Pope Julius II refused to grant him the dissolution of his marriage. Henry VIII therefore founded his own church which, since he was its head, would grant him the dissolution of his marriage. He subsequently had a total of six wives. To this day, the monarch of the United Kingdom is the head of the Church of England. It is this endorsement of a specific religion by the State which led the framers of our Constitution to incorporate the concept that there shall be separation between Church and State. It is this passage in the Constitution which is being today so incredibly misinterpreted that there are those who insist that there can be no recognition of the existence of God and they try their best to abolish the name of God from our society.

My two vacation trips—1955 and 1956—consisted in an initial visit to my relatives in Germany, followed by six to eight weeks with my friends in London and day after day and hour after hour in the Library of London doing the research and gathering the materials I needed to produce my dissertation as part of the requirements for my doctorate. My thesis basically stated and demonstrated that when the Church of England separated from the Catholic Church it fell into complete disarray. This is happening even today when we see the Church of England advocating a female priesthood, has appointed a practicing homosexual bishop and is developing major divisions within itself.

Each year in Canon Law we had to undergo an oral test in each course by the professor who taught the course. The test, of course, covered the entire year of matter. At the end of our third year, the oral test covered all three years of matter, and, as expected, was very difficult. But the Lateran University had a remarkable tradition: As each test took place, an observer (another professor) sat silently to ensure that the examiner was entirely fair. This saved me on one test. The professor was in a foul mood, asked me very difficult questions and appeared to be very angry with me. I thought that this inconsequential subject could lead me to failure in my aspiration for the doctorate. As I left the test, the observer smiled reassuringly at me. When a bell rang and I went back into the class room to receive my grade, I found that I was given 10 points out of a possible 10; the professor glowered at me, and the observer smiled at me. He had intervened in what he must have thought was unfair treatment. My overall score for the final tests was ten out of ten.

When I defended my thesis before a board of five, I also received ten out of ten points. So I passed my doctoral exams with flying colors, was awarded the doctorate (JCD), and made my preparations to definitively return to my diocese. I had gone to Rome as a seminarian in 1950. I came back in 1957 as an ordained priest, a Theologian and a Canon Lawyer. My next visit to Rome came fifty two years later in 1999.

CHAPTER 20

Return to the Sioux City Diocese

Back in the Sioux City Diocese in early summer of 1957, I was assigned to the Cathedral Parish for part time work (evenings and weekends) and immediately began work in the Chancery Office five days a week, 9-5. Not long thereafter, I was named Vice Chancellor of the diocese, *Vice Officialis* (assistant judge) of the diocesan Tribunal (the *Officialis* was an older pastor who was actively involved only once when I served as defending counsel to an errant priest). In all cases, mine was the "hands-on" role of dealing with the petitions which came before the Tribunal; (most of them involved declaration of nullity of marriages). At the same time, I was appointed the Diocesan Director of the Propagation of the Faith. A highlight during that responsibility was a visit to the headquarters of Bishop Fulton J. Sheen in New York City, the National Director of the Society for the Propagation of the Faith; he gave me his instructions on the activities of a Diocesan Director. (I had seen him once before in person when he came to the North American College where he gave a very impressive speech—more like a sermon—to all of us seminarians as a group.) For me, he was even more impressive in person than either in the presentation he made to us in Rome or on his television appearances.

At the same time I was assigned to another duty, which was to ensure that all the young priests who were teaching in the Catholic schools around the diocese, and all those seminarians who in the next couple of years would become priests, received their State of Iowa Teaching Certificates. In preparing for this program, I went to Des Moines, IA to visit the Director of Public Education for the State of Iowa who asked me what I thought was a very pertinent question: "Why are you concerned? Your Catholic Schools are private schools and do not fall under the laws of the State of Iowa. There is no need for your priests to acquire teaching certificates." My own preference was to drop the program and to stay independent of the State. My brother, Msgr. Eugene Kevane, who had built, opened and served as principal of the Central Catholic Heelan High School, serving 13 parishes in Sioux City, agreed. His stand was that the bishops of the U.S. had the power and authority—and the financial ability—to create their own teacher accrediting agency, which would follow the requirements of the Catholic Church and not the State of Iowa. The school he created—Heelan Catholic High School—quickly became the predominant school in the city (there were four large public schools), in every way from scholastic excellence to athletics; and at the time, none of the teachers in Heelan high school were endowed with teachers' certificates recognized by the State of Iowa.

I told Bishop Mueller about the statement of the Director of Public Education, but he was adamant: He was convinced that the State certification of priests would enhance the reputation of the Catholic schools. This was the solitary instance that I know of in which he succumbed to the political pressure from the Conference of U.S. Bishops. In many other matters he opposed the stance of the bishops and became known among them as the *Conscientia Corporis Episcoporum* (The Conscience of the Body of Bishops). It was, of course, a derogatory title. This is one instance in which the bishops of the United States bent over backward to appease the governments in the U.S. by 'fitting in' with American society. This was a heresy identified as Americanism by Pope Leo XIII in his encyclical

Testem Benevolentiae Nostrae (Witness of Our Benevolence) which identified a weakness in the American Church. In my opinion and in my experience, the heresy has grown and gotten stronger in the intervening years since the year 1900.

Since I didn't perceive the program of teacher priests acquiring Iowa teachers' certificates as immoral, in obedience I proceeded as the bishop wished. I'm not sure, considering what I know now, that I should have agreed to do it.

Not long after I started this program, I was assigned the directorship of the Catholic Cemetery which served the thirteen parishes in the city of Sioux City. I had what you might call 'a full plate.'

CHAPTER 21

A Specialized Duty—Chaplain of an Unwed Mothers' Home

A year later, retaining all my other duties, I was re-assigned from the Cathedral, and was appointed chaplain of St. Monica's Home for Unwed Mothers. There were fifteen to twenty girls in the home at all times. It was managed expertly and lovingly by Sister Eugene, a Benedictine nun who originated in a nearby town in neighboring Nebraska and who was revered for hundreds of miles around for the wonderful work she did for young pregnant girls, for her expertise as a nurse, and for her saintliness. The girls came from many miles around, from as far away as New York, Indiana, Ohio, Kansas, Missouri, Nebraska, Colorado, the Dakotas, Montana, Minnesota, even Alaska—actually, I suppose, from nearly every state in the union. It was during this assignment that I had my first experiences with two priests who seduced very young girls. It was one of those girls who, among many others, told me "I didn't know what he was doing." The problem of priests who broke their vows of celibacy was brought home to me when I was a very young priest, and the pain and anguish they caused in their young victims was implanted indelibly in my mind. It seemed to me that I learned to 'read' this kind of priest by simply conversing with him, and I believe I could tell with any young girl, and later young boy, when he or she had been so violated by a priest or, to put it more generally, by someone in whom they had a natural kind of trust—father, brother, uncle, priest, revered college professor, professional counselor. That experience at St. Monica's left an indelible implant in my mind and had much to do with whatever degree of empathy and understanding I have achieved in dealing with people from all walks of life.

Sister Eugene, who managed the pregnant girls at St. Monica's with a firm and loving hand, was a living saint. She had, and was known for, a deep devotion to St. Theresa, the Little Flower. Almost daily she petitioned the Little Flower for special help for one of "her girls". And she always asked for and expected a sign that her petition would be answered. The sign was always a rose. Someone would hand her a fresh rose, and when that happened she assumed that her request would be granted because they always had been. The roses seemed always to come from unexpected sources. A complete stranger would come into the home, ask for Sr. Eugene and hand her a rose. People who knew that she liked roses would bring them to her without any knowledge that she had a special petition in the works. Those of us who knew her were aware that the series of petitions was ongoing, perhaps several times a week, and the accumulation of roses was also uninterrupted. There was one incident which was awe-inspiring. One of the babies born to one of the girls appeared to be a hydrocephalic. His head seemed almost as large as the rest of his body. Several doctors made a cursory examination and each time said that it appeared that the baby was hydrocephalic. The Catholic Charities organization of the diocese, which was responsible for handling the adoption processes for the babies born at St. Monica's, took the position that such a baby would not be adoptable and therefore the baby's mother would have to keep the baby and be responsible for its care. This seemed to me a most uncharitable position for the diocesan Catholic Charities organization to take.

The head of the Catholic Charities (a priest!) had already, long before the baby was born told the young girl that she would have to be responsible for the baby when it was born if there was anything wrong with it. To me this was sheer cruelty; coming from a fellow priest, I found it to be unconscionable. Neither Sister Eugene nor I thought that this stance was very Catholic nor very charitable (and the bishop agreed with me and I thought therefore that we would be able to prevail). The girl's parents had no knowledge of her pregnancy, nor did anyone in the town she would have to return to, and of course she had no means to support herself and a baby. She had come to us for protection.

So Sister Eugene and I did what we could to have Catholic Charities assume guardianship of the baby or find someone who would. But the organization was adamant. Sister Eugene finally insisted that everything should depend on a test of the baby to determine whether he was indeed hydrocephalic. She and I were both privately convinced that the baby had the problem, but we were hoping against hope that something could occur to relieve the mother of a life with the burden of this baby. Sister Eugene initiated one of her special petitions to the Little Flower over a period of several days. On the day when the test was scheduled, Sister Eugene herself took the baby, was driven to the hospital, and, as she told me later, took the baby in the elevator to the floor where the lab was located. As the elevator door opened on the upper floor, a man handed her a bouquet of a dozen red roses, and the baby cried aloud and jerked in her arms.

In the next hour, the baby was given a complete series of tests and no trace of the hydrocephalic condition was found. Over the next week or so we saw the baby's head diminish in size and finally assume a normal size. In the next couple of months, the baby was adopted by a childless couple.

To Sister Eugene and me, a miracle had been performed. American Catholics, including bishops and priests, seem to have lost their belief in an all-powerful God who can and does intervene in miraculous fashion in the lives of His people.

An Uncommon Convent

The group of nuns at St. Monica's was perhaps the oddest assemblage of people I have ever seen collected under one roof.

And I refer in no way to the pregnant girls awaiting the birth of their babies, but to the religious nuns who were assigned to live their lives in this home. The Mother Superior of the religious order told me once that she had no other place to send the misfits and malcontents of her community.

The superior of the nuns at the home was a wizened, aged nun who was four feet something tall and who was a true miser. She hoarded almost everything in the home, especially food. She kept shelves full of old, moldy bread which was never used, nor, as far as I could ascertain, ever thrown away. The stockpile would keep growing until it reached epic proportions. Then (I assume) some enterprising nun, in the middle of the night, would spirit some of it away. Or perhaps the girls did.

Even though this nun was the superior, she ghosted around the home, communicating very little with anyone. I never found her in conversation with any of the nuns who were her charges, and when I tried to engage her in conversation, she would make some monosyllabic response and scuttle away.

Another of the nuns was a kleptomaniac. She would steal anything which was not nailed down. One generation of girls referred to her as "Sister Mary Klepto," and the title carried on among every generation of girls as long as I was there. I was warned when I first moved into my apartment at the home that I must keep my door locked or all my possessions would gradually disappear, because of her. She patrolled the halls of the home dressed in her religious (black) habit and a pair of white tennis shoes. It was a remarkable combination. The look in her eyes would convince anyone that she was mentally unbalanced. When she received communion during the morning Mass, she would lunge forward and snap at the Host. The first few times this happened, I ended up with my fingers in her mouth—and she bit them (lightly). Then, after a few days of this, as she was about to lunge once again for the Host, I quickly drew it away. She nearly fell over. The next morning she became somewhat wary, snapped at the Host, but not as forcefully. Finally, after a few days of having the Host pulled away from her, she became quiescent and simply waited for me to put the Host on her tongue. It was necessary later to repeat the treatment, because after a few days she would lapse back into lunging. (Those were the days when nobody received communion in the hand, as many or perhaps most people do now.)

The other two or three nuns assigned to St. Monica's were not as strange, but they were obviously misfits within the Order.

At one point, fortunately lasting only for 2 or 3 months, there were two French Canadian nuns at the home who were sisters-siblings. One of them arrived alone and was joined after a few weeks by her sister. I know of no other way to describe the two of them except to say that they were insane. There was no light of rationality in their eyes and it was almost frightening to talk to either one of them. One of them threatened one of the girls with a butcher knife. No one thought that she would actually stab anyone, but it was a frightening experience for the girl who was threatened.

Upon her arrival, the first one began subversive activities among the girls in an effort to divide and conquer. She started a whisper campaign against Sister Eugene, undermining her authority and creating dissension. She obviously wanted to usurp the administration of the home.

It was the first and only time I ever saw Sister Eugene's authority questioned or shaken, at least to the point at which she couldn't handle it herself. She asked me to intervene. When three or four of the more level-headed girls understood what was going on, they called a meeting of carefully chosen girls in the home and started to counter the whisper campaign. And the crisis ended. When the sister of the French Canadian nun arrived, together they tried again to undermine Sister Eugene's authority, but the earlier incident was too fresh in everyone's mind so the new effort was quickly quelled by the girls themselves.

Sister Mary Alphonsus, among all the nuns at the home, together with Sister Eugene, was a standout of rationality, personal devotion to her religious life and practical good sense. She was a strong support and friend to Sister Eugene, and probably, in my view, the only reason that Sister Eugene could maintain her sanity in the midst of such a strange kind of convent life. But while she was so strong in support of Sister Eugene, initially she was anything but a support to the girls who were in the home to have their babies. When I first arrived, the girls themselves reported to me that Sr. Alphonsus was mean, irritable and unkind to the girls. At the same time, the girls understood that she was the only support Sister Eugene had within the convent, and for that reason and because she was a good nun with a strong spiritual life, they respected her and were grateful for her indirect support.

Not long after I arrived, Sister Alphonsus had a heart attack and was taken to the hospital. We heard that she would survive, and after a few days she returned to the home. It was immediately obvious that her experience brought about a personality change. Her irritability was gone. She became very friendly and supportive to the girls and spent hours sitting and talking to them in small groups and on a one-on-one basis. Sister Eugene remarked on the change in her and said that, while she couldn't have performed the work without her before, now she had become a great help in working with the girls. Sister Alphonsus tried to tell me what had happened to her, but I was too young and inexperienced to pay any attention. But I do remember what she said. She said that she had an "out-of-body" experience during her heart attack. While the doctors and nurses were working on her, she said, she watched them from above and she had the most peaceful feeling she had ever had in her life. Then she knew she was to go back into her body and return to life. Being very naïve and new to the priesthood, I generally ignored what she was trying to tell me.

But I have regretted it ever since because over the years I have heard a number of stories of what appear to be authentic life-after-death experiences, and part of the experience in every case was a change in the person's outlook and treatment of others. I could have heard a detailed account of this good nun's after-life experience, but my scepticism led me to miss what could have been the opportunity of a lifetime.

Two of the young girls who were sent to be cared for by Sister Eugene at St. Monica's stand out in my mind because of the circumstances which brought them there, and a third whom Sister Eugene referred to me because of unusually difficult health problems complicated by very special circumstances.

The first who stands out in my mind was a special case, not because of any specific physical or sexual abuse, but because she became pregnant when she was only 12 years old. She had not yet begun her menstrual cycles. She became pregnant because she was looking for ways to get her mother's attention. Her mother had sent her father away many years before, and her mother, in total permissiveness, provided neither support nor love nor affection of any kind either to her or to her sister who was two years older. She also stands out in my memory for several reasons, one of which was that she was of genius intelligence, and another that she was impossible to deal with, being supremely arrogant, mouthy, disobedient, and a rabble rouser who created dissension among a sizeable group of the girls at the home at the time. Sister Eugene told me that she could do nothing with her and asked me to intervene.

When the girl came to see me for the first time, she treated me with complete discourtesy, was rude, foul mouthed and refused to answer any of my questions except with unprintable expletives. After a few minutes of that, I simply stood up, told her to leave, and opened the door for her. She was shocked. At the very least I had broken through her shell and got a reaction from her. After a day or so, I asked Sister Eugene to send her to me once again. This time, when she started the same kind of discourteous behavior, I told her what I thought of her behavior and what she was doing to Sister Eugene, to me and to others in the home. I described in detail how she got into the situation she was in (she obviously didn't know that the pattern was similar for all the girls), I told her how she sounded to everyone, how ungrateful she was to the one person who was there to help her no matter how ungrateful she appeared to be. As it sunk in, she began to cry. Then I shifted tactics and told her as kindly as I could what she should do to rectify the situation and make her stay for the next several months as comfortable as possible for herself, for Sister Eugene, and for the rest of the young women who were there at the time. From that moment, there was a startling change in her. She became one of the nicest young women I have ever known. She was thoughtful and kind. The foul language disappeared. She started to attend daily Mass and was frequently on her knees in the chapel. Sister Eugene and I found out that this girl's mother, for as long as the girl could remember, had a succession of men who came to their house, usually staying over night, and her mother paid no attention to her whatsoever except to allow her to do whatever she wanted. So as a young girl of 10 or 11, she began going out at night—and her mother said nothing. She started to stay out all night, coming home only in time to go to school in the morning. And she still heard nothing from her mother. Then she consciously decided that if she got pregnant, her mother would have to pay attention to her. One of the shocking things about the episode was that her mother came up from Missouri, bringing her older daughter whom she dropped off at a convent in Omaha (in my opinion, escaping an untenable situation at home), and the other she brought to St. Monica's to have a baby. After the girl had the baby and she was preparing to leave, I asked her why, after such a terrible beginning, she had become one of the nicest persons I have ever known. Speaking of the session with me when she had cried, she said (I will never forget her exact words): "That was the first time in my life that someone thought enough of me to tell me what to do." She was one of the few who wrote regularly after she left. Sister

Eugene and I had the impression that she was doing reasonably well and was putting her life together in a positive way. She certainly had the intelligence to do so.

The second stand-out in my memory was the case of a 13 year old who had been sexually abused by her own father, who was the father of her baby. Her mother brought her to the home, and it was she who told us (part of) how it happened. The girl had no ill feelings about her father at all and appeared to dearly love him. We assumed that as she grew older and the enormity of what happened to her became clear in her mind, she would lose that love and respect for him. After she had been at the home for a month or so, on his own initiative the girl's father asked if he could visit his daughter, which we permitted with great reluctance because we expected him to be a despicable and loathsome man. Unexpectedly, we found him to be a heartbroken, grief-stricken, likeable man whose anguish and remorse were nearly unbearable for him. He truly loved his daughter (as a father) and would do anything at all to make amends if it were possible. And he told us that more than a year before, his wife inexplicably moved out of the marriage bed, cut off all marriage relations, and left their daughter sleeping with her father. She had been sleeping with her parents since she was a baby. The girl told us separately that her mother no longer slept with her father. Sister Eugene and I were both puzzled (and I remain so to this day) as to which parent was more to blame for the situation: the father or the mother. And I have never been able to imagine that girl having a reasonable life unless she got some very special help. I've often wondered how she fared.

A Very Special Case of Sexual Abuse

After several years of working with the unwed mothers at St. Monica's, including perhaps 3 or 4 other difficult, sometimes incestuous, cases (involving priests, special family friends, uncles, and even brothers) I was well prepared for the most important case of sexual abuse I would ever encounter. Still a young priest, I had gained a reputation as being effective in counseling young teen age girls. So this young woman was referred to me by a counselor at a local college through Sister Eugene at the hospital as one who had an unusually difficult problem and was badly in need of help. While her home was at the other end of the state in another diocese, she intended to go to college in Sioux City, as I found out later, to escape the situation she had found herself in at home.

She had been seduced by a priest who was a friend of her family. She was close to despair, because she felt a huge sense of guilt that she had been the cause of it all. When I learned the details, I assured her that I did not then (and I do not now), believe that she ever committed the least kind of sin because she in fact was forcibly raped. She had always been a religious girl and had a very strong faith which was badly shaken by this episode. But her strong faith was the only thing which saved her. Her self-esteem was non-existent and she felt that she had ruined her life. She had been a virgin, which was extremely important to her, and her virginity had been forcibly taken from her by a trusted figure in her young life. By means of intensive prayer on her part and a great deal of discussion, she began to regain her sense of self worth. But now that she had begun to trust someone again, and was able to trust me as a priest, she began to tell me of other traumatic episodes in her life which left her in a state of abject vulnerability in her relationship with that priest. She didn't want to bring charges against the priest, even knowing that he had seduced other young women, because "it might bring scandal to the Church." An outstanding Catholic, she had, and has to this day, a deep love for the Church.

(It is important that I mention that I have her full permission to incorporate these very confidential matters in this book.)

She is certainly the worst case of abuse in sexual matters I have ever encountered. Several times she said to me, "I didn't know what he was doing!" At the same time, she knew it was wrong. And, unlike many others I have worked with in similar situations, she directly faced the problem (and other problems still to be discussed), making no effort to deny any of it. I believe it is this honesty which allowed her eventually to live the life of a normal woman. As Christ said, "The truth will set you free" (John 8: 32).

Because of problems at home—e.g. her older sister encouraging her to solicit help with her studies from that priest—she frequently visited another sister and baby-sat her children. Then her sister's husband began to molest her, taking every opportunity to fondle her and abuse her sexually.

Caught between two impossible situations, having just graduated from high school, she decided to move across the state intending to go to college in Sioux City. A counselor tried to help her (she saw that she was depressed, completely lacking in self-esteem, and yet was a very prayerful Catholic girl.) She refused to talk to the counselor, so the counselor referred her to me through Sister Eugene at St. Vincent's Hospital.

A remarkable thing happened: She trusted me as a priest, even though it was a priest who had seduced her. ("I never looked on him as a priest.") She began to speak quite freely to me about the episodes with the priest and her brother-in-law, and it became obvious that she was suffering from a very intense guilt feeling—as I had found to be true with most young girls when they get into trouble.

Finally, after many regular meetings, she told me of her most deep-seated guilt feeling and the most shameful thing on her mind.

When she was about 10, in 4th grade, one day she was wrestling with one of her brothers who was about 12 in one of the upstairs bedrooms. Her father came in on them, shouted at her (not at her brother who fled) and left an image which has been burned into her memory ever since. He said "If that's what you want, I'll give it to you." He exposed himself and came toward her, as she says, with a huge erection. She said she had never been so frightened. She went out the window of the second story bedroom, jumped off the roof and didn't stop running for several blocks. She told no one about it. Since that incident she never again felt comfortable alone in the house with her father and for the next 10 years or more always found some pretext to leave when everyone else was gone.

So all her formative years from the fourth grade until after graduation from high school, when she left home, were filled with trauma, stress and anxiety. Her father began to abuse her verbally, humiliating her at every opportunity in front of the rest of the family. When she was in 7th grade, because her mother was away for a few days, it fell to her to get up early and make breakfast for her father. During that time when her mother was away, she consciously thought that perhaps she should give her father another chance, so one day she called to him to come look at what she saw out the kitchen window. He came up behind her, started to rub against her and was obviously becoming aroused. She left the house, never gave him another chance, and spent the rest of her life trying not to hate him. When her mother returned after that incident, her father told her mother that she had done a terrible job of taking care of him and he redoubled his verbal abuse of her.

This, then, was the vulnerable girl whom the priest friend of the family seduced when she came to him for support. She had just graduated from Catholic high school, had known and trusted priests all her life. Her mother spent years as housekeeper in a rectory. She thought this was one contact she could make with complete safety. After this incident, she decided to get away from everything: her father, her brother-in-law and the priest. She moved across the state, using attendance at college as the rationale. Some counselor correctly diagnosed her traumatized state of mind and sent her to me through Sister Eugene. For some reason this young girl was able to trust me, and over a long series of visits, haltingly told me the story of seduction by the priest—a seduction which was clearly a case of forcible rape. Since she was an outstanding Catholic girl, she felt very guilty because she felt she had somehow caused the incident, and she was determined never to reveal the incident to anyone because it would cause scandal, and, she said "most priests are not like that." (She was right, of course, and still is. She is a significant counterpoint to the current victims of pedophile priests, none of whom, at least according to press reports, have shown any inclination to forgive their assailants nor to pray for them.)

She was in fourth grade when her father attacked her; she was about 12 when her brother-in-law began to molest her; she was probably 17 when she was raped by a priest, and about 18 or 19 when she talked to me. Now a woman of 70 plus years of age, understanding the pain of the victims of pedophile priests better than those of us who have never been victims of abuse, she says that none of those victims will ever find surcease until they fully, truly and spiritually are able to forgive their attackers. No amount of court action, no amount of money, no amount of criticism of the bishops and the clergy will ever give them peace. After years of prayer, asking for the grace and strength to forgive her father, her brother-in-law and the priest who attacked her, she finally was given the insight that she had allowed herself to be controlled and shaped by what they did to her, and that those incidents need have no further bearing on the way she now lives and thinks of herself. The day came, just a few years ago, during attendance at Mass, when she realized that she had forgiven the three people who had abused her, and ". . . it was as if a great weight had been lifted off me." Every last vestige of bitterness and resentment was gone, and she made a giant leap in the development of her own personal spiritual life.

During the time that we were talking initially in 1959, she was preparing for serious surgery on her spine at the hospital in which Sister Eugene was a nurse, and she began to worry that she would say something about the incident with the priest while under sedation and might therefore be the source of scandal. I tried to calm her fears by telling her that Sister Eugene would be there throughout the surgery, and, even if she did say something, Sister Eugene would keep the confidence. The surgery took place early in the morning on the scheduled day. At about 3:00 in the afternoon, Sister Eugene called to tell me that the girl had been in a coma all day, they had tried everything to bring her out of it, but nothing worked, and would I please come and see if I could help. They were afraid she would die. When I walked into the hospital room, Sister Eugene called her by name and said "Father's here." She immediately got up on her elbows (she had been lying face down because the surgery was on her back) and turned and looked at me with a radiant smile on her face which I will never forget. I believe she had made up her mind that she would talk to no one except me and simply stayed unconscious until I arrived.

After I went home that afternoon, the implications of this young woman's awakening for me and reliance upon me shook me to the core. She had no one to whom she could look for support. She couldn't tell her parents or her family. (I didn't know why until she finally, some time later, told me about the incidents of abuse by her father and brother-in-law.) To go home would have put her back into close proximity to the priest who had abused her. (I had received a letter from him in which he admitted his indiscretion. I was able to extract a promise from him that he would stay away from her and her family or I would take his letter to his bishop. I had evidence later that he didn't keep his promise—probably thinking I couldn't find out—and had continuing contact with several of her sisters. Even so, she didn't want me to press the matter with his bishop because it would simply become too public and could cause her additional pain.) Her tenuous hold on self esteem at the time revolved around me as a person who knew (part of) the story about her and still held her in high regard. I decided that, since her mental health and perhaps even her ultimate salvation seemed to depend on me, I would continue to give her spiritual direction in order to help solidify her sense of self worth. Later, as my celibate state required, I would find some other kind of support for her at an appropriate time.

It was during these subsequent discussions that she told me about the image implanted in her mind of her father coming at her fully exposed and aroused, and about her sister's husband who began to molest her. She had nightmares about her father for many years, until she was in her late fifties. In terms of destructive power, her father's abuse of her was far more devastating than the violation by the priest. She had nightmares about both, but those about her father caused her considerably more anguish than those about the priest. Throughout her high school years and beyond, she suffered from migraine headaches.

After she was in what I judged to be reasonably good mental and emotional health, I took steps to turn her over to a psychologist/counselor/professor of my acquaintance at a Catholic college in a distant city. He was a married man, a Catholic with an excellent reputation. As we made the transfer, neither she nor I told him about her history. It was her choice to see how comfortable she would be before revealing those things to him. A few weeks later, she called me frantically late at night to tell me that this counselor had tried to attack her sexually. He had called her, set an appointment to see her for the third time, took her out to dinner, then took her to the airport to 'watch the planes.' He assaulted her, forcibly kissed her, and stopped only when she started screaming. He took her home, and she called me. Most of the self-esteem she had recaptured in the past few months was now lost, because someone she felt she could trust—at least partly because I had recommended him—had once again turned on her.

After that dreadful episode, she began a routine of coming to see me (it was a fairly easy bus ride), and I began to realize that her dependence on me was growing, and I wondered what solution was going to be available to cut the ties. During this time, my work as described above continued, and I was additionally assigned as Diocesan Director of the Papal Volunteer program. And also during this time, at my urging, she had gone into nurse's training to prepare a future for herself.

Having completed her training, she decided to get a job in a hospital in Milwaukee, Wisconsin. She visited there, applied at several hospitals in the city, and wasn't offered a single job, in spite of the shortage of nurses at the time—1964. Then, on a visit home, she saw an ad for a nursing job at the hospital in Highland Park, Illinois, a suburb a few miles north of Chicago. She applied and was accepted immediately for the happiest nursing experience of her life. I thought that this would begin to solve the spiritual problem I had as a celibate priest with an attractive young woman so dependent on me. Chicago is five hundred miles from Sioux City and the little I had seen of it I didn't like, so I blithely assumed the potential problem was solved.

Papal Volunteers for Latin America

In 1961-1962 Bishop Mueller assigned me to start a new program in the diocese—on top of all the functions I was performing. The program, *Papal Volunteers for Latin America*—PAVLA for short—was the brain child of Pope Paul VI. It was assigned to the Latin American Bureau of the United States Catholic Conference, from which the appeal went out to all bishops to initiate the program on the diocesan level. I recognized the program as a part of the Lay Apostolate which was so much a part of Vatican Council II, and it was therefore a particular interest of mine. As a start, I organized a committee of three Catholic lay men—a lawyer, an insurance man, and a teacher—all of them recommended by their pastors. After numerous fits and starts and many planning sessions, we began to announce the program and organized an initial public meeting at the principal parish in Fort Dodge, Iowa, situated at the eastern end of the diocese of Sioux City.

At the end of the well-attended meeting, as everyone was filing out, we saw three people—a woman and two men—working their way toward us. They were a nurse, a teacher and a electrician. The first two were in their mid-twenties, the third in his thirties. To make a long story short, after much training in theology, language (Portuguese), the culture of Latin America and in particular of Brazil and acculturation, they ended up in the diocese and city of Manaus, Brazil. I accompanied them. The city of Manaus, although one thousand miles from the mouth of the Amazon, was nevertheless a major seaport. This gives some idea of how huge the Amazon River is—it has four tributaries which are larger than our Mississippi River.

Those three volunteers had a major impact on the area. I received glowing reports from the Redemptorists on the work of each. For example, the nurse prevailed with local religious and medical authorities to encourage people generally (among many other things) to wear shoes. Since the population invariably went barefoot, they were infested with various kinds of parasites which entered their bodies through their feet. Her efforts brought about a major improvement in individual health.

After seeing the three Sioux City volunteers settled in their exotic new duties and having gotten acquainted with the Redemptorist Fathers, I returned to Sioux City and to all my other responsibilities.

About six months after my return from Brazil, a national conference was scheduled in Chicago for the PAVLA program. This was in 1962 or 1963. All diocesan directors and returned volunteers were invited to attend. Because in about a year's time, I had organized the program and sent three volunteers to Brazil, I was recognized during the conference as a successful diocesan director. The National Director of the program at the time was a Father Fernandez, S.J., who led the conference. Candidly, I heard things I strongly disagreed with. Remember, I had only recently completed my own study of Vatican Council II, and I was entirely devoted to the concept of the Lay Apostolate, which was so prominently presented in the Council. What I heard at the conference was a kind of "watered down" social service program with very little, if any, emphasis on the spiritual element which was and is so essential to the lay apostolate, and no emphasis on the admonition of Christ ". . . to go forth and preach the gospel to all nations, baptizing them . . . ." This lack of emphasis on these critical subjects came from the National Director himself, and from a couple of leading members of the Latin America Bureau of which PAVLA was one of four divisions. I spoke out strongly and contradicted those things I perceived as errors in the philosophy of PAVLA as presented, and as the conference ended went back to

Sioux City determined to develop the program there independently of the national office.

Sometime in the next few months, I received a letter from Father John Considine, M.M., the Director of the Latin America Bureau at the United States Catholic Conference (USCC) in Washington, D.C., asking if I would consider replacing Father Fernandez, S.J., as National Director of the Papal Volunteer program. I replied that I was happy with what I was doing, but if he could convince me that for some reason my capabilities rather than some one else's would benefit the program, and, above all, if my bishop would release me for the work, I would consider it. Even if my bishop approved, I had a number of conditions which we could discuss later.

When Bishop Mueller read the letter, he immediately refused, saying that he needed me for the work I was doing in the diocese. Father Considine's direct assistant (he introduced himself as "Director with Father Considine of the Latin America Bureau"), a Monsignor whose name I don't recall, then visited Bishop Mueller to request my services. Bishop Mueller again refused. Some days later, the bishop called me to his office and told me that he had received a letter from Cardinal Cushing of Boston, also requesting my services. Bishop Mueller said, in effect, that when a top ranking official makes a request, one has to take it very seriously. I pleaded with him not to change his mind, and he replied, "You'll do it if I tell you to, won't you?" And I said, "Of course." My two primary arguments had been that I was happy in my current responsibilities, and that I had spent seven years in Italy away from my family, and, since my widowed mother was alone, living in Sioux City, I wanted to stay and be able to visit her at will. But he ordered me to go.

I told the bishop about my own reservations and conditions, and he approved them. If I could be satisfied with regard to them, he wanted me to become the National Director of the Papal Volunteer program. The primary assurance I wanted and received from Father Considine was that I would administer the entire program according to my own understanding of the lay apostolate and make my own decisions without interference from him or any other member of the Latin America Bureau—all this because of what I heard at the PAVLA national conference where there was no emphasis on the spiritual element of such an enterprise and a strong emphasis on the 'social service' nature of such an undertaking. I also had heard from a few at that meeting a strong opposition to the idea of sending members of the laity into Latin America. I knew, as a matter of conscience, that I needed to be completely independent in planning and organizing the program.

With those things settled, it was determined that my appointment as PAVLA National Director at its headquarters in Chicago would be effective on September 1, 1964. This quickly became public knowledge.

Ironically, in June of that year, nearly four months before my appointment took effect, I received a somewhat irate letter from the PAVLA *field representative* named Kevin in Lima, Peru (forwarded to me from the National Office in Chicago), berating me for not yet having taken steps to correct the problems which, in his opinion, needed to be addressed. The letter made a number of negative assumptions about me, was hostile in tone, angry—and seemed to ascribe to the 'social service' approach to the Papal Volunteer program. I found out later that he was closely associated with a Peruvian priest who advocated "Liberation Theology," which I exposed much later to the Bishops' Committee as thinly disguised Marxism. As we'll see in the next section, Pope John Paul II later condemned Liberation Theology during one of his trips to Latin America.

I answered Kevin's letter in as positive and friendly a way as I could, but I didn't know that the letter was something of a forewarning of the less-than-true-Catholic opposition which awaited me.

PART IV

THE PAPAL VOLUNTEER PROGRAM AND THE HERESIES AND WEAKNESSES IN THE U.S. CHURCH

CHAPTER 22

My Move to Chicago as National Director of PAVLA

After packing my car with my few belongings (I had been "home" in the Sioux City Diocese for six years, more or less, and was in my early thirties), I drove to Chicago—about five hundred miles—to become the National Director of the Papal Volunteers for Latin America (PAVLA), a lay apostolate program. It was the creation of Pope Paul VI and was one of four divisions of the Latin America Bureau (LAB) whose Director was Father John Considine, MM., a member of the Maryknoll missionary order which had for many years maintained a strong presence in the countries of Latin America. The Latin America Bureau itself was one of many bureaus with diverse purposes contained within the United States Catholic Conference (USCC) which was (and is) the administrative arm of what is the United States Conference of Catholic Bishops (USCCB). The Director of the USCC was Bishop Joseph Benardin.

My state of mind as I moved into Chicago was very complex. I was looking forward to the new challenge and confident I could handle it. After all, I had adjusted to two vastly different cultures—Italy and Germany. I had become reasonably fluent in three different languages: Italian, German and Latin—I should have little trouble 'getting along' in Spanish and Portuguese (Brazil). In the past six years in my diocese, I had successfully and simultaneously undertaken responsibility for a number of diverse obligations which were described in Part III.

Later, during my first trip into Latin America—a visit to Mexico City—I truly felt as if I was 'coming home', because the atmosphere and attitudes were so similar to my life in Italy for seven years. Nevertheless, I was proceeding into unknown duties which at that time I knew little about except for the experience I had as Diocesan Director of the Papal Volunteer program. I was about to be thrust into a program which potentially encompassed every diocese in the United States and every diocese in every country of Latin America. It would be a great understatement to say that part of my feeling as I moved into Chicago at the time was reverence, intimidation and fearfulness.

My Two Residences in Chicago

The Chancery in Chicago found a residence for me in a large parish—and very large rectory—on the south side of Chicago. I don't remember the name of the parish. All I remember is that the rectory and church were located on Throop Street. The pastor was Father Paul Traut. There were three assistants and another priest in residence who was undergoing spinal surgery which turned out to be considerably less than successful. The three assistants were good priests. The priest in residence and I became friends. The two housekeepers, natives of Ireland, were both efficient and saintly. The pastor, however, was something else, a living example of what a rabble-rousing priest—Andrew Greeley—at a major conference later was to decry in ringing tones as "triumphalism" in the Church. All that I knew for sure that the pastor did was shop for and occasionally buy very expensive furniture for his suite of rooms and perhaps generally for the rectory. It was a wealthy parish.

One morning after my own Mass, as I prepared to go to my office in downtown Chicago where I had a series of very important meetings scheduled throughout the day, he came to me and wanted me to take a sick call in the parish. His three assistants, he said, were not available. I didn't have the time, told him so, and suggested that perhaps he could take care of it himself. He obviously looked on me as simply another of his assistants, shouted at me to do what he told me, and got so angry that I relented even though it destroyed a very important day for me with visitors who had come from different parts of the country and Latin America to meet with me.

The upshot of that was that, in a week or so, he threw me out of his rectory. On the day I left, the two Irish housekeepers, bless them, were crying as they saw me go.

My next residence was at St. Andrew's parish on the North Side of Chicago, where, as you will see a bit further on, I was introduced to true Heresy within the U.S. Catholic Church, and bitter hostility toward Cardinal Cody, the just-appointed Archbishop of Chicago.

CHAPTER 23

Chicago 1964 to 1966—Building the Papal Volunteer Program

The USCC (United States Catholic Conference) was/is the administrative arm of the Body of Bishops (all the Catholic Bishops) in the U.S. The Bishops' Committee for Latin America oversaw the entire Latin America Bureau; four Subcommittees oversaw each of the four divisions of the Latin America Bureau. Therefore I answered to Bishop Joseph Hodges of Wheeling, West Virginia, chairman of the Papal Volunteer subcommittee, and to Father John Considine, MM, director of the Latin America Bureau. My appointment as national director was effective on September 1, 1964. My headquarters initially was in Chicago where I came to know Cardinal Cody, Archbishop of Chicago, who was to give me his unflagging support regardless of the political consequences.

It was with deep satisfaction that I began my responsibilities as National Director of the Papal Volunteer program. Since I had a deeply rooted interest in promoting the involvement of the laity in the overall mission of the Catholic Church—this subject had emerged during my Theology studies as an area of great personal significance—I felt that this appointment put me into the center of what I wanted to do. It seemed to me that this could be perceived as one of the most important programs ever devised for the life of the Church. As the laity can penetrate society in a way that the priests and hierarchy cannot, this would allow specially selected lay personnel to bring their spirituality and the theological and social doctrine of the Catholic Church directly to bear upon their professional counterparts in a way that has not been seen very often since the early Church. And it could and should be accomplished in perfect harmony with the documents of Vatican Council II regarding the lay apostolate. This and programs like it could immediately strengthen the Church and bring about an unprecedented harmony among the hierarchy, the clergy, the religious, and the huge mass of the faithful laity.

Unfortunately, the enemies of the Church must have seen the same possibilities that I did, because they began to attack the Papal Volunteer program as soon as I made my plans known. The attacks were unrelenting up to, including, and beyond July 1, 1969, when I presented to the Conference of Bishops my memorandum calling for action against the organized efforts to discredit the Papal Volunteer program and to subvert the relationship between the Church in the United States and the Church in the countries of Latin America. The frightening and shocking contents of that memorandum will be presented later in this section of this book.

In my role as national director of the Papal Volunteer program, I was responsible for calling upon every bishop of every diocese in the country, requesting the appointment of a priest as diocesan director for the Papal Volunteer program. (I made some exceptions to that where I felt the bishop was himself a Modernist who would appoint PAVLA directors who in turn would recruit volunteers who would have to be rejected.) Thus the strength of the Papal Volunteer program was to be founded in the support of a bishop in the U.S., who through his representative would recruit, and provide financial support for, volunteers among the laity of every profession who could join their professional counterparts in a specific diocese in the countries of Latin America where the bishop requested their services. Their purpose was to join the Latin American laity and work among them.

This was to be a shining example of the concept of the lay apostolate, which had been so clearly delineated and so strongly called for by the Fathers of Vatican Council II. See the Decree on the Apostolate of the Laity, *Apostolicam Actuositatem*, solemnly promulgated by his holiness, Pope Paul VI, on November 18, 1965. Following is a small portion of that Decree, taken from Chapter I, '*The Vocation of the Laity to the Apostolate*':

> "The Church was founded for the purpose of spreading the kingdom of Christ throughout the earth for the glory of God the Father, to enable all men to share in His saving redemption . . ., and that through them the whole world might enter into a relationship with Christ. All activity of the Mystical Body directed to the attainment of this goal is called the apostolate, which the Church carries on in various ways through all her members. For the Christian vocation by its very nature is also a vocation to the apostolate. No part of the structure of a living body is merely passive but has a share in the functions as well as life of the body: so, too, in the body of Christ, which is the Church, "the whole body . . . in keeping with the proper activity of each part, derives its increase from its own internal development (Eph. 4:16) . . . .
>
> "In the Church there is a diversity of ministry but a oneness of mission. Christ conferred on the Apostles and their successors the duty of teaching, sanctifying, and ruling in His name and power. But the laity likewise share in the priestly, prophetic, and royal office of Christ and therefore have their own share in the mission of the whole people of God in the Church and in the world."

In spite of this and the many, many other points made by the Council in that section and others (cf. Lumen Gentium, Chapter IV, *The Laity),* Msgr. Ivan Illich and Father Luis Colonnese (who directed CICOP—one of the four divisions of LAB), and, most likely, Bishop Joseph Bernardin, made continuous statements that the Papal Volunteers had "no right" to go to Latin America, and Father Colonnese attacked the training of the Papal Volunteers including subjects such as theology, the lay apostolate, personal spirituality and cultural adaptation. (To my knowledge, Father Colonnese had no special education in Theology or Canon Law, and no significant experience in intercultural living.) No mention was ever made that PAVLA was founded by Pope Paul VI (except by myself and other members of the PAVLA program). The "signs of the times" mentioned in the Council documents and constantly referred to by Father Colonnese certainly did not point toward a non-religious character of the lay apostolate. He and those he associated with seemed to have a limited vision for the work of the laity in the Church—in his mind, it should be a kind of 'social work' approach. Vatican Council II, however, inculcated a greater and more profound intervention of the laity in the mission of the Church. The following excerpt (from Chapter IV—The Laity) epitomizes how Vatican Council II enunciates the centuries-old tradition of the Church regarding the role of the laity in the over-all work of the Church:

> "But the laity, by their very vocation, seek the kingdom of God by engaging in temporal affairs and by ordering them according to the plan of God. They live in the world, that is, in each and in all of the secular professions and occupations. They live in the ordinary circumstances of family and social life, from which the very web of their existence is woven. They are called there by God that by exercising their proper function and led by the spirit of the Gospel they may work for the sanctification of the world from within as a leaven. In this way they may make Christ known to others, especially by the testimony of a life resplendent in faith, hope and charity. Therefore, since they are tightly bound up in all types of temporal affairs it

> is their special task to order and to throw light upon these affairs in such a way that they may come into being and then continually increase according to Christ to the praise of the Creator and the Redeemer.
>
> "The laity are gathered together in the People of God and make up the Body of Christ under one head. Whoever they are they are called upon, as living members, to expend all their energy for the growth of the Church and its continuous sanctification, since this very energy is a gift of the Creator and a blessing of the Redeemer.
>
> "The lay apostolate, however, is a participation in the salvific mission of the Church itself. Through their baptism and confirmation all are commissioned to that apostolate by the Lord Himself. Moreover, by the sacraments, especially holy Eucharist, that charity toward God and man which is the soul of the apostolate is communicated and nourished. Now the laity are called in a special way to make the Church present and operative in those places and circumstances where only through them can it become the salt of the earth . . . . Thus every layman, in virtue of the very gifts bestowed upon him, is at the same time a witness and a living instrument of the mission of the Church itself "according to the measure of Christ's bestowal".

In the light of these and lengthier pronouncements regarding the laity in Vatican Council II, and considering that the Papal Volunteer Program was ordered into existence by Pope Paul VI, I have never been able to understand how some bishops and clergy not only did not support the Papal Volunteer program, but beyond that, exercised open hostility toward the program and did their best to destroy it. The only reasons I have been able to come up with will be unveiled as we proceed with this narrative.

The Challenge of International Planning

My own job as national director, as I presented it and had it approved by the Conference of Bishops, was seven-fold:

1) to establish the recruiting mechanism in the United States which would take applications from lay people to join the program, and to coordinate the work of the diocesan directors throughout the country in that recruitment effort;
2) to establish a training program for the volunteers before they embarked on their responsibilities in a designated country and diocese in Latin America;
3) to receive requests from the bishops of dioceses in Latin America who wanted to have this specific kind of help;
4) to work with those Latin American bishops as they organized or identified the programs to which the Papal Volunteers would be attached;
5) to organize and administer a moral and physical support system for the American volunteers during their tenure in the foreign environment;
6) to organize the fund raising activities which would at least partially support the volunteers during their tenure (travel to and from Latin America, with the monetary and moral support they needed during their three year period of service);
7) to facilitate their return to their homes, arrange for their replacements if desired by the Latin American authority, and to help them to 're-acculturate' to their own country, encouraging them to bring their spiritual message to their professional counterparts, continuing their apostolate now in their native country.

As the Papal Volunteer program developed, we in the National Office were clearly aware of the phenomenon called "culture shock"—the stress which occurs in a person in adjusting to the customs of a foreign culture—and we did our best to prepare them to deal with it. But when large numbers of volunteers began to return home after serving for three years, we had to help them deal with what we called "*reverse* culture shock." This was more difficult than acculturating to the new country on arrival, because now they had assimilated a great deal of the new culture. They themselves had changed, their own country had changed in ways they were not accustomed to, and therefore they could and did feel initially uncomfortable in their own culture. We found it necessary to have a program to help them speed the process of re-adaptation, and to find perhaps a new way of making a living. It was very helpful in this regard that I myself had personally adjusted to foreign cultures during many years as a student in Italy and in travel throughout Europe and the Middle East; and also having experienced 'reverse culture shock' upon returning to the U.S. after seven years overseas. (To this day I am conscious of certain elements in the Italian and German cultures—and now Latin American cultures—which we do not have in the U.S. and which I miss.) Since I had personally experienced culture shock and reverse culture shock, I could explain in a general way what the volunteers would experience at both ends and establish the means to help them to cope with it.

The Three Start-Up Steps

There were three things which, to my mind, were of paramount importance: 1) To organize and hold conferences in the U.S. on a regional basis with Diocesan Directors, their bishops and as many other bishops as would meet with me to encourage them to establish their own diocesan programs. 2) To tour the countries of Latin America where we had volunteers on the job, to meet with the volunteers and their bishops and local leaders. 3) To establish a sound training program for the volunteers before they went to their assignments so they could more completely understand their mission, understand their role as emissaries of the Church within the professional groups among whom they would work, and to bring their own spiritual lives to bear among their professional equals.

I worked my way through all three of these objectives in that order, interspersing the first with communications directed toward the existing Field Representatives who were there in Latin America to give support to their fellow volunteers: one each in Venezuela, Brazil, Chile, Peru, Columbia/Ecuador, Mexico, Central America, and Jamaica.

My purpose in all these meetings—actually in all three of the undertakings—was to receive and provide input into all segments of the program so as to achieve a meeting of minds, and to make known the number of specific requests we had from dioceses in Latin America for the intervention of Papal Volunteers.

At each of the regional meetings in the U.S., I made available materials for discussion, which contained suggestions for organizing the program at the diocesan level. Each meeting included a few diocesan directors from the region, a few returned volunteers from those dioceses, and in one case a bishop. One important result was about 50 to 60 prospective volunteers attended the National Training Center in Washington, D.C. for the following summer.

In the course of this first step, I spoke with nearly every bishop in the United States or at least his close representative, worked with as many diocesan directors of the Papal Volunteer program as were appointed by their bishops. I also worked with the authorities at the Catholic University of America in Washington D.C. to set up the annual training program which provided each group of volunteers with the basics they needed to begin their work in Latin America.

While most of the U.S. bishops received the Papal Volunteer program with enthusiasm, I did hear a few unsettling things. One of the bishops, on finding that I had originated in the Diocese of Sioux City, told me in a disparaging tone of voice that they called my bishop, Most Rev. Jos. M. Mueller, the '*conscientia coetus episcoporum*'—the 'conscience of the body of bishops'—but it has become evident that the body of bishops needs such a person: They are subject to group dynamics; and while they may feed on each other's strengths, they also, sadly, feed each other's weaknesses and succumb to political pressures. There will be more on this further on. Another unsettling attitude which I occasionally encountered was a pejorative attitude by some U.S. bishops toward the bishops, clergy and faithful of Latin America. For example: "They're very backward there, aren't they? I suppose they need our help."

I looked on this attitude as the concept of the "ugly American" as it operates within the Catholic Church in the United States. I believe it is something of a "We are the master race" complex which is unfortunately a part of the U.S. culture. It was a consequence of the developing Heresy of Americanism as it was identified by Pope Leo XIII in his encyclical letter *Testem Benevolentiae Nostrae (Expression of Our Good Will),* which will be addressed in greater depth as we proceed. (The encyclical is given in its entirety in Appendix B at the end of this book.)

With very few exceptions, I was received courteously and graciously by almost all the bishops. Most of them professed to believe that the Papal Volunteer program was a wonderful undertaking, that it would do a great deal of good for the laity of the United States, give them a positive program to be involved in, and contribute positively to the development of their spiritual lives.

I worked with perhaps 60-70 bishops in 19 countries of Latin America, from Mexico to Chile, established a specialized language training program in Mexico City which was called the "Hogar Interamericano" (Inter-American Home—so named by a prominent Mexican layman) as the final preparation for the volunteers before they began their work at their assigned locations. My work as the national director of the Papal Volunteer program was intensely satisfying because it was so well received in Latin America. It was greatly appreciated by bishops, clergy and laity of the countries in Latin America in which the volunteers were stationed, and it greatly broadened the inter-cultural knowledge and experience I had gained during my seven years of study and travel in Europe and the Holy Land.

One of my highest priorities as I got settled in at my headquarters in Chicago was to establish a training program for the volunteers who would be sent to Latin America. I did my best to organize it in accord with the directives of Vatican Council II on the lay apostolate, and in accord with my years of study in Theology and Canon Law. I approached the authorities at the Catholic University of America to arrange for the National Training Center for the Papal Volunteers to be associated with the university's summer program. (It was of immeasurable help that my brother, Msgr. Eugene Kevane, was the Dean of the School of Education.) The program would therefore gain scholastic credit for each of the volunteers and have the prestige of the university behind it. The curriculum was so designed as to give each volunteer a strong program in the meaning of the lay apostolate, a review of Catholic doctrine (the Deposit of Faith as given to us by Christ Himself), basic tenets of theology, the importance of a personal spiritual life, both as a requisite in every Catholic's life, and as essential in the life of the dedicated lay person such as the Papal Volunteer. This training was particularly important as a means of acquiring the strength to persevere in what would be the challenge of changing cultures, adjusting to cultural differences, and studying guidelines for adaptation to the new culture. A particular point of emphasis was the study of the relationship they would have with the bishop, clergy and faithful of the diocese to which they were assigned. The National Training Center emphasized that the volunteers were to enter the culture as agents of ***support*** for those whose culture it was, not as agents of change.

Unfortunately, there were forces (both individuals and groups) at the time within the Church, both in the United States, and specifically within the Latin American Bureau of the USCC, and in probably every country of Latin America, who wanted to operate in Latin America (and in the United States) precisely ***as*** agents of change. The Spanish was ***desarollo***, i.e. "Change" or "Development." The two training programs operated by Msgr. Ivan Illich—in Cuernavaca, Mexico and in Rio de Janeiro, Brazil—were devoted to indoctrinating all their students in that philosophy. It was easy to conclude that the inner 'spirit' of that philosophy was Communism, particularly since Msgr. Illich was himself revealed to be a Communist, even though ordained as a Catholic priest.

Because I devoted all my efforts to building the Papal Volunteer program according to the directives of Vatican Council II, it was therefore not surprising, in view of the widespread misinterpretation of the documents of the Council, that there were almost immediate efforts to discredit and to destroy the Papal Volunteer program. Those efforts actually began before I took office. As previously mentioned, a letter arrived from the Papal Volunteer field representative in Peru during the summer before I officially arrived in Chicago, berating me for my 'conservative' stance and telling me that such an approach would not work. I found out later that this field representative had been trained under Msgr. Illich in Cuernavaca, Mexico, and was promoted for the post by Father Colonnese. He was closely allied to a priest in Lima, Peru, who was an active proponent of ***Liberation Theology*** and who was personally involved in establishing *communidades de base* (Christian Base Communities) throughout Latin America under the auspices of IPLA (*Instituto Pastoral Latino Americano*—Latin American Pastoral Institute, located in Quito, Ecuador) and Msgr. Ivan Illich. I've often wondered whether someone already knew what my philosophical and theological proclivities were (in that case, it was evidence of a remarkably precocious intelligence-gathering organization), or whether it was a fishing expedition to determine if I could be conscripted as part of their team, or if I would be a problem.

Perhaps the most controversial effort on my part was to train the prospective volunteers in the basics of theology, the theology of the lay apostolate, the development of a personal spiritual life, the need for them to be exemplary Catholics in their work in Latin America, to align themselves with the hierarchical structure of Latin

America and realize that they were sent to Latin America to join the apostolate of the bishop, clergy and laity of whatever diocese to which they were assigned. This, of course, ran completely counter to Liberation Theology and its Marxist intentions. The thrust of my own training program did not recognize the need for Christian Base Communities, which Msgr. Illich and his kind were attempting to establish in every country and diocese of Latin America.

So while it was my intention to conjoin the Papal Volunteer program to the existing hierarchical structure of the Church, both in the United States and in Latin America, this ran completely contrary to the efforts of the new director of the Latin America Bureau—Father Colonnese and those associated with him in LAB, within which the Papal Volunteer program operated, and the efforts of Msgr. Ivan Illich (a priest of the Archdiocese of New York and a proven Communist) and a few other liberation theology leaders in Peru, Chile, Brazil, Ecuador, Columbia, Venezuela, Bolivia, etc. I gradually began to realize that I was up against a massive organization whose purpose was to destroy the existing structure of the Catholic Church in the countries of Latin America and replace it with a new structure whose purpose would be to promote Liberation Theology, which was a thinly veiled form of Marxism—Marxism in Theological terminology—and not really religious at all except in external appearance.

When I had a chance meeting with Msgr. Ivan Illich in the airport at Bogotá, Colombia, we talked for more than two hours, waiting for our respective flights, he acknowledged that his purpose was to destroy the existing Church structure and replace it with a new one of his own (and his associates') design. When I told him that I assumed that he and his associates would be the new power at the helm, he simply looked at me, said nothing, and didn't deny my allegation. He was returning from a visit to the headquarters of IPLA (Pastoral Institute for Latin America)—located in Quito, Ecuador—where he was a major leader and whose purpose was to train carefully selected teams from every country to form in their own countries the afore-mentioned Christian Base Communities whose purpose was to replace the existing structure of the Catholic Church. The basic purpose was simply to transform the Catholic Church into a communist organization.

The National Training Center at the Catholic University was attacked before its first session was completed. It was denounced by Father Colonnese (when he was the director of CICOP, not of LAB) as not conforming to the "signs of the times," (which, though it was a phrase mentioned in Vatican II, was used as a 'tool' of the Heresy of Modernism) and that it would be offensive to "certain groups" (which were not named). One of my most prized staff members at the training program in its second year was Dr. José Baquero, a visiting professor at the Catholic University, a devout Catholic layman, a native Ecuadorian, an expert in Latin American studies, and for years a high ranking diplomat for his country. I spent a great deal of time and effort explaining the Papal Volunteer program to him, trying my best to enlist him as a member of the training school staff. To me he was a prize: An educated Latin American who could speak to the assembled volunteers in training from a fund of knowledge as an ambassador for his country to many other countries of Latin America.

To my astonishment, Dr. Baquero was the most maligned member of my staff—he was maligned by the U.S. priests and staff of the Latin America Bureau. I assumed that he was attacked precisely because he was a powerful member of the Ecuadorian laity and represented a school of thought which the Modernist and Liberation Theology points of view wanted no part of. Apparently, since they wanted to subvert the training program, he had to be denounced. I did not really know initially why the national training center was being attacked, but I certainly knew that it was being bombarded, it seemed, from every direction. I found out later (more on this further on) that the Papal Volunteer program and particularly the content of the National Training Center ran counter to an organized effort to subvert the Church in Latin America—an effort which included the imposition of what was called Liberation Theology, which was thinly disguised Marxism as mentioned above, and the multiplication of so-called "*communidades de base*", which were to replace the parish and the diocese and which would be a widespread training program among the Catholics of Latin America in the principles of Liberation Theology and of the heresy of Modernism. This is what I referred to just above: Msgr. Ivan Illich admitted that he was involved in that subversive effort.

CHAPTER 24

My Introduction to the Heresy of Modernism and False Ecumenism

When I moved into St. Andrew's parish on the North side of Chicago, on my very first day after celebrating my own Mass I proceeded to the dining room to have breakfast before heading to my office in "the Loop." There was a priest there at breakfast who had celebrated an earlier Mass. We weren't acquainted, but said 'Good Morning' to each other. Then he abruptly and passionately made the following pronouncement:

> **"We (Catholics) have to forget about the Real Presence. Otherwise we can never have a true ecumenical movement."**

I was flabbergasted. What he had said was true heresy. I don't remember exactly what I said, but I tried stoutly to defend the doctrine of the Real Presence. I learned immediately that he was a professor of theology at Mundelein seminary near Chicago. The statement is deeply heretical in that it denies the core of the Catholic Church: At every Mass celebrated by an ordained Catholic priest, Christ, the Second Person of the Most Holy Trinity, becomes really and truly present in His Body and Blood, Soul and Divinity, and, in the fullness of His infinite power, retaining the appearance of bread and wine. It is formally called ***Transubstantiation*** (see above Part II, Chapter 18).

The ramifications of a ***seminary professor*** teaching this particular ***heresy*** to his seminary students are nearly unimaginable. Multiply the number of years this professor has taught theology classes to seminarians, add the number of seminarians who sat through his classes each year, consider the unknown number of other seminary professors who hold and deliver the same heretical doctrine, and you will have an educated guess regarding the number of priests who have been ordained in recent years whose belief in the Real Presence is either non-existent or badly shaken. (There is a general assumption that approximately 60% of Catholic priests doubt or have lost their faith in the Real Presence.) And, since all bishops are promoted to that level from among the available priests, the reader can begin to realize how the Catholic Church has been wounded in this time of crisis, and why the aberrations reported later in this book can have happened, *i.e.* the failure of American bishops to stalwartly defend the doctrine of the Catholic Church. But then, even St. Peter denied Christ, and, at the time of His crucifixion, most of His Apostles disappeared. Even the human weakness of bishops cannot lead to the destruction of the Catholic Church which is the Mystical Body of Christ. However, just as the physical body of Christ was wounded and put to death, so now today there are those who can wound the Mystical Body of Christ—the Catholic Church—and be complicit in causing people to lose their souls. See Part VII, p.451, the Judas Syndrome—comprised of those who do not believe in the Real Presence of Christ in the Sacrifice of the Mass.

While I was still a student in Rome, the ecumenical movement was underway. One of my professors made the statement: "The barque of ecumenism will founder on the rock of the Real Presence." While some of the Catholic laity went along with the attitude of this seminary professor and were willing to give up their belief in the Real Presence, they are a small percentage. The vast majority of good

Catholics, I hope and believe, have a rock steady belief in the presence of the living Jesus Christ in our tabernacles, beginning at the words of consecration during Mass. It has been my impression for many years that ecumenism is losing its steam as it confronts the infallible doctrines of the Catholic Church. The Church cannot adjust her dogmatic principles nor compromise her traditional values. Rather, those who are apart from the Church must come to her and become members of what is the Mystical Body of Christ.

That ***'breakfast confrontation'*** was my very first direct experience with a living, breathing practitioner of the Heresy of Modernism within the Church. While some of my school mates in Rome expressed an interest in promoting ecumenism, the Jesuits at that time (1950-1954) were a force for good and they made it clear that the dogmatic doctrines of the Catholic Church could not be compromised.

Heresy Among the Jesuits

The first 'break in the dam' among the Jesuits that I was aware of had to do with Father Leonard Feeney, S.J. of Boston, who publicly held fast to the doctrine of *extra ecclesiam nulla salus* (there is no salvation outside the Catholic church) and its most rigid interpretation. He held that no non-Catholics could be saved. The tradition of the Church, however, always held that people of good faith who, if they knew the truth, *would become* members of the Church, therefore could be saved. Father McCormick, S.J., the American Assistant to the Jesuit General in Rome at that time (1950's), who gave us a weekly spiritual conference, was sent to visit Father Feeney to give him a last chance to recant. When he returned and gave us our next conference, Father McCormick was clearly dispirited and talked to us about intellectual pride, the sin of Lucifer who proclaimed "I will not serve" and was instantly condemned to Hell for all eternity. It was a clear reference to Father Feeney who not long after was excommunicated and relieved of all priestly duties.

My Second Experience with Modernism and False Doctrine

As I began my work as national director of the Papal Volunteer program, Father Louis M. Colonnese was simply one of my associates in the Latin America Bureau and was not a part of the Papal Volunteer program. He had charge of the promotion of a separate entity known as CICOP (I never knew the meaning of that acronym) whose primary function was to promote intercultural understanding in the Americas. One of its most public methods to accomplish that was to hold an international conference each year. Its first meeting, simply announced as CICOP (pronounced see-cop), held in Chicago in the January following my appointment to the Papal Volunteer program, was hugely attended from all over the world. (A British attendee at the conference pronounced it "kick-up"—which didn't stick.)

CICOP had a distinctively liberal stance. The speakers were almost uniformly of a mild to strong liberal bent. Father Andrew Greeley at that first CICOP meeting made his first vitriolic attack on what he called 'triumphalism' among the hierarchy and pastors of the Catholic Church. It was a clear effort, using derision and mockery, to discredit the bishops of the Church because of the nature of their ceremonies, the richness of their vestments and lifestyle and other elements which he characterized as nearly royal prerogatives of everyone from the Pope, through the Cardinals, the bishops, monsignors, and on down through the clergy. (Greeley pretty much "topped" them all with his own outlandish life style.) Much of what was said at the CICOP conference carried the overtones of the heresy of Modernism.

The Papal Volunteer program, although an equal part of the Latin America Bureau, was given no mention at this conference nor was I or any member of the Papal Volunteer program invited to speak, even though I had offered to enlist Latin American bishops and experienced volunteers to join the program. At the next CICOP conference, about a year later, the Papal Volunteer program was openly attacked, by three speakers on a panel apparently appointed for the purpose, and the lone voice in strong support of the Papal Volunteer program was, interestingly enough, a Mexican bishop, who was not a Papal Volunteer. Once again, the Papal Volunteer program was not invited to speak on its own behalf.

I could have known from the beginning that Father Colonnese would be an opponent of the PAVLA program. Shortly after I arrived in Chicago, he invited me to his apartment, he said, for discussion of our mutual responsibilities. At some point during the visit, he put his arm around my shoulders. Having seen in him what I thought were evidences of homosexuality (by now I was something of an expert), I instinctively pulled away. Sensing some hurt in him, I explained, "I think I was born that way; I don't like to be touched." He then proclaimed (I'll never forget his exact words): "That's it! That's what makes a priest! They don't like to be touched!" In all my studies of Theology, among all the references to the special graces involved in the calling by God to become a priest, there was never a mention of reluctance to be touched. Surely this was a 'doctrine' he made up for his own purposes, perhaps as a way to 'save face' in handling my rejection of his homosexual overture.

But even more of a problem, on another occasion Father Colonnese made the statement that "We don't believe in Mortal Sin any more." (I don't know what he meant by "we," nor where "they" got the authority to make such a pronouncement. I later came to know that Bishop Bernardin was the leading support to Colonnese in all of his efforts to destroy PAVLA.) His statement was contrary to two thousand years of doctrine in the Catholic Church. The most important purpose of the Sacrament of Penance is to absolve a person in the state of sin and restore the supernatural life which was lost because of mortal sin.

The second session of the national training center, the following summer, had many obstacles thrown up against it during the months of preparation for it. It was announced by Father Colonnese that there would be an investigatory group commissioned to examine the national training session to determine its adequacy. This was a group of three, two of whom were openly and publicly inimical to the Papal Volunteer program, and a third who was not nearly so hostile and who withdrew from the group before the training session began. And one of the 'volunteers' in training seemed to be a 'plant', who originated in Davenport, Iowa, which was Father Colonnese's home diocese, and who was later identified as a 'spy' for Father Colonnese by the group of volunteers in training.

Knowing that there would be an even greater effort than the year before to discredit the training program, I had sought out staff members who would be strong enough to withstand the pressures of opposition. One of these was Dr. José Baquero, mentioned earlier. Another was a classmate of mine in Rome, who I knew to be an excellent theologian, was sound in his thinking and was a faithful priest, devoted to the Church. My brother, Msgr. Eugene Kevane, the Dean of the Department of Education at the Catholic University, interviewed this priest with a view to having him on his staff as well. When we both agreed that he was an unusually strong and balanced person, we asked him to join us. He would join the staff of the Papal Volunteer national training center that summer, and would begin in the fall term as a full-fledged professor at the Catholic University under my brother. In the next two months before the session started, he and I met frequently to plan the curriculum during the summer. He continued to be enthusiastic throughout this planning period. Then, about two weeks before the session was to begin, he suddenly became distant and cool, and he lost his enthusiasm. Finally a few days before the summer session was to begin, he withdrew both from the Papal Volunteer program and from his candidacy as a professor in the Department of Education at the Catholic University of America. The change in him was so remarkable that my brother and I could only conclude that someone had "gotten to him," perhaps through some kind of threat and/or blackmail process. The sudden turn-about on his part, in a matter of a few *days,* has remained a mystery to me, clarified somewhat by the intimidation which was later directed at me, as I'll explain in due course.

CHAPTER 25

Tours of Latin America—Visiting the Volunteers on the Job

In the course of my first year as national director of PAVLA, I made a fairly quick trip to Latin America, stopping in Venezuela where there was a request for volunteers. They were to be initially associated with an American Missionary order whose headquarters (parish, school, etc.) were situated about midway between Caracas and the north coast.

That religious order was the epitome of balance. During their initial discussions with the bishop of the diocese, they had agreed that the facilities they were to build would be so designed that the poor would not feel overawed nor would the wealthy be reluctant to visit. It was an impressive success because it related the Catholic Church in Venezuela to all of society and was in the process of bringing all levels together. It was a wonderful goal. It epitomized my hopes for the way the Papal Volunteers could meld with the Catholic Church in whatever diocese in whatever country they were assigned to. The Papal Volunteer program would respond as quickly as possible to a request from such a bishop. There were others we would not respond to, for example, a bishop in northern Chile who lived in ostensible poverty in the humblest of conditions, not far above living on the street. The high income and middle income members of his diocese were more than uncomfortable with their bishop. I believe they were actually ashamed of him. He simply did not relate to his complete Catholic membership, and therefore we could not see our way clear to send volunteers to him.

From Venezuela on that first tour, I proceeded to the city of Manaus in Brazil to pay a visit to the original four volunteers I had sent from the Sioux City diocese as its diocesan director. They were doing excellent work, and were highly praised by the Redemptorist Fathers to whom they were assigned by the bishop.

A highlight of that visit was a protracted trip upriver by boat on the Amazon lasting a week or more. It was the superior of the Redemptorists who suggested the trip because, he said, it would give me a very good picture of what the volunteers there were coping with. He stocked the boat with enough food for the journey, a good supply of drinking water (the Amazon River itself was undrinkable, since it was disease-laden and very dirty), including a supply of very large grapefruit which were inedible but contained a large amount of drinkable juice. We visited small settlements on the river bank: three larger ones were, for example, Coarí, Manacapurú, and Codajàz. Because of the tropical climate which was also very humid, the men wore nothing but loin cloths, and the women wore what looked somewhat like a sarong. They lived in houses with roofs but no walls so that the breezes and winds of the area could cool them night and day. As we chugged along night and day to reach those towns, once or twice after nightfall I lay on the roof of the boat to watch the stars, and, of course, I saw the Southern Cross. It was shaped like a kite with four stars forming the outer periphery and another star in the center. It was far more prominent and visible than its counterpart, the North Star.

As I lay on the top of the boat in early evening after dark, I heard a cacophony of screeches and howls, grunts and growls coming from the nearby jungle. It was an unforgettable trip. That Redemptorist superior later was appointed bishop of the Diocese of Manaus.

Manaus is a large city—a seaport—located 1000 miles inland from the mouth of the Amazon. The Amazon is so large as to be almost unimaginable, large enough to carry ocean going ships more than 1000 miles inland—to the city of Manaus.

The four volunteers were working with the Redemptorists to help the native Brazilians develop skills they did not have. The natives to the west of Manaus were impressive. They lived close to nature and coped and survived the most primitive challenges that there are—and it showed in their eyes: A placid acceptance of their way of life and a child-like belief in God and His providence. The most impressive factor in this region was the Redemptorist Fathers (from the Missouri Province in the U.S.) whose dedication to their work was visible, and who clearly had no American axe to grind.

Other Tours

During a get-acquainted three month tour whose purpose was to visit all the Papal Volunteers in the countries of Latin America, and to talk to their bishops and the local clergy and laity with whom they were working, I encountered quite a number of both inspiring and disquieting things.

Northeast Brazil

From Manaus I visited the city of Belem—Portuguese for Bethlehem—on the mouth of the Amazon, and then along the East coast of Brazil to the cities of Fortaleza, Natal, Recife and Salvador. Wherever I went, the volunteers were impressive in the work they were doing and in their personal lives which were exemplary. As far as I could tell, all or most had a strong faith (most said their own faith was strengthened by the unmistakable faith of the Latin American laity among whom they worked), and, wherever it was available to them, they attended daily Mass. They were praised profusely and with obvious sincerity by the local bishop in every case, and by the clergy and religious with whom they worked. But it was on this trip 'around the hump'—the East coast of Brazil—that I met two disquieting figures.

One was an American nun whose personal mission to Latin America appeared to be more the implantation of feminism than it was the salvation of souls. During the two or three days of my visit in whatever city it was—its name has escaped my memory—she sought me out several times in an effort to help me realize that there was no real role for the Papal Volunteer program in Latin America—which sounded as if it were indoctrination inspired by Msgr. Illich in his language training program in Rio de Janeiro—and tried to help me to realize that a valid mission for the Papal Volunteer program would be to help the Latin Americans to realize how important the acquisition of feminism would be in their lives. Finally realizing that she would not convert me, she asked me the burning question which was probably inspired by the Illich/Colonnese axis: "What place does the Papal Volunteer program have in Latin America? (Perhaps she said ". . . Brazil?") And I responded, "Sister, they haven't dug it yet." She dropped her full-bore, somewhat fanatical attack strategy, laughed a bit half-heartedly and ended her dogged questioning of me. I assumed from what I saw that she was one of the worst examples I had ever encountered of the ugly American in religious garb, probably magnified by her Illich training. The Order of Religious Men in Venezuela, the Redemptorists along the Amazon in Brazil, and another order of men I was to meet in Ecuador, stood out as shining examples of Americans who did it the right way: They were there to help the Church in their 'adopted' diocese to strengthen the spiritual lives of their people, and to help the people to improve their economics and life style in accord with their cultural structure.

Another disquieting figure during my visit to the East coast of Brazil, I am sorry to say, was a Papal Volunteer. During that first trip through the east coast of Latin America during which I spoke personally to perhaps 75 to 100 volunteers, I met only three who I wished were not there. This young lady was one of the three. She was perhaps 25 years of age and her name was Camy. I wanted very much to meet her, primarily because she had been named by my predecessor as the Field Representative for Brazil and I was looking forward to her report on the status of the Papal Volunteer program in the country. She had been described as very intelligent, which I found to be true, fluent in Portuguese, which also appeared to be true, and because she had melded very well with the people in northeast Brazil. I found out later that she had been recommended by Father Colonnese and trained at Msgr. Illich's training school in Rio de Janeiro. (The role of the Field Representative was two-fold: Support for the volunteers to whom they could turn and have problems reported to the National Office, and receive requests for Volunteers from local bishops or their representatives and forward those requests to headquarters in Chicago.)

Camy and I got off to a bad start. I had arrived at the airport during the night, about 1:00 a.m., having had 3-4 hours of sleep in the previous 3 days. I settled in for the night about 3:00 a.m. I was bordering on sheer exhaustion. So I 'slept in' until 8:30 the next morning and invited her to join me while I had breakfast. When she arrived, without any preliminaries, pleasantries or introductions, she accused me of committing the worst kind of *faux pas*—rising from bed at 8:00 or 9:00 in the morning was the equivalent, she said, of lying in bed until 2:00 p.m. in the United States. From that point it went downhill. She was clearly a product of the Illich/Colonnese line and said so. She told me that all my ideas about the development of the Papal Volunteer program were wrong, that I must change my plans or resign and do one or the other immediately. She obviously had not heard as much good about me as I had heard about her. I began to realize, of course, that what I had heard about her had come from Father Colonnese, who was instrumental in getting her appointed to her post. What she had heard about me had undoubtedly come from Msgr. Illich during her language training session, and from Father Colonnese who, I was to find out, kept in close touch with two Field Representatives: this one in Brazil and another in Lima, Peru who was a protegé of a Peruvian priest who promoted Liberation Theology and the creation of Christian base communities.

One of the methods used by Camy, in her efforts to adapt to the culture, which I found was unacceptable, was her habit of going barefoot as she made her daily contacts. When I spoke to her about it, she was adamant and told me that it was important to join the "poorest of the poor," in her work as a volunteer. I believe to this day that this approach, which was the approach favored by Msgr. Illich, certain American religious orders, and a very small percentage of Latin American bishops, was wrong for several reasons. Number one, it was dishonest. No American volunteer, no American religious order priest, nun or brother, nor any Latin American bishop, was poor. So it was at least somewhat deceitful, even hypocritical, for such persons to act as if they were. Secondly, it was divisive, showing as it did favoritism by an American visitor toward the poor instead of bringing an even-handed approach to the society, as every good bishop would do and would want. Thirdly, it was not good hygiene nor good example to the people of that locality. The natives who ran around barefoot were subject to many and varied parasites which entered their bodies through the soles of their feet. As mentioned above, the nurse volunteer along the Amazon insisted that, as part of effective education in hygienic practices, that everyone start to wear shoes. For the American volunteer not to wear shoes was to give bad example to those among whom she worked.

When I returned to my headquarters in Chicago, I found a letter of resignation from Camy as Field Representative in Brazil. I accepted with alacrity and immediately appointed another volunteer who had already agreed to replace her if the occasion should arise. He was impressive and very balanced in his approach to his work. I heard later that Camy was devastated that I had accepted her resignation. Apparently she was convinced that she was irreplaceable.

I believe that the identification with the poor is the way certain groups and movements establish and exercise power. A poster I saw while I had my office in Washington, D.C. said it all: "*There's money in poverty*." I think that the poster referred to the political truism that whoever can gain the favor of the poor and of those who favor the poor will have a much higher percentage of public support than someone who does not give that support. So whenever I saw groups of priests and nuns who 'lived among the poor,' ostensibly in the most abject kind of poverty, I felt that it was hypocritical, because they were not poor. And perhaps they overlooked the thought that the wealthy merited attention because they also needed to save their souls. Moreover, they neglected to realize that the wealthy, properly approached, could help transform the lives of the poor. Christ Himself said, "The poor you will always have with you."(Matthew 26:11 and Mark 14:7) And He also said "It is more difficult for the wealthy to enter into heaven than it is for a camel to pass through the eye of a needle." (Matthew 19:23-24)

Brasilia and the Epitome of the Ugly American

My next stop on my first major tour of Latin America was Brasilia, the capitol of Brazil, only because airline schedules took me there on my way to Rio de Janeiro. It was the celebration of *Carnaval—Carnavale* in Spanish—literally meaning "goodbye to meat"—the day and evening before Ash Wednesday and the beginning of Lent. After I landed in Brasilia, I discovered that the pilot who flew in from Recife on the east coast and who was to fly on to Rio de Janeiro, had decided he would stop for the night and join the celebration. Airport people told me they would find another pilot who would take the plane to Rio de Janeiro.

It was during my short wait in Brasilia that I experienced that ugliest of ugly Americans. He was a florid faced man, self-appointed as the leader of his small group, who came into the Brasilia airport, and threatened in a stentorian voice to "contact the Pentagon" and bring the United States Army down to ". . . wipe out you people"—his exact words—because the plane scheduled to take him and his group to Rio de Janeiro had been canceled. When a special flight was finally boarded, I got on last and sat as far away from that small Ugly American group as I could get. I didn't want in any way to be identified with them.

Flying into Rio de Janeiro from Brasilia, I arrived after midnight and therefore entirely missed the festivities of *Carnaval.* All I saw was a very tired individual dressed as an American Indian with full feathered headdress sleeping on a bench in the airport waiting room. And of course there was a huge amount of debris on the streets which would be cleaned up the next day. Aside from the meetings I had with volunteers and bishops' representatives, the most memorable part of the visit was seeing the magnificent statue of Christ standing on the waterfront overlooking the beach and the waters of the south Atlantic.

My meetings with the bishops, clergy and the Papal Volunteers in southern Brazil were very productive and very positive. Those contacts left me with the conviction that I needed to assiduously avoid certain attitudes which were being promoted in all the U.S. Catholic activities within Latin America, and to vigorously adhere to the principles of the Lay Apostolate which were so strongly advocated by Vatican Council II.

CHAPTER 26

End of First Tour of Latin America: Reshaping PAVLA

I came back from my first tour in Latin America and immediately continued my regional meetings with diocesan directors of the Papal Volunteers for Latin America and returned Papal Volunteers, now able to make a personal input of things I had learned in talking to bishops, religious superiors and volunteers in their respective countries and dioceses.

It was clear to me now that the Papal Volunteers could not be sent to the training program of Msgr. Illich either at Cuernavaca, Mexico, nor to the one in Rio de Janeiro, Brazil. The two, while their ostensible purpose was for priests, nuns and laity to learn the Spanish or Portuguese language, they were very little more than an indoctrination process. Their intention was to steep those attending in the Illich view of Latin America, which was Socialistic and, worse, Communistic.

During my first year as national director, I learned that Msgr. Ivan Illich, though a priest of the New York Archdiocese, was a ***Communist.*** I saw a Mexico City newspaper headline which stated "*¡Illich es communista!*"—translation: "*Illich is a communist.*" I asked the Archbishop of Mexico City how the paper could make such a statement, and his simple answer was "Because they have the proof."

Since I had seen a priest in Italy who was a life-long communist 'plant,' and knowing something of Illich's philosophy, this was not difficult for me to believe. Moreover, I knew that Liberation Theology was thinly disguised Marxism, that Illich supported it, and that he was a leader if not the founder of IPLA (Pastoral Institute for Latin America), headquartered in Quito, Ecuador, whose purpose was to train teams from every country who would then form *Communidades de Base* (Christian Base Communities) whose function would be to *replace* the existing structure of the Church.

As we were organizing the National Training Center at the Catholic University in Washington, D.C., I began to search for an acceptable language training program. One of the places I visited in my search was the Catholic University in Ponce, Puerto Rico, where there was a group of priests, nuns and laity (about sixty to seventy total) learning Spanish in preparation for their coming work in Latin America. I found that the director of the program was a very ineffectual priest, and that Father Colonnese had sent word before I arrived that I didn't know much and that I was a very poor speaker. It was becoming more and more evident that Father Colonnese, because of his close association with Msgr. Illich and his membership in a number of very questionable organizations, and as I was to learn fully supported by Bishop Bernardin, was completely hostile to the Papal Volunteer Program.

Clearly, some of the priests at Ponce (with supporting nuns and laity) were *avant garde* in their approach to the "modern" Catholic Church. My first morning at Ponce, I concelebrated Mass with the director. The "host" for the Mass was a roughly twelve inch square of baked bread (unleavened and therefore valid), about an inch to one and a half inches thick. When it came time for the Elevation of the Consecrated Host, the celebrant simply put his hands under the near corners of the 'loaf of bread' and raised them an inch or two off the altar. When it came time for communion, the communicants simply came to the altar and tore off a piece of the host and consumed it. Later, the priest complained to me that it took quite some time to cram the leftover consecrated bread down a *sacrarium*—a vessel designed for the disposal of sacred materials. These leftover materials were the Body and Blood, Soul and Divinity of Christ Himself. I asked the priest why he went along with those things. He didn't have much of an answer. He also told me that they were trying to get him to discontinue use of the pall at Mass. (The pall is a 6" square, flat, stiff, cloth-covered piece of material which is used to cover the chalice during Mass.) He also told me that among a few of the group was an attitude of going into Latin America to help them change the way they practiced their faith.

When I spoke to the group, I started with the pall. The reason for the pall, historically, I told them, was to keep flies out of the wine. Wherever you go in Latin America, particularly the tropical and subtropical areas, "as you see where we are now, there will be windows without screens, and during the day the windows will stand open. This is true here in this room and also in the chapel. As a result, flies abound. The only thing worse than having flies get into the wine before the consecration is to have them get into it after the consecration. What do you do with a fly which is saturated with the Body and Blood, Soul and Divinity of Christ Himself?" And I asked them to please think through why they go to Latin America. I told them the story of the florid faced ugly American in Brasilia on the evening of *Carnaval.* "Wherever you go," I said, "remember that you are there at the request of the ***local Bishop.*** Respect his position and his authority. You go to Latin America, not to Americanize it, but to help it become even more Catholic. Theirs is a simple and solid devotion to their religion. You have more to learn from them than you have to teach them. Avoid the ***desarrollo*** or 'Change' movement. It seems to be fraught with Liberation Theology, Christian Base Communities and the overthrow of the traditional organization of the Catholic Church."

When I finished, I was given a standing ovation. Most of the group were sound and solid Catholics: priests, nuns and laity. But

I went back to Chicago convinced that I couldn't make use of that particular language training facility.

(I have recently come to an uncomfortable realization. As the Communist Party in Italy made a strong pitch for *Cambio* or *Cambiamento—i.e. "Change,"* so also in Latin America the watchword was *Desarollo*, i.e. "Change" by Msgr. Illich, a Communist priest, supported by Liberation Theology, Christian Base Communities—were they the equivalent of communist cells?—and the entire organization of IPLA.)

The *Hogar InterAmericano*

The only reasonable solution for the problem of language training was to establish an independent PAVLA sponsored institution for the purpose. So I talked to the Archbishop of Mexico City, who spoke flawless English. As I explained the problem, he understood it fully (he is the one I asked about how a newspaper could proclaim that Illich was a Communist and who answered "because they have the proof"). He assigned a priest as his representative—Father Hector Samperio—to help me with the project. Father Samperio in turn introduced me to a fully educated successful Catholic businessman who found the real estate and building we needed. When it came time to assign a name to the school, it was this Mexican layman who came up with the title which carried the day: the ***Hogar InterAmericano*** (***the InterAmerican Home***—*casa* means 'house,' *hogar* means 'home').

As the legalities surrounding the acquisition of the *Hogar* were being finalized, there occurred what I simply ascribed to an act of Providence—and in spite of difficulties to come, I believe it truly was. I was introduced to a red-headed American-Irish priest from a diocese in Michigan who spoke, as far as I could tell, completely flawless Spanish. I'll call him Father Mike O'Brien. (This is not his real name in case there is a need to protect any surviving siblings he may have.) I appointed him director of the Hogar. He did a masterful job of opening and directing the first group of about sixty volunteers sent to him after the National Training Center at the Catholic University in Washington, D.C. In opening the Hogar he had the topnotch assistance of a seasoned volunteer who had spent three years in Chile and who spoke Spanish like a native. I'll call her Virginia to avoid any embarrassment to her because of later events. She was totally loyal to the Church, more than excellent in her work, and an excellent Catholic. I was to find out later that I couldn't say the same about Father O'Brien, but more on that later. I appointed both Father O'Brien and Virginia to their posts at the Hogar. However, Father O'Brien was a 'spy' sent to me by Father Colonnese. I suspect one of his responsibilities was to 'indoctrinate' the group of volunteers to the Illich/Colonnese philosophies about what their role was to be in Latin America.

The happy outcome was that Father O'Brien and I became friends and he completely accepted the approach I was taking with the volunteers. I heard later that Father Colonnese was very upset because he felt he had been 'betrayed' by Father O'Brien.

The *Hogar* had its own very small chapel, altar and tabernacle. Father O'Brien celebrated Mass there daily. I personally donated a small ciborium on one of my trips to visit the Volunteers in training, so that the Presence of the Eucharistic Christ would be with them always as they went through their training and daily lives.

The PAVLA National Training Center

The first National Training Center program for the Papal Volunteers was held at the Catholic University of America in Washington, D.C. during its regular summer session. There were sixty volunteers in attendance who were a remarkable group. They were clearly dedicated, focused on their purpose, and more than simply attentive to what was being presented to them. The classes ranged from general theology, specifically the Lay Apostolate, through cultural considerations, personal reactions to cultural adaptation, generalities of differences between the American culture and the Latin American cultures, and what their role had to be in joining a diocese and a parish in whatever country and diocese they were being received into.

Since the National Training Program was part of the summer session of the Catholic University, all the volunteers received college credit for the classes they attended. That was true of all succeeding training programs through 1969.

Just as remarkable as the group of volunteers was the staff who taught them. Three of them were just-returned volunteers who were experienced teachers who brought their very valuable experience in Latin America into the classroom.

One of these latter was a returned volunteer from Green Bay, Wisconsin, who reported on his own experience with the Illich training program in Cuernavaca, Mexico. He was one of those who 'saw through' what he called the 'brainwashing' procedures in play by Illich himself. He said that the common procedures to twist a person's mind were in constant use, i.e. mockery, humiliation to make a person with contrary views feel foolish. One incident he reported was ridiculous. He said that one day, someone strongly opposed what Illich was telling them. Illich then put on an act of devastation, slid down a wall, sat on the floor, and someone put a huge lollipop—about 12 inches in diameter—in his hand and he sat forlornly licking the lollipop. I've never been able to determine what this piece of trickery was supposed to accomplish. This particular volunteer strongly opposed the Illich/Colonnese philosophy and supported the philosophy of our training program. His thoughts firmed up my decision to get away from the Illich training and to establish the *Hogar InterAmericano* that same Fall as a necessary alternative.

I myself taught a course in general Theology, principles and practice of the Lay Apostolate, the role of the Papal Volunteer, and thoughts on cultural adaptation.

Father Colonnese sent three people to evaluate the training program and report back to him. He did this in spite of the fact that he was not my superior. I suppose in retrospect I am forced to face the possibility that Father Considine, Director of the Latin America Bureau, allowed him to take this and other hostile actions. Father Considine was always something of an enigma—no one ever knew exactly where he stood. Openly, however, he always honored the independence I had required as a condition to my accepting the job. Clandestinely, he allowed Father Colonnese to oppose what I was doing with the PAVLA program. I later learned that Father Colonnese had the full support of Bishop Bernardin, General Secretary of the entire USCC.

That first session of the National Training Center, to my mind at least, was a howling success. None of them left the program, and we had no doubts about any of them. This was a tribute to the volunteers themselves, to the staff which taught them so capably during the summer session, and to their diocesan directors who did such an outstanding job of recruiting the right kind of people.

At the end of the session, the volunteers went home for a few weeks and reported to the Hogar InterAmericano in Mexico City on a specific date. As a further tribute to that group of volunteers, none of them left. They completed their studies with varying degrees of fluency in Spanish, and all arrived at their assignments in various Spanish-speaking countries of Latin America. They were also a tribute to the two administrators of the Hogar—Father O'Brien and Virginia—who dealt very ably with a variety of challenges in the first session in Mexico City. There were some ugly rumors at the time, not related at all to the volunteers. I attributed the rumors to the propaganda machine created by Father Colonnese. The rumors were, unfortunately, true, but I didn't know that for two more years. I'll get into that problem a bit further on.

The second session of the National Training Center in 1966, this time with about seventy volunteers, not counting an "inspector" sent by Father Colonnese, attending all the classes, and two "spies" or *false* volunteers from Father Colonnese's home diocese of Davenport, Iowa. Within a matter of days, the actual volunteers recognized the two intruders as being what they were and treated them accordingly. Having been exposed, they left the training program shortly after, undoubtedly with the approval of Father Colonnese.

The staff of this second session was greatly embellished with the addition of Dr. José Baquero, whom I mentioned earlier. He brought a wealth of personal experience to our efforts to prepare the volunteers for the pressures of culture change. Strangely, as I already mentioned, Dr. Baquero became the focal point of the Colonnese Corps' attack on the National Training Center's validity that summer. Certain rumors, i.e. lies, were circulated about Dr. Baquero's personal life which were clearly manufactured to discredit the entire PAVLA program.

A Great Compliment—and the Perception of the 'Ugly American' in the U.S.

If my memory serves me, it was later that fall, after the group had completed their language training at the Hogar in Mexico City, that I was invited by Father Hector Samperio to a meeting of several bishops, including the Archbishop of Mexico City to whom he was a personal aide. The meeting was to be held in a city and a diocese located along the Gulf coast of Mexico. I arrived the night before, checked in at a hotel, and simply expected to be picked up the next morning and driven to the coast for the meeting.

The next morning at 7:00, a bit earlier than I expected, Father Hector Samperio called me from the lobby and asked if he could come to my room to talk a bit. After some small talk and a trading of recent experiences, he told me that the bishops of Mexico (or at least the Archbishop of Mexico City and those bishops who would attend the coming conference that day) had a message for me and a request. They wanted me to know that they greatly appreciated the open attitude that I displayed and with me the PAVLA program toward the cultural differences between the U.S. Catholic Church and the Catholic Church of the countries of Latin America. He very carefully answered my carefully phrased question as to whether the bishops and clergy of Latin America perceived the concept of the 'ugly American' (I did not use the phrase) to be rampant among the bishops and clergy of the U.S. His answer was a very diplomatic '***Yes***.' Father Samperio made it very clear that they did not perceive me as being one of those, and that I approached the Bishops, Clergy, and the Catholic Church in Latin America with great respect. Which, of course, was true. I did and still do. Their question for me was what steps could they take or what help could they give so that when the time came a like-minded successor could follow me in the post. I gave him a brief answer, but told him I'd expand on it more at the up-coming conference.

The reason I had been invited to the conference was to tell the assembled bishops what steps they could take, first to request and acquire Papal Volunteers, secondly how long it might take before they might expect them to arrive, and thirdly what they should do to prepare for their arrival. I gave them answers as best I could; I hoped my answers were satisfactory. Then I told them what they might do to continue the kind of service they were now satisfied with. It was of paramount importance that they, the bishops, directly approach the pertinent bishops in the U.S., tell them of their own satisfaction with the program, and ask how they could help strengthen, broaden and perpetuate the program in such a way as to fit into the Latin American cultures as it was doing so capably now. I gave them the names of bishops on the committee I answered to who I thought would be especially receptive to their request. (I offered to accompany that representative.) And, while this could be done by a specially chosen representative from the Conference of Mexican Bishops, it would be even more effective if the Conference of all Bishops of Latin America (CELAM) would send such a representative. They were certainly aware, I told them, that there were forces in the U.S. Church who were hostile to the Papal Volunteer program, including a number of priests and a few bishops. They had an American priest from the Archdiocese of New York, a known Communist, leading a training program in Cuernavaca who was doing his best to develop a massive program whose purpose was to subvert the Church in Latin America. They already knew that, of course.

In the following three or four years, I never heard that those Mexican bishops made any effort to make the contact I had suggested. After a couple more years of additional work in Latin America, I came to realize that our bishops and priests, as citizens of the world's only remaining superpower, project their own kind of "ugly Americanism"—perceived as arrogance—which makes it difficult for the bishops and priests of other cultures to communicate with them.

Let me give one example of how the Latin American clergy perceived the U.S. Hierarchy and clergy in general. At a CICOP meeting, I believe held in Boston, with a thousand or more attendees, Cardinal Cushing of Boston delivered one of his infamous harangues, proclaiming all the wondrous things that his Archdiocese could do for the dioceses of Latin America. When he was finished, a priest from Chile with whom I was somewhat acquainted, paraphrased one of the Lamentations of the Prophet Jeremiah, "Non est dolor sicut dolor meus" [chap. 1 #12, translation: There is no sorrow as intense as my sorrow] and summed up Cardinal Cushing's speech by saying "Non est dollar sicut dollar meus," meaning "there is no dollar (money) as effective as my dollar (money)." Cardinal Cushing's speech, I am convinced, was perceived by this priest and I don't know how many others as something of an 'ugly American' putdown of the Catholic Church in Latin America.

CHAPTER 27

The 'Ugly American' Bishop and Priest

It pains me to say this, but it is true: I found the Latin American Bishops and Clergy to be in general much more impressive than their U.S. counterparts. (Remember, this was in the nineteen sixties; there have been recent improvements in the caliber of U.S. bishops.) After meeting and talking with bishop after bishop and priest after priest in both the U.S. and Latin America, my impression was that the bishops and priests of Latin America had a greater dedication to their spiritual lives and a better understanding of the dogmatic and moral principles of the Catholic Church than did their counterparts in the U.S. Obviously, there were exceptions in both places, but I'm talking about an overall impression. The bishops and clergy of Latin America (with only one exception I know of) had—and probably still have—a greater respect and level of obedience to the Vicar of Christ than do the general run of bishops and priests in the U.S. I knew of a certain number of homosexual and pedophile bishops in the U.S., while in Latin America I encountered none.

One glaring example of a disobedient bishop in the U.S. who, when the Vatican called for an end to general group confessions, this one refused to obey, saying "He's the Bishop of Rome, I am the Bishop of *My City*; he can do what he wants in Rome, I will do what I want in *My City*." The Theology, Tradition and Canon Law of the Catholic Church ***requires*** that when general absolution is administered to a large number of people *in time of emergency*, each penitent as soon as possible is to make a one-on-one confession to an individual priest. But, properly used, it's a wonderful practice, *e.g.* for troops about to go into battle.

Two recent experiences corroborate what I've just said. A converted Catholic layman who travels throughout Latin America on a regular basis recently said that the priests of Mexico are considerably more impressive than the priests of the U.S. And an American priest who speaks probably flawless Spanish after a great deal of work in Mexico, told me that he recently in two successive years participated in a priests' retreat in the U.S. and one in Mexico. The Mexican retreat, he said, was silent, very devout and prayerful. The U.S. priests' retreat was treated like a vacation; between presentations, the priests met and talked about mostly mundane subjects, went to town to shop, and generally enjoyed themselves as if it were simply time off.

There are three principal forces at work in our country, and a number of lesser ones. I will talk more about them later on, but in general terms the three are 1) the Heresy of Americanism which Pope Leo XIII wrote about; 2) the Heresy of Modernism which Pope St. Pius X described as the summation of the heresies which have attacked the Church over the centuries; and 3) the 'superpower' attitude of the United States which has 'bled off' to the bishops and clergy of the Catholic Church in the U.S.—part of the 'Ugly American' phenomenon which I encountered in Europe for seven years, and in many instances in the various countries of Latin America.

On this latter point, it is unfortunate that the political perception of the United States as the single superpower of the world has somehow infected the minds of bishops and clergy of the Catholic Church in the United States in such a way that we perceive ourselves as the *'superpower'* in the Catholic Church. This leads, I believe to the unspoken thought that we really don't even need the Pope. We are, after all, the most tolerant nation on earth composed as we are of diverse cultures, diverse religions, and we live in harmony with all of these. We tend to forget that we have a command to "preach the Gospel to all nations, baptizing them . . . ." And we seem to think of tolerance as a virtue, even though, of course, it is not. I'll come back to the subject of tolerance.

CHAPTER 28

My Tours of Latin America—Continued

During my five years as national director of the PAVLA program, I took a number of trips into Latin America, some of which have already been chronicled.

In my second year as PAVLA national director, I undertook a three month tour of Latin America, flying directly from Chicago to Rio de Janeiro. This trip took me into Chile, to Bolivia, Peru, Ecuador and into the countries of Central America and Jamaica. It began to puzzle me that in my contacts with the Latin American hierarchy and clergy, and with the volunteers, I received almost nothing but very positive feedback, encouraging me to develop the Papal Volunteer program to its fullest potential. At the other end of the scale, in the United States from Father Colonnese and his staff at the Latin America Bureau, from Msgr. Illich, a few feminist nuns and three volunteers who were by their own declaration attached to the Illich/Colonnese or the Liberation Theology schools of thought, the Papal Volunteer program and I as its director were attacked and pilloried. It was only as I learned more about the more current forms of the Heresy of Modernism and of the phenomenon of Americanism that I began to understand what I was up against. When that began to formulate in my mind, I knew I would have to gather more information, and, as a matter of conscience, I would have to expose the problem to the conference of bishops, even as I foresaw that I would not likely prevail. Excerpts from the memorandum which I presented to the bishops' conference on July 1, 1969 will be presented at the proper place later in this Part of the book. The full text of that report is given in Appendix A.

The next leg of my tour was fraught with difficulties. *Panair do Brazil*, the airline on which my flight from Rio de Janeiro to Santiago de Chile was scheduled, was abruptly terminated by the government and all other airlines were over-booked. It took a day or two to arrange another flight with a change of planes in Buenos Aires, Argentina. Then the plane I was to take from Buenos Aires had a flat tire (which they told us about three days later) and a tire had to be flown in from Boston. When I finally arrived in Chile, I had to reschedule all my meetings, with explanations accompanying each one.

Once again I found the volunteers to be in the best of spirits, doing excellent work, with very few complaints and teeming with excellent suggestions for the future of the program. The Chilean hierarchy were notably different in their general posture than the rest of the countries of Latin America. They seemed to me to be considerably more nationalistic than were the bishops of other Latin American countries.

While enthusiastic about the work of the Papal Volunteers, the Chilean authorities had what they presented as a grave complaint: We shouldn't have American Field Representatives in the country to support the volunteers, but the volunteers should completely merge with the culture and depend on the Chilean authorities. When I told them that I was aware that Chilean representatives were assigned to provide a support system to Chilean students in the United States and that, just as it was important for Chileans in a foreign country to have that support, so it was important for American volunteers to have such an arrangement, they withdrew their objections.

Aside from that concern, the Chilean authorities expressed themselves as being highly satisfied with the work and the deportment of the Papal Volunteers. Not long after my visit, Bishop Pineira, president of the Chilean conference of bishops, wrote to me and clearly reported two outstanding results in Chile as the outcome of the Papal Volunteer presence: 1) They saw a strengthening of the Chilean faithful laity in their participation with the work of the Church, and 2) the Chilean hierarchy were encouraged to resurrect their earlier efforts to engage their own laity in their work. (See Georgia Bulletin, article of May 4, 1967.)

My next stop was in Lima, Peru where there was a center house for the Papal Volunteers and which was the headquarters of the Field Representative for that country.

This representative, whose name was Kevin, was openly hostile to me—one of the three mentioned earlier who took a position of open animosity toward me. He was the one who wrote a rather angry letter to me about three or four months *before* my appointment was effective, upbraiding me for not yet having addressed the problems he perceived in the PAVLA program. A month or so after I arrived in Chicago in the fall of 1964, I received another letter from him. In it, he expressed a great deal of skepticism that I could possibly know what was going on, and he posed quite a lengthy list of questions I was called upon to answer about my attitude toward the program. I sent him back an in-depth response to all his questions and provided a summary of my already-public plans for the Papal Volunteer program, assuming that those plans had not yet penetrated to the volunteers in Latin America. I found out later that he took my letter to a Peruvian priest who was a major figure in the Liberation Theology movement, who advised him to give me a chance to develop the program as I proposed. There was nothing in my plans which could be judged as objectionable by anyone familiar with Catholic theology and the theology of the lay apostolate as proposed by Vatican Council II.

Kevin, the Peruvian field representative, had a direct connection with Father Colonnese who I understood had insisted before I arrived in Chicago that Kevin be appointed to the post. He received his language training at Msgr. Illich's training school at Cuernavaca,

Mexico, and, as just mentioned, was a close protegé of a Peruvian priest who openly espoused Liberation Theology. Kevin quite openly advocated made-in-America *desarrollo* ('development' or 'change') programs for Latin America. It was important, therefore, that he be replaced, and I acted on that as soon as I returned to my headquarters in Chicago.

My tour in Peru included a trip to the *altiplano*—the high plateau running north and south to the East of Lima, extending throughout the country, north to south, and extending into Bolivia. Starting at the town of Cuzco, which is situated at about 11,000 feet above sea level, I went by car on a route that took me to over 14,000 feet, to the city of Puno, Peru, at about 12,000 feet, which is on the north shore of Lake Titicaca, the highest fresh water lake in the world. Midway between Cuzco and Puno we encountered a herd of several hundred llamas and the smaller vicuña, an encounter which slowed our progress to a crawl. It was an unforgettable event. Since it was a hot day, we had the windows in the car rolled down. The llamas thrust their heads into the car, and, like the camel to which they are related, they drooled copiously. So we had to roll the windows up and in effect were trapped inside a sweltering car surrounded by what appeared to be hundreds of llama heads peering in at us.

There were volunteers in Arequipa, Peru, not far from Puno, and others stationed across the border from Peru in La Paz, Bolivia, a city of a million or more which is built upon the internal slope of an ancient volcano, so that a few miles from the city it remains invisible until one comes to the lip of the volcano. (On another trip, I landed on a commercial jet at the La Paz airport, at about 12,000 feet the highest commercial airport in the world, and possibly the longest. Because of the thinness of the air, landing speed was tremendously fast and somewhat frightening.) The volunteers in all these cities in the *altiplano* (the 'high plain') had adjusted to breathing the very thin air. Immediately after landing at the higher altitude in Cuzco, Peru, it was necessary to lie down for about two hours to adjust to the rare atmosphere, and, even so, I developed the dreadful altitude headache which seems to afflict everyone on a first visit. There were people living at 15,000 to 17,000 feet or more, who were born there, who were considerably shorter in stature than most of us, and they were endowed with barrel chests, and, I was told, larger red blood corpuscles than those of us who are accustomed to living at lower altitudes. There were large herds of cattle which developed from calves whose mothers were taken to the high plateau so that their calves could be born there. Otherwise, they could not survive the very thin air at the high altitude.

The volunteers in Puno and Arequipa organized a trip for me by jeep around the area. Several of us rode in the jeep-like vehicle. During the tour, one of the volunteers, an attractive young woman who I believed to be in her late twenties, told me a story which the others had already heard. She was obviously in pain and deeply scandalized. She said that when she had recently visited Santiago in Chile for additional language training, one of the Jesuit priests who was also there for language training tried to seduce her. He used the 'free love' arguments which were becoming so common at that time and which have become even more common as time has gone on. They continue to be the same arguments used by homosexuals to this day to justify their sexual activities. He told her in whatever terminology he had found to be effective that for the two of them to go to bed together and engage in love-making was itself an act of love and therefore was a good thing, because, after all, "God is Love." She rejected him, of course, but was deeply shocked by the incident. I myself was shocked. I have no doubt that what she told me was absolutely true, and, in all likelihood, was more despicable than she described. The only thing I remember saying to her was to ask if she wanted me to press the matter with his superiors. I admire her for her response: in effect she said: "I've been trying to forgive him for what he did and I've been praying for him every day. I wouldn't want to open up a scandal for the Church." (Her response is a wonderful counterpoint to the victims and alleged victims of pedophile priests in the years around 2002 who seem to think that the acquisition of large sums of money will ease their pain and anguish. The only thing that can give them surcease, as was true with my wife, is somehow to forgive them for what they did and to pray for them.) I haven't the slightest recollection of what else I may have said to her, but I simply hope that I said something reassuring which was truly helpful to her. After all, I had learned a lot in a home for unwed mothers where a significant percentage of those young mothers were seduced or raped. As recounted before, I had developed additional understanding in another connection working with a young woman who had been raped by a priest she trusted. The young woman volunteer in southern Peru was badly shaken by her experience and I suspect it colored the rest of her stay in Peru as a Papal Volunteer. Almost all of my daily Masses at that time were celebrated for the welfare of the Papal Volunteers as a group, and oftentimes for particular individuals such as this young woman.

The next stop for me was Ecuador where again I experienced unmistakable and genuine enthusiasm for the Papal Volunteer program on the part of the bishops, the clergy and the volunteers themselves. An exception to this was an American religious order—a group of religious men who opened a new monastery in the city of Guayaquil, Ecuador. I thought at the time that their negativism toward the volunteers was rooted in some kind of jealousy because they felt that their own contribution was going unnoticed. They brought overtones of ugly Americanism to Ecuador. At some point during the construction of their new establishment, a ship docked and unloaded all their furniture, beds and bedding—manufactured or at least purchased in the USA. It was an appalling way for them to begin their entry into the new culture. They could have purchased an equal quality of furnishings much more cheaply in Ecuador itself and demonstrated their respect for the culture they were entering.

The Papal Volunteers themselves were painfully aware of the attitude of this religious order and, as far as I could tell, did not socialize with them, which probably contributed to the negative attitude of the religious order toward the Papal Volunteer program.

This unimpressive religious order was in direct counterpoint to another order in the city of Quito, Ecuador, whose approach to the culture of Ecuador, as far as I could tell from the brief conversation I had with its superior, was very similar to the very impressive order I had met in Venezuela.

CHAPTER 29

Confrontation With The Enemy

My next stop was mind boggling—Bogotá, Colombia. I was scheduled simply to change planes there on my way back to Chicago. But my connecting flight was delayed by several hours. Msgr. Ivan Illich was also waiting for a delayed connecting flight. We met for the first time and spent more than two hours in the waiting area of the airport throwing verbal darts at each other. I was traveling with the newly-designated Field Representative for Peru, Ecuador and Colombia who sat silently and listened to the debate. Possibly because I was his boss, he spread the word that I had won the debate hands down. It was wonderful to have his support.

At any rate, I learned a great deal about the mind of Illich. I learned that he was indeed involved in dismantling the Church in Latin America and rebuilding it into a new order. I told him later that I assumed that he would be the leader, or at least one of the leaders, of this new order once it had been constructed. He made no response to that. I found that he and Colonnese had what sounded like identical agenda for bringing about change in Latin America. He was involved in establishing *Communidades de Base* (Christian Base Communities) in several locations in each country of Latin America—he had just come from such an organizational meeting in Quito, Ecuador—and he strongly favored Liberation Theology. I also learned that he was involved in establishing IPLA, an acronym for a

Spanish title meaning Pastoral Institutes for Latin America. Several of these were to be organized. The institutes would serve as training programs for those who would, after proper indoctrination, return to their home areas and organize the Christian Base Communities. (The concept of these IPLA institutions comes up again in my memorandum to the Bishops' committee—in a later chapter.) I never heard a single Latin American bishop speak in favor of those institutions. When I asked Msgr. Illich why he and his cohorts would not simply use the existing structures—the diocese and the parish—within which to work rather than creating new ones, he had no answer. I assume that the problem was that the bishops, pastors and the Vatican controlled those traditional structures, and he and his disciples wanted a new order which they would control.

During our discussion, Illich spoke against almost every power in the U.S. Church and the Latin American Church—the two notable exceptions: Father Louis Colonnese—and Bishop Joseph Bernardin. Even though Colonnese had publicly broken with Msgr. Illich, I think it was a public relations move and that there never was an ideological break. Colonnese said that just once, and never again to my knowledge spoke against Illich. Certainly Illich never spoke against Colonnese—to me. Msgr. Illich espoused most of the doctrine which Father Colonnese promoted, which I heard *ad nauseam* for five years.

When I returned to Chicago, I found that our requests to bishops to establish diocesan Papal Volunteer programs had resulted in the appointment of a large number of diocesan directors.

CHAPTER 30

Chicago and Cardinal Cody

I believe I arrived in Chicago shortly before Archbishop Cody did. He encountered instant enmity. When I went to lunch with two other priests, we were at a table beside four women with southern accents. They were from New Orleans, they said, and had come to Chicago to warn the city about the nature of Cody. As far as I could tell, their argument with him was that he was too traditional and not in tune with the 'modern' thinking within the Church.

My own first encounter with Cardinal Cody was not too pleasant, although it ended well. After some weeks or months, he became aware that I was headquartered in the archdiocese and that I published a small magazine called "*The Papal Volunteer.*" He asked me if I had sought permission from his predecessor to publish the magazine. I told him that when I came to Chicago, the See was vacant, but I candidly confessed that the need to seek permission had never crossed my mind. So I asked him for permission to continue. He had many questions about the Papal Volunteer program, and, after I had explained at some length, he gave his approval to what I was doing, and he specifically included publishing the magazine, with the stipulation that I add him to my mailing list.

Later on, he became my strongest supporter among the hierarchy. During a meeting held in Venezuela, attended by bishops from both the U.S. and countries of Latin America, the Colonnese forces were bad-mouthing the PAVLA program. Cardinal Cody made it a point, during a lunch break, to walk with me so that every bishop and priest at the conference saw him and me together. It was a magnificent demonstration of support for me and the PAVLA program.

As a Theologian myself with an advanced degree, I felt that I could with reasonable objectivity analyze the Catholic stance of bishops and clergy, depending on what they said or wrote.

At the time—1954 to1959—only about four or five of the bishops out of the many I met with were ***not*** infected with Modernism and what Pope Leo XIII identified as Americanism. The *leading* priests in Chicago were infected with anti-authoritarianism, Modernism, Americanism, open disloyalty and hostility toward their bishop (there were, of course, among the general run of priests, many top-notch ones). As I write these lines, things have greatly improved. I believe that there are twenty five to thirty solid bishops who are not infected with the errors I just mentioned. And there may well be more. I say this because I don't have the kind of contacts I used to have.

All this was intended to lead up to the statement that at the time I was in charge of the PAVLA program, I perceived Cardinal Cody as one of the best—perhaps the very best—bishop in the U.S. He was a spiritual man, a very devout priest, totally loyal to the Pope as the Vicar of Christ, and in addition he was an excellent administrator whose primary purpose was to take care of the priests in the archdiocese, and therefore, through them, of the faithful of his archdiocese. And yet, from the moment he arrived, he was vilified, lies were told about him, and he was attacked for everything he did and for everything he was perceived as not doing. Among the lies told about him had to do with a woman in his life. The 'woman' was his adopted sister. His parents adopted her when they were both children, they grew up as brother and sister and were brother and sister when he was Cardinal Archbishop of Chicago.

Before he died, he was vilified and mentally tortured. As someone remarked at the time, "God certainly knows how to put the finishing touches on a special soul." Cardinal Cody was given the honor and privilege of suffering with Christ on the Cross.

Two Years of Growth of PAVLA and Growing Opposition

In the course of the next two years the Papal Volunteer program continued to grow. As a program of the lay apostolate, it caught the imagination of bishops around the U.S., of the clergy and laity, and of religious orders of men and women, particularly of those with missions in the countries of Latin America. It appeared to fill a need among the Catholics of the United States, and it filled a need among the bishops, clergy and laity of Latin America. The number of dioceses which established a local Papal Volunteer program nearly doubled, and the number of laity volunteering for the program continued to grow.

According to records of the Papal Volunteer program, in the spring of 1967, Archbishop Vagnozzi, apostolic delegate to the U.S. at the time, was quoted as saying that the program has been a brilliant page in history; it was, he said, one of the most outstanding examples of lay apostolic action in the entire history of the Church. At a meeting of Papal Volunteer diocesan directors held in the Archdiocese of Atlanta, Georgia, I was quoted as saying, "We follow the judgments of the Latin American bishops and authorities—as to what projects they need, and what programs in their judgment are necessary to strengthen their countries—whether in the areas of medical, socioeconomic, education, co-op programs or missionary work." PAVLA recognizes that "we are to assist in the development of the Latin American nations; it is always implicit in this program that the PAVLA personnel work with Latin Americans to help them develop their own culture and heritage."

The Latin American bishops and other authorities—both religious and secular—responded enthusiastically to this approach. While there were more than 300 volunteers at work after two years at diverse locations in Latin America, there were more than 2,000 requests for more personnel. One of the PAVLA field representatives wrote to me that "no matter what I do—hide in the house, or travel, I keep getting more requests."

The National Training Center in Washington, D.C. became continually more effective, and the *Hogar Interamericano*, the Papal Volunteer Spanish language training program in Mexico City, under the able direction of a priest and a very capable and experienced Papal Volunteer as co-director took shape and grew stronger. Since this *Hogar* was a remodeled residence in the heart of Mexico City, it had the volunteers not only taking formal classes on a daily, intensive basis, but it provided for them to simply go out on the street and immerse themselves in speaking with the people of Mexico City as they went about their daily lives.

Of course, as the Papal Volunteer program grew stronger, so also did the opposition to it. Msgr. Ivan Illich questioned the effectiveness of aid to Latin America in general, and in a special way attacked the validity of the Papal Volunteer program, and he wrote that "many (successful Americans) fail to ask whether the ethic of the 'achieving society' is suited to the needs of contemporary Latin America." I was quoted at the time as saying that his statement is a broad generalization. While I have always decried the 'ugly American' in whatever guise (tourist, military, missionary), there are many people who love the Latin American culture and who respect all other cultures and do not try to change but to learn from them. The Papal Volunteer program had the support of the Latin American bishops and other authorities because one of its fundamental principles was to adjust and to adapt to the culture in which it worked, always under the authority of the local bishop.

In spite of this general support from Church authorities both in Latin America and in the Vatican, opposition grew stronger from those hidden 'ugly Americans' (Illich, Colonnese, Sidney Lens—more about him later—and their associates, and, of course, Bishop Bernardin) who wanted not only to change the Latin American cultures, but change the Church itself. The second session of the National Training Center, as mentioned earlier, was burdened by a "committee" formed by Father Colonnese to scrutinize its methods and report to him on its findings. It also had a "volunteer" who originated in Father Colonnese's home diocese who was anything but cooperative with the teaching staff of the Center. He became known by the rest of the Papal Volunteers in training as a 'spy' for Father Colonnese.

I'd like to re-emphasize the attacks we were afflicted with. At one of the meetings of CICOP in Chicago, the Papal Volunteer program was attacked mercilessly by a panel of *avant garde* 'experts'—both lay people and clergy. One Mexican bishop had been asked to join the panel. Several Papal Volunteers offered their experience for that presentation, and they were refused. This resulted in the strange anomaly of a panel of non-Papal Volunteers and non-Latin American people who vilified the Papal Volunteer program, and the lone *Mexican* bishop on the panel strongly supported it.

A year later, the CICOP conference was held in Boston where a similar but more concentrated attack was made on the Papal Volunteer program. This time it was joined by Kevin, the Papal Volunteer Field Representative who was so hostile toward me during my extended tour of Latin America, who was the protegé of the Peruvian priest who was a proponent of Liberation Theology. Throughout all this, the Papal Volunteer program was able to hold its own, because the volunteers themselves had built up a great deal of good will both in Latin America and in the United States.

I therefore was able to apply my energies enthusiastically to the administration and development of the Papal Volunteer program, and I was quite blithely unaware of the ferocity of the opposition which was building toward it. And I now know that the opposition had the full support of a few key bishops in the United States, the principal one of whom was Bishop Bernardin.

In retrospect, I have come to believe that the bishops who rather clandestinely opposed the Papal Volunteer program were of two types: 1) those who in varying degrees espoused the heresy of Modernism, and 2) those who were uncomfortable with the development of a lay apostolate which would quite obviously become very powerful in its own right—and this was true, even though the volunteers pledged themselves to work under and in unison with the established hierarchy. Now unfortunately we are seeing groups of Catholic laity who are forming in varying degrees of opposition to the hierarchy. The Papal Volunteer program would have ushered into the Church a group of laity who were dedicated to working in harmony with the bishops and priests. A great opportunity was lost when the bishops failed to act to forestall its destruction.

CHAPTER 31

Move to USCC Headquarters, Washington, D.C.

After about eighteen months in Chicago, I personally had taken an exhaustive look at the PAVLA program's income and expenses. When the analysis was concluded, I couldn't help but realize that the income I could foresee would cover a little more than half of the expenses I would incur in developing the activities I had already planned. Operating on blind faith and hope with an underlayment of fear and anxiety, I proceeded to do what I wanted to do, hoping against hope that somehow the means to pay for it all would be forthcoming. The result? After about two years of implementing and generally completing those plans, and when I was ordered to move my office to Washington, D.C., the PAVLA program had $75,000 in the bank which was of considerably greater value at that time than it is now. Once I turned that money over to the USCC as required, the PAVLA program never saw it again, at least not while I remained in charge for the next two years.

As I knew then, and am even more convinced now, the move was intended to control me and the PAVLA program, and either destroy it as some wanted, or shift its emphasis from the lay apostolate to simply a social service program with no religious purpose. As I think about it now and as I have pondered it for the last forty years, I find it almost incredible that a group of Catholic priests, supported by a few bishops, would be so anti-Catholic as to oppose a program of the Lay Apostolate initiated by a Pope (Paul VI) and so strongly advocated by the Second Vatican Council. The only explanation, so far as I can understand, is that these bishops and clergy had allowed themselves to be strongly infected with the Heresy of Modernism, and the Heresy of Americanism as predicted by Pope Leo XIII, to the point that perhaps they had lost the supernatural virtue of Faith and were acting as tools of the Devil. Since Ivan Illich was a proven Communist, I more than strongly suspect that all those who bought into his philosophy—Bishop Bernardin, his assistant, Father Colonnese, the 'groups' he was so much a part of—was a Communist group intent on destroying the Catholic Church.

At any rate, on instructions from Father John Considine, MM, Director of the Latin America Bureau of the United States Catholic Conference, I moved my headquarters from Chicago to Washington, DC in the fall of 1967. Since the rumor was strong that Father Considine would soon retire and Father Colonnese would succeed him, I told Bishop Hodges, chairman of the PAVLA subcommittee of bishops at the time, that it would be better that I resign and return to my diocese rather than undertake what I believed would be a losing battle with Father Colonnese. Bishop Hodges prevailed on me to make the move, saying that the Papal Volunteer program would die if I were to leave it at that juncture. Reluctantly, I agreed and immediately started to make the move.

Into the Snake Pit

My first step was to move into a residence known as the 'staff house' of the USCC (United States Catholic Conference), where Bishop Bernardin, appointed as director of the USCC by the conference of bishops also had his residence. He was known to be the personal choice of the president of the conference of bishops at the time—the Most Rev. John Dearden, Archbishop of Detroit, soon to be Cardinal Archbishop. I was assigned a suite of rooms, transferred my personal belongings from the north side rectory in Chicago where I had been living, and got settled in Washington, D.C.

My first action was to place an ad in the Washington Post seeking an assistant who could help me organize the new office. I was fortunate in that a young Catholic married woman who had served on the staff of Congressmen answered the ad. With her help, I was able to quickly replace the very efficient staff I had in Chicago, and we began work in remodeling the office space which would house the entire Latin America Bureau, except that Father Considine remained in his office at the USCC.

Now that I had moved within close proximity to the administrative center of the Catholic Church in the United States (the United States Catholic Conference), I was to have a number of odd experiences not directly related to the Latin America Bureau nor the Papal Volunteer program.

Since I had residence in the USCC staff house, I quickly became acquainted with quite a number of priests and monsignors who were the national heads or administrators of various responsibilities in the Church—akin to the fact that I was the national director of the PAVLA program. While I don't remember all their names, there were those relating to the liturgy, Catholic education, civil rights—to name a few.

An early experience, as I recall in the first few weeks that I lived there, a meeting was arranged by some of the priests to consider the matter of their financial compensation. Bishop Bernardin, director of the USCC, chaired the meeting and appeared to support its purpose. The contention was that, as national heads of these various responsibilities, we were deserving of larger salaries than we were receiving. As the meeting proceeded, enthusiasm for this idea grew apace, and it began to be suggested that we each were the equivalent of a CEO of a large corporation in the business world and therefore should be the recipients of similar salaries. Throughout the meeting,

Bishop Bernardin smiled and nodded in such a way that everyone (myself included) assumed that he was in full support of the ideas being presented. After it seemed that everyone in the meeting (and remember, these were all priests!) was looking forward to achieving some level of wealth in their lifetimes, Father Bernard Law (who later became the Cardinal Archbishop of Boston) administered the *coup de grace* to the meeting. In an act of what I consider to be great courage (he hadn't lived in the staff house much longer than I), he asked the group what they were trying to do. He said that all of us were priests; we were not there to earn high salaries, or to earn any salary at all. We were there to serve as priests and any effort to compare our financial value to the salaries paid in the business world was completely out of harmony with our vocations. On that note, the meeting ended, and, as far as I know, the subject never came up again. It therefore hurt me deeply when Cardinal Law, who I knew at that time to be a deeply devout and courageous priest, was so publicly criticized later for failing to adequately restrain pedophile priests in his archdiocese. One of the great responsibilities of any bishop is the care, especially spiritual, of his priests. I have no doubt that any mistakes he may have made were made in his effort to care for the salvation of the souls of his priests and his people. And, knowing how these things work after my years in a chancery office, I am sure that in each case he sought, and was given, professional reassurance that the priests involved had been rehabilitated and that they were no longer a danger to anyone. If this is true, how much more of a good steward can anyone be?

At any rate, the arrogance of a number of those priests at the meeting on priestly salaries, and the *prima donna* (ugly American?) attitude that seemed to prevail among them was appalling to me. The bishops do not need priests like that to represent them, and there is a great need (I hope this is no longer true) for them to exercise the oversight which will keep those kinds of priests out of the USCC and ensure that those kinds of attitudes do not develop among them.

I quickly began to realize what relationship existed between the United States Catholic Conference (USCC) and the United States Conference of Catholic Bishops (USCCB), the latter, of course, being the supreme power of the Catholic Church in the United States and the former being their administrative instrument. The Body of Bishops (as the USCCB was commonly called) probably felt they could rely on that group of priests in the USCC because it was itself headed by a bishop—Bishop Joseph Bernardin—as its Secretary General. Unfortunately, therefore, the bishops in general who headed committees of bishops dedicated to a given cause (e.g. the head of the PAVLA Subcommittee—a division of the Committee for Latin American Affairs—was initially Bishop Hodges with whom I conferred frequently) gave their 'rubber stamp' approval to whatever declaration was formulated in the USCC.

As a very personal example: When my own bishop—the Bishop of Sioux City, Most Rev. Jos. M. Mueller—at first refused to release me to become national director of the PAVLA program, he later changed his mind when he received a letter from Cardinal Cushing, Archbishop of Boston, directly requesting that he release me for the position. Bishop Mueller then told me that he thought he should release me for the purpose. When I strongly urged that he not change his mind, he said, in effect, "When someone at the level of Cardinal Cushing makes the request, it's important to re-think the decision." As I lived and worked within the USCC, anyone can imagine my chagrin when I learned that the letter to my bishop was not written by Cardinal Cushing, that he had not signed it himself, and that he probably never knew that it was composed, signed in his name, and sent by Father Considine. I've always considered it likely that Cardinal Cushing did not even have a copy of the letter. Instead of thinking of how I might have avoided all the ignominy of the last few years, I began to realize that it all was somehow providential and that perhaps it was my obligation to reveal the many things I had learned about problems in the Catholic Church.

The Special Case of Bishop Joseph Bernardin

When I moved into the USCC, I knew that the priests who headed up the various 'bureaus' were in large part infected with the heresies of Modernism and Americanism, but I knew that I would not be required to deal with most of them in my work. My "boss" was Father John Considine, Director of the Latin America Bureau, who was ostensibly supportive of what I was doing. I knew I would have ongoing battles with Father Louis Colonnese, but he didn't live at the staff house and wouldn't be a concern until and unless he succeeded Father Considine as Director of the Latin America Bureau.

My most implacable and powerful opponent, of whom for several weeks after I moved in I had not the slightest inkling, was Most Rev. Joseph Bernardin, only recently appointed the first General Secretary of the fairly newly created United States Catholic Conference (USCC).

A fairly recent example of the flawed interaction of the USCC and the Body of Bishops was the statement of Cardinal William Keeler, Archbishop of Baltimore, who was a fellow student in the North American College in Rome and whom I know to be an honest man, but not necessarily a good Theologian. The statement, filled with doctrinal error, absolved the Jews from the need for baptism, that the Old Covenant with them was still in force, and generally releasing them from any obligation to recognize Christ as the Messiah. After my experience at the USCC in Washington, I believe that the statement was formulated by the pertinent Modernist group of priests at the USCC, and Cardinal Keeler in an unwarranted act of trust simply 'rubber stamped' it.

In another example, the Body of Bishops later had to specifically and publicly retract that portion of the American version of the Catechism which contained the same doctrinal error. The Catechism, I believe, was formulated by the USCC and again was 'rubber stamped' by the Body of Bishops.

Another unsettling event at the USCC staff house occurred one night around midnight when some of us who couldn't sleep were gathered in the dining room. One of the priests came in and began to describe his night on the town. He had been out on a date. With a woman. There were those of us there who were greatly taken aback (I could see the signs of shock in the faces of a few), but, unfortunately, there were those who seemed to enter into the spirit of the occasion and enthusiastically asked for details. And they received them. I do not believe that the priest in this instance had sexual intercourse with the woman he went out with, but it sounded as if quite a number of activities which might have led to that did in fact occur. The most appalling part of that evening, to me, is that Bishop Bernardin participated in a way that could have easily been construed as approval. He certainly voiced no kind of disapproval. It occurred to me later that the priest who had the 'date' may well have been a homosexual, and therefore ran no risk of committing fornication.

A growing realization as I continued to stay at the USCC staff house was that there may have been a great deal of homosexuality among its residents. The reader will recall that I had had a rather significant number of contacts with homosexuals. Apparently I was attractive to them until they discovered that there was no taint of the same impulse in me. The number of contacts and the discussions I had earlier with homosexuals led me to rely on a number of important conclusions I had drawn: 1) I could quite accurately identify a homosexual man, 2) homosexuals could easily recognize each other, 3) they tended to 'flock together', for example, a superior would choose a homosexual subordinate, and 4) there was a deeply buried—and unconsciously denied—anger and bitterness that every homosexual I encountered carried around with him because he knew that he was 'different.'

This—again deeply buried and unconsciously denied—caused (perhaps in every case) a very strong but carefully muted animosity toward a heterosexual man. This would explain probably a *small part* of the hostility toward me throughout my entire tenure as national director of the PAVLA program. Most of the hostility and antagonism, however, was grounded in philosophical differences.

It was difficult for me to conclude (in the sense that I was reluctant to face the fact), but I came to realize after considerably more than a year that Bishop Joseph Bernardin was himself the core of the problem at the USCC. Extremely intelligent and politically accomplished he very astutely and credibly portrayed himself as an orthodox Catholic and pretended to be loyal to the Pope. However, when Pope Paul VI promulgated his encyclical ***Humanae Vitae*** (on Human Life) on 25 July, 1968 in which he opposed all forms of abortion and artificial birth control, Bishop Bernardin was heard to comment about "That damned encyclical." I concluded after experiencing the atmosphere of the USCC staff house that many of those priests, following the lead of Bishop Bernardin, were infected with the Heresy of Modernism, the Heresy of Americanism, and the arrogance of power. I have never been able to determine whether, how much or why this was magnified by homosexuality. (See Chapter 34 on the weaknesses of the Catholic Church.)

It was easy to conclude from the early approach that Father Colonnese made to me that he himself was a homosexual. The Director of the USCC, Bishop Joseph Bernardin, however intelligent and politically adept he was, had the earmarks of the homosexual. (Later on, he was identified from a number of sources as a pederast /pedophile, and according to some, he died of AIDS.—see the references given just ahead). From that, it was easy to suspect that at least a number of the priests at the USCC who worked under Bishop Bernardin, were themselves homosexuals. As time progressed, I did indeed encounter some of them. After Bishop Bernardin was appointed as Archbishop of Chicago, there were charges against him by a young man whom he allegedly had molested as a young boy. That former young boy never retracted his charge. However, he reportedly received a settlement of about three million dollars. Cardinal Bernardin said that he did retract his charge. Then stories began to spread that the Archbishop was suffering from terminal cancer. He appeared in photographs, however, very similar to those whom I had personally observed who were dying of AIDS. In support of my perceptions at the time, I present excerpts from Randy Engel's recent book "The Rite of Sodomy":

> This segment on Joseph Cardinal Bernardin was originally incorporated into the previous chapter on homosexual members of the American hierarchy. However, because of his extraordinary influence on AmChurch, I decided Cardinal Bernardin deserved a chapter all his own.
>
> To do real justice of Cardinal Bernardin and his entourage of clerical homosexuals and pederasts and ancillary hangers-on who made up the Chicago-Washington, D. C. Homosexual/Pederast Axis would require more than one full size book.
>
> This highly condensed summary of information on the role played by Bernardin in the building of the Homosexual Collective within AmChurch is intended to dispel the fiction that the late Cardinal Bernardin managed to fool all of the people all of the time.

If anyone would like to pursue the subject in greater depth, I refer the reader to Randy Engel's book, "The Rite of Sodomy," Chapter 15, *The Special Case of Joseph Cardinal Bernardin.* See also the syndicated column by Matt Abbott, *Renew America* [Chicago, IL], August 18, 2006.

The USCC and Abortion/Contraception

On yet another very questionable occasion, the assistant director of the USCC, Msgr. Frank Hurley (later named bishop of Juneau, Alaska) invited Father Charles Curran over to dinner at the staff house. And certainly he would not have done so without at least the approval of Bishop Bernardin, who was present at the dinner as host.

Father Curran was notorious, as a self-styled Catholic Theologian, for advocating two anti-Catholic positions: 1) abortion and 2) artificial contraception as a legitimate and moral means of family planning for married couples. These two positions stood in opposition to the uninterrupted centuries-long tradition of the Catholic Church on the two subjects. As a result of Father Curran's public stand on the subject, Archbishop Boyle of Washington wrote a well-reasoned and strong letter condemning abortion and artificial contraception. In addition, my brother, Msgr. Eugene Kevane as the Head of the Education Department at the Catholic University, also took a strong stand against Father Curran's position on both subjects. That my brother and Father Curran were at odds on these subjects was a matter of public knowledge, certainly within the Catholic Church and at the USCC staff house. That Father Curran should be invited to dinner as an honored guest at the staff house points up the attitude of both Bishop Bernardin and of the general attitude among those clergy. That evening, Father Curran was treated, as I said, as an honored guest, and Msgr. Hurley seemed to take great delight in introducing him and me, identifying me to him as Msgr. Kevane's brother. It seemed to me at the time (and it still does) entirely inappropriate for the USCC staff, representing the U.S. bishops as they did, to invite such a priest who publicly stood opposed to accepted Catholic moral doctrine into their place of residence, which gave the appearance of condoning his approval of abortion and artificial contraception. Bishop Bernardin, of course, was very much in evidence as the presiding host at that dinner. The Vatican stripped Curran of his status as "Theologian" on August 1, 1986.

Msgr. Hurley's handling of the matter might have given me forewarning as to the stand he would take during the later meeting when I presented my memorandum to the bishops' committee. There will be more on that later.

CHAPTER 32

The United States Catholic Conference and U.S. Politics

Another disturbing component of life at the USCC and its staff house had to do with politics. Occasionally, members of the House of Representatives and the U.S. Senate were invited to the staff house for dinner and discussion (and more often to the various offices of the USCC). It seemed to me that there was a tendency to convey some kind of parity between the top legislative branch of the U.S. government and the top administrative arm of the Conference of Catholic Bishops. While it could be argued that it was important to maintain a reasonable form of communication between the government and the bishops, it was disturbing to me that *all* of the congressmen invited to the staff house were members of the Democratic party. I do not recall a single Republican coming to the staff house while I was there. And most, if not all, of the Democratic senators and congressmen who visited the staff house were, at least in their political stances, pro-abortion. Which, of course, may have bearing on the USCC's receptivity to Father Charles Curran.

On July 25, 1968, Pope Paul VI promulgated the encyclical *Humanae Vitae* which clearly condemns both abortion and artificial contraception. Not long after that, as mentioned earlier, Bishop Bernardin was quoted to me as proclaiming, "That *damn* encyclical," (his own emphasis) which succinctly represents his own erroneous attitude, and that of many of his followers at the USCC, toward abortion and artificial contraception. It should be clear from the foregoing why I would in retrospect feel that in moving into the USCC environment that I was entering into enemy territory among those who adhered to the Heresy of Modernism and Americanism and why I would start this segment of my personal history as entering into the Snake Pit.

I always believed that it was important for me, as a priest, to maintain a stance of neutrality when it came to politics. (See what was said above—Part II, Chapter 20—about the concept of the Perfect Society.) I believe they call that being an independent. Therefore, I could simply vote for the *person*, for his (or her) stand on policy, on principle, and on matters of morality without being pressured one way or another by a blind allegiance to a specific political party. It is a fact that Catholics in general, particularly those who live East of the Appalachians, and even more particularly those of Irish descent, tend to support the Democratic party, and they somewhat blindly support even those Democrats who are pro-abortion. Most of the bishops who were willing to talk to me about their political affiliation told me that they tended toward the Democratic party, and had done so since childhood, and they spoke very vaguely about Democratic politicians who were pro-abortion but whom they seemed to support in the elections. One bishop told me, in defense of his political leanings, that the particular politician in question might for political reasons make pro-abortion statements in public, but in his private life was pro-life. I believe that to be a hypocritical distinction: pro-abortion public statements by any Catholic politician can and do promote scandal. A young woman with an unwanted pregnancy might use such a statement, coming from a known Catholic politician, as justification for procuring an abortion as a means of birth control. Such a politician, therefore, would commit the gravely serious sin of scandal, and would be complicit in an act of murder.

Now today, as I write this book, we have a Democratic president who openly supports abortion, whereas his predecessor was a Republican president who spoke and acted more forthrightly against abortion than many of the bishops, and he seemed to be more forthrightly pro-life.

At any rate, it was clear to me during my years in Washington, DC with the USCC that the powers of that organization favored the representatives of the Democratic party far more than they did those of the Republican party.

Another unsettling episode during my tenure among the administrative representatives of the U.S. bishops had to do with the ecumenical movement. One day as I was sitting in my office between meetings (my life was a continuing round of preparing for meetings, attending them, or assessing and acting on them—or contrary to them—afterwards), an impressive gentleman knocked at my door—my secretary was momentarily absent—stuck his head in and asked if he could have a few minutes with me. It turned out he was a 'Rev. Mr.'—a member of the Council of Churches whose purpose was to make contact with various denominations to explore ways and means of enhancing the ecumenical movement. We talked about many subjects, and he asked me directly what I thought of the chances of success in bringing the churches together in the ecumenical movement. Among other things, I told him that whatever each Church group held to be eternal truths taught by Christ himself they could not compromise on those beliefs and retain their identity. As far as the Catholic Church was concerned, I mentioned a few such doctrines, such as the validity of the Sacrament of Orders, the Celebration of the Mass, the doctrine of the Real Presence of the living Christ in the Eucharist, the number and efficacy of the Sacraments, and the Primacy of the Pope in an unbroken succession since St. Peter.

Before this non-catholic minister left my office that day, he told me two extraordinary things. First, he told me that he had talked to every priest at the head of all the bureaus, agencies and secretariats of the USCC (this included Bishop Bernardin), and, he said, "You are the only honest man I have met here. I know all these things you told me about the Catholic Church are true, I know that we can get nowhere unless we honestly face these areas of difference, and yet no one but yourself has even hinted at them." He was clearly disheartened by this experience at the USCC. As was I. It made me think that the attitude expressed at the breakfast table in Chicago by the seminary professor—that in the interests of ecumenism we needed to downplay the doctrine of the Real Presence—was far more widespread among the clergy (and perhaps among the bishops whom they represented) than I believed could be possible.

The other thing he told me was that Father Colonnese was making veiled references to a letter I had written (this was either the memorandum I presented to the bishops in Mid-1969 exposing him as a Modernist who was supporting Liberation Theology and Christian Base Communities in Latin America. Or perhaps he was referring to an earlier letter I had written to the diocesan directors of the PAVLA program explaining the organized opposition to the program). He said that Father Colonnese was condemning me because of the content of the letter, but, he said, Father Colonnese told him that he was not permitted to show him the letter nor to reveal its contents. His opinion, therefore, was that Father Colonnese was indulging in gossip mongering, which might be in the nature of bearing false witness, and that he should not even mention the letter, particularly in any derogatory tone, if he was not permitted to reveal its contents.

Going back to an earlier time—almost immediately after it became known that Father Colonnese would succeed Father Considine as director of the Latin America Bureau, and after I had completed combining the offices of the Latin America Bureau and the Papal Volunteer national headquarters, Father Colonnese approached me and suggested that I undergo a "training program" in Montana. The Latin America Bureau would pick up the expenses for that training. I was not told what the training would consist in, nor why it was important. I declined, on the basis that my Licentiate degree in theology and my doctorate in canon law should be enough schooling for anyone, and that I was far too busy to undertake such a program. I suspect that on the basis of that training, I would either be ruled 'in' or 'out' depending on my response to what I suspected was an indoctrination program. Since I declined to participate, I believe that I was immediately ruled 'out', and this was the point which determined that the Papal Volunteer program had to be destroyed. From that point on, I no longer had control of the PAVLA budget, and a total of $75,000 which I had brought from Chicago and turned over to the central accounting system of the Latin America Bureau, which had been donated by various dioceses in the country, was no longer available to the program.

Papal Volunteer Program Caught Between Two Forces

From the time in 1964 when I arrived in Chicago to administer the Papal Volunteer program, and until I resigned in fall of 1969, the program itself and I personally were subject to intense hostility from specific identifiable forces, and to intense support from a great majority. I have witnessed things like this in many cases, but never before was caught between them. The hostility made it difficult to effectively administer the PAVLA program, but somehow it captured the imagination of the people who really counted—both in Latin America and in the United States.

My own contacts with American bishops were almost universally positive about PAVLA. Before I told them that the program was initiated by Pope Paul VI, the most common response can be summed up this way: "It will be very good for our own people to be actively involved in apostolic Catholicism, and it will certainly be good for the people of Latin America." The bishops supported the National Training Center and its content, specifically relating to the theological content, the training related to a more perfect spiritual life, and, of course, training in adapting respectfully to a different culture. Those positive responses were turned into action as bishops regularly appointed their own diocesan directors for the PAVLA program. The closest I heard to a negative response was a lukewarm: "I suppose those people are in bad shape and can use every bit of help they can get." The positive response was further augmented by the steady inflow of U.S. lay people who applied for the program and whose diocesan directors and pastors vouched for their high level of spirituality and sincerity.

Among the many, many contacts I made with Latin American bishops there was nothing less than open enthusiasm, usually accompanied with an immediate request for volunteers and a statement that they could be immediately assigned to work with such and such a group—and he would name an American missionary group already in his diocese; in some cases the bishop would name a priest whose English was excellent who could coordinate the work the volunteers would undertake.

There was a steady flow of expressions of gratitude from bishops in Latin America, thanking us for the presence of Papal Volunteers in their dioceses, either by letter or in person when I visited them on my tours.

The hostility to the Papal Volunteer program began upon my arrival in Chicago, or, if it existed before that time, I became fully aware of it immediately. Since Msgr. Ivan Illich was deeply opposed to the concept of lay people being sent on an apostolate to Latin America, the opposition existed before my arrival. Since, as I found out later, Father Louis Colonnese and Msgr. Ivan Illich shared the same philosophical principles, it should have been no surprise that the opposition as I first experienced it, came directly from Father Colonnese. After I resigned as PAVLA director, to my chagrin the thought belatedly occurred to me that perhaps Father Considine was complicit with Father Colonnese in opposing what I did with PAVLA. As a specific requirement for me to accept the position as director of PAVLA, Father Considine had agreed that I would have a free hand in building the program. Since most of the priests who comprised the total staff of the USCC were either homosexual or Modernist or both, I have to acknowledge at this writing that Father Considine, perhaps regretting that he had chosen me, very likely used Father Colonnese as a tool to oppose me and get me to change my ways. He therefore ostensibly kept his bargain with me. The internal enemies of the Catholic Church in the United States were clearly headquartered in Washington, D.C. in the offices of the USCC, with Bishop Bernardin, the homosexual, pederast-pedophile Modernist/Americanist who clandestinely supported abortion and artificial contraception as its principal head.

The people (bishops and priests!) who opposed the PAVLA program and me were all infected in greater or lesser degrees with the Heresy of Modernism, who, in keeping with their leanings, wanted to 'modernize' the Church, as Father Colonnese frequently said, according to the "signs of the times." All of these efforts to 'modernize' the Church (and there were and are many such efforts) were completely contrary to the words of St. Paul, "O Timothy, guard the deposit"(2 Tim. 1:14; and see 1 Tim. 6:20). All of the Apostles were clearly conscious of their responsibility to maintain the treasured knowledge which Christ had personally given them, not to change it, but rather to make it known to the whole world, making sure that everyone was baptized into His Church.

It became obvious that Father Colonnese answered to a superior or superiors who in general used him as a tool to oppose whatever I did in accordance with the orthodox activities of the Roman Catholic Church. I was to learn later, as I prepared my Memorandum to the U.S. Bishops, what these groups were which were so often cited by Father Colonnese. And, belatedly, I realized that Bishop Bernardin, Director of the USCC, was himself an ardent Modernist to whom Father Colonnese reported.

We'll talk about these 'groups' a bit later on. Aside from these groups, Dr. Baquero's chief opponent was a Dr. Manoel Cardozo, also on the staff of the Catholic University, and also a native Ecuadorian, who I believe was a known Marxist.

One of the ploys Father Colonnese used was to report on a meeting he purportedly had with a number of U.S. bishops who were strongly opposed to the PAVLA program. At the time I believed, and I still do, that the meeting was fabricated and the opinions expressed by those bishops were also fabricated. As I said above, all of the bishops I met with—and they were very, very many—were enthusiastic about PAVLA with the exception of only one who was lukewarm and somewhat biased against Latin Americans in general.

The "*American*" Catholic Church

I wasn't certain at the time. When I moved reluctantly into the staff house of the USCC, I was surrounded by a bishop and priests who I identified as belonging to the American Catholic Church. They were in the process of pulling away from the ***true*** Catholic Church, as they and their associates had been doing for years. As I was to realize rather quickly, as a group they were Modernists, Americanists . . . . and homosexuals.

The only truly ***Catholic*** Church in this country is the one whose precise title is the '***Roman*** Catholic Church in the United States,' the one which recognizes, and is obedient to, the current Pope in the Vatican, who is the legitimate successor to St. Peter designated by Christ Himself as the "Rock" upon which He would build His Church.

Pope Leo XIII on January 22, 1899—more than a century ago—wrote an encyclical which warned of a growing aberration which has since been called the Heresy of Americanism. That encyclical has been generally ignored by the U.S. bishops since the day it was promulgated. The encyclical was called ***Testem Benevolentiae Nostrae*** (Witness to Our Good Will) and warned against a growing tendency in the United States to make unacceptable changes in the Eternal Doctrine of the Roman Catholic Church. (The full text of that encyclical is given in Appendix B of this book.) Dissenters from the Magisterium of the Roman Catholic Church, dating back to 1970 or earlier, began referring to themselves as American Catholics. While there's a remarkable mix, they tend to accept artificial contraception, and even abortion, as good things. (As we've already discussed, I personally knew a priest(!) theologian(!) who promoted these two ideas as good for family planning. They push for women's ordination, generally discard belief in the Real Presence, and flirt with Communism by their attachment to Liberation Theology. And there are many more ways in which they deviate from the traditional teachings of the Roman Catholic Church. There will be much more about those beliefs in a later section.

Malachy Martin, S.J. (1921-1999), a prolific writer of the last century, coined the word ***"Amchurch"*** to designate this group of dissenters who referred to themselves as American Catholics. Paul Likoudis, a reporter for the Catholic Newspaper *The Wanderer* has published a book called ***Amchurch Comes out*** (Publ. Roman Catholic Faithful, 2002). Randy Engel, author of the 1281 page book ***The Rite of Sodomy (***Publ. New Engel Publishing, 2006) uses the word 'Amchurch' extensively. Personally, I don't like the word. I prefer simply to identify such people as heretics who have allowed the Heresies of Modernism and Americanism to twist their thinking. She devotes Chapter 15 to "The Special Case of Joseph Cardinal Bernardin," and his entourage of homosexual/pederasts who apparently followed him wherever he went.

Bishop Joseph Bernardin, the first General Secretary of the newly created United States Catholic Conference (USCC), replacing the National Catholic Welfare Conference (NCWC), was appointed to the post by Archbishop (later Cardinal) John Dearden, Archbishop of Detroit, who was a that time President of the United States Conference of Catholic Bishops (USCCB).

At any rate, my initial (and growing) impression of Bishop Bernardin was that he displayed the earmarks of the homosexual man, although, in him, they were so subtle as to be nearly undetectable. He was an artful politician and a topnotch actor. I had some initial doubts. And he chaired some meetings and made some statements which made it highly questionable that he was loyal to Rome and that he ignored several orthodox doctrines of the Church. He was in the catbird seat with reference to the hierarchy of the U.S. Catholic Church. It was as if the Body of Bishops (USCCB) in business parlance was the 'board of directors' and he himself was their CEO. And once a board has appointed its new CEO, their mind set is to approve his actions and they are highly reluctant to countermand his decisions. There are those in recent years who profess that they have evidence that Bishop Bernadin exercised his influence on Archbishop Jadot, the Apostolic Delegate, to have a number of homosexual bishops appointed, thereby increasing his power and authority over the Body of Bishops. This all began when he was General Secretary of the USCC, and gained increasing momentum after he became president of the USCCB. (See R. Engel, ***The Rite of Sodomy***, pp. 895ff)

After I presented my report to the bishops subcommittee, of course, Bishop Bernardin could 'spin' the matter any way he wanted, both against the Papal Volunteer program and against me personally, to that subcommittee of bishops and later to the entire USCCB. It has saddened me greatly, during the past year particularly as I've begun seriously to finalize this book, to ask several prominent Catholics about the Papal Volunteers for Latin America. One very apostolic Catholic asked me "What's that? In every case (only about 4 or 5), each one in effect responded the same way: "What's that?" The work of those incredibly devoted Papal Volunteers has been buried alive and they are now as if they had never been.

When Cardinal Madeiros told my brother that "Your brother was absolutely right, we should have listened to him," I believe he was deeply embarrassed and perhaps humiliated. As a result he couldn't bring himself to contact me personally, and it was apparently important to him and whatever group of bishops agreed with him to begin a process of denial that the Papal Volunteers had ever existed.

There is no doubt in my mind that in all of his activities designed to destroy the PAVLA program, Father Colonnese had the direct and positive support of Bishop Bernardin who was clearly ***in charge*** when it came to the entire USCC. No good, truly *Catholic* bishop would have permitted Colonnese to publicly attack the PAVLA training program because, following theological doctrine of many centuries and the dictates of Vatican Council II, we provided for the Papal Volunteers in training courses in theology, principles of the spiritual life and cultural adaptation.

It therefore was obvious: Bishop Bernardin himself opposed the Papal Volunteer program, which he knew was initiated by Pope Paul VI. In those days, therefore, he was the leading force in what some have called Amchurch. As he moved to another diocese, became president of the USCCB, became Cardinal Archbishop of Chicago, taking with him his entourage of homosexual priests and (I assume) other associates, as an Americanist, became ever more powerful in developing this new American Catholic Church with little or no allegiance to the Vicar of Christ in Rome.

When Father Colonnese said to me, "We no longer believe in mortal sin," it was clear that he was voicing a stand he had heard Bishop Bernardin and other Americanist colleagues articulate. It was necessary for active homosexuals to justify their actions by creating a church which would not see those actions as sinful, and, moreover, to say that such sexual activities are acts of love, and since God is Love . . . Etc. One is reminded of Henry VIII who wanted Rome to annul his marriage so he could marry another woman to have a male heir. When Rome refused, he created his own church: The Church of England, the Anglican Church, the Episcopalian Church. Homosexual bishops and priests in a similar fashion, in order to justify their sexual activities, were forced to excuse their actions by using the ". . . after all, God is love, and this is an act of love" subterfuge and also to avow that "we no longer believe that there is such a thing as mortal sin." It was therefore apparently an easy step to create an ***American*** Catholic Church because the Pope would insist that sexual activities outside of marriage are morally sinful, and that artificial contraception and abortion totally unacceptable.

CHAPTER 33

The Latin America Bureau and the Papal Volunteer Offices

When after two years I was instructed to move my offices from Chicago to Washington, D.C. and combine them with the Latin America Bureau, I knew that the forces which opposed the Papal Volunteer program were consolidating their energies in order to bring about the change they wanted to see in the PAVLA program, or bring about its destruction. For some unknown reason, it fell to me to find the appropriate office space, organize the remodeling, and prepare for the day that the headquarters for the Latin America Bureau and for the Papal Volunteers for Latin America were combined in one office space. I designed the space so that there would be a large office at one end of the space for the Director of LAB, and an equal size office at the other end for myself. And at each end were smaller offices for subordinate personnel, for example Father James Eron was my Assistant National Director, and at the other end an office for the office manager who would be responsible for pay checks for all personnel, and for the office services that all LAB programs would require, such as copy machines, etc.

Independent Observations—John Muldoon and Madeleine Creason

On my staff in Washington, D.C. in 1968-1969 were two experienced Papal Volunteers who had completed their three years of duty on their assignments and then agreed to help me in the National Office. They each wrote an independent report of their personal day-to-day observations. They sought no approval nor input from me, and I believe each prepared the report without the other's knowledge. They corroborated everything that was happening to the PAVLA program and reported a few things I had no knowledge of. If I had had these reports at the time I presented my memorandum to the bishops, of course I would have used them, but they were written after that meeting with the bishops and didn't come to my attention until many months after.

John Muldoon

John Muldoon was the Coordinator of Projects and Personnel. One day when I was traveling he was involved in an incident which to him was so appalling that he felt he simply had to report it in writing. He begins: "No one has asked or ordered me to prepare this memo." He continues to explain an incident of June 12, 1969 and a related matter. Since most of the PAVLA staff were away preparing for the upcoming National Training Center program for that year, only he and his secretary and a few others were present. He goes on to say ". . . . the event of June 12 was so unbelievable that I hesitate to prepare a report on it because anyone not present at the time probably would not accept it as possibly happening in an office under the directorship of a sane person." He explained that on that same morning a Diocesan Director had called requesting information regarding a problem on a project where a volunteer from his diocese was working. "It was necessary" he wrote, "for me to call Father

Kevane to ask permission to forward copies of the information to the Diocesan Director requesting it."

I remember the incident, recognizing it as deeply personal, and highly confidential. I gave permission to John Muldoon to send copies of the information to the Diocesan Director, emphasizing the need for confidentiality and stressing that no one on the PAVLA staff who knew about it should discuss the matter with anyone else. John Muldoon then reports ". . . I asked Miss Suarez (his secretary) to make Xerox copies of the various letters and reports that made up the information. My instructions were that all this was confidential matter and if anyone else wanted to know what it was to return it all to me and we would proceed from there." He went on to explain the incident:

> ". . . . I had just picked up my phone to answer another long distance call when I heard extremely loud shouting. Shortly Miss Suarez ran into my office crying, very upset and very frightened. Immediately behind her was Father Colonnese who was doing the shouting and demanding of her who had given her the instructions that the matter was confidential. He also shouted that he was boss—that nothing was confidential to him—that he was going to fire any number of people etc. All this time Father Colonnese was waving the papers which he had taken from Miss Suarez and which I had requested her to Xerox. Miss Kathy Knara (Father Colonnese's secretary) entered my office at the same time as Father Colonnese and she was trying to console and help Miss Suarez. Mr. Boxler (office manager for the LAB complex) also came into my office at the same time but he remained silent and did nothing to intercede in this verbal attack on Miss Suarez or to try to do something about the situation. Finally Father Colonnese left, still raging, and Mr. Boxler began to question me and Miss Suarez who, at this time, was sitting in a chair in my

> office still crying, still very terrified and in no condition to answer the questions Mr. Boxler directed at her. Everyone then left my office. Father Colonnese returned . . . . At the end of our discussion I informed Father that the papers were still of a confidential nature and he agreed. I further informed him that Miss Suarez was in no way to blame, that anything that happened was not her fault that she was in no way responsible for anything that may have caused the incident. He also agreed with this and upon leaving apologized to Miss Suarez.
>
> Later in the afternoon when a relative calm atmosphere prevailed after the morning action I asked Miss Suarez what had happened at the Xerox machine. She said that she was in the process of making the copies I requested when Father Colonnese came and took some of the papers and demanded to know what they were and what she was doing. Not knowing what to answer she said they were confidential and belonged to PAVLA. He then screamed at her and she ran to my office with Father immediately after her at which time the aforementioned episode took place. I want to stress the point that Miss Suarez **was *throughly frightened and made the statement to me that she was afraid that Father was going to strike her as he seemed so completely out of control of himself.*"** *(*Emphasis added.*)*

To digress for a moment from John Muldoon's statement, having heard eventually about this incident, it was and remains incomprehensible to me that a priest, hearing that another priest had identified certain information as confidential, would ignore the possibility that this was serious matter and first talk it over with the other priest. Instead, Colonnese allowed his own ego and his personal need to have his power recognized; he "blew up" and attacked a newly hired young woman, shouted at her, terrified her, when she was simply doing what her manager told her to do. Because of this and other incidents, I began to believe what John Muldoon hinted at in the beginning of his statement: "(it could not possibly happen) . . . in an office under the directorship of a sane person." Similarly, I began to be certain that the bishops had appointed a person of unsound mind as Director of the Latin America Bureau.

Back to Mr. Muldoon's statement:

> "I think it is also relevant to mention the attitude of Mr. Boxler which I feel was expressed in answers to some questions I asked him later that afternoon also the next morning in an unplanned discussion . . . . Because it is always being brought up that PAVLA does not cooperate with LAB I asked Mr. Boxler if he could tell me of any one time that I did not cooperate. He answered 'no' but that there were a few times that someone from PAVLA did not cooperate in the use of the memograph (sic) machine. I next asked him if he thought that Father Colonese (sic) had handled the incident June 12 in a proper manner. He answered that Father did things his way, that he would have done it different and that I probably would have handled it differently. The next day he told me how he would have handled it. He said that he would have fired the person (on) the spot. This statement, with a history of Mr. Boxler's management from the time that LAB and PAVLA were coordinated in one unit indicates to me his complete incompetence. He did not at any time inform Miss Suarez of the office set-up or procedure nor, for that matter, have any of the other employees in the PAVLA received this information. I hold that this is one of his duties. Yet Mr. Boxler would have fired any person who had acted without knowledge of what the correct procedure was."

This was one of the many examples of how Father Colonnese harassed the PAVLA program from the time that I arrived in

Chicago, and how this hostility increased in intensity, culminating in what appeared to be near hatred after he became director of the Latin America Bureau.

In a second report, undated but signed, Mr. Muldoon reported on a number of incidents which underline the animosity of LAB (Father Colonnese) toward the PAVLA program:

1. Office Manager was uncooperative in arranging transportation for the Papal Volunteers to their destinations. Mr. Muldoon had to make the arrangements himself.
2. Paychecks to PAVLA Field Representatives were provided a month or more later than they were due.
3. Budget checks were consistently delayed each month.
4. Staff transportation costs were not reimbursed in timely fashion. Mr. Muldoon received two complaint calls that their bills were not paid. He himself had to make a number of requests to the office manager before the bills were finally paid.

He cites several more examples of delay and inefficiency, closing with this statement:

> "I have pinpointed some prime examples of inefficiency and lack of cooperation that I have experienced in the period from April 1968—the time of our move to the present office. I would also be hard put to think of an example of any procedure relating to this department which was performed with any indication of a desire to cooperate or which was done without delay or was done in a business-like manner. A number of things I have initiated on my own either because I was constantly put off or I learned from experience that the necessary results would not be forthcoming if I relied on the people who were supposed to perform those duties. I might add that

> in some of these cases better arrangements were arrived at than might have been expected and they resulted in a saving of not only time but money."

Madeline Creason

Madeline Creason was another senior staff member at the National Office of the Papal Volunteer program. She herself was a Returned Papal Volunteer having spent three years on her assignment where she did a superlative job. The excellence of her service is what prompted me to ask her to accept a position at the National Office. Her job, as she herself described it in her report dated February 19, 1969, was ". . . coordinator of recruitment, some promotional work and liaison between the offices of Father Kevane and Mr. John Muldoon, Projects and personnel director. My work is to prepare materials for the annual recruiting drive, information on the program to Diocesan Directors, handle all inquiries to the program, evaluate prospective candidates and assist in the processing. I also work in whatever capacity Father Kevane asks me to."

She opened her statement in this way:

> "The subject of this paper is the lack of cooperation I personally have experienced in respect to the necessary work I am assigned to accomplish as a member of the staff of the National Office of Papal Volunteers. The lack of cooperation I am speaking of is not on the part of any of the personnel attached to PAVLA, but specifically from the Latin America Bureau side of the office."

She confirms what John Muldoon had explained as the administrative functions of the combined LAB and PAVLA offices, saying that . . . "the mail room services and the ordering of necessary materials, plus duplication and collating of materials is to be handled and scheduled through the secretary of Mr. Ken Boxler, the Office

Manager." She starts with a summary of all of the difficulties to which PAVLA was subject:

> "It is my distinct impression that there has been a deliberate ignoring of the needs of our program and a definite relegating of Papal Volunteer work, as it pertains to the above mentioned services, to a lesser priority than any other branch of this whole Latin America Bureau. Below are some specific examples of this as it has occurred since I began working here the latter part of August, 1968."

She continues in her report to enumerate those attitudes and actions on the part of the LAB administrative department which are most vexing to her and which badly curtail the functions of PAVLA in the latter's daily efforts. I will recite a few of the incidents which she describes as real problems for the PAVLA program, most of them unwarranted interference in the PAVLA program by members of LAB (principally Father Colonnese) who knew very little to nothing about what the PAVLA program is all about.

One of the strange incidents was a film strip which was injected by LAB into the PAVLA national convention. I personally never saw the film strip, but it was such that it insulted Latin American students who were present and it angered and insulted the Returned Papal Volunteers. The word from LAB was that the film strip would be useful for recruiting, but, Madeline Creason says, "[the film] as we saw it, was offensive and in no way desirable to be used for recruiting. We decided to make an issue of this, but Father Kevane and Fr. Eron were not in the office when this came to the attention of Fr. Colonnese. Father Colonnese stormed down to our end of the office shouting at the secretaries in general and to me in particular. He said he was sick and tired of the lack of cooperation from PAVLA with the Latin America Bureau. 'The PAVLA program is in jeopardy of its existence. I have just been to a meeting of the Bishops and I was on the carpet because of PAVLA. We had only 30 minutes to discuss various matters and we talked about PAVLA for 23 of those minutes . . .'

What Father Colonnese was reported to have said about his 'meeting' with the bishops runs absolutely counter to my own experience in meeting with many, many bishops who uniformly expressed enthusiasm for the program and who thereafter appointed Diocesan Directors for the PAVLA program. It made me wonder if the meeting actually took place or was manufactured to support Colonnese's position in the current fracas. Madeline Creason continues with her report:

> "I tried to explain to Fr. Colonese (sic) that there had been a mistake and tried to explain why the returned volunteers were offended by the film strip. His reply was ***'What do a bunch of stupid returned volunteers know about Latin America?'*** [Emphasis added to simulate shouting] When I explained to him the facts of the situation, that the film strip had been taken out of context, he suggested that we owed an explanation in writing [to] all the Diocesan Directors who were in attendance. I agreed . . . . (but) . . . the explanation should have come from LAB and not from PAVLA."

Had I been present at that meeting, I would have told him that using the word 'stupid' was insulting and completely inappropriate since, having lived and worked among the Latin people of their assignment, they knew much more about the culture of Latin America than he did. Madeline Creason continues: "This lack of cooperation he mentioned is not on the part of PAVLA but on the part of LAB."

She goes on to explain how many of the PAVLA projects had to be undertaken by PAVLA staff when it should have been done (by) LAB services whose purpose it was to do those things, and in fact, she gives examples of several times when the PAVLA staff pitched in and helped with LAB preparations for major meetings.

Another item of concern which she reports had to do with raises in salaries. They were promised for January/February of 1969, but she said, as of April 1969 they had failed to materialize. "To my knowledge," Madeline continues, "no one in the PAVLA office has yet received a raise of any kind and some have been here a year. I have heard that some personnel in LAB have received these raises."

She goes on to a number of other subjects (it was a rather lengthy report consisting in five single-spaced pages). One example was *The Papal Volunteer*, a magazine I had initiated during the years in Chicago. Father Colonnese attempted to take control of the magazine, wanted to change its name, overrode my decisions as to its content. (These things occurred in spite of his earlier agreement to abide by the understanding I had—in writing—with Father Considine that I would be completely independent in the way I administered the PAVLA program.) While I was out of town, he issued orders to replace some of my decisions about content of the magazine and had them replaced with some oftentimes questionable articles by a head of one of the "groups" he spoke of so often. In a discussion with Jim Campion who had been hired as editor of all LAB-related publications, including *The Papal Volunteer,* Madeline Creason reports the following:

> "During the course of our conversations, a suspicion began to grow in my mind that the Latin America Bureau was making a deliberate attempt to take over completely our magazine and the Newsletter . . . . Jim told me that an article had been substituted for one approved by Father Kevane in an upcoming issue. When that issue was printed (Feb. 1969) Father Kevane was again out of the office. A copy was given to me. I noted 4 changes that I was certain Father had not approved and confronted Jim Campion with this. I told him that I doubted that Father Kevane had seen any of these 4 changes and I did not think he would have approved. He said that Father Colonnese had

> approved all of these things before he left for Latin America. I stated that Father Colonnese was not deciding what went in the magazine and there exists a very basic difference of thought theologically and philosophically in what Father Kevane and PAVLA as a program wish to promote and in what Father Colonnese is trying to promote."

The last thing she said was, of course, absolutely true. I remember the article well. It was written by Sidney Lens, the head of one of the "groups" Father Colonnese constantly alluded to. As will be recounted later on, Sidney Lens was the subject of a report by the House Unamerican Activities Committee as a less than savory person. My own assessment of the article that had been published without my approval is the same as that of Madeline Creason: "My own objections to the substituted article have to do with the subject of revolution, violence or non-violence in Latin America . . . . the manner in which it is written leaves one with the impression that non-violence is ridiculous."

She closes her report as follows:

> "I further wish to state that the writing of this paper has been most distasteful to me, but life has been extremely difficult in this office. I work here only because as a Returned Papal Volunteer, I am extremely concerned with the future of our program, of Latin America and of the church. It is only a sense of loyalty that keeps me here and the fact that I am convinced of the basic soundness of our approach to Latin America. There are many other incidents which have occurred in this office, not mentioned here, but I do not have the "stomach" to write them."

It saddens me as I record these reports and write these lines to "re-live" the two things I knew at the time: 1) that Father Colonnese was probably Marxist/Communistic in his philosophy—because his stated policies and beliefs were in total accord with Msgr. Ivan Illich who was a proven Communist, and 2) that Father Colonnese was mentally and emotionally unbalanced, which, combined with his supreme egotism and need for control, created havoc in the National Office of the Papal Volunteer program.

This assessment of his character is further demonstrated by two of his parishioners who told of an incident that occurred when he was assigned to a parish in his home diocese of Davenport, Iowa. At an Easter Sunday Mass at which he was celebrant, he started with a procession down the center aisle of the church. He himself wore vestments with a throng of butterflies on them and he was carrying a live lamb. While it is true that there was a somewhat accurate symbolism in what he did, it was nevertheless a flamboyant noncompliance with the liturgy of the Roman Catholic Church. And what did it mean in terms of his own attitude regarding the doctrine of the Real Presence at the Consecration of the Mass? Father Colonnese was neither a Theologian nor a Canon Lawyer. I am both. While this may have been part of his problem with me, my belief at the time and now is that he was basically a Marxist/Communist who wanted the Papal Volunteers to be simply social service workers in Latin America with no religious purpose at all.

CHAPTER 34

Heresies and Weaknesses in the American Catholic Church

I didn't understand the complexities of ecclesiastical politics in 1968-1969 as I wrestled with the forces of Americanism, Modernism and Liberation Theology to keep the Papal Volunteer program alive and thriving. Albeit nervously, but trying to believe that the bishops would support me, I assembled the facts and the documentation I would need to make a good case to the American bishops to seek the protection the program would need to survive. I quite naïvely assumed that if my presentation was clear, the bishops, one of whose major purposes was the protection of Holy Mother Church from heresies and heretical activities, would quickly act to guard the Deposit of Faith. As it turned out, I could not have been more wrong. For a number of reasons:

1. Bishop Bernardin, General Secretary of the United States Catholic Conference, I was quite sure at the time, was a homosexual. The reader will remember that I had more than my share of encounters with homosexuals, beginning with my first year in college, and I had in-depth discussions with at least one of them. I knew the signs.

2. Since Father Colonnese was almost certainly a true homosexual, it should have been a foregone conclusion for me that Bishop Bernardin would support Father Colonnese. Homosexual superiors almost uniformly seek out and favor homosexual subordinates.
3. Bishop Bernardin's adherence to legitimate theology was, to say the least, questionable—perhaps even heretical. As mentioned earlier, he presided over a dinner at the USCC staff house at which Rev. Charles Curran, a pro-abortion and pro-artificial contraception 'theologian' was the honored guest. He also was heard saying "that *damned* encyclical" (Humanae Vitae of Pope Paul VI which condemned abortion and artificial contraception), which fairly clearly exposed his thinking along that line.
4. Bishop Bernardin, the story was told, was chosen by Archbishop Dearden of Detroit who at the time was President of the USCCB (the 'body of bishops'), and not yet a Cardinal. Dearden was said to be "deeply impressed" by Bernardin. He presented Bernardin to the Body of Bishops who duly elected Bernardin to the directorship of the USCC. Dearden at the time was known as "Iron John" because of his strict adherence to the traditional doctrine of the Church. After he became a Cardinal, having achieved the pinnacle of his career, he immediately changed into a 'liberal churchman' and was identified in local reporting as the 'Red' Cardinal, meaning that his doctrine had at least some 'overtones' of Marxism/Communism. This at least would suggest that Cardinal Dearden, before his ascension to the Cardinalate, secretly adhered to the Heresy of Modernism. (This 'before and after' pattern is also true in the ascension of Cardinal Mahoney in Los Angeles.)

   This information, of course, would explain why Dearden was "deeply impressed" with Bernardin, why Bernardin would support Father Colonnese rather than me, and why

Bernardin had an ". . . entourage of clerical homosexuals and pederasts and ancillary hangers-on who made up the Chicago-Washington, D. C. Homosexual/Pederast Axis . . . ." (Taken from Randy Engel's book *The Rite of Sodomy*, Chapter 15, 'The Special Case of Joseph Cardinal Bernardin, ***Introduction***.') I believe that many of the priests at the USCC (the Bernardin 'entourage') were homosexuals, and almost all were Modernists.

5. Professional Solidarity. As professional groups, *e.g.* medical doctors, rarely acknowledge that a colleague made a mistake, in a similar manner bishops tend always to defend their colleagues and almost never take a contradictory stand. Most of them are expert at "talking around" such a subject. I was certain that Bishop Bernardin would find a way to support Father Colonnese rather than me. And I was fearful that the bishops would support a fellow bishop, who, after all, they had in some fashion (they thought) elected to his post.
6. The political nature of the United States Conference of Catholic Bishops (USCCB). Unfortunately, as an offshoot of the Heresy of Americanism which has infected the U.S. hierarchy for many years (there will be more on this later) the Conference of Bishops is strongly political, exerting pressure on each member to follow the trends of that body, and they are strongly tempted to adjoin themselves to the United States government and culture rather than to their own Church as its own Perfect Society. (See above, Part II, Chapter 20. A Perfect Society is one which has within it all the means required to meet its own goals)
7. There was speculation at the time that some form of blackmail was involved, first in getting Father Colonnese appointed as director of LAB, and second in overriding all the documentation and evidence I presented in support of my memorandum. The rumor surrounded personal indiscretions on the part of some member(s) of the bishops'

> subcommittee for PAVLA. The bishops of the subcommittee would, in a very human fashion, protect a fellow bishop if at all possible.

When it became clear, not long after I had moved the Papal Volunteer headquarters to Washington, D.C., that I would not be allowed to administer the program as I had in the preceding three years in Chicago, then I began to rethink my position. I started to question whether I should quietly resign and return to my diocese, or whether I should expose what I firmly believed to be heretical groups which were trying to discredit the program and create havoc in Latin America. More than $75,000 which had been given by the faithful of many dioceses throughout the country was taken from me and I was not allowed to use it for the purpose it was intended—the sending of volunteers to Latin America—and, since Modernism and Liberation Theology activities were underway whose purpose was to undermine the Catholic Church both in Latin America and in the United States. For those reasons, I felt I could not, in good conscience, simply leave without bringing both of those problems to the attention of the proper authorities. I had a fairly clear understanding of what the consequences would be for me. While I was sorely tempted not to proceed, I felt in conscience that I must continue regardless of the likely negative outcome for me.

CHAPTER 35

My Written Report to the Bishops of the United States

In the Fall of 1968 and the early months of 1969, I began to amass the documentation that I felt I would need to present my case accurately. I studied the public pronouncements of those who had been opposing my efforts and who I knew espoused principles of Americanism, Modernism, Liberation Theology, the Pastoral Institute for Latin America (IPLA) and the Christian Base Communities which sprang from that organization. I looked at the affiliations of people who apparently were grouped under those philosophies. After several months of preparation, I was able to prepare a seventeen page memorandum and then arranged for a presentation of that material to the entire Bishops' Subcommittee for the Papal Volunteer program. The date for that presentation was set for July 1, 1969 at, if my memory serves me, 10:00 a.m. in the conference room of the USCC. The four non-members of the bishops' subcommittee were Father Colonnese, Bishop Bernardin who chaired the meeting, Msgr. Frank Hurley, the Assistant Director of the USCC, and, of course, myself.

The night before the meeting, presumably prompted by Bishop Bernardin, Msgr. Hurley came to my room at the USCC staff house, in what was disguised as a show of friendly support, and asked me to tell him the nature and details of my presentation the next morning. I tried to respond in a similarly friendly way and suggested that it was quite complex, it would take a good deal of time to explain it properly, I was very tired, and it might be best if he would wait for the meeting itself. But I went on to explain to him that I was very nervous about the meeting, that I had many misgivings, primarily because I knew that when a management structure is in place, usually the one with the superior position would prevail. So, I explained, I had no illusions. He responded by saying that he didn't feel that this would be true in this case because I had a good deal of public support and prominence as the national director of the Papal Volunteer program.

At the meeting the next morning, Msgr. Hurley was the only one present (except of course for Father Colonnese) who would try to undercut my presentation. Bishop Madeiros of Brownsville, Texas, was the only member of the PAVLA Subcommittee who was absent. The remaining four bishops, during and after my presentation, were completely silent.

The report was generally addressed to the Conference of U.S. Catholic Bishops, even though it was presented orally to the Subcommittee for Papal Volunteers. The subject matter was given as "Difficulties in the Division for Latin America, United States Catholic Conference." I made it clear in the beginning of the presentation that I was taking action at the behest of many people in the program:

> "I do not say the following things lightly, nor do I say them for personal reasons. There have been complaints from several sources regarding the position in which the PAVLA program is placed, particularly during the past year. These complaints have come from Papal Volunteers working in Latin America, from PAVLA Diocesan Directors, and, most recently from PAVLA's National Planning Committee."

> *(The full text of this report is given as **Appendix A** at the end of this book.)*

The National Planning Committee for the Papal Volunteer program was a group of eight carefully selected Diocesan Directors, returned Papal Volunteers whose term of service in Latin America had been outstanding, one Latin American priest, two Latin American lay people, and members of the lay boards of diocesan programs. They met regularly every quarter, with extraordinary meetings scheduled as required.

My memorandum continued:

> "It was in March of this year that the Planning Committee appealed to the bishops through Bishop Hodges. Its members, as well as returned volunteers and Diocesan Directors throughout the country, are waiting for an answer. They have been patient, trusting in my judgment, but the time for an answer is past due. I ask for immediate clarification of the position of the Papal Volunteer program.
>
> "A most serious issue lies at the root of the current difficulties in the Division for Latin America. I want no one to mistake the gravity of this issue, and I hope never again, after this presentation, will it be lightly brushed aside as a "failure in communications" between Father Colonnese and myself. The problems that plagued the PAVLA program and the rest of the Division for Latin America at the time of my memorandum to Father Colonnese of February 20, 1969, remain unresolved at this presentation four months later. I believe that at least an investigation should have begun immediately."

The February memorandum just alluded to, with copies to Bishop Bernardin as Director of the United States Catholic Conference and others, including the members of the PAVLA subcommittee, and the National Planning Committee members, addressed several problems. As stated in my memorandum I did not have access to the sum of $75,000 I had turned over to the Latin America Bureau as I moved my office to Washington, D.C., that I was unable to have a budget assigned to the Papal Volunteer program, that another session of the National Training Center was due to get under way at the Catholic University during the summer session and planning for that training program was well behind where it had usually been in previous years at that same time. The only response I received to that memorandum was, in a chance meeting in a corridor, Bishop Bernardin told me to wait for Father Colonnese to return from his travels and "work it out." When at the end of March I had received no word of any kind, it was necessary to take strong action. Hence the meeting with the bishops' subcommittee was scheduled for July 1, 1969.

Most of the members of the bishops' subcommittee attended the meeting. Bishop Joseph Hodges as chairman of that subcommittee was present. Three other bishop-members were also there, although my memory of this event is so hazy that I do not remember their names. Bishop Medeiros of Brownsville, TX, had sent his regrets. The meeting took place forty plus years ago so that some parts of it escape my memory. Bishop Bernardin, of course, as Director of the United States Catholic Conference chaired the meeting. Father Colonnese was there as Director of the Latin America Bureau and against whom the proceedings were directed, at least in my mind. Msgr. Frank Hurley, assistant director of the USCC, the one who had visited me in my apartment the evening before, was in attendance.

I was, quite naturally, very nervous. The future of the Papal Volunteer program which I had worked so hard on for five years was at stake, and I was very much afraid that the things I had to say would either sound bizarre and non-credible, or, if they were perceived as credible, the state of affairs I was about to expose would be so frightening to the bishops that they would sweep it all under the rug and fail to act on it. I have never felt so alone in my life.

I have no recollection as to how the meeting was introduced. All I remember is that after a very few minutes I was reading from my memorandum. I read aloud the paragraphs repeated above and then proceeded to present the problem on a point-by-point basis:

> "PAVLA is now facing problems, and has been facing them for the past year. The problems are literally destroying the Papal Volunteer program. Immediate action is imperative. If it is not taken, not only will the Papal Volunteer program be destroyed, but all hope of rapport between the Church in the United States and Latin America will soon die. The principles established by a succession of Popes are being undermined. There is likelihood that the Christian heritage of Latin America, mentioned so explicitly by the present Pope *(Paul VI)* and his predecessor (cf. the PAVLA founding document and other sources), will not only be destroyed, but, ironically, will be destroyed at the hands of an ostensibly Catholic organization operating under the aegis of the Bishops of the United States. During the past year in which the programs of the Division for Latin America have for the first time been consolidated in Washington, the Papal Volunteer program has been subjected to a series of administrative failures, to harassment of its personnel and to delays in its programming. Evidence of these things will be submitted as this paper proceeds. This to a program which for several reasons enjoys the special commendation of Vatican Council II. (Decree on the Apostolate of the Laity, ch. IV, nos. 20-22)

The remainder of the memorandum was devoted to how the opposition to the Papal Volunteer program was ideological in nature, and that it came from the united efforts of like-minded people whose allegiance was uniformly to the Heresy of Modernism and its child, Liberation Theology. It was most unfortunate that the effort to undermine the Papal Volunteer program was also aimed at *desarollo* (the Spanish word for d*evelopment* or *change*) in Latin America and of the Church in Latin America. Liberation Theology, which was little else but Marxism dressed in religious garb, intended to *replace* the structure of the Church in Latin America—and presumably in the United States as well—with IPLA training programs (the Spanish acronym for Pastoral Institutes in Latin America), where people would be trained in the new order and prepared to go forth to specified locations in Latin America and establish *communidades de base*—known in English as Christian Base Communities. These bear a remarkable similarity to the age-old concept of the communist 'cell.' Since the Papal Volunteer program was publicly engaged in sending assistance to the existing Church structure in Latin America—to the bishop and his diocese, and to his clergy in their parishes and other activities—those who intended to replace that structure with the slant of Modernism and Liberation Theology could not sit idly by and allow the PAVLA program to flourish.

The most outspoken and well-known opponent of the Papal Volunteer program was Msgr. Ivan Illich. He was also well known for opposing every form of religious help to Latin America. He was an outspoken advocate of the destruction of the current order in Latin America and its replacement with another order which, presumably, he would control. His philosophy and his ideology was explained to me in depth when he and I met and talked for two hours in the airport in Bogota, Colombia during one of my visits to the Papal Volunteers in service. He was born behind the Iron Curtain. I believe he was most likely a communist 'plant' much as was the Jesuit 'Golden Voice of the Church' in Italy whom I encountered as a seminarian in Rome. I believe he was the ideologue around whom various people such as Father Colonnese and his associates revolved. Therefore, the report goes on to say:

> "Father Colonnese's opposition to the Papal Volunteers is in the order of ideology and is similar to the anti-PAVLA stance of Ivan Illich through the years. This is clear after a cursory reading of Father Colonnese's paper "Imperialism or Servanthood" which was distributed, in English and Spanish, at the Interamerican Bishops' meeting in Caracas,

June 3-5 just past. See, for example, pp. 2-6: the criticisms listed (and approved by Father Colonnese: "while I do not negate the general validity of such criticism . . .") have all been enunciated at one time or another by Ivan Illich, many of them aimed at the Papal Volunteer program. It is remarkable that the Director of the Division for Latin America singles out the PAVLA program for special criticism (p.7). There are other groups, both lay and non-lay, not LAB programs, which have demonstrably failed or limped and which could have been the subject of his criticism. And he would have it that PAVLA (as also other activities) was "spawned" by a "sudden burst of enthusiasm." This is a gross misstatement. The Papal Volunteer program—Colonnese and Ivan Illich share an unwillingness to recognize—was "spawned", to use his term, by action of the Holy See with direct approval of Pope Paul VI. Father Colonnese's entire paper reflects the Illich ideology, such as is to be found in his (Illich's) letter to me in 1965, and in his two celebrated articles "The Seamy Side of Charity" and "The Vanishing Clergyman," both of which appeared in *America* magazine.

"Father Colonnese's views as reported by the National Catholic Reporter a year ago had the familiar Illich ring. Starting in about 1958 or 1959, Father Colonnese acted as editor of *CIF Reports* (Center of Intercultural Formation) which emanated from Illich's training center in Cuernavaca. Although Father Colonnese has stated to me that he broke publicly with Illich in the early sixties, I suggest that the break may have been opportunistic and not at all ideological. During the intervening years, I never heard Illich speak against Father Colonnese, although I personally heard him attack every other LAB official."

One of my earliest responsibilities as national director of the Papal Volunteer program was to make sure that the first group of volunteers to go under my responsibility had the proper kind of preparation in a number of areas including language training. The National Training Center at the Catholic University was established for this purpose. It was designed to help the volunteers prepare for their work in the lay apostolate. In addition to that, of course, they needed to understand the culture they would live and work in, and they needed to be as proficient in Spanish (or Portuguese) as a reasonable amount of language training would permit. The only recourse I had—and I did not know at the time that this was not a good option—was to send them to the two training programs run by Msgr. Illich, one in Cuernavaca, Mexico, and the other in Rio de Janeiro, Brazil. I was appalled at the result, because these programs were not simply language and culture schools, they were indoctrination centers. The memorandum goes on to explain:

> "It is a matter of record that in 1965 I terminated the training of Papal Volunteers at Cuernavaca, Mexico, under Ivan Illich, and opened a special training program for PAVLA in Mexico City. I did this because I could not countenance the manipulatory nature of Illich training. I personally saw the effects among personnel trained there: people whose minds had been warped, whose confidence was shattered, who had been filled with the "proper" (i.e. conceived in Cuernavaca) solutions for Latin America and who then became rebels on assignment where the local Church's ideas did not coincide with those learned at Cuernavaca. In April of 1965, I found that an entire group of Papal Volunteers in training (the last group to train there) had been filled with doubts about their right to go to Latin America, that they had become anti-Church, anti-institution, and anti-PAVLA. Since I had known some

> of those people earlier, their apparent personality change appalled me."

My memorandum to the Bishops continues:

> "Father Colonnese's paper presents a similar viewpoint. All of Illich's criticisms, he says, are valid, but if personnel receive the proper training, only then will the sending of U.S. personnel to Latin America be relevant. The clear implication is that the proper training is that outlined in his paper and administered by himself."

The subject of preparation and training of the Papal Volunteers was a matter of great sensitivity for me. Believing as I did that the most important element that the volunteers could take into their assignments in Latin America was their own personal spiritual lives together with the firm purpose to strengthen them and the spiritual lives of those with whom they made contact and worked, it was important to me—and this I believe was the major message of Vatican Council II—that they be chosen because of their exemplary lives and that they be given an intensive foundation in the Church's Deposit of Faith, in the basics of the spiritual life, and a basic understanding of and respect for the culture they were about to enter.

Since I had heard Father Colonnese and some of his associates make very questionable assertions about the Catholic Faith, I had to be wary of the kind of training they (including Illich) wanted to impose. Father Colonnese had said at one point: ". . . we no longer believe that there is such a thing as mortal sin . . ." And one time when I visited him in his apartment, he put his arm around my shoulder in a way which caused me some discomfort; I pulled away, saying that I had never liked being touched (it was simply my way of backing away from what I perceived as a homosexual approach). And he said, very forcefully: "That's it! That's what makes a priest!" He was placing the call to the priesthood on some physical proclivity rather than attributing it to a true vocation—a calling from God. And he had said many times that the sending of personnel to Latin America should be based upon a proper interpretation of the "signs of the times."

The Heresy of Modernism, first identified by a papal encyclical in 1835, has continually endeavored to 'adjust', i.e. *change*, the Deposit of Faith, the word of God given to the Church by Christ himself, giving it a new meaning which is in accord with a changing world.

I had experienced the Jesuit priest who was perceived as 'the Golden Voice of the Catholic Church in Italy' who revealed himself as a life-long communist, and I had a seminary professor in Chicago tell me that the Catholic Church should downplay the doctrine of the Real Presence in order to foster ecumenism. Therefore I was wary of anyone who sought to destroy a training program whose major thrust was Theology, the Spiritual Life, the Lay Apostolate and cultural adaptation. Father Colonnese, Msgr. Illich and other associates of theirs had revealed their philosophy of training and sending personnel to the point that there had to be real concern that their ideology was strongly socialistic, perhaps Marxist, and partaking in many respects in the Heresy of Modernism. Therefore, in the memorandum, I went on to say:

> ". . . . The person (or group) who controls the nature of training controls the kind of personnel who are sent to Latin America. Manipulation of people is always a danger in any training program. But the danger of manipulation is far greater when we are dealing with dedicated groups going overseas to a strange culture. This is because of the peculiar psychology involved. There is ignorance, there is fear of the unknown, there is the unusually intense desire to do well, there is the fear of failure and attendant embarrassment—all of these factors make it possible for those in charge of training to reshape the individual to an extraordinary degree. Father Colonnese's reference

> (pp. 13-14) to the missionary's need for a "re-tooling" according to the "signs of the times," in this context, is rather disturbing. One wonders what this "re-tooling" really is, who designs it according to the "signs of the times," and who interprets the "signs of the times."

This "re-tooling" idea, when it first came up from Colonnese, truly disturbed me in the light of the radical changes I had seen in personnel who had attended the language training sessions at Cuernavaca, Mexico. As previously stated, they had lost their confidence, doubted their "right" to go to Latin America to join Church activities there, and they had become anti-Church, along with other 'anti' stances in which they had obviously been indoctrinated. In other words, they had been 're-tooled.' I believe that Father Colonnese wanted me to be 're-tooled' when he offered to send me to a 'renewal' program in Utah. It became quite clear that the Christian Base Communities which were in the process of being established throughout Latin America as 'supra parochial' training programs were designed to quickly and on a gargantuan basis 're-tool' the masses of the Latin American faithful. It began to appear to me that, just as Latin America was being organized for change, the same thing was happening in the United States.

The so-called renewal programs for priests and the Catholic faithful were designed to instill the Modernism interpretation of Vatican Council II, and, while I have never attended one, they undoubtedly emphasized ecumenism and downplayed the Real Presence, they emphasized the concept of social service and downplayed the need for and the efficacy of the Sacraments, and all the other things which the Heresy of Modernism has determined must be 'modernized' to fit the exigencies of the 'signs of the times.' I tried to emphasize these things in the memorandum to the bishops:

"Our major challenge is to find and prepare people, not "re-tool" them. We need to find people (leaving aside for a moment the question of professional qualifications) whose spiritual lives are of such dimension that they love both God and His People enough to adjust to the latter wherever they are in the world and in whatever condition. Such people, once found, need preparation for culture change, and need to be provided with various tools, such as language. Far more important than a "re-tooling process" (if it is indeed acceptable in concept) is an adequate selection and preparation process designed to protect both the candidate and the project in Latin America."

In retrospect, I know that the reason that Father Colonnese and all his associates (these names will come up frequently: Thomas Quigley, James Lamb, Sidney Lens, Glen Smiley, Dr. Manoel Cardozo—and a few others) opposed the training program I had planned and implemented for the Papal Volunteer program was that it was entirely too Traditional and helped the volunteers adapt to the life and culture of Latin America and to the bishops and Catholic dioceses of those countries. I was to learn that the powers at the USCC and LAB intended to ***change*** the culture and ***modify*** the structure of the Church in Latin America. This could spring from an "Ugly American" attitude toward those 'poor, benighted, backward' people of Latin America, or, in my experience, could be the product of a socialistic or Marxist attitude toward governmental structure, civil or ecclesiastical.

The first National Training Center opened in the summer of 1965, coinciding with the summer session of the Catholic University. At the meeting of the PAVLA Board of Directors prior to the opening, Father Colonnese strongly pushed for an investigation of the training program. An investigating committee was appointed whose members (Father Colonnese and James Lamb—Virginia Leary withdrew) appeared at the site of training during that summer. The report continues on this subject:

> "In January of 1966, at a meeting of the LAB Advisory Committee, Father Colonnese spoke out strongly against the "thrust" of the PAVLA National Training center. Its

> greatest error seemed to be that it was teaching theology and spiritual life, that it was not attuned to the 'signs of the times,' etc."

With the success of the first National Training Center, the opposition to the Papal Volunteer program and its training methodologies grew fiercer. During the preparation for the first National Training Center, and during the session itself, while administration officials at the Catholic University were most helpful, it was vigorously opposed by Dr. Manoel Cardozo, Head of the Department of History at that same University. He personally opposed Dr. José Baquero, who had joined the staff of the National Training Center. Both Dr. Baquero and Dr. Cardozo were native Ecuadorians. While Dr. Cardozo was said to oppose Dr. Baquero's work in International Education, I assumed that, since Dr. Baquero had held high level posts as a diplomat for his country, there was a good deal of political ideology behind the antipathy.

At the CICOP meeting in Boston in 1967, when Father Colonnese for the first time had full charge of that organization, he scheduled a panel on foreign lay apostolic action in Latin America. James Lamb was it's chairman and Thomas Quigley was a principal speaker—both were in public opposition to the Papal Volunteer program. Another member of the panel was the Papal Volunteer who had been stationed in Lima, Peru as Field Representative, who was allied with a Peruvian priest who promoted Liberation Theology. (I had replaced him because of his adherence to those principles of Modernism.) Dr. Manoel Cardozo was also a member of the panel. Neither I nor any other representative of the Papal Volunteer program was consulted or asked to join the panel. The session was described as an open attack on the PAVLA program—as might have been expected in light of the panelists' outspoken opposition to the entire concept of sending Papal Volunteers to Latin America. The only panelist who defended the Papal Volunteer program that day was, ironically enough, a Mexican bishop; he expressed his strong support.

On February 20, 1969, because of all the harassment incidents perpetrated by Father Colonnese, I sent a memorandum to him summarizing all those incidents and reporting that his opposition had grown more pronounced since he had become the director of the Latin America Bureau. It seemed to me that in his new position of responsibility he should support rather than try to tear down one of the four principal divisions of the Latin America Bureau. Since he took over, as I said in the memorandum, I had been rendered virtually powerless, had no budget, and had no access to the approximately $75,000 in PAVLA money which I had turned over to LAB as I moved from Chicago to Washington, D.C. as I had been told to do. In that same memorandum to Father Colonnese, I raised a number of questions which were never answered, and which I now posed again in my memorandum to the bishops:

At this time I would like to raise again some of the questions posed in that earlier memorandum:

"1. Why is Father Colonnese so opposed to Dr. Baquero? Which are the "groups" that do not accept Dr. Baquero? What "stance" of Dr. Baquero's was objectionable to these groups? Who "practically gave orders" to exclude Dr. Baquero? (Memorandum, pp. 8-9)
2. Why does Father Colonnese belittle the abilities of Papal Volunteers? (Memorandum, pp. 5 & 7)
3. Why did Mr. Hegy, trainee during the 1968 PAVLA training session, insist on relating directly to Father Colonnese rather than to Father Eron or myself? Why did the same Mr. Hegy clandestinely circulate a questionnaire to the trainees, and why did many of the trainees feel that he was a "spy" for Father Colonnese? (Memorandum, pp. 7-8 and various reports)
4. Why was it necessary that a layman teach the course on "Role and Spirituality of the Layman"? Which are the "groups" that would otherwise object? Why was Thomas Quigley

> proposed by Father Colonnese as the man to teach the course? (Memorandum, p. 9)"

It made no sense to me that Thomas Quigley should teach the course, since he, like all associates of Father Colonnese, had publicly opposed the very concept of sending lay people as part of an apostolate to other countries. Beyond that, as far as I know, he had no training in Theology, nor in Scripture Studies, nor even in catechetics; it was not at all credible that he should teach the course on the 'Role and Spirituality of the Layman.'

It was during this last year when I was in charge of the Papal Volunteer program that I came to a full realization that I was dealing with a movement which was truly evil—evil in its methods, evil in its purpose and goal, and based on an effort to control the minds of men and women and so to control and change the Church (and the culture) in all the countries of Latin America. It was a huge undertaking, encompassing as it did the entire Western Hemisphere (and beyond, for all I ever knew), organized in such a way as to penetrate in some fashion or other the principal activities of every government in the western hemisphere, every diocese in that vast area, with tentacles into as many seminaries as it could so that the selection and training of priests could be manipulated. Many, many religious orders, both men and women, were infiltrated and filled with ideas which were contrary to the Eternal Truths which were given to us by God Himself through the Prophets and scriptures of the Old Testament and through the Truths which Christ Himself left with the Church that He founded to retain those Truths for the rest of time. It was clear that all of this had to have the full support of Bishop Bernardin.

A Special Returned Volunteer

One of the volunteers from a diocese in Wisconsin went through the training by Msgr. Illich at Cuernavaca, Mexico. He was an outstanding volunteer, having served, if my memory is accurate, in Peru. He was unusually intelligent, an exceptional Catholic, devoted to his Church and he was visibly devout in his personal spiritual life. After returning from his three years as a Papal Volunteer, he served on the staff of the National Training center, where he also excelled. His experience as a volunteer was of special interest and importance to those volunteers in training who were about to begin their service. He told us incredible stories about the nature of Illich's training program at Cuernavaca, Mexico. He himself was intelligent enough and educated enough to perceive the methodologies at the training school at Cuernavaca as manipulative. He saw the curriculum for what it was, and was not himself infected by it. Msgr. Illich, he told us, used techniques designed to warp someone's thinking, to tear down their self-confidence, to cast doubt in their minds about what they intended to do. Illich used techniques of shame, embarrassment and ridicule—all designed to raise doubts in the participants, to change people's minds, even to change their personalities, which I saw myself in a group of volunteers who were dramatically different after they had been through the Cuernavaca training. It was very clear after a study both of the training programs of Illich at Cuernavaca and of the training envisioned by Father Colonnese that they were both ideologically and methodologically the same. So my memorandum to the bishops proceeds:

> "It is clear from what has been said that Father Colonnnese's ideology of training differs from that of PAVLA. In order to understand better what his ideology of training is, I would like to direct attention to Father Colonnese's program for training in Mexico City and in the pastoral institutes (the third stage), which are projected to branch from the parent institute (IPLA) in Quito, Ecuador."

The memorandum goes on to report that Father Colonnese himself said that the new training program in Mexico City would use a number of Illich's former staff, which, of course, was less than reassuring. The Mexico City training program was to be a 'second stage' (the 'first stage' was not yet identified), and the 'third stage' was to be the developing 'pastoral institutes' which were to be set up in each country, patterned after the International Pastoral Institute which had been established in Quito, Ecuador, through subsidies received from the U.S. Bishops. I have never been able to determine whether the 'pastoral institutes' to be set up in each country were the *communidades de base* (Christian base communities) which would be supra-parochial and replace the Catholic administrative system, or whether the pastoral institute in each country (diocese?) would be responsible for organizing those smaller training cells.

My memorandum to the bishops proceeds:

> "According to a written report I have received, there are priests in Ecuador who describe the new training center as "Cuernavaca transplanted." The same report described positions taken by the IPLA staff. For instance:
>
> 1) IPLA has no official position on violence; the staff sees to it, however, that the students are informed on both the "theology of violence" (even guerilla warfare) approach to development, and the "non-violent" approach. According to this report, the staff does not subscribe to the position of Pope Paul VI made public in his visit to Bogotá during which he called for an end of violence.
> 2) All IPLA staff members reportedly say that the role of the Church in social development (desarrollo) is limited:
>   a. to becoming the mystique of development, and
>   b. to denouncing injustices.
>
>   There seems to be no sign of the positive role of the Church in training human resources for development,

as envisioned by Pope Paul VI *Populorum Progressio* (The Development of Peoples).

3) According to this same report, the director of IPLA maintains that development (*desarrollo*) is *non-violent revolution.*"

This is a threatening statement to conferences of bishops in Latin America who depend a great deal on the foreign personnel already in their countries. They can envision the time when, subject to this kind of influence, the U.S. Church will remove its personnel from their countries and dioceses unless they take immediate action in establishing pastoral institutes locally.

The Memorandum continues:

> "It is not surprising, therefore, that at the meeting in Caracas last month, it was proposed that these pastoral institutes be established in every country. An investigating team, as you know, under the auspices both of CELAM and USCC, is to visit countries of Latin America to conduct a feasibility study. It will not be surprising to me if in nearly every country, there will be found alumnae and alumni of IPLA in Quito, to whom it will be entirely natural for the investigating team (and the local conferences of bishops) to turn for assistance in opening a pastoral institute or "updating" an existing one. Assuming the accuracy of the report I received about IPLA and its ideology, it will not be long until that same ideology will be planted in every pastoral institute in Latin America. As a result of that, the leading clergy, religious and laity of each country (as well as in-coming foreign personnel) will have been exposed to the same doctrinaire training. The end result, of course, is clear: local personnel will have been exposed to the doctrines summarized above. The natural outcome, one would suspect, would be that they would be promoted

> or not according to their degree of conformity with this doctrine. Such personnel could easily become excessively negative and destructive."

On a massive and unprecedented scale, *desarrollo,* development and change, was to be brought about in the cultures of Latin America through the preparation of personnel who were trained in non-violence as a tool to be used as part of mass demonstrations.

To continue:

> "In addition to this wholesale identification of development with non-violence, these carefully trained personnel will reportedly have been taught to form "communidades de base". Those "communidades" are supra-parochial, formed of "like-minded people", and who strive toward their own personal conversion in order to develop the community. The "conversion," in all likelihood, would include (if not comprise) adherence to the concept of "non-violence as development," of denouncing injustices, and of being the mystique of development. It would not be surprising if the group has as a primary purpose the promotion of non-violent movements."

The urgency to establish pastoral institutes became ever greater. The team organized to study the feasibility of pastoral institutes was originally scheduled to make the trip in September. At Father Colonnese's insistence, this has been re-scheduled to July. This urgency to establish the pastoral institutes (and the training in Mexico) has been characteristic of Father Colonnese for the past year.

My central point in presenting this report to the bishops was that a massive movement was being organized to export to Latin America on a wholesale basis a very questionable doctrinaire training program. It was much more than simply objectionable for two reasons: 1) it was a depraved form of Ugly Americanism, since its purpose was to implant a 'made in America' form of change on the Church and the cultures of our neighbors to the south who were in such dire need of our 'enlightened' help, and 2) it sought to change the everlasting Deposit of Faith which Christ has given us through His Church by encouraging what has become so prevalent in the U.S. culture: situation ethics, loss of the sense of sin, free love, abortion on demand, Liberation Theology with its overtones of thinly disguised Marxism. Each passing day made it clearer in my mind that I was jousting with the devil in the person of his close representatives. St. Peter in his epistle wrote *"Diabolus sicut leo rugiens circuit, querens quem deveret."* (1 Peter 5:8) (Translation: The Devil, like a roaring lion, circles, seeking whom he may devour.) It became fully obvious that if the forces working on Latin America were to succeed, tens of thousands, perhaps hundreds of thousands, even millions, of people would lose their Faith and as a result lose their souls. They would be devoured by an organized program spawned by Satan himself. I was trying to alert the bishops to this awful possibility.

I proceeded in the report:

> "I believe it will be clear, after my few remarks on this subject, that the new LAB training program needs a careful review. This will also give some idea why PAVLA's training has been strongly criticized by the advocates of that new program. And surely it is understandable why PAVLA's Planning Committee—and I wholeheartedly with them—want PAVLA to be responsible for training its personnel (religious and laity by no means excluded). We certainly agree that final training should take place in the country of assignment, but it should be clear why we are reluctant to have this carried out by the local pastoral institutes until their validity is demonstrated."

The next segment of the memorandum deals with the available documentation regarding the various interlaced "groups" who were involved in exporting questionable training methods into the countries of Latin America. And the memorandum made the point that, even if the other considerations already presented were not in question, the following information standing alone would open up suspicions about infiltration of the Latin American Bureau of the U.S. Bishops' Conference by questionable ideologies.

> "My next point is, I believe, closely related to what I have already said. But if none of those things had been said, it would still demand your very special attention. I submit to you, first of all, two documents. The first is a letter from Mr. Glenn Smiley relating the success of his efforts to carry the non-violent movement to Latin America. While I think the U.S. effort to carry the non-violent movement to Latin America is of highly questionable validity, the body of the letter is not its most pertinent part. The letter itself is written on the letterhead of the "Coordinating committee of Latin America." At the left side, Mr. Smiley is listed as Executive Secretary. There follow the names of the Executive Committee members. The chairman is Sidney Lens. Also listed are J. Hugh Anwyl, ***L.M. Colonnese,*** Dana S. Green, George Lakey, Elaine Mikels, Thomas E. Quigley, Esteban Torres, Brady Tyson, Herman Will, Jr., and Carl Zietlow."

The most important consideration in that letterhead is the name of L.M. Colonnese as a member of that group. While the point is not made in the report, the letter cited is an example of "made in America" political activism which is being exported to the countries of Latin America by an agency representing the U.S. Bishops. If my many conversations with the hierarchy in a variety of countries are credible, this attempt to transfer an ideology to the cultures of Latin

America was not at all appreciated. It is an example of the Ugly American attitude which I experienced in every country of Europe and nearly every country of Latin America. It was more despicable than most other examples, however, because it was being foisted upon the Latin Americans under the guise of religion.

At any rate, until that letter arrived, I had never heard of the Coordinating Committee on Latin America, and I had been immersed in things relating to Latin America for nearly five years. And, as I pointed out, having heard of it, I did not know what it coordinated. The only members of its executive committee whom I had met were, of course, L. M. Colonnese, Dana S. Green (who was closely associated with CICOP), Thomas Quigley (who had been suggested to teach the spirituality and role of the layman at the National Training Center for Papal Volunteers), and Brady Tyson (who was in charge of the Interamerican Forum).

The second document submitted with the memorandum to the bishops was one which announced the establishment of the "National Information Network on Latin America." By definition on that document, the "Network" was designed for all those "concerned about the urgent need for changing present U.S. politico-economic policies (public and private) toward Latin America." The first two pages of that document gave some standard organizational information. The final page listed the organizations and the people who were the founding fathers of this network, both those who were present at the initiating meeting and those who were preliminary consultants. Some of the organizations, judging simply by their titles, were quite clearly political in nature. Among the people who are listed as founders of the National Information Network on Latin America: Elaine Mikels, Dana Green, Glenn Smiley, Sidney Lens, Thomas Quigley, ***L. M. Colonnese***, Brady Tyson. A comparison of the two documents raises some pertinent questions which the memorandum proceeds to pose:

> "One wonders what precisely is coordinated by the "Coordinating Committee." Is it non-violent movements in Latin America? Is it the Information Network? Is it both of these and more than these? And the question naturally arises: Are these, perhaps, the 'groups' that thought Dr. Baquero's stance disqualified him for our training program? Are they the ones which insisted on a layman teaching the course on the Role of the Modern Christian?"

And, while the question was not raised in the memorandum, it might have been asked whether the leadership of one or both of these groups were the ones who "practically gave orders" (as Father Colonnese reported it) that Dr. José Baquero, a prominent educator, a practicing Catholic, an experienced diplomat for his native Ecuador, and a full professor at the Catholic University, be excluded from the staff of the National Training Center for Papal Volunteers.

While it never crossed my mind at the time, it occurred to me as I have again reflected on those incidents during the writing of this book: I believe it is quite certain that there were bishop(s) and other powers at the USCC—principally Bishop Berrnardin—who clandestinely gave their support to Father Colonnese, to these groups and their questionable activities. Such things have not been unknown in the history of the Church. And if it were true, it would explain what happened in the weeks following the presentation of this memorandum—or rather, what didn't happen. It would explain why Cardinal Cody finally called me from Chicago and told me: "We've lost. You had just as well return to your diocese."

Many centuries before Christ founded His Church, there were forces at play among the Israelites which turned them from the message of the Prophets and had them expecting a Messiah who would help free them from the bondage of the Roman Empire; but Christ was to say to Pilate: "My kingdom is not of this world."

There were forces at work in the early Church which would change the message that Christ left behind; this concern led St. Paul to tell Timothy: "Guard the deposit"—meaning the deposit of Faith which Christ taught to the Apostles and which they were to maintain until the end of time. The history of the Church—2,000+ years—is interlaced with heresies to the extent that from time to time Councils have been called to condemn the heresies and infallibly declare, with the approval of the Holy Father, what the true Faith really is. The Heresy of Modernism in 1865 was described by Pope Pius X as the sum of all the heresies which had plagued the Church through the centuries since the time of Christ. It should not be surprising that these heresies are still with us and that those who promote them—some of them perhaps in good faith—will cause political turmoil within the church. All of these considerations in the memorandum to the bishops were enough, I believed at the time—and on re-reading and re-visiting the matter forty years later still do believe—that these groups and their members shared a purpose, a motivation, and indeed an ideology which was nefarious, not at all in keeping with the doctrine of the Catholic Church, which intended to export from the United States a program designed to change the cultures, attitudes, politics, structure of the Catholic Church in the countries of Latin America. It was the most awful kind of Ugly Americanism which I have seen, far surpassing the florid faced American in Brasilia who threatened to wire the Pentagon and bring the U.S. Army down to "wipe out" those people. That involved one irascible frightened man and the small embarrassed group who were with him. This was a carefully planned, astutely structured and very efficient *organization* whose clear purpose was to destroy the existing structures and engage in what they called, euphemistically, *desarrollo—i.e.* development, undoubtedly chosen because it is a nice, *modern* word.

The final consideration in the memorandum along these lines emphasizes everything that has gone before:

"Now, as a final point relating to these groups, close attention should be given to the background of Mr. Sidney Lens, Chairman of the Coordinating Committee on Latin America. I draw attention to a number of documents. One is an excerpt from the book "Fabian Freeway" by Rose L. Martin, on Lens' alleged connections with the "Fair Play for Cuba Committee", and relating that he took the Fifth Amendment when asked if he has ever belonged to a Trotskyist organization.

"A second set of two documents are excerpts from reports by the House Committee on un-American Activities. Both deal with the "Fair Play for Cuba Committee" and the name of Sidney Lens appears in both; and in the one dated June 15, 1961, he is reported as a member of the group which started the Fair Play for Cuba Committee. In view of recent statements on Cuba made by Father Colonnese, this raises some most important questions which are entirely obvious.

"A final document of great interest in this context is a four-page confidential report produced on October 31, 1962 by the American Security Council. The entire issue is devoted to Sidney Lens, and goes into detail about his past life, including his double identity. Under one name, he was associated with the Revolutionary Workers' League which the report indicates stood for the violent overthrow of the U.S. Government. Under the other name, as the report says, he has been connected with the Fair Play for Cuba Committee and characterizes himself as a "Ghanian", favoring non-violent resistance.

"It is noteworthy that Sidney Lens is featured on the front page of the May,1969, issue of "Latin America Calls", (the principal) publication of the Latin America Bureau."

And I said that I was sure that the U.S. Bishops did not want the Papal Volunteer program associated with unknown or questionable groups. And I suggested that perhaps we were looking only at the tip of the iceberg:

> "All these considerations make one wonder how many activities of this nature the Latin America program of the U.S. Bishops has been or is being associated with."

The report went on to conclude with a recitation of the difficulties which had plagued the Papal Volunteer program for the past year, since the move to Washington, D.C. It enumerated harassment of staff, lack of budget, wholesale layoffs of PAVLA personnel without reference to me, delays in implementing planned activities, accounting discrepancies, the financial support system for the volunteers terminated without being replaced by another system, disappearance of more than $75,000 in Papal Volunteer funds, a report on these same items submitted in February now five months later with no response. In spite of a record number of Papal Volunteer applicants, the number of actual Papal Volunteers in the field was at an all time low because the ability of the national program to process, prepare and support them financially had become non-existent. I therefore called upon the bishops, if they wanted the Papal Volunteer program to continue, to take it completely away from the jurisdiction of the Latin America Bureau so long as Father Colonnese was in charge and provide it with its own autonomy.

Father Colonnese in late February, 1969, left for an extended tour of Latin America, leaving many unanswered questions about how the national training center was to be organized and financed; when I appealed to Bishop Bernardin, he simply told me that I had to wait until Father Colonnese returned, several months hence, and it was already too late to organize effectively.

Remarkably, Msgr. Frank Hurley, who had approached me in such a friendly fashion the evening before, during the presentation of my report told me that I was indulging in "guilt by association." This phrase, 'guilt by association,' was currently being used by the Democratic party in both houses of Congress as a means of defending themselves against charges of being soft on Communism. To have such a charge made against me, coming from someone who had been so supportive just the evening before, actually blind-sided me. I had been under great stress during the entire presentation of the memorandum, and his sudden attack weakened me even further. I didn't have the presence of mind at the time to counter with such thoughts as "By their fruits you will know them" and "Birds of a feather flock together." I also could have pointed out that to be listed on these 'groups' as a member of the executive committee and apparently one of the 'founders' of such an organization is considerably more than simple 'association.' And to feature the chairman of two or more of these questionable organizations on the cover of the principal publication of LAB, one could argue, is to identify with his ideology. What he said, I believe, gave the bishops present at the meeting whatever excuse they needed to ignore what I had said. I don't recall anyone else saying a word, except at the start of a break, one of the bishops asked Bishop Bernardin whether he had the kind of security he needed to leave all that material behind on the conference table. Bishop Bernardin, showing anger, simply ignored him and walked out.

I believe I was in something of a daze during and after the presentation of this report. It seemed to me an enormous thing I had to do, but it was a matter of conscience that I had to do it. My own belief was that very little, if anything, would come of it, because I knew by now that the Heresy of Modernism was alive and well among the staff of the USCC, and, as I was beginning to suspect, even among some of the bishops. As recounted above, there were a number of incidents which inescapably led to that conclusion. I thought perhaps the bishops would be solid, except for Bishop Bernardin whom I had seen and heard, do and say some very questionable things, as said before. Now, forty years later, I don't remember how the meeting ended, and I don't remember anyone talking to me afterward. I remember only four things: 1) Msgr. Hurley's accusation that I was indulging in 'guilt by association'; 2) a bishop asking Bishop Bernardin how good his security was as we took a break with these documents lying upon the conference table; 3) because I was under great stress, I laughed nervously when Father Colonnese made some statement directed at me; and 4) immediately after the meeting, as everyone stood and prepared to leave the conference room, Msgr. Hurley and Father Colonnese (with someone else standing by) were talking about people who were called before congressional investigating committees and took the fifth amendment, not because they were trying to hide anything, but because they felt in principle that those committees had no right to question any one on those matters. This was a familiar method of refutation: take one small part of an argument, cast doubt on it, and ignore the rest of the incriminating evidence. This demonstrated that at least a few of those at that meeting that day were not interested in determining the accuracy of what I had said but in undermining my entire presentation. They certainly gave to those bishops who might have been inclined to act on what I said but were afraid to do so, an excuse not to act.

While I have no clear recollection now of the mood of the assembled bishops, I do remember saying on several different occasions to several people shortly after it was over that the "fear in the room was palpable" (my exact words). The bishops knew the gravity of what I had presented, and, having had no chance to discuss it among themselves, had no idea how they were going to handle it. They were completely vulnerable to any solutions presented by Bishop Bernardin.

CHAPTER 36

The U.S. Bishops

I have known a number of bishops and two Cardinals (the only two I really knew) who were truly humble men. One of them, Cardinal Humberto Madeiros, the Archbishop of Boston, approximately two years after I presented my report in 1969 to a committee of bishops of which he was a member—he was bishop of Brownsville, Texas, at the time—told my brother, Msgr. Eugene Kevane, that "your brother was absolutely right and we should have listened to him." My brother described Cardinal Medeiros as "eating humble pie" during that conversation. I must confess that it still rankles with me that the Cardinal did not contact me directly—all he needed to do was pick up the telephone, use the National Catholic Directory, and contact me at the Sioux City Chancery where I was Chancellor. But in my more forgiving moments, I know that would have been extremely hard for him, as it was extremely hard for him to summon the courage to talk to my brother, knowing that my brother would make sure that I knew. So I've come to be grateful to the Cardinal for his honesty.

Cardinal Humberto Madeiros, the Archbishop of Boston, mentioned just above, before he was appointed to the Archdiocese of Boston, was bishop of Brownsville, Texas. As bishop of Brownsville, he was a member of the Bishops' Subcommittee for the Papal Volunteer program. He was unfortunately unable to attend the meeting at which I presented my memorandum. Since I looked on him as one of the more solid members of that subcommittee, during my period in 'limbo' after the meeting, I wrote him a letter asking him to carefully examine the contents of the memorandum. He answered with a letter which I can only describe as 'wishy-washy'—clearly pursuing a 'party line' which, I believe, had been articulated by Bishop Bernardin, director of the USCC and Father Colonnese's superior; it was then simply accepted by the members of the bishops' subcommittee. Within the next year or so, he was assigned as Archbishop of Boston, and, not long after that, he was named as a Cardinal.

It helped me a great deal to have a major figure in the Catholic Church in the United States finally acknowledge that I had been right in what I exposed. It was an even greater consolation to know that the problems I had uncovered were in the process of being corrected. It explained why, for some time, I had heard no more about Christian Base Communities, why Msgr. Illich retired to Germany, why Liberation Theology apparently was no longer credible. However, it remains a sadness for me that those Papal Volunteers were no longer enhancing the relationships between the Latin American Church and countries; they would have continued to do an immense amount of good. I know that most (all?) of the volunteers who went to Latin America during my tenure retain a deep respect for the deeply religious people of Latin America and for their culture. However, it hurts and will continue to hurt that it took so long for the bishops to recognize the problem. It also rankles to know that the Papal Volunteer program simply died of disorganization about a year or so later under the direction of Thomas Quigley, who was perhaps instructed to destroy it. We'll come to this later on, but the Communist effort to destroy the Church in Latin America also died.

The other Cardinal was the Archbishop of Chicago—John Cardinal Cody. As I mentioned before, he was always honest and direct with me, with the people of the Chicago Archdiocese, and he gave his full support to me and to what I was doing. Before he died, while he had many supporters, he was vilified and excoriated, surrounded by enemies (Modernists) on all sides. He was, in my view, a Modern Day Martyr. As someone said about Cardinal Cody's final suffering, "God certainly knows how to put the finishing touches on a special soul."

Bishop Jos. M. Mueller, bishop of Sioux City, I knew very well because he was the bishop of my own diocese. It was he who sent me to Rome, who appointed me Vice Chancellor, Chancellor, Vice Officialis of the diocesan tribunal, etc., and released me to be national director of the PAVLA program. It is he who another bishop called the 'conscience of the Body of Bishops'—an unintended compliment. And it was he who asked me my opinion of things he said and heard at the bishops' conferences. The most important memory I have of him (an incident which epitomizes the kind of a person he was) was a time when he called us all together (about 20 people at the chancery, the diocesan newspaper, the central cemetery office, etc.) and told us that if he ever told us to do something we felt was wrong, then we were bound in conscience not to do it, but he would appreciate it if we would tell him why we disagreed. I couldn't imagine that there were many (if any) bishops who would say such a thing to their staffs.

Bishop Hodges, who was a special soul, I came to know very well because he was chairman of the subcommittee of bishops who had oversight of the PAVLA program. He was a truly humble man, very supportive of the PAVLA program and of me. When I was told to move my offices from Chicago to Washington, D.C., and conjoin them with the LAB offices, I told him I would prefer to resign rather than do that, because it was hard enough operating the way I had been, but it would be insufferable with Father Colonnese in the same offices. Besides that, I told him, it was rumored that Father Colonnese would succeed Father Considine as Director of the Latin America Bureau, which would make it impossible for me to do my job. He pleaded with me not to resign, because, he said, if I didn't stay with it, ". . . the Papal Volunteer program will die."

Needless to say, I moved to Washington, D.C. and suffered the consequences I had expected.

Comparing: U.S. Bishops & Clergy vs. Latin American Bishops & Clergy

In the course of five years as national director of the Papal Volunteer program, I met and talked to between 50 and 100 U.S. bishops; and an equal number of Latin American bishops in 15 to 20 different countries. I met and worked with more than twice that many Latin American priests (i.e. 100 to 200).

And of course I had much more than passing contact with a huge number of Latin American Catholic laity in all those dioceses and countries. I'll say a word about the laity before proceeding on to the bishops and clergy of the Latin and U.S. cultures. In all the countries I visited, the Latin (perhaps I should say Hispanic) laity freely and openly talked about their religion, their own internal spirituality, and their relationship with Jesus Christ. In the U.S. we are reluctant to expose those innermost feelings and values and are quite undemonstrative in regard to them. As an example, it wasn't long ago that I witnessed an obviously Hispanic father, carrying his 5 or 6 year old son, who went up behind the altar to the tabernacle in the Blessed Sacrament Chapel at the Basilica of San Juan del Valle, and together they stroked the tabernacle, and, while I didn't overhear their conversation, the father I'm sure was whispering to his son about the presence of Jesus Christ—God—within. This basilica is located about 10 miles from the Rio Grande border with Mexico. The population of the cities along the Rio Grande River is mostly Hispanic. The people in this area approach their religious faith exactly as do the faithful in all Latin American countries which I've had the privilege to visit.

The bishops and clergy of Latin America, like their laity, have a similar openness, humility and deep spirituality. It saddens me to say that the Catholic bishops and clergy of Latin America far outshine their U.S. counterparts in their religious devotion, their loyalty to the Pope in Rome and in the degree to which they do not allow the politics and governments of their countries to sway their own devotion to their God, their religion, and their people. But please don't misunderstand me: there are U.S. bishops and clergy whose devotion to their religion is strong and beautiful; there are Latin American bishops and clergy whose positions are heretical or nearly so—as an example, the adherents to Liberation Theology, which presents communism under the thin disguise of Theology.

As an example I used earlier, the Archbishop of Salvador, Brazil, a major city located on the northeast coast of the country, was one of the kindest, most charitable and devout individuals I have ever met. On my first visit to him, he invited me to spend the night in his house, even though, he warned me, he had no comfortable place for me to sleep—which was true. The second time I visited, he had to be out of town, but through his assistant, he offered me his own bed in which to spend the night. It was a much more comfortable place to sleep than I had during the previous visit. Other bishops in Latin America expressed concern as to where I might spend the night, and, since I had it already taken care of, they pursued it no further. In all my travels in the U.S., no bishop showed any concern for my overnight plans, and, of course, none ever offered me the opportunity to sleep in his guest room.

As to the clergy of Latin America, most of them were impressive in their devotion to their responsibilities. During the 1960's when a priest was ordained in Mexico, he was immediately stripped of his citizenship. They were not allowed to wear the Roman collar in public. Such priests clearly attached greater importance to being Catholic priests, than to being Mexican. Fortunately for the priests of the U.S., they have not yet had to face such a choice, and I hope they never do.

The Latin American bishops were clearly aware of how the U.S. hierarchy looked upon them, but were supremely gracious in staying silent on the subject. When they did broach the subject, it was with the most sensitive kind of diplomacy. For example, the time when they had their representative, Father Hector Samperio, ask me if there was any way I could ensure that my successor would have the same approach to, and respect for, the cultures of Latin America that I did.

In all my travels, and they were extensive, I came to have great respect for every culture which I encountered: Italy perhaps most of all, Germany, Austria, Switzerland, England, Scotland, Ireland, and now, most recently, certain elements of every Latin American country. Even as I am an American and proud to be one, there are elements in almost every other culture which to this day I wish that we had in the U.S.

I saw some of the U.S. bishops and many of the clergy at their worst. There is evidence that now, perhaps 30 to 40 years later, the less-than-impressive bishops are gradually being replaced by much stronger ones, and students in our seminaries appear to be a much stronger group who will not be taken in by Modernist professors. I would like now to cover at least some of the major forces operative in our country which make it difficult for our very human bishops and clergy to be what Holy Mother Church, down through the ages, has wanted them to be.

Bishops belong to an unusual and elite fraternal club and therefore are subject to a sort of 'professional entrapment' which puts pressure on them to conform to what they perceive to be the wants and desires of their fellow bishops. They are priests. More than that, they each have been ordained into the "fullness of the priesthood," and it is part of their responsibility to protect and defend the priests who are under their care, both in their physical well-being and in their spiritual growth. They are responsible in a way we probably cannot understand in this life for the salvation of the souls of their priests. But then they are equally responsible for the salvation of the souls of the faithful in their dioceses, and of the religious men and women who reside in their dioceses. It is unfortunate that, being human, a certain percentage of them fix their focus on their worldly obligations and become overly political, overly administrative. St. John Chrysostom made the statement that a very large percentage of bishops lose their souls because they didn't take care of their spiritual responsibilities. If this book can help some bishops to quietly reassess how they are living up to the demands of their offices and in all humility strengthen their personal and spiritual lives—even if it is only one such bishop—it will be well worth the time and effort I put into this writing and whatever vilification may result from it for me.

CHAPTER 37

Ugly Americanism, Heresies of Americanism and Modernism, Politics

The bishops of the United States, both as individuals and as a group, possess a level of human frailty, differing from person to person, and differing for the group depending upon the intensity of outside pressures. The one I knew best was Most Rev. Jos. M. Mueller, Bishop of Sioux City, who is the one who was in charge of my diocese. I attended Trinity College and Loras College as a seminarian, then was given the privilege of studying at the North American College in Rome, Italy.

On completion of studies in Theology and Canon Law, I was appointed Vice Chancellor and other posts mentioned earlier. A few years later, Bishop Mueller released me to become the national director of the Papal Volunteer program, and then appointed me Chancellor of the Diocese of Sioux City when I resigned PAVLA. Bishop Mueller was a good bishop, a truly humble and prayerful man who had very few pretenses. He wanted to do what was right, and, while he was very decisive, always faced the possibility that he wasn't objective in some of his decisions. Because I had a degree in Theology and a degree in Canon Law, and because he asked me to do so, I used to be quite candid in giving him my opinion on many of the subjects which were discussed in the Chancery. I began to realize that this caused him a good deal of trouble and he became rather testy with me.

Finally, and again very forthrightly, I told him what ***obedience*** meant to me: "If I think you're wrong, Bishop, on a given point, I believe it is my duty to tell you why I think you're wrong. And if I think that you do not understand what my position is, then I believe it is my duty to make sure that you do understand. Then if, knowing what I am trying to get across, you still hold to your position, then I will do whatever you tell me to do." After that statement of mine, he began to trust me entirely, and I was subsequently told by many priests in the diocese that I had become "the power behind the throne."

It was then that I had a beginning awareness of a weakness among the body of bishops in the United States. He began to call me to his office after each of the annual conferences of bishops to solicit my opinions as a theologian. It became clear that at each of these conferences he delivered statements regarding points of doctrine and morals.

On one memorable occasion when he called me to his office, having just returned from one of the annual conferences, he was noticeably agitated. He asked me to explain the difference between a mortal sin in a matter of morals and a mortal sin against the virtue of faith. I told him that a person who commits a mortal sin related to morals can quickly regain the state of grace by going to confession in a spirit of repentance and receiving absolution; but if a person commits a mortal sin against the virtue of faith, he thereby loses the gift of faith, and, because of the heinousness of the sin, is unlikely even to seek absolution unless he receives a special grace from God. Bishop Mueller visibly relaxed and said "That's what I told them." I assumed from this that the matter was debated at the bishops' conference, and that a sizeable number took an opposing view—whatever it may have been. Bishop Mueller was an accomplished theologian and in his humility was well aware of the admonition that our minds as human beings are so clouded that we must at all times ensure that our theological thinking is in tune with the infallibly teaching Church.

Politics Among the Bishops

One of the weaknesses of the body of bishops in the United States is precisely that it is a *body* (and this, of course, is true of the conferences of bishops in every other country in the world), and therefore, however unconsciously, they exert political and psychological pressure one upon the other. Therefore, when one bishop makes a statement which is in error, and a few others immediately support the view of the one, it is easy for the remainder to lend their support to the statement, or at least not publicly oppose it. Those few whose theological thinking is more accurate, if they oppose the statement, become a 'minority'—and we all know that if the majority of Americans support a given concept by voting in favor of it, then that doctrine is 'right'. A bishop in the minority who opposes a theologically erroneous concept becomes, as Bishop Mueller was, the 'conscience of the body of bishops', which was something of a derogatory term, at least in the mind of the bishop who said it to me.

Bishop Frank Greteman, who succeeded Bishop Mueller as Bishop of Sioux City was an example of a weaker bishop who 'went along with the crowd.' He is yet another example of how the group psychology operating within the conference of bishops can lead them to a biased interpretation of matters affecting doctrine. He came back one year from the meeting of bishops and said to me, "We no longer think that there is the Real Presence of Christ in the crumbs left over from the hosts, because the crumbs are not recognizable as bread." He was referring, of course, to the crumbs which are sometimes left in the bottom of a ciborium after communion is distributed to the Faithful at Mass. "We" in this case quite clearly meant at least some of the bishops at the conference who were at least talking among themselves, perhaps not during a formal session. This was barefacedly heretical. The Council of Trent long ago (1545-1563), in response to the Protestant Reformation, among many other things, clearly defined the Real Presence and declared that in Transubstantiation the entire Christ—body and blood, soul and divinity—was fully present in the smallest particle of the consecrated host and in the minutest drop of the consecrated wine. All of the decrees of the Council of Trent were formally confirmed by Pope Pius IV in 1564.

Two things are particularly frightening about Bishop Greteman's pronouncement: 1) the particular group of bishops involved (whether one or two, several or all) were usurping the infallibility of the Pope in making that determination; 2) as just mentioned, they contradicted the solemn definition by the Council of Trent that the entire Body and Blood, Soul and Divinity of Christ is present in the consecrated host and chalice of wine, and in every particle of host and wine. This is what permits a priest to break a host into many pieces in order to distribute communion to an unexpectedly large number of communicants. And even if the particle were so small that only through the use of a microscope could it be determined that it had the appearance of bread, then we must assume, as a matter of faith, that it is the Living Christ.

It is most important to me at this point to go on record as having a total measure of respect for bishops (and certainly an incomplete understanding of the pressures upon them) as they endeavor to carry out the responsibilities which have been placed upon them. They are the visible successors to the Apostles. The Apostles, being entirely human, had their problems. The worst of them, Judas, destroyed himself by betraying Christ to the Roman and Jewish authorities. Peter, already designated as the first Pope, denied Christ three times, even though Christ predicted that he would and Peter vehemently asserted that he would not. A message in the story of the crucifixion is that none of the Apostles stood by Christ, with the exception of John, who stayed with Christ's mother.

The bishops of the United States have forces acting upon them which, taken in combination are perhaps far more difficult to deal with than the forces acting upon the bishops of any other country in the world. I offer an explanation of those forces hoping that the U.S. bishops may use those ideas for personal meditation in order to steel themselves to become as completely as possible the loyal, obedient leaders of the Roman Catholic Church in the United States.

'Ugly Americanism' Affects the Bishops and Clergy in America

Underlying all the weaknesses of the United States Catholic Conference of Bishops is that they are *American*, and, as a group almost certainly have at least a taint of the 'Ugly American' attitude. Actually, very few Americans escape it. When I was a student in Italy and Europe fifty years ago, whenever we encountered a group of American tourists, we oftentimes feigned an inability to speak English, so that we need not talk to them. Far too many—obviously not all—American tourists assumed a superior posture, treating native Italians, Germans, French, etc., with a patronizing attitude, embarrassing those of us who had learned to respect each of those cultures. ("Why can't these people learn to speak English?"—I heard that on more than one occasion.) So we tried to avoid them. Later, as national director of the Papal Volunteer program, I saw the same attitude wherever I traveled in Latin America. In Mexico one morning, having breakfast at the restaurant of the hotel in which I had stayed, an American at an adjacent table complained bitterly to the waiter that his eggs were not properly done, treating him like an indentured slave. It was so bad that after that very ugly American left the restaurant, I apologized to the waiter, telling him that most Americans were not like that, and, in fact the Mexican people were widely admired and respected in the United States.

At another time, in Brazil, I encountered probably the worst incident I have ever seen, which I have already described. It was an American who shouted "I'm going to bring the U.S. military down here and wipe you people out"—because his flight to Rio de Janeiro had been canceled on *Carnavale.*

I had decided many years earlier in Italy that underlying the ugly American attitude was a certain amount of fear. And perhaps all the American tourists at that time and probably since had a normal kind of fear of the unknown and different culture. And there is a certain amount of fear and intimidation related to the older cultures in the world, whose length of existence and accumulated wisdom makes our culture seem like an upstart in the world. In order to hide and manage the fear, many of them would remind themselves that they were citizens of the most powerful nation on earth, had more money than most of the citizens of most countries, and therefore they need not feel intimidated. Their fear then, because of the need to hide it, drove them into some degree of arrogance.

I cannot imagine that the U.S. bishops would be entirely unaffected by certain world political pressures. As belonging to the most powerful nation on earth, the U.S. bishops, I am sure, feel the internal need to stand out among the various other conferences of bishops in other countries. As citizens of the United States, they can be infected by the 'master race' attitude which the ugly American portrays. As national director of the Papal Volunteer program, I faced an occasional diplomatic challenge: To cope with the disdainful attitude which some U.S. bishops expressed toward the people and cultures and the Church of Latin America: "They're so backward," I heard on a few occasions, "I suppose they really do need our help."

Attitudes like this, especially coming from bishops whose spiritual lives, I thought at the time, were supposed to be better than those of the rest of us, always raised my hackles. Over the years, I had developed the profoundest kind of respect for the depth of faith which I saw among Latin Peoples—Italians and Spanish, and now in the years with the Papal Volunteer program, the peoples of the many countries of Latin America. To me the economic development, or lack of it, of the Latin American countries was relatively unimportant compared to the absolute desirability of helping the Latin American hierarchy and clergy help their people to maintain their child-like faith in God. They lived and live in the presence of God; they are devoted to the primacy of the Pope in Rome; they are a prayerful people. It was my absolute and conscious intention to ensure that the Papal Volunteer program, through the people who would be sent to assist in Latin America, would in no way tarnish that faith. They would instead enhance it, and, in turn, have their own faith enhanced and somehow strengthened through contact with the peoples of Latin America. I was convinced that the interaction of the beautiful faith of the Latin American people and the professional know-how of the clergy and laity from the United States would greatly enhance both cultures.

The Latin American bishops and clergy must have felt the patronizing attitude of the Church in America, such as the one described just above, and they must have been aware of my attitude, because, through Father Hector Samperio, they paid me the greatest compliment I have ever received. Father Samperio was a priest of the Archdiocese of Mexico City, apparently designated by his Archbishop to deal with the Church in the United States. He spent a good deal of time in Washington, D.C., making contact with the USCC, and in particular with the Latin America Bureau, both with Father Colonnese and with me. When I wanted to meet with a bishop or his representative in Mexico, I always made the arrangements through Father Samperio. On this particular occasion, described earlier, I had been invited to attend a meeting of a number of bishops—a meeting which was to be held on the Gulf Coast—and I would be taken to the meeting by car.

As I explained before, arrangements were therefore made, and a time was set for me to be picked up in Mexico City. Father Samperio came to my room to talk about the attitude toward the Church and culture of Latin America which I was bringing to bear on the Papal Volunteer program.

This was the magnificent compliment they paid me.

I was particularly saddened by recent events which, in my opinion, were spawned by the 'ugly American' attitude of the U.S. hierarchy. Since the Catholic Church in America resides in the last remaining superpower in the world, it seems to me that the conference of U.S. bishops somehow subconsciously looks on itself as a Catholic "superpower" whose decisions should be applicable to the entire world and must to a certain degree participate in infallibility.

It was therefore a major blow to the collective episcopal pride to have their 'zero tolerance' policy relating to pedophile priests countermanded by the Vatican. And after the special commission met to review and amend the policy, it was particularly lamentable that two American members of the commission—one cardinal and one bishop—attempted to put a face-saving 'spin' on the results by saying that the decision of the American bishops really had not been changed, we needed to rethink it a little bit, etc. etc. The American bishops need to realize that the only ecclesiastical superpower is the Pope himself in the Vatican, and they participate in infallibility only when they are in union with the Pope. The reaction of these two prelates smacks of disobedience to the Holy See, or at least a lack of loyalty, which is a terrible example to give the Catholics of this country. They would have gained a tremendous amount of respect from the Catholic faithful if they had honestly and humbly made a public statement to the effect that: 'We made a mistake. In our efforts to avoid and repair scandal in the Church, we condemned certain priests without a hearing, and now, in complete obedience to the Pope we must correct that mistake.' Christ himself told his first Pope—Peter—"Turn back from time to time and strengthen your brothers." (Luke 22:32) The Pope was doing precisely that, and the bishops should have made it clear that they understood the Pope's supreme role, and they should have assured him and the American people that they would obey him. As a canon lawyer myself, I cannot understand how the bishops—many of whom are themselves canon lawyers and who had scores of canon lawyers at their beck and call, as well as advisors at the Vatican available to them—could have decided on a course which was in so many ways contrary to the Canon Law of the Catholic Church, a course which did not allow priests the due process of law. How could they have embarked on a course that condemned *priests—their* priests—without a hearing? Unfortunately, because they appear to be more afraid of the press and of public opinion than they are of God, and because they wanted to save their own secular hides, they were ready to throw their priests to the wolves.

The only *Christian* stance for the bishops to have taken, it seems to me, is that they are in the business of the salvation of souls. In this case, they had two groups of souls which demanded their attention in terms of salvation: the allegedly pedophile priests, and the victims of those priests. Just as God, by Church doctrine has a universal salvific will—he wants all souls to be saved—so must the Church want all souls to be saved. As a U.S. Congressman once somewhat famously said: "We can walk and chew gum at the same time," so can and must the Church, especially in the person of her bishops, actively strive toward the salvation of the souls of her priests *and* the salvation of the victims of those priests. The bishops can try their best to strongly encourage celibacy among their priests, both by example and by exhortation; and by the same means and with the threat of severe disciplinary action they can deter those who have a tendency toward sexual aberration and pedophilia, insisting that such priests seek the spiritual counseling and build the personal spiritual lives which will bring about their rehabilitation. And the bishops must devote at least an equal amount of energy to providing support, solace and comfort to those who have been the victims of the abusive acts of priests and bishops. And while we can understand how the victims of abusive priests naturally feel abused, wronged, outraged, vengeful, vindictive, and furious, we can also exhort them to apply the principles of the spiritual life to their situations. Christ himself shows us the way: "Father, forgive them for they know not what they do." Pope John Paul II actively and publicly forgave the gunman who tried to assassinate him. To the question how often one should forgive his oppressors, Christ said "7 times 70 times," or, in other words, without limit. "Turn the other cheek," Christ admonished us. As I said before, my wife was threatened with rape by her father when she was in grade school. She was abused by her brother-in-law. And in fact she was raped by a priest when she was barely out of high school. For years she hated her father and that priest, but knew that it was wrong to hate anyone. She struggled to set the hatred aside and to forgive both. I heard her argue with herself many times that she knew all priests were not like that, that she would never bring charges against him because of potential scandal within the Church. I told her countless times that because she *wanted* to forgive them, she had already done so, because forgiveness is an act of the will, not of the emotions. But even though I believe she had already forgiven them, it remained important to her to *feel* that she had forgiven them. The time came not long ago when the burden was finally lifted from her soul.

Two things occurred which contributed. I may have finally said the right thing to her: "You know, it doesn't really matter what your father or that priest did to you or thought of you; there's no way they should be able to control your life or what you think of yourself, particularly now that they are both long dead. You can be completely independent of those episodes in your life. The only thing that really matters is what God thinks of you." And I could tell that these thoughts had a positive impact on her. The other thing occurred not long ago when she received communion during Sunday Mass at the Basilica of the Virgin of San Juan del Valle in San Juan, Texas. She told me that at Mass she had asked once again for the grace to forgive, and, after receiving communion that day she felt as if a great weight had finally lifted from her and she realized that she had fully forgiven her father and the priest. And when victims and groups of victims began to rage against the bishops and priests and to seek financial recompense, she said "No amount of money nor apologies from the clergy and bishops in general, nor from the Pope himself can ever give the kind of surcease which the effort to forgive their oppressors can provide." Surely the bishops in their combined intelligence and wisdom can find an effective way to exhort both the abusive priests and their victims to overcome their problems through an effort which proceeds from the depths of their spiritual lives.

Simply from an administrative point of view, the bishops could well take a lesson from the military society. No top officer will ever allow his troops to feel that he doesn't give them his full support. To do so would be to destroy the morale and the fighting spirit of the military as a whole. If a soldier is caught in some transgression, he will not be punished until the allegation is proven—and the rest of the troops know that in general terms the top brass will never railroad anyone. The bishops, unfortunately—both according to things I have heard from priests themselves and from things I have read on the subject—have given the impression to the clergy that the bishops are ready to ignore the needs of their priests in order to save their own reputation among the press and society in general. The only way for the bishops to reestablish their credibility completely is to engage in complete honesty and humility. They need to recognize publicly that, like Christ, their kingdom is not of this world, that they have made egregious mistakes in the administrative handling of pedophile priests, that they acted in a way that was disobedient to the Pope and the Church, that they have not taken proper care of their priests, nor have they taken proper care of those who are victims of abusive priests. Instead, when they come across as 'spin doctors' in a crass political way, they engender anything but loyalty among the faithful and the priests for whom they are responsible.

The religious superiors of the various religious orders in the United States, meeting about eight weeks after the ill-fated meeting of bishops which adopted the 'zero-tolerance' rule, had a much more balanced approach to the problem, according to an Associated Press report by Rachel Zoll, date-lined Philadelphia, August 11, 2002. They decided that abusive priests should be kept away from children, but not expelled—a stance which was considerably less restrictive than the zero-tolerance plan of the bishops. The report stated that their approach was grounded in the Catholic belief in the redemption of sinners. The stance of the religious superiors was nicely balanced between concern and care for the victims of pedophile priests, and care and concern for the priest perpetrators themselves, who were sinful fellow priests. One thing they did not do was suggest to the victims that Christian charity might require them to forgive the priest perpetrators: To forgive; to build their spiritual lives in spite of what had been done to them; to join the bishops and priests in a joint effort to help save the souls of those priests rather than, in some form of self pity, to wallow in the harm that had been done to them and exact some kind of compensation for that damage. It is a cross which for some reason they have been asked to bear. If they forthrightly pick up that cross and follow Jesus Christ, if they offer up their pain and suffering for the salvation of souls, the benefits to them and to the remainder of the Church Militant and Suffering will be beyond measure.

The Heresy of Americanism

These attitudes all contribute to what we can call the developing 'American' church. It is frequently referred to as Amchurch. Pope Leo XIII in his 1899 encyclical "*Testem Benevolentiae Nostrae*" (Witness to Our Good Will) warned of a developing heresy of Americanism. The following excerpt summarizes the concern of the Pope:

> "The underlying principle of these new opinions is that, in order to more easily attract those who differ from her, the Church should shape her teachings more in accord with the spirit of the age and relax some of her ancient severity and make some concessions to new opinions. Many think that these concessions should be made not only in regard to ways of living, but even in regard to doctrines which

> belong to the deposit of the faith." (The full text of this encyclical is given in Appendix B of this book.)

I have had the impression for many years that the U.S. Bishops have largely ignored this encyclical; some may not even be aware of its existence. Americanism can be identified as a consequence of 'ugly Americanism' among the American bishops. After all, we are the one super power left in the world. We are the richest, strongest society on earth, and we lead the world in (almost) every respect. It is very human, I suppose, for the bishops as a group to feel that they must uphold this image even in things religious, and that the Vatican, after all, is simply a small city-state which, as Stalin once stated in denigrating the power of the Catholic Church, has no military might at all. It is probably very easy, therefore, for the American bishops to skirt the edges of disobedience when dealing with the Pope as they did when they tried to 'save face' after the Vatican rejected their policy relating to pedophile priests.

Something like that, as I said before, probably contributed to the attitude of a given bishop in the South who wanted to continue the practice of general absolution in his diocese in spite of the papal directive to discontinue it. When pressed on the subject, the bishop said about the Pope: "He's the bishop of Rome, I'm the bishop of *My City*; He can do what he wants, I can do what I want." saying, in effect, "the Pope has no power over me. I owe him no obedience."

The *American* church, unfortunately, tends to downplay the primacy of Peter. Will the Catholic Church in the United States of America some day become known as the American Catholic Church with no real allegiance to the Pope in Rome, much as happened to the Church of England and to the Eastern Rite orthodox churches? Some day the history books may tell us that it has already happened.

If only the bishops, having had their newly minted policy regarding pedophile priests rejected by Rome, had acknowledged that they had made a mistake and announced that they would now, in total obedience to the Pope, correct the error. The elected leaders of the conference of bishops should have taken that stance, but they did not. In my view the bishops would have instantly regained whatever respect and trust they had lost among the majority of the faithful. Instead they were perceived as a group of ordinary humans who, in the paucity of their spiritual lives, had to save face at all costs, even if it meant throwing their own priests "under the bus." It is very likely that among the priests of the United States there is a real fear that the bishops would turn on them in order to save their own skins and will not ensure that their priests will receive justice. Priests I have talked to take consolation from the fact that the Vatican quite clearly understands and appreciates the importance of the simple priest in the life of the Church.

Heresy of Modernism in the U.S. Catholic Church

Pascendi Dominici Gregis (On the doctrine of the Modernists) was a Papal letter promulgated by Pope Pius X on September 8,1907. In the encyclical, the Holy Father identified and defined the Heresy of Modernism which he described as the summary of all heresies. During the two thousand year history of the Roman Catholic Church there has been an almost uncountable series of heresies—some came briefly and disappeared after pronouncements by the Church, i.e. Ecumenical Councils; others, such as Protestantism, have lasted from the Middle Ages to the present. The image of a combination of all those into one heretical undertaking is a soul-shattering concept. (The full text of the encyclical is given in Appendix C of this book.)

The American bishops and clergy, because of all the factors listed here, are unusually vulnerable to the Heresy of Modernism: The 'Ugly American' attitude; the Heresy of Americanism; Politics Among the Bishops; Patriotism. This heresy, originating as almost all of them do with the clergy and the bishops, has trickled down to certain groups of the laity.

As has always been true, it will once again be true, that the heresy will be destroyed by the magnificent figure of the Pope at his end of the spectrum and the broad base of the faithful laity around the world. Together they will identify and ultimately destroy whatever errors come into the Church.

The Heresy of Modernism has members of the Church, principally bishops and priests, questioning and intending to change some—even most!—of the traditional doctrines of the Church which have been handed down from Christ. However, it has been clear for 2000 years that Revelation from God ended with the death of the last Apostle. Over the millennia, God in His Infinite Wisdom and His care for His people, has revealed an immense body of His Eternal Truths to mankind. With the Incarnation, when the Second Person of the Divine Trinity became man and dwelt among us, He revealed for the first time that, indeed, there are three Persons in One God. The Jews had no inkling that this was true, nor did any other religion up to that time.

Christ Himself instituted seven Sacraments which are defined as Sensible (i.e. observable) Signs which Impart Internal Grace to the individual. These seven were discussed earlier: See Part II, Chapter 18.

During the lifetime of the Apostles, additional Truths came to light. However, the Tradition of the Church has maintained for two thousand plus years that the Deposit of Faith was complete with the death of the last Apostle—i.e. the Revelations God has given to His people were closed for all time. (See Revelations 23:18)

Even the revelations given to individual saints were simply fuller explanations of Truths already revealed. Christ left behind a body of knowledge which He wanted His Church to provide to her people as she took the Gospel to all nations. That truism was expressed when St. Paul commanded Timothy, "Guard the Deposit." (1 Tim. 6:20; 2 Tim. 1:14) When Pope John XXIII convoked the Second Vatican Council, I am sure he did not know the extent to which the Heresy of Modernism had tainted the minds of the Fathers of the Council. It was said that the Pope was astounded at what can only be described as the 'Modernist' thinking which was so much part of the debate. It finally took Pope Paul VI to make certain appropriate changes and then to close the Council. Under the guidance of the Holy Spirit, the Council said what God Himself willed it to say.

The Documents of Vatican Council II

The Second Vatican Council (1962—1965), which identified itself as a *Pastoral Constitution on the Church in the Modern World,* immersed itself into American society at a time when the Catholic Church in the U.S. was tainted by its own form of politics among the bishops, Ugly Americanism, the Heresy of Americanism, the Heresy of Modernism, Feminism, and its own peculiar kind of Patriotism. Because of these inclinations, the documents of Vatican II were vastly misinterpreted, with different groups focusing on whatever their particular bias happens to be. Human nature and journalism being what they are, it is not at all surprising that the misinterpretations have been more widely disseminated than have the calmer, more objective interpretations which emanate from the two thousand year history of unchanging doctrine.

For example, there were (and are) those who think that the major emphasis of the Council had to do with Ecumenism. Those who thought that way would focus on that part of the Council and ignore everything else. This perception had a seminary professor in Chicago telling me, as I already said, that we had to forget the Real Presence if we were to have any real success with Ecumenism; to favor his particular bias, he was ready to destroy the core of the Catholic Church. These attitudes had Father Colonnese saying that "we don't believe in mortal sin anymore," constantly talking about the "signs of the times," words actually taken from the Council documents but he used them to promote a non-religious agenda in shaping relationships with the Church in Latin America or changing it. I suppose it was these same attitudes which had priests (and at least one bishop), in their private interpretation of the 'signs of the times' supporting abortion and contraception as 'made in America' methods of birth control. It had a bishop proclaim that the Pope is the Bishop of Rome: "He can do what he wants in Rome, I'll do what I want here." Another bishop: "We don't believe that there is the Real Presence in the crumbs, because the crumbs do not have the appearance of bread"—in contradiction of the Council of Trent which clearly and infallibly stated otherwise. And so on and on . . . and on.

For some reason, known perhaps only to God and Satan, those who were tainted with Modernism leaped upon the documents of Vatican Council II, found their favorite subject and then utterly misinterpreted it. Weakened by all the 'isms'—as enumerated just above—they interpreted what they read in the way they *wanted* to read it, rather than what the Council text actually said. This is man, once again, creating God in his own image.

What they did—and do—had specific earmarks of Protestantism and its prejudicial reading of the Scriptures. Their (very human?) tendency is to concentrate only on those texts which, they believe, support their position, and to ignore or blatantly misinterpret those passages which would not substantiate their position.

As an example, I recently spent a good deal of time discussing Catholicism with a young Calvinist. His name was Moses. He wanted to know more about the Catholic Church, he said. On one occasion, as together we contemplated the Promise of the Eucharist in the Gospel of St. John (6: 35-71) we could see that Christ repeated approximately eight times that unless his followers eat His Flesh and drink His Blood, they cannot be saved. The text clearly said that his disciples began to leave him because they could not imagine this to be true. How could they eat the flesh and drink the blood of this robust man before them? It must have sounded to them like cannibalism. This young Calvinist, as we talked, interpreted the text as saying that the disciples left because Christ said no one can come to Him unless the Father draws him. He was blind to the actual interpretation, no matter how often I pointed out the obvious meaning. He himself, with his failure to understand what was before his eyes, was a clear example of what Christ meant when He said that no one can come to Him unless the Father draws him. The ability to understand the content of Revelation is a matter of the grace of God working in each of us. Weak human reasoning can't understand it in its fullness.

To continue on that same subject: There are four levels of human knowledge:

1) sensory knowledge, i.e. sight, hearing, touch, taste;
2) reason, intelligence;
3) prophetic knowledge attained by those in the State of Grace with the indwelling of the Holy Spirit and the Trinity—theirs is a knowledge that goes beyond the weak human mind; in prophetic knowledge there are many levels of understanding depending upon the person's participation in the spiritual life and closeness to God.
4) The Beatific Vision, when those of us who are saved see God face to face, and all knowledge is before us.

When the documents of Vatican Council II were available, I did my own private and complete study of their contents. With my Licentiate in Theology obtained after four years at the Gregorian University in 1954, and my Doctorate in Canon Law after three years of study at the Lateran University (1957), I felt fully qualified to do so. When I had completed my analysis, I stood in awe of what I had read: All the doctrines of the Church established at the time of Christ and the Apostles—moral and dogmatic theology—were explicitly retained unchanged, and it was written in modern language, easily understandable. This was inescapably beyond the abilities of the human mind, no matter how intelligent nor how many such people were involved. As a matter of faith, we know that the Holy Spirit ensured that the Council documents contained exactly what God Himself wanted.

It must be concluded that the central theme, the core issue, of Vatican Council II is the Universal Call to Holiness in the

Church. Depending on individual prejudices, the interpretation of the Council's documents has ignored the call to holiness and concentrated on what the Council identifies as the *tools*, for that level of holiness, e.g. Ecumenism, to bring other faiths into the Church; Judaism (Nostra Aetate), to absolve the Jews of today from charges of the death of Christ; Muslims, to hail their recognition of the One True God, and of the Blessed Virgin. The Council also emphasizes the Laity and the Apostolate of the Laity, to call for their spiritual immersion into the world. The true spirit of the Vatican Council has been ignored by many as they call for the Catholic Church to modify itself in order to become more acceptable to those of other faiths. I cite again the example of the Mundelein Seminary professor in Chicago who said "we must ignore the Real Presence if we are to have any true Ecumenism." In effect he was saying, 'we must destroy the Catholic Church if we expect any other faith to join us." This was the voice of the true Modernist. There are converted (Catholic) Jews who say that in becoming Catholic they become more Jewish, or they bring Jewish rites into their lives, such as the Seder meal which brings true meaning into the Holy Thursday services, even though to do so is contrary to the decrees of the Council of Florence. There are those who make their own determination of what the 'Signs of the Times' are and strongly urge that both abortion and artificial contraception are permissible, e.g. Rev. Charles Curran some years ago in Washington, D.C. who presented himself as a 'Theologian.' Among a very vocal minority of both bishops and priests is the urge to 'modernize' the Church in its moral and dogmatic theology and in its liturgy. Some bishops and some clergy very loudly promote doctrinal error. In this atmosphere, the true Catholic finds it difficult to maintain his or her faith in its true form, composed as it must be of the Eternal Truths which have been handed down by Christ to His Apostles.

It has been the doctrine of the Church since the time of Christ that the Deposit of Revelation was closed with the death of the last Apostle. Therefore, no amount of wishful thinking can change the

Moral and Dogmatic Theology of the Church. The documents of Vatican Council II must be read and interpreted in the light of those two thousand years of constant adherence to the teachings of Christ who said that even though heaven and earth will pass away, His words will never pass away.

Misplaced Patriotism

> "Render unto Caesar the things which are Caesar's, and unto God the things that are God's" (Matthew 22:21).

With those words, Christ, whose words will never pass away, established what the relationship should be between His followers and the government of the country in which they live and in which they are citizens. It is important to remember that even that government in all its power is God's. Pilate said to Christ before he was given up to die that he had the power to put Christ to death. Christ said to him that he would not have that power unless it was given to him from on high (John 19:11). Therefore, even the civil government in any sovereign country in the world belongs to God. A Catholic, therefore, has a dual citizenship: A member of the Church and a member of the civil society in which he resides.

It is important, however, to understand fully what the priority between the two-fold 'citizenship' really is. The truly devout Catholic will ardently believe the principles upon which the United States was founded and which are incorporated in her Constitution. Therefore such a person will be intensely patriotic. If that civil society should stray from those principles, led either by the government or by groups within society, then the Catholic in true patriotism both to his Church and to his country must fight against those false principles. And yet, for example, how many Catholics actively join in the fight against abortion? How many priests and bishops do so? In my own direct experience, the answer is: Far too few. Even one who 'tolerates' abortion would be too many. It may well go into the tens, the 50s, even the hundreds. We have been badly wounded by the enemies of the Church—enemies of the Mystical Body of Christ—but even if the Church becomes even more disastrously wounded than she is now, she will 'resurrect' again as did the physical body of Christ, because Christ promised that he would be with His Church "until the end of days." (See Matthew 28:20)

Our devotion to God must take precedence over our dedication to our country, which should be a matter of simple common sense. Unfortunately, though, it doesn't seem to work that way. In the days in which I was national director of the Papal Volunteer program, I met with a bishop in Peru who was only recently selected by the Pope to be a bishop, was newly ordained as a bishop, and, within the past few months, had been assigned to his diocese. He was American born, but had served as a missionary in Peru for many years and was therefore fully acculturated, completely fluent in Peruvian Spanish. As we talked, he told me something I hadn't heard: In order to serve as a bishop in that country, Peruvian law required that he give up his American citizenship and become a citizen of Peru. He had done so. With tears in his eyes, he told me that he felt as if he had killed his own mother. I told him that I felt sorry for him because of his sacrifice, and that of course he did the right thing because his service in the Catholic Church was the higher calling. I've done my best not to pass judgment on him, because, after all, he made the right decision: To serve God rather than his country. But, having become comfortable in several cultures—the Italian, German, British, Swiss, Austrian, and several Latin American countries—I don't believe if I were called by the Church which Christ founded that I would have any major difficulty in adopting any other culture in which I could live with reasonable comfort, giving up my U.S. citizenship. Not that I would want to. Since my many years of living, studying and working in other countries, I have always been aware of a subtle underlying dissatisfaction that we do not have in this country many of the indisputably advantageous elements which I experienced in those cultures.

Various attitudes of mind can be considered associated with the concept of Misplaced Patriotism and will illustrate the dimensions of the problem. For example, Judaism. I will address this concept much more completely later in this book. But I had the opportunity a few years ago, over a period of about six months, to communicate by letter, telephone and email with David Moss, a converted Jew, who was taking his organization not only close to the edges of heresy, but, in some ways, is directly involved in heresy. At some point in our six months of communication, I asked him two questions: 1) Did he agree with my definition of the Magisterium of the Church, and he said he did: "I understand and am in agreement with your description of the Magisterium." 2) I asked him which is more important to him: Retaining his Jewish identity, or being a Catholic? Depending on one's mind-set and hidden loyalties, this can be a difficult question, but the only acceptable answer should be obvious. His answer to this question was: ". . . in response to your question about what is most important to me, the answer is simple: that I am in union with our Lord and Saviour in accord with the teachings and discipline of His Catholic Church." I suppose in his own mind, this settled the matter. But to me it was a non-answer. A direct answer could only be: "It is more important for me to be a Jew" or "It is more important for me to be a Catholic." In other words, he waffled and he is not completely the Catholic Jesus Christ wants him to be.

Pope Benedict XVI can be a major role model in this regard. When he was asked by journalists during his visit to Poland how he felt about visiting Auschwitz as a German, ". . . the 79 year-old Benedict said, 'I am above all a Catholic. I must say that this is the most important point.'" (Reported by Victor L. Simpson of the Associated Press, May 26, 2006.)

The Pope's response was incredibly direct, honest and humble. I take for granted that most of us will fail to reach that level of humility. He could have said, "I am the Pope, after all." Or he could have said, "I have been a Cardinal . . . a Bishop . . . a priest . . . ." Or "I was never associated with the Nazi party." Or "I am a Head of State." He was simply saying (to paraphrase), "I am simply a member of the Roman Catholic Church; nothing else is that important."

Which is More Important: To Be a Catholic, or To Be an American?

As I said above, depending on one's mind-set and hidden loyalties, this can be a difficult question, but the only acceptable answer should be obvious. I suggest that all Catholics—Cardinals, bishops, priests, religious and laity—ponder this question and determine at the deepest level of their consciousness what their answer *really* is. If every Catholic in the United States were asked this question—again, Cardinals, bishops, priests, religious, laity—I wonder what the answer would be. Personally, based on the many contacts I have had, I believe there would be a diversity of answers: 1) Some who have a well-grounded understanding of Catholic Theology would give the answer that it is much more important to be a Catholic than to be an American. For some of these, and I believe a very few, it would be not only an intellectual answer, but also a profoundly heartfelt personal part of their total Faith. 2) For many others, I fear, they would say that it is more important to be a Catholic, but it would be simply an intellectual 'politically correct' statement. They would know that *Theologically* the Church founded by Christ Himself is the most important society on earth, therefore it stands above all civil societies; yet they 'feel' otherwise. 3) Yet another group would be badly torn by the question, somewhat like the American bishop of a Peruvian diocese, and they might, with tears in their eyes, acknowledge reluctantly that it is more important to be a Catholic. 4) Another group would answer, in varying degrees, that it is more important to be an American, or at least equally important, or 5) they would dodge the issue much as David Moss did. These are the members who would (will) as soon as possible be involved in the creation of the *American* Catholic Church, which, in its independence, they feel, will be better equipped than the Vatican and the Pope to organize and lead the Catholic Church in the United States.

What I have just now written I base on the many contacts I have made over the years. But there is another measure which I present to you now. The following is truly frightening:

According to the Catholic Radio
Association (November 2006):

- only 10%of lay religious teachers accept Church teaching on contraception;
- 53% believe a Catholic can have an abortion and remain a good Catholic;
- 65% believe that Catholics may divorce and remarry
- 77% believe one can be a good Catholic without going to Mass on Sundays;
- a New York Times poll found that 70% of all Catholics (age group 18-44) believe the Eucharist is merely a "symbolic reminder" of Jesus.

Aside from a recent mailing from them, I did not at the time know anything about the Catholic Radio Association, but if their figures are only half right, it's all very ominous. What a wonderful thing it would be for all *bona fide* Catholic laity and apostolic lay organizations to undertake the re-education of their fellow Catholics. (These statistics will be considered in greater depth in Part VII.)

Looking once again at those figures from the Catholic Radio Association, when one considers the atmosphere in which we live, it should perhaps be not at all surprising. Most of us, if not all, are tainted with a number of 'isms' which we have lived with since our early years: Ugly Americanism (after all, we are the only superpower left in the world); the Heresy of Americanism (as the leading power in the world, we should be the predominant figure on the landscape and there's no need for us to be subservient to the Vatican); the Heresy of Modernism (trash the 2000 year old doctrines of the Church and bring them up to date so that they're in tune with the modern world). There is also politics among the bishops—what a strong group among the bishops proposes is likely to be supported by the weaker ones. The widespread and very public misinterpretations of Vatican Council II is a major factor. False Ecumenism (meaning: if the various religious groups are ever to be united, then we must downplay certain truisms of the Roman Catholic Church and accept the often repeated thought that all religions are equal). Etc.

Tolerance

The Catholic Catechism lists eight virtues. Most protestant religions identify the same ones. The Jewish, Muslim and Hindu religions recognize their own. But all are similar. Nowhere does one find a virtue called 'Tolerance.' I believe that only in the U.S. culture has tolerance been elevated to the level of a virtue. As such, it detracts from and contaminates the purity of the Roman Catholic Church in this country, and it derogates from the pure virtue of Charity.

We in the U.S. were founded in diversity. Because of this, over the years, we have adopted an attitude of tolerance toward all other persons, whatever their ethnic origin, whatever their religion, whatever their philosophy of life. And we accept the fact that the U.S. law is supposed to apply toward all persons no matter who they are. And, we think unconsciously, if it is the law of the land, then it must be accepted as applying to all with equal impact. In simpler terms, we are conditioned to 'put up with' whatever other people do, so long as it is not unlawful, no matter how repulsive it may be to us.

Unfortunately, this has tainted our attitudes even in something so immorally monstrous as abortion on demand. We can and should tolerate, *i.e.* have charity toward, the sinner, and pray for him or her, but we must never tolerate the sin and should fight against it with all our strength. Abortion is murder, pure and simple. Yet as a culture we have permitted ***fifty three million*** babies to be murdered in the womb since Roe v. Wade. And we accuse other cultures of atrocities when they put perhaps a few thousands of their innocent citizens to death. As we should. Because to murder even one innocent person, let alone five or five thousand is a crime that cries out to heaven for vengeance. But as we point the finger of blame at other societies, we must remember that *three* fingers point back at ourselves.

Christ said that we should render unto Caesar the things that are Caesar's, and we should render unto God the things that are God's. We in the United States seem to have gone overboard in rendering unto Caesar many of the things which are God's. Surely the lives of the unborn belong to God, who created each soul at the moment of conception, yet our society takes their lives by law and without compunction. According to various studies, 53% or 54% of Catholics in recent years have voted for politicians who are publicly pro-abortion, and even for self-styled 'Catholic' politicians who support abortion. Something is dramatically amiss with the Catholics in the U.S. society when they allow things like this to occur. And we can only point to the bishops and clergy who have failed to address these problems with the people they are responsible for.

For example, I wonder what kind of Catholic is the Most Rev. George H. Niederauer, current Archbishop of San Francisco, who without saying much (as far as I know) allows Nancy Pelosi, one of our most powerful politicians, clearly a feminist proponent of abortion, to call herself a 'Catholic.' She publicly misinterpreted the Fathers of the Church (she's hardly a theologian) and tried to find support for abortion from that source. Of course, if he were to publicly denounce her, he might be fearful of the consequences. St. Peter was afraid to be associated with Christ and denied Him, but later redeemed himself. Any bishop can be afraid to deal with the powerful politics of the United States. But surely they should take whatever steps are required to redeem themselves if necessary.

A succession of archbishops of Boston allowed the politically and financially powerful dynasty of the 'Catholic' Kennedys to support abortion on demand, and, again as far as I know, those archbishops did little to oppose the Kennedy position. Even Cardinal Law, whom I saw forthrightly oppose a group of Modernist priests who were seeking salaries equal to those of the top executives of major corporations, did little, if anything—as far as I know—to oppose the Kennedy pro-abortion philosophy, and, unfortunately, he appeared publicly at the site of an abortion clinic which had been bombed and, in effect, he apologized for the atrocity, as if the Catholic Church had committed the barbarity.

I believe it is the very American concept of tolerance which leads to these kinds of 'political' activities on the part of the leaders of the Catholic Church in the United States.

Another bishop I know (I won't mention his name because I personally did not hear him say it), defended a 'Catholic' politician, because, he said that politician in his personal and private life is opposed to abortion, but, must support abortion publicly because of his obligations to his constituents. Again, if I'm not mistaken, this is an example of the 'American virtue' of tolerance.

Should not that bishop have insisted on the obligation of every Catholic lay person, including every politician, to live an *apostolic* life in the workday world? This means, of course, that we all are conscience bound to oppose whatever is immoral, and, in the case of a public person like a politician, to do so publicly.

I wonder how many 'Catholic' politicians who support abortion on demand, and the bishops and clergy who defend them (such as the bishop just mentioned) ever give much thought to the concept of ***scandal***. The definition of Scandal: A word or action evil in itself, which occasions another's spiritual ruin. Apparently neither do they think of ***complicity***, i.e. participating in the sin of another.

In this context we can think of people like Sen. John Kerry, the late Sen. Ted Kennedy, Vice President Joseph Biden, former Speaker of the House Nancy Pelosi, and many others, all of whom support abortion and allow it to be publicly known that they think of themselves as "Catholics." I recently found a web page entitled "U.S. Catholic Politicians." It was last modified on Nov. 11, 2005. There were 35 pages of names, listing all from the 50 states. There were about 50 names per page, therefore about one thousand seven hundred fifty politicians—mostly senators and congressmen if I'm not mistaken. As an aside, if such a large number of Catholic politicians, were to live their lives as lay apostles (obeying the command of Christ, "Go forth and preach the gospel to all nations, baptizing them . . . .") then this nation could quickly become *truly* great, as they believe it already is.

The point I want to make is that if (perhaps I should say 'when') a young woman with an unwanted pregnancy is aware that a publicly well-known 'Catholic' figure supports abortion and is therefore influenced to procure an abortion, there is at least a certain amount of scandal committed by that public figure. It must also be said that the bishop or priest who defends the abortion stance of that politician (for example, see above: ". . . in his personal and private life, he doesn't believe in abortion, but publicly he is responsible to his constituents.") Those public politicians and the bishops and priests who defend them, insofar as they influence a woman to abort the child in her womb, are they not in some fashion complicit in, *i.e.* guilty of, the murder of that unborn child? In addition to everything else, in weighing the heinousness of the sin of abortion, we must take into account that the child's life is ended without the possibility of baptism. We can only hope, as some theologians *believe*, that God gives such a baby the full use of his or her reason before death in order to make an act of the will to receive Baptism of Desire.

It is important that Catholics be aware of and fight against the verbiage that pro-abortionists have developed to soften the evil that abortion really is. I recently heard a Catholic talk show host succumb to that force by speaking of the fetus in the womb as "a potential human being." In actual fact, from the moment of conception, because God has created a soul, the fetus is an ***actual*** human being, going through the first of his or her many phases of life, preparing for a more independent life outside the womb. The phrase "potential human being" is designed to reduce the horror of killing an actual immortal creature of God.

Only God can accurately judge the consciences of such politicians, bishops and priests (and perhaps I should add lay feminist groups). God is infinitely just, and at the same time He is infinitely merciful. Our weak human minds cannot understand how these divine attributes mysteriously interact as God scrutinizes the individual conscience. One can only hope that our poor human understanding will allow the Mercy of God to favor the individual who has not foreseen the consequences of what he has done or failed to do.

And now on to another American attitude which is interpreted by some within the Heresy of Modernism as the most important emphasis of Vatican Council II.

Ecumenism

There have been and are many priests and bishops, tainted with the Heresy of Modernism, for whom Ecumenism is the primary message and call to action of Vatican Council II. Such people apparently are willing to discard all the doctrines of the Church in order to promote their pet project which is Ecumenism. As is presented in some depth elsewhere (see Part II, Chapter 18), the ***Core of the Roman Catholic Church*** is the Sacrament of the Eucharist, the Sacrifice of the Mass, the rock-solid belief in the Real Presence of Jesus Christ, body and blood, soul and divinity in the bread and wine which is consecrated in the course of the Holy Mass. If this sacrament and this Real Presence is cast aside, we have nothing left. In effect, we become a protestant church. If we allow this, we have become victims of what, as you have seen, I refer to as the ***Judas Syndrome***. Judas, unlike the rest of the Apostles, could not bring himself to believe what Christ repeated over and over: Unless we eat His flesh and drink His blood, we cannot have everlasting life. It is sad to think that there are perhaps many who would give up that central truism in order to fulfil their own erroneous definition of Ecumenism. How many priests and how many bishops (and laity?), in their heart of hearts, actually feel this way? I hope that those who do will read these lines and re-think their theology.

Ecumenism became a strong subject for discussion during my years in the study of Theology in Rome. It became something of a 'pet idea' among some of my seminary colleagues sixty years ago. One of our professors, aware of the intense discussion among his students, said "The barque of Ecumenism will founder on the rock of the Real Presence." But he might have added, "In some cases the Rock of the Real Presence will be shattered by the torpedo of ecumenism"—witness, for example the Mundelein Seminary professor who said to me that we must forget or set aside the Real Presence in order to foster ecumenism.

Within the documents of Vatican Council II, the Decree on Ecumenism presents its approach to Ecumenism very carefully (Decree on Ecumenism: *unitatis redintegratio*). Following are excerpts from the decree:

Introduction

1. The restoration of unity among all Christians is one of the principal concerns of the Second Vatican Council. Christ the Lord founded one Church and one Church only.

CHAPTER II—
THE PRACTICE OF ECUMENISM

5. The attainment of union is the concern of the whole Church, faithful and shepherds alike . . . .

6. Every renewal of the Church is essentially grounded in an increase of fidelity to her own calling. Undoubtedly this is the basis of the movement toward unity.
7. There can be no ecumenism worthy of the name without a change of heart. For it is from renewal of the inner life of our minds, from self-denial and an unstinted love that desires of unity take their rise and develop in a mature way. We should therefore pray to the Holy Spirit for the grace to be genuinely self-denying, humble, gentle in the service of others, and to have an attitude of brotherly generosity towards them. St. Paul says: "I, therefore, a prisoner for the Lord, beg you to lead a life worthy of the calling to which you have been called, with all humility and meekness, with patience, forbearing one another in love, eager to maintain the unity of the spirit in the bond of peace". This exhortation is directed especially to those raised to sacred Orders precisely that the work of Christ may be continued. He came among us "not to be served but to serve".

   All the faithful should remember that the more effort they make to live holier lives according to the Gospel, the better will they further Christian unity and put it into practice. For the closer their union with the Father, the Word, and the Spirit, the more deeply and easily will they be able to grow in mutual brotherly love.
11. The way and method in which the Catholic faith is expressed should never become an obstacle to dialogue with our brethren.

   It is, of course, essential that the doctrine should be clearly presented in its entirety. Nothing is so foreign to the spirit of ecumenism as a false irenicism, in which the purity of Catholic doctrine suffers loss and its genuine and certain meaning is clouded. *(*Emphasis added*)*

I saw it myself: certain priests and theologians leaped upon the inclusion of Ecumenism by Vatican Council II, especially the sentence: "The restoration of unity among all Christians is one of the principal concerns of the Second Vatican Council" (cf. Introduction above). The professor at Mundelein Seminary in Chicago told me "We have to set aside the Real Presence if we are to have any kind of Ecumenism." The representative from the Council of Churches, after I had enumerated the doctrines of the Catholic Church which had to be acknowledged as unchangeable as the various churches discussed Ecumenism, told me "You are the only honest man I have talked to here." He had talked to about twenty (modernist) priests and one (modernist) bishop. All, I deduce from what he said, expressed their willingness to compromise the doctrinal positions of the Catholic Church in order to proceed toward unity of the Christian churches. As someone put it: ". . . certain priests and theologians . . . became interested in this 'Movement of Unity,' and that many were literally straining at the leash to take part." The Decree on Ecumenism must be studied carefully and in depth. It contains all the admonitions and cautions which Pope Pius XI identified in his 1928 encyclical Mortalium Animos (*On fostering true religious unity*). Primarily, the encyclical warns against the temptation, in the effort to promote unity, to compromise or 'soften' Catholic doctrine in an effort to accommodate to our non-Catholic brethren's thinking. Pope Pius XII also sounded the alarm to this error in his great 1950 encyclical ***Humani Generis*** (*Treating certain false opinions that threaten to ruin the foundations of the Catholic Faith*). He warned of those who wished to "reduce to a minimum the meaning of Catholic dogmas . . ." and "the desire to do away with the barriers that divide good and honest men." Pope Pius XII cited the "serious danger" in the Movement toward Unity (i.e. Ecumenism) because "it is concealed beneath the mask of virtue."(See *Humani Generis* par. 12 ff).

Pope St. Pius X identified Modernism as a heresy within the Church, described it as the synthesis of all heresies, and condemned it as such. He also pronounced it as being alive and well "within the very bosom of the Church." It has been speculated that Modernist members of Vatican Council II—bishops and *periti* (experts)—'pushed through' the Decree on Ecumenism. Personally, I do not believe that anything is 'pushed through' any ecumenical council, because it is the Holy Spirit who ensures the content which God Himself wants. The providential oversight of a council is perhaps identical to—certainly similar to—the inspired nature of the Holy Scriptures: God so inspires the human writer so that he writes in his own style, but writes exactly what God Himself wants to reveal. When the Pope ultimately approves the documents of that ecumenical council, which was done by Pope Paul VI, we therefore know that it is the infallible Word of God.

Ecumenism, properly understood and promoted, is nothing else than one of the tools which the Church can use to pursue the final command of Christ: "Going forth, preach the Gospel to the entire world . . . ." Quite clearly, He meant not only every nation in the world, but He meant the Jews, Muslims, separated brethren, heretics, schismatics, atheists . . ., everyone, in other words, without exception. And he prayed that those who follow Him might be one . . . "as you and I, Father, are one." He wanted them all to be one as members of the Church He founded—which is His own Mystical Body. Ecumenism, therefore, in the only acceptable definition of the word, means to bring about the conversion of all peoples into His Church.

In bringing into the documents of Vatican Council II what they wanted so badly to have—the Decree on Ecumenism—those Modernists who promoted it began immediately to attach their own definition to it, namely to 'modernize' the doctrines of the Church, to 'change' them and 'amend' them so as to make them more palatable to our separated brethren.

The way that Modernists before, during and after Vatican II have promoted and interpreted Ecumenism is absurd. How could any true Catholic accept the preposterous notion that an acceptable religious unity is possible by denying any part of God's revelation concerning

Himself, His Church, and our salvation? It's as if two thousand years of Catholic Teaching and Tradition should give way to the 'magnificent modern idea' of ecumenism. It's as if the proponents of false Ecumenism are saying: "Ecumenism must increase, and the Church founded by Christ Himself must decrease."

But the Holy Spirit, perceiving the progress of the Church founded by Christ from the vantage point of Eternity, determined that the time was at hand for the churches once again to reunite. He therefore used the enthusiasm of those in error to bring Ecumenism strongly into the Church so that it can become a tool to bring the masses of non-Catholics back into the true Faith. God, we have been told so often, works in wondrous and mysterious ways.

The Decree itself provides all the safeguards required to obviate the errors which Pope Pius XI and Pope Pius XII warned against. Any person—bishop, priest, religious, and lay person—as a matter of conscience should study the Decree on Ecumenism carefully and look for all the safeguards which are designed to ensure that the dogmas and doctrines of the Catholic Church will remain exactly what they are and have been since the time of Christ. The central safeguard, of course, is to observe the principal message of the Council: That we are all to strive as never before to achieve personal, spiritual holiness. If we succeed in doing that, all religious people will be drawn toward us and begin to join us. The personal holiness of every member of the Catholic Church and complete adherence to her traditions is the key to the only valid form of Ecumenism.

In my years as PAVLA director I met with and spoke to many bishops, diocesan priests and order priests, many religious men and women and certain specialized lay groups—both in the United States and in the countries of Latin America. In the United States, I encountered many bishops, and many more diocesan and religious order priests, a large number of women religious who espoused Ecumenism in its erroneous forms as described and denounced by Popes Pius XI and Pius XII. With a good deal of mixed emotions I must report that I encountered no cases of false Ecumenism in Latin

America, neither among her bishops, clergy and religious—except in a lesser degree among the *American* missionaries, men and women.

Judaism

The Jews have succeeded in intimidating most of the Christian world—and much of the rest of the world. The holocaust, of course, was certainly one of the most heinous crimes ever perpetrated in the history of humanity. I don't know from any personal research how many Jews lost their lives in that barbarity. Perhaps it was the millions the Jews have put forth; perhaps they exaggerated the number. Whatever the number, it was a profoundly horrifying episode in history. It has been said recently that Mao Tse Tung put 80 million people to death. If that is true, then the Jewish holocaust comes at least second to it. However, another outstanding example of horrifying atrocities is the number of innocent children put to death in this country since Roe v. Wade. The number is commonly estimated at ***fifty three million,*** which makes the United States the perpetrator of one of the world's great atrocities. There are those, of course, who respond that abortion on demand is 'legal' in this country. But the real question is, is it morally justified? There were those in Germany at the time of Hitler who would say (did say) that the extermination of Jews was 'legal.'

The Jews have adroitly used the holocaust to build sympathy for themselves. It has been and continues to be a masterful effort at public relations so that almost any criticism of the Jews is branded as 'anti-semitic.' This has become such an ugly concept that almost everyone bends great energy in order to avoid being stigmatized with it. It is entirely true, of course, that a person can be 'anti-error' when the error is perpetrated by a Jew and not be at all 'anti-semitic.'

The power of this stratagem—branding people as antisemitic—cannot be overrated. It induced William Cardinal Keeler, Archbishop of Baltimore (who was two years behind me in Theology in Rome) to approve a theological error. Since I personally observed how these things work, I assume that the error was formulated by the appropriate group of (Modernist) priests in the United States Catholic Conference who were acting out of their ecumenical enthusiasm. At any rate, however it came about, he approved a statement which stated more or less the following: The Jews, since they were still living under the earlier covenant made with them by God, can be saved without being baptized. But according to Christ Himself, the New Covenant which He announced at the Last Supper superceded the Old Covenant; subsequently, all the Sacraments, including Baptism, were instituted by Him. As I observed myself during my years at the USCC, the Modernist priests of that organization proposed material for the bishops to approve—which they commonly did in something of a 'rubber stamp' mode. I reported similar incidents earlier in this writing. Unfortunately, at the time, there was a Cardinal in the Vatican who took the same position, *i.e.* that the Jews did not need to be baptized. If this wasn't heretical, it was at the very least the deepest kind of theological error. According to the Acts of the Apostles and other parts of the New Testament, thousands of Jews were baptized and thus became, as they were called in those days, 'Followers of Christ.'

The Greatest Atrocity of All Time (and Eternity?)

Far outstripping both of those inhumanities, *i.e.* the holocaust and the atrocities of Mao Tse Tung, and even the millions of abortions in this country, was the crucifixion of Christ, the incarnate Son of God, second Person of the Holy Trinity—in other words, God Himself was tortured and put to death at the instigation of an angry mob of Jews. They put to death the Man who proved He was God by the many miracles He performed, in spite of the general knowledge in the land about those miracles, His acts of kindness, in Whom Pilate found no fault, and Who fulfilled in Himself the prophecies about the Messiah. What greater atrocity can there be than for His own creatures to kill the God Who came among them to save them? As He hung on the cross, He said, "Father, forgive them, for they know not what they do."

Is there a strong percentage of the Jews who have an inkling that Christ was indeed the Messiah? I believe this to be so. Do they continue to deny that Christ is God in order to assuage the guilt feeling that may be under the surface in each of them? It seems to me that I saw among Jews in my active years in the priesthood that they were looking to the Catholic Church to give them some kind of absolution from this guilt feeling.

The Catholic Church has recognized from the very beginning that not all Jews took part in the crucifixion of Christ. In fact, it was a small percentage who actively promoted His death. And the Church has recognized that the Jews since the time of Christ have no responsibility for His death. Vatican Council II explicitly states this to be true. I strongly suggest, however, that all Jews individually, even those who have become Catholic, should examine their minds and hearts in great depth to determine if there is some residue of discomfort in the realization that it was *their people* who were responsible for the crucifixion. They might use as a somewhat similar example the very race of people whose forbears were responsible for the holocaust. I spent many years visiting relatives in Germany. I saw then what I saw recently: Germany is a *wounded* culture. While no one in the modern world attributes the rise of Hitler and the atrocities committed by him and the Nazis to the modern day German, all Germans are painfully aware that it was *their people* who allowed him to take power and, over a protracted period of time, commit a series of atrocities which the world will never forget. I believe that evidence of this deep-seated and enduring guilt lies in the German legislation which recognizes denial of the holocaust as a heavily punishable crime. The German nation continues to make atonement.

In a similar fashion, I believe that the Jewish people are a *wounded culture*, knowing as they do that it was *their people* who put

Christ to death. It can therefore be important to them to deny that Christ was the Messiah even though all the prophecies of the Old Testament were fulfilled in Him. In their denial that Christ was God, it follows that there is no need to become His followers. And even some (many?) of those who have become Catholic find it difficult to completely leave the Jewish religious practices behind. They need to embrace one of Christ's most famous sayings, "The truth will set you free." If they can face how they *really* feel, they can finally do what all Jews should have done at the time when Christ walked among them—become His followers.

We will return to the subject of converted Jews in the next major section of this book.

Feminism

The feminist movement has led at least one bishop astray, and very likely a goodly number of priests. On the face of it, feminism is a good thing, calling as it does for equality for women in the social order. It is defined as a) the theory of the political, economic, and social equality of the sexes; and b) organized activity on behalf of women's rights and interests.

However, somewhat akin to Ecumenism, its enthusiastic promoters have led the movement in strange directions. I have the impression that nearly every feminist is pro-abortion. I'm sure there are exceptions, but feminism seems to harden a woman's heart and convinces her that she should have her own choice whether to let a child grow in her womb. Such a woman doesn't seem to stop to think that she had a prior choice not to have had sexual relations—which, in the light of the Sixth Commandment, is the only valid and acceptable pro-choice stance.

If she were to use artificial contraceptives, that too is morally unacceptable even if she is married. In the case of the killing of the innocent unborn, at least God exercised His Will to create a soul, and we hope that soul will be given the full use of his or her reason and the opportunity to receive Baptism of Desire. In the case of artificial contraception, the will of God is thwarted and He has no occasion to create a soul. It is difficult for the very limited human mind to know which is more morally reprehensible—artificial contraception or abortion. Many Catholics in the U.S. seem to have convinced themselves that contraception is acceptable in order to limit the size of families. A few priests have told me that for several years they have never heard contraception confessed in the confessional.

One of my unforgettable experiences took place in Brazil. An American Religious Order woman—a nun—who, while arguing with me against the Papal Volunteer program, was clearly in Brazil not to enhance the spiritual lives of those among whom she worked, but rather to promote feminism, which was unacceptable in the Brazilian culture.

Another unforgettable incident was at a Mass I attended (I had celebrated my own Mass earlier), a nun in her habit stood at the door of the chapel on some kind of guard duty. She was built like a smaller-scale football fullback, and carried herself like a man who lifted weights—arms somewhat akimbo, shoulders squared, with a determined and dedicated scowl on her face. She had a mission. Her mission was to tell everyone who came into the chapel that anyone who received communion was to receive in the hand and not on the tongue. One had the impression that this was vital, not only to her, but also to the celebrant of the Mass. In her mind, apparently, this was a *dogmatic* change that had to occur in the Church. Her behavior was most unseemly.

Feminist groups have sought ordination to the priesthood. The Vatican has declared such ordinations to be invalid, and have declared that there is an automatic excommunication levied on both the woman who permits the ordination ceremony and on the bishop who performs it.

There was a bishop (now deceased) who had declared that he would never ordain another seminarian to the priesthood until and unless the Vatican permits the ordination of women. Obviously he contributed somewhat to the shortage of priests in recent years. I wonder how many bishops (and priests) have been affected by the Feminist movement to believe that women should be ordained as priests.

Many religious orders of women no longer wear the religious habit, but have allowed their hair to grow, have their hair done, wear shorter skirts, and generally dress like women of the world. The only thing that identifies them as nuns, perhaps, is that some wear a cross which hangs around their necks. It used to be, many years ago, that a nun, dressed in her religious garb, could safely walk through any section of any city in this country and be absolutely safe because they were revered and respected. This remains true for those who have retained their religious habits, but they have become few and far between.

Do they think any more of the Blessed Virgin Mary, Mother of God, who is the most respected and revered woman ever born—simply the greatest woman who has ever lived. For all eternity, she is intertwined with the Trinity in a way that no other human person can ever be: She is the daughter of the Father, spouse of the Holy Spirit, and the Mother of the Son. It is defineable doctrine, in addition to all the things which have been defined about her, that she is the Mediatrix of all Graces. As Jesus Christ came to us through her, so every grace which comes to us in the world comes to us through her. This continues what started at the wedding feast in Cana when they ran out of wine. She told her Son who said His time had not yet come. Nevertheless, she told the wine stewards to do what He told them, and at her behest He performed His first miracle, turning water into wine. She is there in her special relationship to the Trinity, where, ***as our Mother***, she is always ready to intercede for us. I don't think that the Feminist movement has any real reverence toward her, yet all women should have her as the most perfect role model of all time.

I don't know if the following incident exemplifies the attitude of the Feminist Nun and her tendency to be charmed by the Heresies of Modernism and Americanism. I was national director of PAVLA at the time and we were attending some important function in Chicago. To her credit, this woman was wearing a religious habit which clearly identified her as a person dedicated to the religious life and associated her with a specific Religious Order. At some point, however, she asked me how my Faith had changed since my training in Rome so many years ago. She was visibly skeptical when I told her that my belief in the doctrines of the Church had not changed at all from the time my parents taught them to me using the Baltimore Catechism. My ***understanding***, of course, of those doctrines was much deeper as a result of my studies, and I now knew ***why*** the Church's Magisterium had, for two thousand years, held them to be true. No matter what I said to her, she remained skeptical, even when I quoted to her the watchword of St. Paul: "O Timothy, Guard the Deposit." (2 Tim. 1: 14)

Since that time I've wondered if Feminism carries with it a leaning toward the Heresies of Modernism and Americanism.

CHAPTER 38

"We've Lost!—You Had Just As Well Go Back to Your Diocese"

Immediately after my presentation of the memorandum to the Bishops' Committee, there was a deafening silence. There were no questions, no discussion. The meeting was simply adjourned. In the days and weeks following the meeting, there was a very unsettling series of occurrences: I was followed, night and day, wherever I went. Every day when I drove in my car for any destination whatever, someone was following behind me. No matter where I turned, that car turned after me. After I relaxed somewhat about being followed, I did my best to 'lose' whoever it was. By then, I knew the area well and was familiar with all the twists and turns of the city of Washington. I believe I succeeded whenever I tried to get them off my trail.

Whoever it was, quite clearly wanted me to *know* that I was being followed. That went on for the next four or five years—during a month or two as I was winding up my affairs in Washington, D.C., and after I returned to my diocese for two years, and for another two or three years after I was laicized and moved to the Northwest. In Washington, D.C., my telephone was tapped. Whether that was true later in Sioux City, I do not know. Someone who understood the Washington scene told me to be very careful or I might easily end up as an accident on a lonely country road. I didn't know, and do not know to this day, whether that was a warning from a friend, or a threat from an enemy. The fact that I was under surveillance was very frightening and I was afraid of coming to physical harm. But as I became accustomed to it and was able to think more clearly, I concluded that the surveillance was too obvious and was meant simply to intimidate me and probably serve as a warning that I shouldn't go to the press with the things that I knew.

For several days, which turned into several weeks, after the meeting, I heard nothing. Although I don't remember it, I am sure I spoke with Bishop Hodges, but I don't know whether he or I initiated the contact, nor do I remember the nature of the conversation. But I do clearly remember speaking with Cardinal Cody who, in his customary stance of strong support, told me that he would initiate efforts to have the Papal Volunteer program taken out of the Latin America Bureau and established in another division of the United States Catholic Conference, probably the Office of the Lay Apostolate. I heard nothing from Bishop Bernardin who, I thought, would have been the one to keep me informed as to what was happening, but, although we lived in the same house, he avoided me and didn't speak to me for several weeks. At one point I spent a few days with a priest-friend in Baltimore (Msgr. Claire Dwyer, Baltimore PAVLA Director), played golf with him, and told him the entire story of what I was going through. When I was done, he whistled and said, "You've pushed at the power tower," and didn't hold out much hope that I could possibly win. In mentioning the 'power tower', he was referring, I believe, to the fact that Bishop Bernardin was chosen as director of the United States Catholic Conference by Cardinal Dearden of Detroit who at that time was the elected President of the Bishops' Conference. In exposing what Father Colonnese had done, I was casting aspersions on Bishop Bernardin who put Father Colonnese in his position as director of LAB and continued to support him. As time went on, my hopelessness grew and I became convinced that the Papal Volunteer program would be terminated. After what seemed like many weeks of waiting, accomplishing nothing, feeling humiliated and ostracized, I received a call from Cardinal Cody who said, "We've lost. You had just as well go back to your diocese."

I therefore wrote a number of letters of resignation, had a final meeting with the volunteers in training at the National Training Center and began to pack my things, ready to drive back to Sioux City, Iowa, to rejoin my diocese. Eerily, as I was about to drive away with my car packed, Bishop Bernardin came out of the USCC staff house, all smiles, and for the first time in several weeks, spoke to me. He wanted to wish me well, he said. He was obviously the consummate politician, one of just a very few I had met in the Church, all of whom seemed to be striving toward political perfection rather than spiritual perfection, even as they gave every external evidence that they were striving toward a strong spiritual life. Much to my chagrin, he later was elected as president of the Conference of Bishops, then was moved to another diocese, and finally was appointed Archbishop of Chicago where eventually he faced a charge of pedophilia. The young man who accused him of sexual abuse, eventually dropped the legal charge after payment of three million dollars (cf. *Op. Cit*, p. 889), but never retracted his statement. Bishop Bernardin contracted an illness which looked suspiciously like Aids (his followers circulated the rumor that he had cancer). He maintained the outward appearance of a holy man, right up to his death. He was an accomplished actor.

The 'spin doctors' at the USCC and elsewhere, in the weeks and months (years?) following my testimony before the subcommittee, were hard at work to negate the effect of what I had presented. I personally had no access to any spin doctors who would support me, and I certainly was neither capable of, nor inclined, to do any spinning myself. That the tide turned against me, however, I had no doubt. There were two principal pieces of evidence for this.

In the first instance, the members of the Papal Volunteer Planning Committee, in the first few weeks after their meeting, met with the Archbishop of Miami, who was the newly appointed chairman of the committee on Latin America. He told them that I had no staying power and generally criticized what I had done. He clearly had no idea of what had transpired. He also was not very intelligent in criticizing me to a group who knew exactly what I had been through and who gave me their full support. This was as fine a group of laymen (and priests) as I have ever had the pleasure to work with, a group whom that Archbishop should have listened attentively to, but who, as a group of (mostly) lay men and women, were generally ignored. They reported to me on the nature of the meeting and told me what the Archbishop had said about me.

The second piece of evidence—that the tide had turned against me—came from my own bishop after I returned to my diocese. When I visited with him after my return, he told me that he had some idea of what I had gone through, told me that he and the priests of the diocese gave me their full support, and he asked me to take over the post of Chancellor of the Sioux City Diocese. "This," he said, "will show them what we think of you and the work that you did." It was clear that by "showing them" he meant members of the bishops' conference who apparently had been given an erroneous understanding of what had transpired with the PAVLA program and my part in it.

In those days I was (and perhaps still am) the victim of a magnificent naiveté. I had hoped simply by presenting evidence of what was wrong, the bishops, being good, honest men who possessed the fullness of the priesthood, would simply perceive what was wrong and take action to correct the problem. I should have known (and I think I did—they were simply following a story contrived by Bishop Bernardin) that they were ordinary men who had been elevated to great responsibility and who, because of that, were capable of great fear and ordinary human weakness which caused them to take the path of least resistance. In retrospect, I believe that the information and documentation which I presented was conclusive, but, since the bishops chose to do nothing about what I presented, their only recourse was, in effect, to 'kill the messenger,' so that in a face-saving maneuver, I became the culprit.

It is the same series of factors which I believe were, and still are, operative among the bishops and led them to the 'zero tolerance' stance toward alleged pedophile priests—a stance which the Holy See didn't like, which they were forced to modify. Subsequently they 'spun' the situation to say that, after all, the Vatican generally accepted what they had decided and they simply had to modify a few unimportant parts of their policy. The humanity of the bishops needs to be recognized, accepted, understood (after all, St. Peter denied Christ three times)—and every effort needs to be made by the clergy and laity to show them the respect they deserve because they have received the Sacrament of Orders in its fullness. They need whatever help we as clergy and laity can give them to be strong as they face the trials of the modern age. They need to be strong to stand up to the press, fear God more than the press, politicians and Federal, State and Local Governments, and to remember that their real 'kingdom' is not of this world. It is important that they keep in mind what St. John Chrysostom said many centuries ago: that bishops lose their souls in greater numbers than most others because they have greater responsibilities on their shoulders, but also because they don't act on the greater abundance of grace they receive to help them successfully shoulder those responsibilities.

Return to My Diocese after Five Years

The priests of the Diocese of Sioux City at that time formed the finest group of priests I have ever known in the United States, and it was an honor for so many years to belong to that group. And it was now a pleasure to be back with them. Very few of them, if any, were infected with the Heresies of Modernism and Americanism. Most of them retained their strong belief in the efficacy of all the Sacraments; none of them had fallen prey to the movements to downplay the Real Presence; they unwaveringly supported individual sacramental confession, and they opposed the Modernist revision of the liturgy.

In a word, they were all good, devoted priests, dedicated to the care of those entrusted to them.

Therefore, my next two years as Chancellor of the Sioux City Diocese were perhaps the most comfortable period of my life in the active priesthood. Wherever I went in the diocese, I was received with open arms by all the priests with very few exceptions—the pastors, the school principals, the assistant pastors, the teachers, the hospital chaplains—they all received me without reservation. While we never spoke of it, I believe they all thought that I was given a raw deal. As one of them put it some time later, the bishops had "hung me out to dry."

Chancellor of the Diocese of Sioux City

As Chancellor of the diocese, I had many responsibilities, many of them routine for the administration of a diocese, some of them unusual. For example, the bishop gave me the overall responsibility for the planning and implementation of a new retirement home which was to be a model of efficient physical and spiritual loving care for the elderly. It was a very large home. As I recall it was designed for 300 beds. Once the home was built, it became my next responsibility to seek out and find an unusually capable administrator. This person, I knew, had to be a standout as a manager, had to know how to organize the staff of such a home so that it could provide nearly the equivalent of hospital care on less than 25% of a hospital budget. Whoever was chosen would be required to establish a public relations program which would 'sell' the home to the priests of at least three or four different surrounding dioceses, to the priests and parishes of Sioux City, to the doctors of the city and surrounding areas, and who would understand the psychology of people who would live in the home and of their children who would urge them to live there.

After a few unsuccessful interviews and giving two or three candidates a chance to show what they could do, I finally in desperation ran an ad which brought the right person to me. She was a nurse, in the prime of her professional life, who had been a head nurse in a hospital, a nursing director, and, most importantly, had worked for years under a very successful nursing home administrator.

In the course of a few interviews, she told *me* what had to be done to make the home a success. She told me everything I had thought of on my own and many things besides. Among other things, she told me that she would have to have the unswerving support of both Bishop Mueller and myself in order to make it work. She told me that it would have to become the home where the priests of the diocese would be willing to send their mothers and fathers, the place where the good nurses would want to work at a lower salary to gain the kind of experience available there, a place where all the doctors would feel comfortable in sending their patients. She accomplished all that and more. She did such a wonderful job that, as I learned while writing this book, I am given credit to this day, forty years later, for the excellence of that retirement home. In addition, she provided for her own successors who have carried on the tradition of excellence.

One incident will exemplify how capable she was. She and I were waiting in one of the rooms for a new resident to be brought in. When she arrived, she was accompanied by her forty plus year old daughter who was fussing over her mother, giving her physical support as she came into the room, and helped her into bed. The new director watched this for a short time and then told the nurse who had been part of the transfer to walk the woman to the cafeteria and make sure that she got a good meal. The daughter began to object, saying that her mother was in no condition to walk but had to have a wheel chair. The director insisted, and the woman left with the nurse. A confrontation ensued: the daughter insisted that her mother had to be treated in a certain way. The director finally stated very firmly that unless the daughter was prepared to allow her mother to be cared for by the staff of the retirement home without interference, then she would be best to simply take her away and find other accommodations. While they were arguing, the mother walked back into the room, without assistance, took off her robe and cheerfully climbed into bed with no help. The director explained briefly to the daughter what had happened, and gave me a much longer explanation later on: She had seen the same phenomenon several times, that the daughter felt such an overwhelming guilt for not being able to take care of her mother, felt so badly at the need to place her in a home, that her care for her mother became overdone and actually turned her into a psychological invalid. If I had needed proof that we had made the right choice for a director of the home, that one incident would have been more than sufficient to tip the balance in her favor.

CHAPTER 39

The Forces Which Led Me to Seek Laicization

During the two or three years when I was Chancellor of the Sioux City Diocese, a number of things coalesced to cause me to begin to question whether I could save my soul in the active priesthood.

One of these elements was the fact that I continued to be followed wherever I went. In Washington, D.C., whoever followed me wanted to make sure that I knew this. Again, knowing the area well, I was frequently able to 'lose' whoever it was. The entire procedure was obviously very important to whomever instigated my being followed. A great deal of time was spent by the person or persons who actually followed me, and therefore a great deal of money was being spent in the exercise. I assumed the follower or followers were being paid a significant salary and had to receive living expenses. I don't know whether my telephone was tapped, but, since that had been done in Washington, D.C., I simply assumed that it was done in Sioux City, both my telephone at the Chancery and where I lived.

A second factor which I would later realize was important in my ruminations regarding my future in the priesthood was that Bishop Mueller told me that many of the priests of the diocese told him that I was doing a fine job as Chancellor, far better, he was told, than my predecessor. Among those priests who praised my work were the

Deans and Consultants who played a special role in advising the bishop as he undertook his many responsibilities. It was they who recommended to him candidates to be bishop, and I thought they might well recommend me.

A third incident which weighed very heavily in my thinking at the time was information which came to my attention entirely by accident. Being canonically correct in everything that he did, Bishop Mueller at one point began to gather information from his Deans and Consultants as to whom they would recommend as candidates for the episcopacy. He did this in secret; I don't think he used his secretary for this except perhaps to acquire the special stationery he would use to contact his advisors. He wrote each letter himself to make his request and enclosed a form asking them to name one person and send their recommendation back to him in an enclosed self-addressed stamped envelope. When the letters came back, it was my job to assemble them and present them to him unopened. Unfortunately, or from my perspective very fortunately, the high quality return envelopes which I was gathering were almost completely translucent so that I read my own name within the envelopes in those cases where the form was folded in such a way that it showed through. Mine was the only name I saw in a large enough number of those envelopes that it caused me grave concern. As required, I turned the envelopes over to the bishop and tried to forget what I had seen.

When one is trying *not* to think about a given subject, I believe it is impossible to keep it out of your mind. I had no idea what the chances were that I would be so chosen. I had some idea how long such processes take—a long time. I assumed therefore that I could take all the time I needed to think things through.

It was possible by now that the stigma surrounding me had been lifted—a stigma which had been imposed due to the disinformation following my resignation as national director of PAVLA. I felt this could be true because Cardinal Medeiros of Boston (who had been a member of the PAVLA subcommittee to which I had presented my memorandum) as my brother reported "ate humble pie" and told him that "Your brother . . . had been absolutely right and we should have listened to him."

Since it was remotely possible that I could be named a bishop, the question occurred to me, "Did I want to be?" and "Could I save my soul as a bishop?" I mulled over all the topics mentioned above about the heresies, politics and weaknesses which were rampant among the bishops and clergy of the United States at that time. Did I want to become part of a group which had just discredited me? Was I strong enough to maintain my Faith against those pressures? I knew that if the Pope were to designate me to be a bishop my own sense of loyalty and obedience would not permit me to refuse (not to mention my own ego).

When I saw my name on so many of the recommendations to the bishop suggesting candidates to become bishops, it threw me into an instant mental and emotional, and (probably more accurately) *spiritual* turmoil. Could I in good conscience allow such a thing to come to fruition? Until that point, I had been content. I was back among true and honest friends. My bishop gave me his open support; all the priests of the diocese appeared to support and respect me. The one exception was my predecessor as chancellor—probably because he had been asked to resign to make way for me. Another plus: I no longer had the incredible burden of the international Papal Volunteer program weighing on me as it had for five years.

The motivations which were pushing at me at the time were so numerous that I would never attempt to list even the conscious ones; and I'm sure that there were many unconscious forces at work within me. I was ordained a priest forever. I intended initially to remain all my life in the active priesthood. But now there was a question whether I could save my soul—of greater importance than any other consideration. If I sought laicization, I would remain a priest ("Thou art a priest forever, according to the order of Melchisedech"). If I were to do that, it would cause immeasurable anguish to my mother who in my mind had already had far more than her share of suffering. The pride she took in her two sons being in the priesthood was nearly tangible; it would be difficult to explain the problem to her. And yet I would still be a priest.

Yet another factor weighed heavily on me. There was a deeply devout young woman whom I mentioned before—see Part III, Chapter 21. She says to this day that I saved her from spiritual destruction, who, I began to think, would probably consent to become my wife if I were free to marry. Her presence in my life would help provide the healing which I was trying so hard to achieve.

So my thoughts went, over and over, back and forth, for six months to a year. Underlying all of that was my own deep-seated anger and bitterness about the betrayal by the bishops. I tried my best to erase those feelings and I believe I succeeded, although it might simply have been some form of denial. The bishops' intransigence in failing to act on what to me was incontrovertible evidence caused me an indescribable amount of internal pain. It also resulted, more importantly, in the failure of what had been an outstandingly successful program of the lay apostolate which was contributing mightily to intercultural understanding in the western hemisphere, and one that had been initiated by the Pope. It helped me, of course, to hear that Cardinal Medeiros had said that the bishops made a mistake. I had been absolutely correct, he said, and they should have listened to me. Yet, I suppose, it still festered within me. Perhaps it does to this day, although I am conscious that facing it all and writing about it has helped me immeasurably.

Later, after I had declared my intention to seek laicization, when Bishop Greteman, who had succeeded Bishop Mueller, offered to intercede to have me named a bishop if I would remain in the active priesthood, it very candidly disgusted me. I'm not entirely sure I know why I reacted so strongly, but I believe I took it as something of a bribe.

These last thoughts prompted a memory which I think deserves to be recorded here, although it is an aside. In my early years in college I read a study which underlines the infinite wisdom of Christ as He established the Seven Sacraments as the source of the special graces needed for all the stages in our lives. The study found that Catholics who regularly confessed their sins in the Sacrament of Penance suffered significantly fewer psychological and emotional maladjustments than others. When we routinely acknowledge our sins and weaknesses, forthrightly express them to a priest, and receive absolution, we cannot indulge in denial. The ability to deny what we have done wrong is one of our great weaknesses, which is another application of what Christ Himself said: "The truth will set you free." It is my fervent hope and prayer that recording all of those things in depth will lead me to a greater self-honesty, enhance my spiritual life, and lead me to a more profound forgiveness of the bishops than I hope I have already attained.

Petition for Laicization

While I was fretting about what I should do, at some point I began to formulate my petition for laicization, so that when the time came and I decided to proceed, the petition would be ready to give to the bishop for transmittal to Rome. In retrospect, I believe I had already made the decision, but actually writing the petition was very difficult.

During the formulation of the petition, I finally and with great hesitation told my future wife, Lillian, what I was doing, and asked her if she would become my wife if my petition were granted. She sat in silence for so long that I began to think I had made a huge miscalculation and that she would refuse. She was silently crying and finally told me that for years she had given up hopelessly praying that we could somehow eventually be married, but, knowing how dedicated I was to the priesthood, she felt it was completely impossible. Aside from my dedication to the priesthood, she was convinced that it would never be permitted.

At any rate, I submitted my petition to Bishop Greteman and suggested to him that he might ask for the intervention of Cardinal Cody in Chicago who might be willing to expedite the procedure.

(It was at this time that Bishop Greteman suggested that he would help me become a bishop if I would stay in the active priesthood. Of course, as I already mentioned, I refused.) I really do not know whether Cardinal Cody actually got involved, but the petition was granted much more rapidly than my experience as a canon lawyer led me to expect. In submitting the petition, I set a date two weeks later when I would actually leave the diocese and my position as chancellor.

Departure

On a chosen day in the Fall of 1971, I rented a U-Haul trailer, attached it to my car, and parked a block or two away from my residence. That evening, with the help of a young priest who was aware of my plans, I filled my car and the trailer with my belongings, leaving a large number of my books behind. After dark I simply drove to Omaha, Nebraska, where Lillian and I had agreed to meet, transferred her belongings to the trailer, and we headed west with California as a vague destination. We are convinced we were, once again, followed. This continued for years—at least three to four. Once again, I believe, whoever it was, was afraid that I would go "public" with what I knew.

And so my career in the active priesthood in the Catholic Church ended. As I have been forced to explain a number of times, I left the active priesthood with honor, but I never left the Catholic Church. My faith in the Church is as strong as ever, actually stronger. I revere the Pope, respect and pray for the bishops and the clergy and all good Catholics. I am proud of the fact that I remain a priest, that I did good work in that capacity. I left with the knowledge that while the program I had built was terminated about a year after I left, in the process of defending the Papal Volunteer program, I believe I helped destroy a major effort of enemies within the Church in their determination to subvert and destroy the Church. (See Part VI of this book.) Not long after I left, Ivan Illich retired and moved to

Germany. Archbishop Bernardin was exposed as a homosexual/pedophile bishop. I have never again heard of Father Louis Colonnese, who, as a closet Communist, failed in his purpose and I assume was punished in some fashion. I never again have heard of Christian Base Communities, except for one instance in a southern diocese of the U.S. After its condemnation by Pope John Paul II, I only once heard of Liberation Theology which apparently has some 'hangers on' among a small number of Latin American Bishops. So while I remain saddened at the loss of a superlative Lay Apostolate program—Papal Volunteers for Latin America—I believe there may have been a much greater good come out of it of which I am just now becoming aware.

My new career, as the reader will see, was to employ my knowledge, experience and training as a priest to help as many people as I could to better their personal economic and, in a major number of cases, their spiritual lives. And so we come, in the next major part of this document, to my new life as a married priest, a beautiful life with a beautiful wife, children who are in their thirties as this is being written, three grandchildren and a fourth on the way, and the continued development of my own spiritual life.

PART V

LIFE AS A MARRIED LAICIZED CATHOLIC PRIEST

CHAPTER 40

Moving to the West and Adjusting to a New Life

As my future wife and I moved to the West we sought anonymity and secrecy, and some measure of peace until we were settled and married. Therefore, about at the half way point, we changed our plans and decided to move to Portland, Oregon. Neither of us felt any particular attraction to California. We were simply looking for a place to live which would be far enough from the Diocese of Sioux City so as to reduce the likelihood of scandal to a minimum. I was unwilling to target Seattle because I had a nephew who, with his wife and family, was stationed at an Air Force base near there. Not yet having informed my mother of my plans (with no idea as to how I was going to handle that), I didn't want to risk a chance meeting with him which might allow a premature announcement. Portland at the time seemed to be a good middle-ground choice: a relatively small city, yet large enough to provide the anonymity which was important to us at the time.

Arriving in Portland, we took temporary lodging and went about the business of finding a more permanent place to live. We set up a P.O. Box address so we could not be easily found. Having accomplished those things, we began to furnish an apartment with the basics and set up an appointment with the Chancellor of the Archdiocese of Portland, asking him to perform the marriage ceremony for us—which he did.

It was a major shock to have him tell us at the time we visited him that he had been out to our apartment a couple of times, but didn't find us home. (This was probably because we had not yet moved into it.) The 'shock' occurred because the only person who had that address was our landlord on whom we impressed the need for anonymity. We left our street address, of course, at the Post Office when we applied for the post-office box, but the actual street address they had on file was to remain unidentified. The telephone line we set up was unlisted. What this told us, *i.e.* his attempts to visit us, was that we had been followed all the way from Sioux City, Iowa, just as I had been followed wherever I went for three or four years—in Washington, D.C., in Sioux City, Iowa, and now, apparently, this was going to continue. This demonstrated even more strongly than before that, in my report to the bishops, I had tapped into something which enemy forces within the Catholic Church had determined would be damaging to them if I were ever to make a public issue of it. But then, once again, it occurred to me that I did not know whether it was hostile or friendly forces who were watching me so closely.

I finally decided that if I simply went about getting my marriage and personal affairs in order, this fixation on my activities would eventually end. Which seems to have occurred, although not for a considerable time, and we do not know exactly when 'operation watchdog' was disbanded.

My wife with her nursing experience, and in particular because of her specializations in intensive care and coronary care, easily and quickly found work in one of the local hospitals. Our landlord offered me the management of the small apartment complex in which we were to live, reducing our monthly rental by fifty percent. Between us we had pooled fifteen thousand to twenty thousand dollars, which we wanted to save for emergencies. With her income from nursing and our reduced rent, we were financially comfortable for the time being. Once that much was accomplished, it became necessary for me to determine what I was going to do to ensure our financial growth as a couple and future family.

CHAPTER 41

Developing A New Career

Since in the course of my twenty years in the active priesthood I had encountered a substantial number of men and women who were not at all happy with their lives—from quite troubled to deep depression—we were determined to avoid that possibility in our marriage. The causes of desperate lives, as far as I could ascertain, ranged from incompatibility to the way the couple made a living.

Actually, many of the unhappy marriages I had come in contact with were *caused by* dissatisfaction with their work. Most of them—unmarried men and unmarried women, and married men whose wives did not work, and married men and their wives who worked simply by choice or to enhance the family income—were dissatisfied because, consciously or unconsciously, they were unhappy with whatever work they did to provide the income they needed to live. I believed and hoped I could help people with that problem.

My very first effort to find a job in Portland, Oregon, was successful. I answered an ad by L & S Placement, Inc., which purported to be a very sophisticated employment agency. It was located in the Georgia-Pacific Building which was a major downtown skyscraper. When I arrived for my first appointment, I found a receptionist, a large empty space with a few desks and an empty inner office. The receptionist asked me to be seated and left. When she came back, she directed me to the building cafeteria a few floors down and said the two principals would like me to join them there.

When I came into the cafeteria, they must have assumed I was the one they were waiting for, because they rose and introduced themselves as Doug Longbotham and Harold Steubs (hence, *L & S Placement*). I must have been the kind of person they were looking for, because they hired me that day after less than an hour of discussion. Their intention, so they said, was to put together a highly professional agency which would not stoop to simply matching a person's background experience with the job description received from a company. My own purpose was to match as carefully as possible, the person, the actual responsibility of the position and the philosophy and ambience of the company. My first 'placement', I believe, did precisely that and I received my first commission check with a sense of great pride. That first check was for something more than five hundred dollars which at that time (1972) was a significant addition to our assets and was proof to myself that I should be able to accomplish what I wanted to do.

After about a month at L & S Placement, the feeling of being watched once again raised its ugly head. A priest walked into the office and came over to me. I recognized him instantly. He was a classmate of mine from my first four years in Rome. If I had remembered that I had a classmate in Portland, we probably would not have moved there since both my wife and I were concerned about maintaining anonymity. After he came into the office, for a while, it was old home week. Twenty five years earlier, we had known each other well during four years in Rome. He told me he found me because he had a habit of walking into the principal buildings in Portland and looking at the directory to see if he recognized any names. So he found mine. It struck me as a strange practice. I didn't find it credible, particularly in view of the fact that the Chancellor visited us in our apartment before we had moved in. (Later on I came to believe that, acting under instructions, this classmate had consciously sought me out—we'll come to why in a moment.) So I introduced him to my wife, and, as they arrived over the next six years, to our children. We invited him for dinner several times, and he did the same for us. He was a solid, good priest, and practiced a very sound Theology. Then came the day after about five years when he was sent to an extended program at Notre Dame for 'updating', preparing, as I've heard it said, to work in the 'modern' church. He came back a changed person with what were now quite obviously Modernist views. He had been successfully indoctrinated in, and had visibly accepted, false doctrine.

After he came back from Notre Dame, he once again invited us to his place for dinner. By this time, we had three children, the oldest being about 6 or 7, who remembers him after nearly thirty years. In the course of that dinner, my wife brought up the subject of my years with the PAVLA program, explaining what I had gone through during those years. As she talked, I saw evidence of a major discomfort in him, so I said, "Honey, he may have heard only the other side of the story and has never heard ours." There followed what we have referred to ever since as the ***Great Silence.*** He sat in complete silence, looking down at his plate, and said not a single word. The silence lasted, it seemed, for several minutes, and it was extremely uncomfortable. He might well have said something like, "You're right, I did hear something about that, but I'd like to hear your side of the story." Or he might simply have said, "Why don't you tell me about it." One of our children after what seemed like an eternity created a diversion and the subject was changed. I would have liked to hear what was being said about me and the PAVLA program. His handling of the subject raised the image for me of being used in indoctrination programs as an example of the "old," "antiquated" Catholic Church as the Modernists in the Church went on their merry way in promoting their misinterpretation of Vatican Council II. This was now more than ten years after I resigned my position with the Papal Volunteer program, and the old, uncomfortable feeling of being followed and watched returned to plague me.

Getting back to L & S Placement, it didn't take long for me to realize that the level of professionalism I was looking for simply wasn't there. In their efforts to make as much money as possible, the two principals were quickly transforming L & S Placement into a 'body shop'—to use the lingo of the employment agency world—*i.e.* their simple purpose was to move as many people as possible into a job opening, collecting as many fees as possible. The promised 'sophistication' simply did not develop.

In voicing my concerns, apparently I created a fear in the two principals that I would look elsewhere (which I was seriously considering). Apparently it was very important to keep me aboard, since I had a documented doctorate, and thus greatly enhanced the image of their enterprise. The result was that I was quickly promoted in a few steps to being named a Vice President in charge of something or other, and finally was named Chairman of the Board, even though I had no ownership in the company. My guess is that they were trying to allow me to turn the agency into the more sophisticated entity I wanted it to be, or, more probably, simply trying to keep me as a member of the firm because they perceived me as 'impressive.'

During the time that I spent at that agency, which I believe was about six months or so, an occasional visitor was a Dr. Ralph Warren who would from time to time sit at a desk and do some placement work. He presented himself as a doctor of psychology, although I never saw any documentation of his degree, and he certainly seemed to have no real knowledge of the field of psychology, whereas my own educational and practical background gave me a major proficiency in the field. I concluded that he was a fraud. It turned out, however, that he did me a good turn, because he introduced me to another office where he also did some temporary work: J. Frederick Marcy & Associates. The Portland office was the only sub-office of a franchise office of the same name in Seattle, where the owner of the franchise had authority in the states of Washington and Oregon.

The owner of the sub-office franchise of J. Frederick Marcy in Portland, Oregon, was C. H. (Pat) Patterson who simply served as his own salesman to encourage an individual, for a fee, to join the program. Beyond that, Patterson depended on people like Ralph Warren, and, a short time later, myself to know how to work with his clients. He apparently believed, after a short interview, that I could do the necessary work for his clients. He offered me that position. What the Marcy office did with its clients was much more to my liking than what was done at L & S Placement, and I was convinced that I could, if allowed to do so, modify the program so that it would do for people what I envisioned needed to be done. A major advantage, in my eyes, was that I received a specific salary for joining the firm. The salary, while relatively small, joined with my wife's income as a nurse to give us a more comfortable standard of living.

The Marcy program, using a simple testing device, initially helped every client to examine his or her own capabilities, personality traits, personal needs and positive or negative habit patterns and begin to develop a more open mind as to future possibilities. There was even a fairly sophisticated program to help the client develop more professional and effective interview techniques. While it was a major improvement over what I had been doing, it still remained, as I later understood to be true with all the Marcy offices nationwide, nothing but a sophisticated placement agency. Whatever field the client had been involved in, he or she continued in that same work, oftentimes with the palliative of a more responsible position and/or higher pay. If the client didn't *like* or *take pride in* the work he/she did or field he/she was in, the program didn't give him or her a positive solution. Therefore I wanted to make some major changes, but, because of the franchise nature of the business, felt that I couldn't do so.

One of my early clients at the Marcy office was a lawyer, Steven Hughes, who was trained as a tax lawyer. He worked for a large firm and found the tax work to be stultifying. Recently married, he was so dissatisfied that he was concerned that his state of mind would affect his relationship with his wife. He initially had no idea what he might do; he simply wanted to change the way he made his living. He ultimately realized that he had no idea what the 'practice of law' really was, but really understood only what taxes and tax laws were. He decided, therefore, to set up his own law firm, and he paid me the compliment of patterning his practice after my own: he offered a no-cost no-obligation first appointment, during which he presented in depth to a potential client what would need to be done and the likelihood of success, and then specified a flat fee up front for the work he would do. As far as I know, he never used the concept of 'billable hours' except perhaps in working for large corporations. He was hugely successful. He and I became good friends, and he was to perform two major favors for me in the next few years, in addition to a number of lesser ones.

My wife, Lillian, and I, because there was a need to take care of our children as they began to arrive, and because of my dissatisfaction with the work I was doing, began to look at a number of ways to bring in the income we needed and wanted. Because she is a nurse, we gave serious thought to setting up a day care service. Her nursing expertise would give us a strong competitive edge in providing that kind of service. We didn't pursue the idea because it would require too much of a monetary investment up front. We examined a mail order opportunity selling a large range of commodities. We actually had that enterprise going quite well, but in the final analysis couldn't see ourselves taking pride in that kind of career.

We were aware that J. Frederick Marcy & Associates was doing well and that the owner, Pat Patterson, was taking home a large percentage of the revenue, while I received what I began to perceive as a paltry percentage of the income. So the thought crossed our minds that perhaps we could purchase the business from Patterson, so that I would become self-employed.

At this point, Steve Hughes, the lawyer/client I mentioned above, performed his first huge favor to me. I went to him to explore what would be involved to buy the Marcy business. My first question to him was, "What do you think that business would be worth?" His answer was a classic: "About fifty cents." Surprised, I asked him what he meant. He said, in effect, that Patterson never did a thing in that office except sit, read the newspaper, take occasional phone calls and 'sell' the program to a new client. After an individual became a client, some of whom I brought in on my own initiative, I worked with that individual from start to finish. Steve Hughes ultimately said that I personally was the only thing of real value in that office. He and other clients urged me to open my own independent career counseling service. After researching the legalities involved, Steve Hughes ultimately gave me the go-ahead with the warning that Patterson might ultimately take me to court, but even then, judges were reluctant to take away a person's means of livelihood. While I had signed a non-competition agreement with the national J. Frederick Marcy & Associates organization, that firm was completely disbanded a few months after I had signed that agreement and I was never informed of its demise; therefore there was no valid non-competition agreement.

Accordingly, R.A. Kevane & Associates, Career Consultants, came into being with its watchword "The Self-Directed Career[SM]", a phrase which identified the specific difference between our firm and its competitors. As I proceeded to formulate the procedures of the new firm, Pat Patterson began quickly to offer me a much higher percentage of the income in the Marcy firm, but now, with the bit in my teeth, I was unwilling even to discuss how we might continue our arrangement. It had become crystal clear to me that I needed no one except a secretary/receptionist in order to succeed in what I wanted to do. My wife, initially on a part time basis, and later after our children were old enough, on a full time basis, fulfilled that need admirably. Later, my oldest daughter handled the role for a year, and much later my youngest daughter did the same for several years.

CHAPTER 42

The Self-Directed Career℠

Next I rented and furnished a small office space/reception area, small office for myself, conference room for instruction in interview techniques. Then I sent a letter to each of the clients I had worked with at the Marcy offices, offering them continuing consultation at a no cost basis and offering, at very low cost, a new feature which would allow them to make a free decision as to what they wanted to do as opposed to being restricted in some sense to what they already had experience in, as most people are. I also ran a (very small) daily ad in Portland's *Oregonian* and placed a small ad in the forthcoming new edition of the Yellow Pages.

As I worked on the materials I needed for the complete program my firm would present, Pat Patterson took me to court, citing the non-competition agreement I had signed. It was a major distraction and I was very nervous about it, even though (and my lawyer assured me) it was no longer in force since J. Frederick Marcy & Associates was terminated as a national firm just a few months after I signed the agreement. The judge agreed and ruled in my favor.

The trial continued for over a month. When it was done, having been exonerated and completely free to do as I wanted, I attacked the preparation of the materials for my new business and professional service with renewed energy.

Freedom of Choice

The concept of the Self-Directed Career[SM] was to be built upon one of the major doctrines of the Roman Catholic Church: That we are all created in the image and likeness of God, which means that we have intelligence and free will as our prominent capabilities. We are capable of intelligently exercising that freedom of will to do good, or to do evil, and we will be rewarded or punished depending on how we exercise that power.

In my years in the active priesthood, I encountered very few people who were truly happy in the work they did. When an occasional person took pride and self-satisfaction in the way he made a living and supported himself and his family, such a person stood out and was in every case exceptionally capable at what he did. And invariably his/her personal life was filled with peace and contentment. This included doctors, lawyers, retail store managers and workers in general, nurses, lab workers, priests and nuns . . . . and I could go on and on. Those, on the other hand, whose dissatisfaction was obvious, were less expert, treated their customers and clients impatiently, and, in many cases, unprofessionally.

These latter were, in effect, trapped in unsatisfying careers, simply pursuing what their parents had pushed them into, what their education led them to believe was the only thing available to them, or finally what their years of experience in a given line of work led them to believe was their safest career course. I firmly believed then, and I now know, that individuals could make a free decision either to radically change their career course, either into another field entirely, or make a major move within a given field. In order to help my clients make such a decision, it was necessary to devise a way to help them completely open up their minds to the possibility of change. In other words, they must have a way to modify the image they had of themselves, oftentimes since childhood, certainly since they had finished their education, and inescapably after years of experience in the field in which they had worked. Therefore, they needed to identify and make a decision based on their *inborn and developed* ***talents***, rather than on the *skills* developed through education and repetitive actions.

It was also extremely important that their decisions be based on their own personal hopes, aspirations and desires—*i.e.* their *personal needs*, on their own *personalities*, their own *functional capabilities,* and their own identifiable *talents—i.e.,* the roles they were comfortable and proficient in performing.

Having revised their own self-image and opened their minds to the possibility of change, then they needed to look at *all the industrial concepts* available in society, and, using a careful methodology, *choose what they* ***wanted***, studiously avoiding the comfortable, *safe,* attraction to things they had already proven they could do.

Having made that (very difficult) decision, the clients would go on to learn completely professional methods of setting up interviews with principals in the field they had chosen, establishing full credibility with those they chose to contact. I called this 'self-marketing.' It's purpose was to ensure that a client knew how to present his *current* capabilities and *future potential*, instead of being perceived (usually misperceived) simply for what he or she had done in the past.

To summarize, the program I presented to my clients, in a period of five to six weeks, proceeded through the following steps:

1. Re-examine, modify and broaden their own self-image, examining their range of *talents* instead of concentrating on their developed *skills*, preparing for an open and free decision. This kind of open-mindedness was achieved usually in two to three weeks.
2. Choose, in order of preference, a small list of industrial concepts, with the choice depending on personal hopes, desires, aspirations—and not on demonstrated skills and experience. This decision required one to two weeks.
3. Develop the professional ability to penetrate what might prove to be an entirely new field. This third phase was to be

called Self-Marketing. This phase required four to six formal weekly sessions, usually as part of a small group for mutual support, with an intense interview program beginning after the very first session.

It might well be appropriate at this point to quote from a book I published in 1994 at the height of my career guidance service:

> "Many years ago, a man came to me for counseling who had himself been a counselor—a guidance counselor in a local public school system. We took him through a number of exercises designed to help him determine what his true needs and talents are and then explained the goal-setting process that would allow him to more fully take charge of his career.
>
> "At the end of our session he looked at me and said, 'I guess we've been doing it back-wards all these years. We've been telling them what to do instead of letting them make their own decisions.' (Author's note: what he actually, literally said was 'I guess we've been doing it bass ackwards . . . .' I guess I didn't at that time feel it was appropriate to use that exact quote.)

"'We' in this case is our country's educators. 'Them' is the millions of students whose career paths are indelibly influenced by their educational experiences. The quotation continues:

> "No doubt about it: Education as it's now construed contributes as much to inappropriate career decisions as any other factor. For the most part, our schools don't help with career decisions—they program. And many of us spend the rest of our lives either succumbing to or fighting that programming.

> "Let me be clear that I am not at all opposed to tests and grading systems as means of motivation, encouragement, and discipline, and of ascertaining whether a student has learned the given material. What I am opposed to is that the system in which people who score well on tests in certain areas are automatically pushed to pursue further training and careers in those areas." (Quote taken from *Employment Power: Take Control of Your Career*, 1994, Peanut Butter Publishing, pp. 127-128.)

On another occasion, a client who was a bishop in a major Protestant religious group—I don't remember which—when he had completed our entire program said the following—and I will never forget his exact words: "The *genius* of your program is that it is a study in applied *Theology*" (emphasis added). He was one of only two people who, when they first came into my office, looked carefully at the parchment documents which—entirely in Latin—recorded my advanced degrees in Theology and in Canon Law and said, "You're a Catholic priest, aren't you?" The other who came to the same immediate conclusion was a Jew.

I report these incidents and provide these quotations to demonstrate the reason why I founded a service whose watchword and philosophy were simultaneously wrapped up in the concept of 'The Self-Directed Career[SM].' I looked on the service as an informal continuation of my work as a priest.

Over the years, ***exactly three clients*** (among several thousand) alleged that we had not fulfilled our promises and took their complaints to the Small Claims Court. In each case, the judge decided in our favor, asking one woman, a former university professor, "Did you read this contract? I urge you to read carefully anything you sign." Another was a former dentist who hated being confined to a small area, peering into people's mouths, and he wanted completely out of the field. I don't recall the third complainant, but it was a woman to whom the judge said she could simply take advantage of our no-cost on-going consultation guarantee. These three (and there may have been others who made no complaint), in my opinion, came to us with a preconceived notion of what our services would entail, hoping that we would find them a job, and, in spite of our contract, our careful explanation before they started, and in spite of all we said about the Self-Directed Career[SM], simply failed to understand and proceeded under a false interpretation. My wife said about one of the three when he came into a self-marketing session that he (the dentist) was paying no attention, not taking notes, but apparently day-dreaming.

After a few years as a Career Consultant, another major adversary reared its frightening head: the State of Oregon. For a number of years, the Oregon legislature attempted, pushed by some lobbying group, to enact a law which would require any "job consultation" service to be licensed as an "employment agency." This would require a firm like ours to conform to the precise methodologies of employment agencies: Acquire 'job orders' from companies, make the orders public, talk to candidates, match their résumés with the job orders, and charge fees based on the level of salary paid by the company. These and many other stipulations would effectively make us change the nature of our service. In this particular session of the legislature, the measure was 'pushed through' in the dark of night, i.e. the last session of the legislature before it went on vacation. In the fullness of time, some weeks later, I received a letter from an employment czar who was affiliated with the State Attorney General's office, telling me that as of the first of the following January (it was early Fall) I would be forced to comply with the new law.

By this time our service was widely recognized and respected, I had become something of a public figure, and our firm was a complete success. From the incident I'm about to explain, I learned a lesson I should have learned many years earlier: Anyone in power, *viz.* Governments at any level—local, county, state, federal, *and* in the Church from pastors to deans to bishops to conferences of bishops—in their own minds must maintain a minimum of control over those who are their responsibility. I was helping people to develop a complete independence of mind, and therefore must have been considered by some an 'enemy of the state.' At any rate, for some reason, it was important to someone that I should no longer continue to do what I was doing. While it was a nerve wracking experience from the moment I received the fateful letter until the matter was settled, I was firmly determined to fight for what I had developed.

I first called Steve Hughes, my lawyer/client, and was told that he was out of town for the better part of a week. So I left a message and sent him a copy of the letter I had received. Then I called all the lawyers in Portland who had excellent reputations. Time after time, these lawyers suggested solutions which were untenable to me. They ranged from "You will simply have to comply with the new law," To "You can move across the river to Vancouver, Washington, where you can continue to carry on your business and still draw upon the Portland area market." In the midst of the anguish we felt, my wife and I began to seriously contemplate moving our offices to Vancouver. We weren't happy about it, and we were not at all optimistic that the location would entice potential clients to cross the bridge to come to our offices.

Then Steve Hughes embarked on the second major favor he was to do for me. In the middle of the following week, shortly after he came back from his trip out of town, he called me three times in one afternoon when I was tied up with clients. He didn't leave a message; he insisted on talking to me personally. The third time he called, I was free. He sounded somewhat angry and wasted no time. He said, "That new law is unconstitutional; they're trying to put you out of business. It's essential that you fight it. What we'll have to do is threaten to make public what they are trying to do to you." He put his focus immediately on the crux of the problem which his learned colleagues didn't even advert to. Since we were challenging the constitutionality of the law, he told me that I could continue to work with clients and acquire new ones beyond the January 1st deadline. Which I did. He wrote to the Attorney General of the State of Oregon, and to the woman who had written to me earlier.

In mid-January, Steve Hughes called me to say "We have a nibble; they would like meet with you." "They" it turned out was not only the woman I referred to earlier as the 'employment czar', but also the Attorney General himself—not one of his assistants. A stenographer came with him to record the 'minutes' of the meeting.

The Attorney General, of course, opened the meeting; and, after some discussion with Steve Hughes, turned to me and said, "Why don't you tell me what you do?" I said, "Let me give you an example. Suppose an Attorney General came in to my office, dispirited, telling me that he no longer took pride in his work, for a number of reasons. Number one, he was forced to give too much attention to being re-elected at the end of his term. For that reason many of his decisions had to be at least unconsciously weighted in the direction of pleasing the public, rather than objectively meting out justice." I gave a number of other reasons why such a person might be disgruntled. "And he didn't want to simply leave the public sector and go back into the private practice of law, because he felt he couldn't take any real pride in doing so." I then gave the Attorney General a fairly comprehensive description of what I summarized above regarding the processing of a client. After asking me a few questions, he turned to my attorney and asked him, "What do we need to do?"

I'll never forget the image of what happened next. Steve Hughes brought out a yellow legal tablet on which he had written thirteen items in the newly enacted law which would have to be formally waived. He read them all, the stenographer recorded them, there were a few questions, the Attorney General agreed, and the meeting ended. I was now completely free to proceed with my business practices with no changes.

There was a lasting benefit, completely unexpected and unforeseen. Since my firm and I were now legally registered as an employment agency, I was invited to join a private association of employment agencies. At the first meeting I attended, one of the owners whom I had befriended over the years explained to the other members what my firm did. This started a flow of referrals from those agencies of people who approached them and for whom they had no solutions. The increase in my business from these referrals was truly significant.

Now, in retrospect, I know that about 80 per cent of the roughly 5000 clients I worked with over the years moved successfully into fields they had no prior experience in. Invariably, they made this revision without loss of income, and usually with an increase both in responsibility and income. Perhaps it can be of interest to read about a few examples of career changes. The first one is simply a reminder of Steve Hughes, an unhappy tax lawyer who remained a lawyer, but shifted to his own practice in general law. He became completely contented and (I have always assumed) greatly increased his income.

There was a physician who became a disc jockey.

I worked with the manager of a Portland radio station who moved to southern California, immediately became the manager of an amusement park (roller coasters, merry-go-rounds, etc.), moved up to being a partner, and finally the sole owner. He undoubtedly became a wealthy man.

A few more examples:

> In the early 70's, an oil company executive came to me, one who was earning in the neighborhood of $90,000 a year. He had grown tired of the international manipulation, as he saw it, by the oil companies within the market. He left the oil company with the rather common attitude that he would simply find himself a top level executive position in something like steel or heavy equipment—just so it wasn't oil! He became a university professor. He had no more than a bachelor's degree at the time, he had to do some very effective negotiating with university officials, which he did, and he negotiated quite effectively among a

few different universities. He had to agree that he would go on for higher studies, although he was under no time line for that.

He called me in his first year of teaching and told me that he and his wife were happier than they had ever been before. He said they had not realized how much they disliked the social and political pressure of top corporate activity. He said they had changed their lifestyles and he said if he didn't have the figures in front of him, (it must have been tax time) he wouldn't believe it. He said that on a third of his previous salary, they were putting more money away than they had ever done in their lives before. He said apparently the reduction in social expenditures, the lower cost of a different life style, and the different tax bracket all combined to have them in better shape financially than they had ever been. This was certainly one of the exceptional success stories.

There was a retired Army Colonel, Joe Piortrzkowski, who I believe would have soon become a general, but he opted out. He was elected mayor in a small Oregon town near Portland, and, some years later died of cancer. At the time that Mt. St. Helen's erupted, as I walked in the rain on a Portland street, a hooded figure suddenly took me by the arm, pulled me under an overhang, and said, "I cheated." She removed her hood, and I saw that it was Joe's widow. She told me that she listened to all the tapes that her husband had recorded during our sessions, and, using what she heard, got herself a job as liaison officer between Mount Hood and the Portland military headquarters. In that position, she made daily visits by helicopter to the mountain and reported back what the situation was at the site. Obviously, she loved it.

Another Colonel, stationed at the Colorado air base, wanted to decide whether to stay in the Air Force or pursue

> a different career. One of his responsibilities was to fly once a week to Washington, D.C. to brief the Joint Chiefs. He was not very happy with what seemed a routine job. He knew that if he waited, he would be promoted, but he wanted to look at other possibilities. When the time came for a decision, he waffled. After a few weeks I told him bluntly, "Paul, you can't make a decision." He got visibly upset and said, "Ray, I've been making heavy decisions during all my years in the Air Force." To which I said, "That may well be true, but the point is that you're not making *this* decision." About a week later I received a letter from him saying that I was absolutely right, that he had decided to leave the Air Force, come back to the Willamette Valley (the river that runs through Salem, Oregon and Portland, emptying into the Columbia). He had decided to settle in Salem and pursue a life-long hobby: the collection and restoration of antique cars. He maintains a large fleet of vintage cars, and he travels the country finding additional cars and attending antique car association meetings. And he serves as a counselor to nearby university students. We hear from him every Christmas.

For a number of weighty reasons, in 1990 we closed the office in Portland and moved to Seattle. We took over an existing office run by a woman who had acquired the rights to use my material. She was no longer physically capable of handling the clients and asked me for help.

As I said earlier, about 80% of my clients over the years accomplished a successful redirection into another field, in most cases with an increase in responsibility and income. Those who stayed in their field, whether it was a valid decision or not, invariably repositioned themselves into a higher level with increased income. Many of those simply started their own businesses.

Certain clients found it more difficult than others to cast off a hardened self-image in order to make a truly free choice. Lawyers always found this to be difficult. So also bankers, engineers, doctors, university professors. It was always necessary with people like this to work harder to help them to break the mold that their education and experience had put them in. A few (three) found it so difficult that they chose to ignore what the contract they signed said we would do for them, and what we would *not* do for them. Actually, I felt sympathy for these, because they were unhappy in the knowledge that they were not doing what they knew they were innately capable of doing.

In the Fall of 1998, at the age of sixty nine, I sold the business and retired. The woman I sold it to was under contract, and made a personal promise to pay us over a period of years, but she made some rather puerile mistakes, closed the business, walked away from it, and never did pay the full amount of the contract.

After retirement, we moved to an apartment in Seattle. After less than a year we moved to a town house in Las Cruces, New Mexico. Then we purchased a small house in Horizon, Texas, a suburb of El Paso. When we had determined that we could sell that house at a break-even level, in September of 2000 we acquired a 1.75 acre property in the outskirts of McAllen, Texas, about ten miles from the Rio Grande/Mexican border. It was the ninth move we made during our marriage. It will almost certainly be our last. My wife and I are very comfortable here. I think it's true that "You can take the boy out of the farm, but you can't take the farm out of the boy." So even though I'm old enough that I don't get around as much as I used to, it's nevertheless a nice feeling that I'm surrounded by open land, with a paved city road and unimproved land on the other side of the road to our west, an unimproved acre and a large orange grove to our east, with neighbors north and south no closer than a quarter mile. When we first moved to an acreage (8 acres with a small herd of cattle and some chickens) west of Portland near North Plains, Oregon, my wife was at first intimidated by the country, but grew to love it as much as

I. Both of us would feel confined if we were to live in an apartment, or even in a house in town.

As we grow older, even though we are living on our Social Security incomes, we can afford to hire the help we need occasionally to maintain the house and property.

As we've moved across the western part of the United States, we have seen many examples of the Heresy of Modernism in the parishes. We have had to "shop around" for parishes in which the pastor was a good traditional Catholic. Pope John Paul II astutely added a proviso to the New Code of Canon Law, allowing the faithful to register in any parish they choose, rather than be restricted to the parish within whose boundaries they lived. As we moved, we found it necessary, for our greater comfort, to 'pick and choose.' While we knew that any parish which offered the Sacrifice of the Mass with its essential parts, and if the priest pronounced the proper words of consecration over the bread and wine, it was a valid Mass, and therefore we fulfilled our obligation to attend Mass every Sunday and Holyday of Obligation. In many cases we were uncomfortable with what we heard—or didn't hear—from the pulpit, or with changes and additions to the liturgy which were improper, so we looked around until we found what we wanted.

The parish, Holy Spirit Parish, whose boundaries we live in here in McAllen, Texas, when we first moved into it, was a perfect example of the *Christian Base Communities* I had heard of in Latin America. So we chose another parish.

As the director of PAVLA, I had experienced inappropriate attitudes among a good number of the U.S. bishops; I had fewer contacts with priests. In my attendance at Mass as a laicized priest, Theologian and Canon Lawyer, now I was to see how different pastors presented the Faith to their people. In the interests of helping to identify the good and not-so-good priests and bishops, and helping priests and bishops become more orthodox in their Catholic thinking, I'd like to describe some of the different experiences we have had in the variety of parishes we have encountered.

CHAPTER 43

Ongoing Experiences with Modernism and Americanism

All the ***ism's*** described earlier in Part IV of this book affect the Catholic Church with a greater or lesser impact, depending on the philosophy, knowledge of Theology, Scripture and Canon Law, and the depth of Faith of each bishop, each priest, each pastor in every parish, and each professor in every seminary and Catholic school. As I said before, the bishops of Latin America uniformly projected a greater loyalty to the Pope and Rome than do many of the bishops in the U.S. The same can be said of the pastors, oftentimes independently of the attitude of their bishops, but, of course, frequently shaped by the bishop and the messages which he openly and sometimes unspokenly communicates to his priests.

While in this chapter the emphasis is on the time after we sold our business and moved away from Seattle, I will give an account of a number of the earlier experiences, dating back to the time immediately following my laicization.

A reminder to the reader for his or her personal study: The encyclicals on Americanism and Modernism by Popes Leo XIII and Pius X are given in Appendices B and C respectively at the end of this book.

The Northwest: Portland & Seattle

Our first parish in Portland, Oregon, was not comfortable for us. The pastor, who was also Chancellor of the Archdiocese, was too liberal for our taste. If he was not an outright Modernist priest, he was strongly contaminated by that Heresy. To some degree, we found out later, he set the tone in the Archdiocese of Portland. At any rate, not feeling entirely comfortable in the parish, we began to shop around.

First, we attended what was called the Downtown Chapel. It was a parish, and its small church was centered in the main shopping area of Portland. The pastor was a good priest and we were satisfied. One Sunday, however, an incident occurred which sent us further afield. The Assistant Pastor was preaching all the sermons that week. (Many pastors who have one or more 'assistants' share the celebration of the Masses each week with the assistant(s), but take all the sermons in a given week, and assign the sermons to another priest for the following week; this allows two weeks or more to each for preparation.)

As the pastor seated himself for the sermon, this young priest publicly announced his departure from the priesthood, and, one could infer, from the Catholic Church. In the process, he attacked the Pope, the bishop and many other things about the Church. I don't recall that he attacked his pastor, but obviously the pastor had no idea that his assistant was going to make this announcement. He was visibly agitated and uncomfortable. What that assistant did to his pastor was one of the cruelest things I have ever seen done to anyone.

That incident somehow changed the dynamic of the parish—it seemed to take the heart out of the pastor—and so we did some more shopping. We spent several years attending Mass at the parish administered by the Dominican Fathers where the liturgical rites were meticulously observed, and where we heard some of the finest sermons of our married life. A memorable one was delivered by the

Pastor on the subject of the Mass, the Eucharist, and the Real Presence. That sermon was one of only three on those special subjects I have heard in my more than fifty years as a laicized priest. And yet the concept of the Real Presence of Jesus Christ in the Eucharist is the absolute Core of the Catholic Church. He pointed to the tabernacle and said very bluntly, "This is not a bread box."(See Part II, the Sacraments, Chapter 18.)

We had moved from an apartment into our first house in Portland when our first child was about two years old. Some time later, a love-sick student from the public school about a block away rammed his car against his girl friend's car, which was shoved across the street and onto our lawn. My wife was frightened out of her wits because she thought our daughter was under the car, but, fortunately, she had disobeyed orders to stay in our yard and was on the neighbor's lawn.

That incident coupled with other lesser ones told us we had to take action: We decided we had to move into a safer neighborhood. (There had been a murder in the school in the year prior to the car incident.) By this time, our second child, a boy, was born, Lillian was pregnant with our third, a girl, and we were now intent on providing them with a better environment in which to grow up.

Move to North Plains, Oregon

We began looking—East, South and West. North would have taken us across the Columbia River into the State of Washington, which, for some reason, we didn't even consider. We ended twenty miles west of Portland near the small town of North Plains along what was known as Sunset Highway leading directly westward from Portland to the Pacific coast. We settled into what had been a logger's cabin on a strangely configured eight acres, with McKay Creek in the rough configuration of a backward 'S' along the east and south boundaries of the property. The house itself left much to be desired. It was the kind of house which I believe in real estate terminology is frequently referred to as a 'fixer-upper.' Oddly enough—in retrospect I believe providentially—both my wife and I felt comfortable the first time we sat in the living room of that house which was several levels below that of the top quality house we had lived in for the past few years.

To make a long story very short, in a few years' time we remodeled the house, doubling it's size. The house itself stood on high ground. The pasture, where we kept twelve to thirteen head of cattle, flooded two or three times a year as McKay creek overflowed its banks during the rainy season. There was a barn in which the cattle congregated at flood time, waiting for the water to recede. We at first rented a bull, finally purchasing one, and had several calves born on our acreage. As I looked back on my own childhood, I realized it was a wonderful learning experience to see calves being born and growing on the farm I myself was born on. I was certain that same experience on our new acreage would be good for our children. Our youngest, Mary, was born shortly after we moved onto the acreage.

Our home was about two miles from the small town of North Plains, which had its own parish church, making it very convenient for us. Its pastor, as we moved in and for several years after, was Father Manik, an excellent, spiritually outstanding priest who completely accepted me and my wife and family after I told him in depth about my background. Unfortunately, his good parishioners took advantage of him because he was very slow. Injured many years earlier in an automobile accident, he spoke ***v-e-r-y s-l-o-w-l-y***, and all of his actions were equally slow.

A parish committee determined to build a parish hall and prevailed on Father Manik to approve it. When it was built, the committee began to formulate plans to turn it into a restaurant as a means of increasing income to the parish. Fortunately, those plans never came to fruition and the next pastor squelched the restaurant plans and made good use of the hall.

Since all three of our children were now old enough to attend the religious training program of the parish, my wife attended a CCD (Confraternity of Christian Doctrine) meeting. There were two groups representing the religious training program for the parish: a six-member board of directors whose only purpose apparently was to meet once a year and decide on the text books which were to be used; and a group of eight or nine teachers who would handle the classes. The book being suggested by the board at that time was, in my wife's estimation (I agreed), simply a book on sociology with very little on religious doctrine. My wife insisted that the text books chosen should at least be derivatives of the Catechism of the Catholic Church, and that it should be the teachers as a group who should decide, with approval of the pastor, which text books they wanted. The teachers supported this idea, and the members of the board were strongly opposed. After extended argument, everyone turned to Father Manik, who, in his inimitable way, said "I . . . . support . . . . Mrs . . . . Kevane." With that, the board of directors was disbanded; all stood and left the meeting. The teachers, as the newly constituted board of directors, elected, and Father Manik approved, my wife as Director of the CCD program.

My wife spent six relatively thankless years organizing and maintaining the program, ensuring that they had a sound set of textbooks, finding and training teachers, arbitrating disputes, and enduring criticism for her work. She found it to be very demanding, but her primary purpose in doing it was so that our own children could be assured of a sound religious training program at an early age. We were both very mindful of the words of Christ Himself, on an occasion when a number of children wanted, or their parents wanted to take them, to come to Christ; the Apostles were trying to keep them away from Him, when He said, "Suffer the little children to come to me." (See Luke 18:16 and Matthew 19:14) In other words, children were to learn about Him and His Church at the earliest possible age. Our children probably will never fully understand the anguish and distress that their mother endured for them.

When Father Manik passed away, Father McMahon who originated in a diocese in Pennsylvania, was appointed to succeed him. At the earliest opportunity, I met with him, identified myself as a laicized Catholic priest, and told him about everything that had happened to me in Sioux City, Chicago and Washington, D.C. I told him nothing about my perceptions of the parish. Of course I told him about my wife and her work as Director of the CCD program. He fully supported both of us, and, of course, agreed to keep my secret. Again, we were blessed with an outstanding pastor who apparently 'read' the parish at a glance, disbanded the plans for a restaurant in the parish hall, installed moveable walls within the hall so that there could be classrooms for CCD, and at the same time the full hall could be used for other functions. It was too bad, in my opinion, that the parishioners never understood what saintly priests they had in those two pastors.

Every small town in Oregon, in the view of all other small towns, was filled with 'Red Neck' Oregonians. While North Plains didn't see itself that way, it's residents were 90% of a 'Red Neck' attitude. If your family could not trace its origins in the parish back several generations, in some subtle way you were never accepted, even though you were Catholic as were most people in North Plains. This was all counterbalanced for us by the fullest kind of support we had from the two pastors who were there during our time living in North Plains.

Move to Seattle

We moved onto our country acreage near North Plains in 1977 and then spent years of running our business in Portland, including daily commuting twenty miles to the office. In those years, we won a court suit against C. H. Patterson at J. Frederick Marcy & Associates, and we came out on top when the State of Oregon tried to modify our business. We helped a client establish a similar office in Seattle, and then eventually we saw the opportunity and the need to move our business and our residence to Seattle.

Judy Louderback, owner/operator of the Seattle Office, while doing an excellent job of working with her clients, was wearing down and wanted me to take over. While her knowledge of and instinct for business was excellent, her one weakness was that she took her worry about every client home with her every night, and lost sleep over them. She gave me a wonderful deal in turning her office and her entire business over to me.

We made the move to Seattle in several steps. I began to commute between Seattle and Portland. Jim Ellis, who had been my second in command in Portland for many years, simply couldn't handle the Portland office. The upshot was that my wife took the steps to sell our acreage and find a house in Seattle. Whenever I was in Portland, the office there flourished, and, of course, the office in Seattle produced nothing unless I was there. Again, to make a long story short, we sold our home, closed the office in Portland, moved into a beautiful house in Bothell, Washington, a suburb of Seattle, and saw the business in Seattle prosper.

A major marketing tool was to publish a book entitled *Employment Power: Take Control of Your Career.* Its purpose was to serve as a somewhat expensive brochure which explained an employment-seeking option which very few people knew how to use. The motif of the book was the slogan I had used for years to explain briefly what our service consisted in: ***The Self-Directed Career***℠. If individuals could broaden their self-image to concentrate on their inborn and developed ***talents*** rather than their historically developed *skills and education*, they could accurately decide upon a more suitable career direction. Once having determined the career path they really wanted, they could learn the professional methods of tapping into the 70%-80% of positions in the market place which are filled without ever being advertised or made known publicly in any way.

The book described the three-part service involved in the *Self-Directed Career*^{SM}: See Chapter 42 of this book.

Unexpectedly, the book functioned at an entirely different level than simply an expensive brochure. I'll give one example: A professor at Central University of Washington used it as a textbook in a private course he offered. He worked with five lumberjacks who had been laid off. The timber industry was in great difficulties at the time, at least partly because of the spotted owl controversy. These five men, using their professor and this book to rethink their situations, ***all*** in approximately two months' time, had well-paying jobs in different fields outside the timber industry. To me, that one example proves a point I have been making and proving for the many years I worked with people and their career decisions. There is a resiliency in the human mind, which, unenclosed by a system, allows that mind to 'think outside the box' and open up to new thoughts and to new levels of creativity which the 'standard job hunt' system suppresses.

Another step which we took with the Career Consulting business in Seattle was to join an annual 'Job Fair' which was very well attended. This move was the brain child of our oldest daughter who made the contact for us. Our involvement, in our best year, included a highway size ***'Dead End'*** sign prominently displayed at the entrance to our booth. The booth was attended full time by my wife and one of our two daughters who suggested to visitors that they attend my speeches. In another part of the arena, I was giving as many speeches as I could on The Self-Directed Career^{SM}; the Unadvertised Job Market; the importance of re-thinking one's career; talents vs. skills, etc. etc. I explained in summary how it could be done, and then suggested that my audience visit our booth, identifiable by its ***Dead End*** sign, where they would be given materials on the program, and/or sign up for an initial no-cost meeting to discuss their career situation. The interaction between our booth and my speeches was more than productive.

The Church in Seattle

Even as our business flourished, we were hard pressed to find a Catholic parish, Church and pastor in which and with whom we could feel comfortable. We knew as we moved to Seattle that this would be a problem. As a matter of fact, during the five years (1964-1969) when I was director of the international Papal Volunteer program, I studiously avoided approaching the Archdiocese of Seattle to request the appointment of a Diocesan Director for the program because the Archdiocese under the leadership of Archbishop Hunthausen was infamous for its observance of principles of the Heresy of Modernism. I was concerned that a Modernist priest would be appointed to the post, and it would follow that he would recruit young volunteers whose philosophies would take into Latin America attitudes which would harm rather than help the beautiful faith of the Catholic people of the Latin American countries.

Archbishop Hunthausen was infamous for two aberrations. One was the liturgical practices which he allowed if not actively promoted. A major story in *Time* magazine in that era reported on a funeral in which, as the casket proceeded down the main aisle of the parish church, a person dressed as a clown danced around the casket. The "clown" was the deceased man's wife. This was, as every Catholic must know, in no way in accord with the liturgical rites of the Church. The second aberration by Archbishop Hunthausen is that, in accord with certain tenets of the Heresy of Modernism, he began to sell many of the properties which the Church held in order to give away the monies from these sell-offs to the poor. A good pastor we finally found in the city of Everett, WA, told me that by this action, the Archbishop had severely weakened the Church in Seattle.

As we shopped for a parish we could be comfortable with, we found that the Cathedral parish had a Rector who was generally more acceptable than most, but some of his liturgical practices were questionable. We attended the Redemptorist parish adjacent to the

Space Needle which was generally better than most, but when the time came for our youngest daughter to receive Confirmation, the pastor forgot to contact us, which was most disturbing. She quickly got to an age where we couldn't arrange it for her, and to this day she has not received the Sacrament of Confirmation.

We were fortunate ultimately to find a pastor—Father Petosa—in Everett, Washington, a short distance north of Seattle, who was the epitome of the good, spiritual pastor whose sole purpose in life was to take care of his people and to save his own soul. He and I spent hours discussing the situation and how he could ensure that the people of his parish were not affected by the Modernism of Archbishop Hunthausen. After a few years, Father Petosa retired. His parish and a neighboring parish were united, and the new pastor was a Modernist priest whose liturgical practices were anything but theologically correct, and he inaugurated a preparation program for Confirmation which was nothing more than a social work training program. Every candidate, as *the* principal element in their training, was required to undertake several weeks of home visitation to the elderly—akin in my mind to a preparation for social work. As so many priests seem to have forgotten, each Sacrament is a matter of the acquisition of internal grace for a special purpose within one's soul and spiritual life, and not intended for some external mundane social activity. Once again, our plans to have our daughter receive the Sacrament of Confirmation were thwarted.

As we closed our business and were going into retirement, and since our children were all old enough to fend for themselves, we decided we would move away from Seattle and the State of Washington, for two reasons: 1) We were uncomfortable in the Archdiocese of Seattle because the Catholic Church there was too taken up with the principles of Modernism. While individual priests maintained their devotion to the traditional Catholic Church, the atmosphere in the Archdiocese of Seattle was tainted with Modernism and therefore was uncomfortable for us. 2) The cost of living in Seattle had risen in the past few years and we were concerned that our retirement income would not sustain us there. We had decided we would move to Mexico if necessary, but, having researched the cost of living in various parts of the country, we found that perhaps southern New Mexico (specifically Las Cruces) and southern Texas might work out for us.

Having sold our home in Bothell, Washington, we spent the best part of a year in an apartment in the south of Seattle and finally began the long trek to Las Cruces, New Mexico, with quite a number of stops along the way. After renting a town house in Las Cruces, we discovered that there was a state income tax in New Mexico, but that Texas, just a few miles away, had none. So, after six months, in the fall of 1998, we moved to the town of Horizon, a suburb of El Paso, Texas. We bought and lived in a beautifully designed small house and, for a time, reveled in the steady warm climate and the nearly cloudless skies—the rainfall was reported to be twenty four inches per year.

As a neighbor told us, we were living in what he called the "high desert." However, in spite of the pleasant weather, we began to realize, after a few months, that we had not yet found our final resting place.

Two things made the location uncomfortable for us. First of all, while the parish church was a block or so away and made it very convenient to attend Sunday Mass, the pastor, a young priest, had no daily Mass and had one communion service each week—on Tuesdays. We never understood why he did not celebrate Mass daily. During Holy Week in 1999 he permitted someone to write a skit about the Passion of Christ which bore little resemblance to the Gospel narratives and impressed us as at least somewhat sacrilegious, certainly irreverent. And the pastor, along with many other pastors we encountered over the years, belabored the need for the congregation to form a "community" which to him (and most others) would be accomplished by special get-togethers such as, in his case, a coffee-klatch after Mass on Sunday.

Another factor which caused us great discomfort was sand. Whenever there was a high wind, the abundance of sand would pile up in drifts as if it were snow. From time to time, the drifting sand would close the nearby Interstate Highway 10; it would fill a road from curb to curb with a leveled sand drift, and it crept into the house through cracks and crevices we didn't know were there.

On a positive note, our stay in Horizon gave us the platform from which we launched our trip to Rome and Italy which was and continues to be one of the most important of our experiences. More on this in Chapter 45.

The Taint of Modernism in the U.S. Church

Wherever we have been in our travels—starting in several churches in Portland, Oregon, in a number of parishes in Seattle, Washington, at the Cathedral in Las Cruces, New Mexico, in El Paso and Horizon, Texas, and finally in several parishes in McAllen, Texas—we have seen religious and liturgical practices which were undoubtedly inspired by Modernism, simple Americanism, or the direct insubordination of the individual priest.

On a happier note, now that we are living in South Texas, where the Hispanic culture along the Rio Grande border prevails, we find the practice of the Catholic religion is much stronger and deeper than any other section of the U.S. in which we have lived.

Invalid Materials for the Eucharist

Probably the worst thing we have heard about but not personally experienced was a pastor who made his own hosts out of cookie dough—not the required unleavened wheat bread—and, while his bishop knew of this practice and had to know it was wrong, did nothing about it.

Reconciliation vs. the Sacrament of Penance

Somewhere as we moved about, we were introduced to what seemed to be the latest 'fad' word which we began to see more and more: Reconciliation. Quite a number of parishes display in front of their churches a billboard with the times of Masses and what they refer to as the day(s) and time(s) of the 'Sacrament of Reconciliation,' or simply "Reconciliation.' For centuries, since the time of Christ, the Church has counted among her seven sacraments instituted by Christ Himself, the ***Sacrament of Penance***, in which we are to confess both our venial and mortal sins and receive absolution of those sins from the priest. Whenever I see or hear the word 'reconciliation,' I am instantly reminded of Father Louis Colonnese, a Modernist priest who was my major nemesis in the Papal Volunteer program. As I've stated before: During one of the first times we met, he said (I'll never forget the words): "We no longer believe in mortal sin." If there is no such thing as mortal sin, why ever would Christ have instituted the Sacrament of Penance? While one can accurately say that a *result* of confession of sin is 'reconciliation with God,' it has been more commonly said for centuries that when a person is absolved from a mortal sin, that person is returned to the State of Grace, is returned to friendship with God, and once again becomes a 'child of God.' I've always been concerned about the way people (priests and bishops particularly) talk about the Sacrament of Reconciliation, that they are tainted with the Heresy of Modernism and have lost the sense of sin.

The Sign of Peace (i.e. the Handshake)

Another practice which always seems wrong to us is the ***frenzy*** in some parishes with which the 'Sign of Peace" (usually a handshake) is performed. Sacred Heart parish in Edinburg, Texas, a few miles east of McAllen, is a particularly exaggerated example. The impression was (and this is not much of an exaggeration) that everyone in the congregation were at pains to shake hands with everyone else in the church. It seemed to us that the attitude in the parish was that this 'sign of peace' was far more important than the consecration of the Mass and the reception of communion. While we saw no significant liturgical aberrations, we nevertheless were uncomfortable with what we saw and moved to another parish.

[New] Liturgical Music

The pastor of St. Joseph parish in Edinburg was the vicar general of the Diocese of Brownsville. Still in shopping mode, we began to attend Mass at his parish. The pastor's liturgical practices were impeccable. More than this, at one time he delivered one of the finest sermons on the Real Presence I have ever heard, and it was only the second time in forty years that I heard a sermon on the subject. Unfortunately, he was an innovator when it came to liturgical music. At some point, after a few months, he began a practice of appearing in the sanctuary ten minutes before the scheduled time for Mass, wearing his vestments and carrying a guitar, with a 'key board' set up in front of him, and began to play and sing religious music, asking the congregation to join him, and he continued this until ten minutes after the time scheduled for Mass to begin—a full twenty minutes. We're quite sure that initially he did not notice that people began to stay away in large numbers. We were two of those who stopped attending Mass there.

A 'Christian Base Community'

We attended Mass once at the Holy Spirit parish in McAllen, within whose boundaries we live. But it was instant turn-off, because the pastor had turned over the management of the parish to a group of elected parishioners, and the result was almost nauseating. I had seen such parishes in Latin America, part of the new order inspired by Msgr. Ivan Illich, the communist priest in Cuernavaca,

Mexico, which were called *communidades de base*—Christian base communities—which in my estimation were intended to turn each parish into a communist cell, independent of the bishop and diocese. When the bishop of Brownsville replaced that pastor, certain lay members of the parish initiated a court suit against the bishop and the new pastor. Those laity who felt in control of the parish had developed the mind set that the bishop had no right to intervene in their parish life.

Two Outstanding Experiences

We found the basilica of San Juan de Valle to be an excellent place to attend Mass, but it was much too long a drive for us, so we settled finally in the parish of Our Lady of Sorrows. Msgr. Agostinho Pacheco was the pastor, an excellent priest, who was appointed to the parish many years ago, and, in a period of some ten years, saw it grow from a relatively small parish to one with 5,000 families and a grand total of over 20,000 parishioners.

I don't know how we found Father Patrick Meaney, a priest of the diocese of Corpus Christi, who founded the ***Rancho Maria,*** a hermitage located on several acres a few miles north of Hebbronville, Texas. Each of its hermits, including a few priests, live in their own independent huts, living a life devoted to prayer, both individual and communal. It is a most impressive group.

Liturgical Aberrations

After Father Gus (as he was affectionately called) retired from Our Lady of Sorrows Parish in 2008, the new pastor was and is a good priest with a specific idiosyncracy which I don't believe is serious, but it bothers both my wife and me. At the consecration he lifts the host and the chalice of wine, and, while turning with both the host and then the chalice from his left to his right, pronounces the words of consecration. The Pope himself, and most other priests, will devoutly pronounce the words of consecration over the host and chalice, and *then* (as the Pope does) elevates and, turning, presents the *consecrated* host and chalice before the congregation for adoration by the people. I personally wish our pastor would refrain from making such a show of the actual consecration. Of course, there is nothing serious about this—the consecration is not invalidated—but it bothers me in that it detracts at least a bit from the devotion which should surround Christ coming onto the altar.

Social Community vs. the Mystical Body of Christ

Catholics all over the world are bonded in a special supernatural relationship because, as members of the Church, they are together members of the Mystical Body of Christ. This concept was undoubtedly taught by Christ Himself to the Apostles, because more than two thousand years ago, St. Paul mentioned it several times in his epistles. For example: ". . . just as the body is one and has many members, and all the members of the body, though many, are one body, so it is with Christ." (1 Corinthians 12: 12) The body of Christ in the Eucharist is what nourishes us and makes us all one universal community with each other.

The passages from 1 Corinthians 10:1-22 depict the Church as consisting of faithful individuals who are members of Christ and temples of the Spirit. Their unity is achieved in the sacrament of baptism and in partaking of the Body of Christ. This culminates in the image of the body presented in 1 Corinthians 12, in which St. Paul emphasizes the unity of Christians in the body of Christ.

In 1 Corinthians 6:15, St. Paul stated that our bodies are members of Christ; in this passage he goes further and explains that those who are individually united to Christ form one body.

Such has been the traditional doctrine of the Church for two thousand years. All this was corroborated by Pope Pius XII in his Encyclical *Mystici Corporis Christi* (The Mystical Body of Christ) promulgated on June 29, 1943.

Starting with the pastor in Horizon, Texas, it has been disheartening to hear a number of priests promote in their parishes a kind of 'social' community that had nothing to do with the concept of the Mystical Body. Some pastors promoted a 'coffee klatch' after Mass to 'build community'. Others have promoted parish get-togethers on various evenings of the week to accomplish the same thing. This all sounds too similar to the protestant groups I have studied who had little else to do than strengthen the local communities of which their congregations were composed. I have seen far too much of this effort, in the promotion of ecumenism, to adjust the Church to the practices of other religions, from Christian groups to Judaism. We must remember that we have a bond with Catholics all over the world, even though we have not met them, that is supernatural in scope, mystical in its nature. We Catholics should take great pride and pleasure in that knowledge.

Important Contacts

Since we both felt that this would be our permanent residence in retirement, I began to make some contacts which I now had time for. These were contacts given to me by my brother, Monsignor Eugene Kevane—people and groups he had worked with during his lifetime, and with whom he developed a special relationship. There remained three of whom I have not met to this day, but have communicated with extensively by telephone and email.

Scott Hahn

A standout among these contacts is Scott Hahn, founder and director of the St. Paul Center for Biblical Theology, who was an ordained Presbyterian minister and a bluntly outspoken critic of the Catholic Church, was converted, and now is, in my mind, one of the very few outstanding Catholic apologists in the United States. He tirelessly travels the country giving—almost weekly—major presentations on the Catholic Faith. In a telephone conversation with me, he told me that one of my brother's books and a personal telephone conversation with him were the principal reasons for his own conversion. He never personally met my brother. I asked Scott to continue to pray for my brother, who died in 1996, and he responded, "I don't pray *for* your brother; I pray *to* him because I'm convinced he is a saint in heaven."

H. Lyman Stebbins

H. Lyman Stebbins and his wife were the founders of Catholics United for the Faith. My brother, Msgr. Eugene Kevane, was close to them, as I understand it, worked closely with them as they founded the organization in response to the Second Vatican Council's call for the laity to join in the apostolate of the Church. Since I knew that Mr. Stebbins had passed away, I contacted the President of CUF. I found out that Mrs. Stebbins was currently a member of the CUF board (I never tried to contact her but wish I had) and that Scott Hahn was currently the Chairman of the Board; he resigned the post a couple of years later.

Richard Bradley, S.J., Beaverton, OR and Robert I. Bradley, S.J., Austin, TX

It was my privilege to know and to spend time conversing with two outstanding Jesuit priests who were siblings (they had a third brother, also a Jesuit, who died before I got to know them). A group of Franciscan Sisters in Beaverton, Oregon, whom my brother had chosen to establish one of his Catechetical Institutes designed to train catechists, had Richard Bradley, S.J. as their chaplain. My brother's final two books, mentioned further on, were designed to be text books for these institutes.

These three Jesuits and a few others, as I understand it, maintained the purity of their Faith when the Society of Jesus as an organization slipped into Modernism. The Rev. Malachi Martin, S.J. wrote a book entitled *The Jesuits* which exposed most or many of those errors. When I asked Father Richard Bradley, S.J., whether he thought the book was factual, he said, "There's some poetry in it, but essentially it's accurate."

Anyone who watched the inner workings of the Catholic Church became aware that the Society of Jesus (the Jesuits) lost its way and as a group meandered into the realm of the Heresy of Modernism. Because of this, Pope John Paul I, whose papacy was very short lived—it has been said that he was murdered—had drawn up the papers to have the Jesuits suppressed. What Pope John Paul I started, Pope John Paul II completed and turned to a powerful organization called the *Opus Dei* ('Work of God) to be the stalwart force within the Church which the Jesuits had been.

The education of any Jesuit priest is—or at least used to be—unparalleled. This means, of course, that their knowledge of Theology and Church doctrine was beyond the norm. For that reason, they should be able to 'see through' any heresy that arises before them. But for that reason, also, they may be tempted more than most to individual pride.

In my early years as a student in Rome, we attended a weekly spiritual conference given by Father McCormick, S.J., the American assistant to the Jesuit General (known in Rome as the 'black pope' because of the extent of his power and influence). At the time, a Jesuit priest in New England, Leonard Feeney, S.J., was known for his harsh—and heretical—interpretation of a doctrine of the Church, *"Extra Ecclesiam Nulla Salus" (There is no salvation outside the Church).* His interpretation: Unless a person was literally and visibly a member of the Catholic Church, he or she could not be saved. At a certain point, we were told that Father McCormick would be gone for a few weeks. When he came back, he was visibly in a somber mood; the subject of his conference that day was 'intellectual pride,' which, as he said, was the downfall of Lucifer who was consigned to Hell when he said "I will not serve." St. Thomas Aquinas ventured the opinion that Lucifer was given a vision of Christ on the Cross and was given to know that he must worship the God-Man. He couldn't bring himself to do this because a human being is on a much lower level in all creation than the pure spirit which Lucifer was. Now, as Satan, he is on an unceasing effort to destroy the Mystical Body of Christ.

It is my belief that the outstanding intellectualism and knowledge of the Jesuits led them into the temptation toward intellectual pride. The Bradley brothers I knew escaped or overcame that temptation and kept their faith intact.

I came to know Father Robert Bradley, S.J. after getting settled in McAllen, Texas. I wanted to meet him because he was my brother's direct assistant in his final efforts to establish Catechetical Institutes around the country.

CHAPTER 44

Heresies of Modernism And Americanism Among Catholic Jews

To complete the contacts that I could make as a result of my brother's work, I called David Moss, President of the Association of Hebrew Catholics (AHC). My brother had spoken favorably of him to me and he told me that he had encouraged and helped David Moss found the AHC. My brother was therefore listed on the AHC's website as a founder of AHC (more on that later). When I first called David, he greeted me with great enthusiasm, and even more so when I disclosed that I was an ordained priest who had spent twenty years in the active priesthood. In response to that, he said in hushed tones, "then I should call you Father." I pleaded with him not to do that since it could create confusion among some people in that I had been laicized by Pope Paul VI. In that same conversation, he also said, "I loved your brother." Those two statements created a positive response that caused me, as I look back on it, to delay my recognition of a number of errors he was introducing.

Now let's turn to the extensive and in some ways disheartening relationship that developed between David Moss, his AHC and myself, even though we have never met in person. As I pondered what I heard in our phone calls and what I read in the publications of the Association of Hebrew Catholics, I grew more and more concerned about certain errors I perceived in the stance of the AHC, and more than concerned that my brother, Msgr. Eugene Kevane, was identified as a founder of the AHC on the organization's web site and therefore being associated with those errors. As a result, I wrote an Open Letter to the Hebrew Catholic Conference which was scheduled to be held on Jan. 27-29, 2006, in Jacksonville, Florida.

I am convinced that the Hebrew Catholics, in varying degrees, particularly those who have assumed leadership positions, are tainted by the heresies which corrupt too many of the clergy and hierarchy of the United States—the heresy of ***Modernism*** and the heresy of ***Americanism.*** Modernism and Americanism want to ***change*** the doctrines of the Church in order to keep up with changing times and to make it ***easier*** for American Catholics to *dialogue* with American non-Catholics, thereby promoting Ecumenism. The philosophy of Hebrewism prompts Jewish Catholics, aided and abetted by a clergy and hierarchy in the U.S. who are heavily tainted by Modernism and Americanism, to endeavor to ***change*** Catholic doctrine so as to incorporate Jewish theology and ritual. Such people apparently have a dual allegiance: they try to be both Jewish and Catholic at the same time.

In the course of that first telephone conversation Dave Moss asked me to serve as a consultant to him and his organization. I accepted, primarily because he had said, early in the conversation and with what I believed was true sincerity, "I loved your brother."

His singular relationship with my brother blinded me to certain disquieting things he said (and omitted) in the course of that first conversation. As a Theologian and a Canon Lawyer, and having been asked to serve in a consultative role to the AHC, I felt obliged to watch closely in the AHC publications for evidence of my concerns following that first telephone call. David had assured me that he would make use of me as a consultant, but after a year, he had not contacted me; therefore I called him. He told me that he would be in touch with me "soon"—"about several subjects." After yet ***another*** year or more of watching and waiting (I was receiving the AHC monthly publication, *The Hebrew Catholic)*, I became much more than concerned about the accuracy of his Theology. In my opinion at that time, he and they—the AHC—were promoting Heresy or at least skirting the edges of it—and I'm not talking about 'judaizing,' a word that I believe causes major irritation to Mr. Shoeman, if not to David Moss. (Mr. Shoeman is also a Jewish convert whose Catholicism is severely colored by his allegiance to the Jewish religion. More on him is coming up in a few pages.)

After I finished the Open Letter, mentioned earlier, I sent it first to David Moss with a cover letter which summarized the four major points of the Open Letter:

1. "On EWTN last March you stated that the Church taught an 'erroneous theology' for many centuries. No good Catholic . . . could possibly make such a statement without revealing some deep-seated problem with his own Catholicism.
2. "The 'erroneous theology' you identified was that the Catholic Church replaced the people of Israel. You probably meant the *religion* of the people of Israel. The enclosed (Open Letter) will show that there are plenty of scriptural citations, definitive statements by ecumenical councils, and pronouncements by Popes which demonstrate that you are wrong. The Fathers of the Church generally supported what you call an 'erroneous theology.'
3. "Along the same line, you stated that the Church no longer teaches that the Jewish people have been superseded . . . . (t)hey are an eternal people."

   I don't know how you reached that conclusion . . . . It bothers me that someone, in defense of his own theories, will *manufacture* evidence to support them, and will *twist* what is written or said by someone else.
4. "The following came, I believe, from my first conversation with you: You do not believe that Hebrew Catholics should

> try to convert the Jewish people . . . . (However) (y)ou know as well as I do that to more completely ensure their salvation, everyone ***must*** be baptized. As Catholics, we are bound by the command of Christ to go forth to all nations, baptizing them . . . ." How can you not want to obey that command of Christ, particularly with the very people you feel so close to and so much a part of?"

As I summarize my communications with Dave Moss, I should mention that in that context there are two other Jewish converts to Catholicism of whom I became aware. Ronda Chervin, a personal acquaintance, is the only person, aside from David Moss, who responded to my Open Letter to the Hebrew Catholic Conference. Her response was entirely positive. Among other things she said, "I wish that we (meaning, I think, herself, David Moss, and others) could sit down with you and your brother and discuss every paragraph of your letter." Later I asked her why she could be so positive about my letter while others were either negative or non-responsive toward it. She answered, "My parents were atheists, so I wasn't raised with any allegiance to Jewish ritual as others were." She also told me that I should write continuing articles for *The Hebrew Catholic*, the magazine published by the AHC, but at the same time warned me that if I did so, I would have to be very circumspect because of the sensitivity of the Jewish male ego. When I last met with her, she was (and I'm sure still is) a daily communicant.

The other principal Jewish convert of whom I have some knowledge is Roy Shoeman who wrote a book entitled *Salvation is from the Jews* and who maintains a website under the same name. One major problem with both book and web site is that their titles are, in fact, heretical. The title repeats what Christ Himself said (John 4:22)—"Salvation is from the Jews"—using it in support of his thesis. Christ made that statement to the Samaritan woman before he died on the Cross, at a time when, indeed, salvation was from the Jews. However, once he had died on the Cross, salvation came uniquely from Jesus Christ Himself—a statement made by St. Peter, the first Pope (Acts 4:12). This is a *twisting* of the Scriptures in order to support an erroneous doctrine, much as I have encountered among, for example, Calvinists who go to outlandish lengths to ignore certain scriptural passages such as the Primacy of Peter and the Real Presence and to read something into them which is not there.

In his Preface to the above-cited book, Shoeman says (p.9): "If there is one theological issue that both Jews and Christians should be able to agree on, it is that "salvation is from the Jews . . . . And Christians, or at least Christians who believe in the accuracy of the New Testament, have no choice but to believe that 'salvation is from the Jews,' since those are the very words that Jesus spoke to the Samaritan woman at the well" (John 4:22).

On the contrary, I can't disagree strongly enough. As I just said, before Christ's death on the Cross, salvation was indeed from the Jewish religion. After His death, salvation was, has been, and is now uniquely from Jesus Christ and His Mystical Body, the Catholic Church. Simeon (cited above—Luke 2: 32), holding the Christ child in his arms did not say salvation is from the Jews; rather, he spoke of the *Christ Child* (not the Jews) as being a light to the Gentiles and glory for God's people Israel (to the extent that they would accept Him). In Part II, earlier in this book, Chapter 18, *The Incarnation*, is a presentation of the doctrine of Original Sin, which, committed by finite human beings, was infinitely evil in that it was perpetrated against our infinite God. Reparation for that sin therefore had to be performed by a human being to be efficacious, but infinite reparation required that the human also be God. So the Second Person of the Trinity became Man and died on the Cross. The liturgy of Holy Saturday refers to Original Sin: "O happy fault. which merited for us such an incredible Redeemer" (personal translation from memory of the Latin).

It should be enough for Mr. Shoeman simply to be a Catholic, but in order to promote the Catholic Jews and their former religion, Mr.

Shoeman has *twisted* the Scriptures in order to support an erroneous doctrine, much as I have encountered in my work with converts.

The salvific power of Jesus Christ as God and Man ***infinitely*** surpasses what were centuries (and millennia?) of Jewish rituals and animal sacrifices. For explanation and clarification of Shoeman's book title as heretical, see above Part II, Chapter 14 of this book—The Principal Doctrines of the Church: Original Sin and The Incarnation.

The following question must be addressed by Shoeman and those who follow him: Does he believe that the Sacrifice of Christ on the Cross is truly perfect and that it *replaces* the incomplete and insufficient sacrifices of the Old Testament? Every heresy that I have studied (beginning with Judas) has its beginning in someone who does not humbly accept the Real Presence of Christ in the Sacrifice of the Mass—the Perfect Victim who, as God and Man, finally and fully on the Cross made atonement for the sins of all mankind. He is the "Lamb of God" who died once in a bloody sacrifice, and is now the self-same victim in every unbloody Sacrifice of the Mass. A true Catholic knows that this is the centerpiece of our religion, the source of the power of the other six sacraments. There is no need for other victims, for other liturgical rites, other than those which were given to us by Christ and established by the Church in conjunction with the Mass and the confection of the other Sacraments.

To reinstate, in the Catholic Church, any of the Judaic rituals of the old Testament would be to suggest that the Sacrifice by Christ is not perfect. Can it be that the suggestion to reinstate Jewish rites of any kind is rooted in a less than strong belief that Christ is present in his body and blood, soul and divinity in the Sacrament of the Eucharist? Or—perish the thought!—is there in such a mind a doubt that Jesus Christ was and is actually God? Judas turned against Christ because he could not accept the thought that we must eat His Body and drink His Blood.

Let me digress a moment to say that in the first pages of his book, Mr. Shoeman clearly is trying to be a true Catholic. The same must be said for Dave Moss. And for that I salute them. But Mr. Shoeman trips himself up, unfortunately, by endeavoring to make a theological statement when he is clearly not a Catholic theologian. That he is a Jewish theologian—perhaps. But he should be applying Catholic theology in order to reach an acceptable Catholic conclusion.

And he claims: "a Jew who has become Catholic is the best person to explore the true meaning of Judaism . . . ." But what reason is there for him as a Catholic to explore the true meaning of Judaism? It would be far more productive to explore the true meaning of Catholicism which as Christ intended *replaced* Judaism. From these considerations, it would appear that none (or very few) of the converted Catholic Hebrews who choose to 'go public' have undertaken an exhaustive study of Catholic Theology. Rather than undertake such a study, they attach themselves to a bishop or cardinal who will support them, forgetting that no one bishop or cardinal is infallible, nor is he necessarily a Theologian or Canon Lawyer.

In our initial conversation, Dave Moss insisted on the need to maintain the identity of the Jewish religion within the Catholic Church. Not just the Jewish people, but the Jewish *religion*, with some kind of retention of Jewish rites within the Catholic religion, somehow intermingled, as I understood it, with the Catholic liturgy. He didn't say this outright, but his meaning was clear. At some point in our conversation, he advocated a special Jewish Catholic Rite. Out of deference to his relationship with my brother, I didn't ask him, "Why should this be important to you, in the light of eternity?" The Apostle to the Gentiles said that there shall be neither Jew nor Greek . . . . *etc.* (Galatians 3:28) The leaders among the Jews who have become Catholic are remarkable. All of us have the imperative need to save our eternal souls and Christ Himself showed all of us the way to do that: To become "Followers of Christ," *i.e.* to become members of the Church which He created and left behind. And this must be accomplished through Baptism—for the Jews as well as everyone else.

There was no mention in that initial telephone conversation between David Moss and myself, nor in subsequent conversations, nor in any publication of the AHC that I have seen, of the outstanding Jewish converts of all time: the Twelve Apostles. The two principal Apostles—St. Peter and St. Paul—have major monuments to their lives and works which stand in the City of Rome, which is the New Jerusalem. A uniform stance of any committed non-Catholic, be it atheist, Calvinist, etc.—in short, any one who is fixated on a given philosophy, including a heretical one—is to ignore or to subject to private interpretation any Scriptural fact which does not support their thesis. The sole exception among the Apostles is the Epistles of St. Paul, but even in his case, what he wrote is sometimes taken out of context, and, among apparently contradictory texts, the one supportive of their thesis is chosen. It is noteworthy that I have not seen St. Peter even alluded to, either what he is recorded as saying in the Acts of the Apostles or in his two Epistles. It has been a puzzle to me that Jews who have become Catholic seem to have little or no reverence toward St. Peter, the very first Pope of the Church Christ founded, and the very first Vicar of Christ on earth. A reading of the Acts of the Apostles shows that St. Peter, knowing he is now a Follower of Christ, implies that he no longer considers himself a Jew. On several occasions, he refers to his audience, in effect, as "You Jews . . . ." For examples, see Acts of the Apostles, 2:23; 2;36;3:14; 4:10; 5:30; 10:39; 13:27-28.

David Moss wondered as we talked the first time how Jews who have converted to Catholicism could maintain their identity as Jews. I assumed at the time that he meant the Jewish *culture*. (It has become clear to me since that time that he probably meant their *religious* identity as Jews.) I told him, drawing on my studies and knowledge of Theology and Church history, that the answer to his question has been available in the Church for many centuries. When he failed to comment on this, I did not at the time pick up on the significance of his non-response. In retrospect, I suspect it was something he didn't want to deal with. In my experience, this has been the classic reaction of the non-Catholics I have dealt with, *i.e.* they do not acknowledge the Primacy of Peter as the first Pope; they gloss over the clarity with which Jesus pronounced, "Unless you eat my body and drink my blood . . . ." This kind of thinking clearly puts a person in danger of becoming a non-Catholic and wasting the agonies he or she underwent in the process of conversion.

As I pondered these things and became more and more concerned about them and the consequences for Dave Moss's own spiritual life, certain things began to register which accelerated my concerns for him as a close friend of my brother. For example, he has not once approached me as a consultant for my input on anything—in more than two years—even though I called him fairly soon (a bit less than a year after my previous contact) and asked about it. He told me at that time that in a short time he would be coming to me about several subjects. Now, several *years* later, that has never happened. He may have known from our very first conversation what my stance would be; perhaps he did not want to hear it.

I wonder if Dave Moss or any Hebrew Catholics who personally knew Msgr. Eugene Kevane, whom they held in high esteem, have ever asked themselves what he would say about the things the AHC and other converted Jews are contemplating? There can be no doubt: He would have said that they were toying with ideas which were (are?) of questionable orthodoxy and which can blossom into a full-blown heresy.

Anyone who wants to fight against the Heresy of Modernism which wants to *'modernize,' i.e.* ***change*** the immutable doctrine of the Catholic Church has two very good tools (among others) immediately at hand: Msgr. Kevane's final two books: 1) *"Jesus the Divine Teacher: What the Prophets* ***Really*** *Foretold"* and 2) *"The Deposit of Faith: What the Catholic Church* ***Really*** *Believes."* In my Open Letter, I suggested to converted Jews that a deep study of these two books would give them some answers which they might not want to face. Actually, I went beyond that and urged those who were in leadership positions among converted Jews to spend the time and money on high quality courses in Catholic Theology and Canon Law. This could wipe away any unconscious inappropriate adherence to Jewish ritual. I suggested that it would not be wise to rely on Catholic priests because priests and bishops who are infected with the heresy of Modernism—there are many of them—are drawn to and tend to sympathize with what the Association of Hebrew Catholics and other groups are trying to do, because it sounds so "modern" and so "ecumenical." Consider again what I said above about the seminary professor who wanted to reject the concept of the Real Presence in order to foster ecumenism.

The Open Letter I sent to the Hebrew Catholic Conference sparked six months of back and forth communication between David Moss and myself.

Following is a quotation from my Open Letter to the Hebrew Catholic Conference:

> "**Not too long ago** (March 2005), in a public statement on EWTN, David Moss rejected the idea that the Church replaced the people of Israel. He clearly identified the latter idea as an "erroneous theology" that was taught for 2000 years by the Catholic Church. He further stated that the Church no longer teaches that the people of Israel are superseded. They are an eternal people with an irrevocable calling. How can any *individual* declare that the Catholic Church (". . . whatever you bind on earth will be bound in heaven . . .") has taught erroneous theology for 2000 years? Both statements are heretical. The 'irrevocable calling' the Jews have is the same as it is for the rest of us—to save their eternal souls.
>
> In one stroke he denied the Scriptures as inspired by God, the infallibility of the Pope and Ecumenical Councils, and the fact of Tradition (the office of the Magisterium of the Catholic Church). No Catholic can say that the

> Church has held an erroneous theology for 2000 years and still remain a Catholic."

He later recanted and acknowledged that he was wrong in saying that the Church taught an ". . . erroneous theology . . . for many centuries." I rejoice for him in his retraction, hoping that it is complete and truly heartfelt.

However, his troubles, in terms of accuracy of doctrine, do not end there. While many of the things I heard from David during those months of communication demonstrated the general accuracy of his knowledge as a Catholic, my uneasiness grew about certain subjects as he expanded upon them.

David Moss' Theological Errors and PR Disasters

Dave Moss, starting in February 2006—I assume because of my Open Letter—started calling me and emailing me in an effort to convince me that his Catholic Theology was completely 'kosher.' We traded messages and phone calls through May of 2006. The documentation I have of those communications (mostly emails, some USPS 'snail mail' letters) fills a two inch loose leaf notebook. At some point he sent me a tape of the interview he had with Marcus Grody at EWTN on March 7, 2005. If my memory serves me, it was he who suggested that he obtain and send the tape to me—he was that sure the tape would convince me of his doctrinal soundness.

In a moment, I will simply list the questionable attitudes toward Catholicism which he, the AHC, and a few Hebrew Catholic "leaders" are promoting. I want to emphasize that I am personally acquainted with, and I know of, a few Jews who converted to Catholicism who apparently have adopted the attitude of St. Peter in the Acts of the Apostles: They present themselves simply as Catholics who are no longer Jews. As reported elsewhere, they have a perfect role model in Pope Benedict XVI who, when asked why he as a German visited Auschwitz, he said "I am a Catholic; that is the important point." In my opinion, every German, Italian, Spanish, Polish, Mexican . . . etc. Catholic can and should say, with the Pope: "I am a Catholic . . . that is the important point."

When the tape arrived, I simply listened to it and heard a number of disquieting things. Then my wife and I sat and, word for word, transcribed four kinds of information: 1) Statements which could easily irritate or anger a devout non-Jewish Catholic. 2) Statements which in fact were untrue. 3) Statements which were theologically and canonically at least questionable if not indefensible. 4) Statements which were unquestionably heretical.

Earlier, Dave Moss had asked me to send him a listing of those things I was aware of which could be questionable or poor public relations as stated by him or other Hebrew Catholics. After developing a transcription of the tape of his interview on EWTN, and gathering information from a number of other sources, including publications by the AHC, I prepared and sent to him a 21 page critique. I suggested that he take all the materials he and I had shared to Archbishop Burke in St. Louis, since very few bishops are accomplished Theologians or Canon Lawyers, and none of them are individually infallible. (Case in point: William Cardinal Keeler, Archbishop of Baltimore, "rubber stamped" the conclusion of those priests who were in dialogue with Jews that they—the Jews—did not need to be baptized in order to be saved. Although the decision was heretical, it was supported by another Cardinal in the Vatican. Cardinal Keeler was a classmate of mine in Rome; while he was a man of strong faith, he was not a knowledgeable Theologian.)

Now ***after more than six years***, David Moss has not replied, though he had said he would do so by the following spring. His only reply was to say it would be some time (a few months) before he could give it the thought it required, but for now, he said, it is clear that since 1996 some errors had crept into his work, and "I will study them and act on them independently." (I took this to mean that he didn't want my help in trying to correct the situation.)

The document analyzing the interview and statements from other sources was sent to Mr. Moss on May 16, 2006, I will simply list the objectionable topics which have come to my attention.

- **Supersession:** David Moss said: **"Part of the *supersession* was that the Church replaced the People of Israel**—that was an ***erroneous theology*** that was taught for many centuries." (Emphasis added.) No true Catholic can believe that the Church, in the light of the promises of Christ, can teach an erroneous theology. Fortunately, David Moss recanted, I hope with full sincerity.
- **Gentiles are "Grafted on . . . to the root which is Israel."** This was given as an effect of Baptism, but it has never been part of Catholic doctrine. Among the effects of Baptism: We are raised to a supernatural life, original and actual sins are wiped away, we have the indwelling of the Holy Spirit; we live a life in Christ, and become members of the Mystical Body of Christ.
- **The Jews are an Eternal People.** Perhaps, as I said before, this arrogance, even on the part of *Catholic* Jews, is designed to ignore the fact that their forebears committed an atrocity even greater than the Holocaust: They put the God-Man to death. See Gal.3:28: "There is neither Jew nor Greek . . . . for you are all one in Christ Jesus." Since each of us has an immortal soul, all of us are an "eternal people."
- **The Root of the Church is Israel.** The root, rather, is Christ Himself.
- **For a Jew to become a Catholic is to become a complete Jew.** There is no such concept in Catholic Theology. As Pope Benedict XVI said, the important thing is to be a Catholic.
- **Mass and Synagogue are Similar**. This reflects a very shallow understanding of the Catholic Faith. The Mass is the unbloody reenactment of the ***infinite*** atonement performed by Christ as God/Man, and He becomes truly present at the

Consecration. The difference between the two is ***infinite*** because of the Real Presence of God in the Mass.

- **Catholicism is Living a Jewish Way of Living.** Why would one want to go back to what was an incomplete religion?—No Trinity, no Eucharist and Real Presence, no Seven Sacraments, no Blessed Virgin . . . and on and on. It takes most converts a great deal of time to fully accept that they are members of the Mystical Body of Christ and what that *really* means. After many months of discussion with Hebrew Catholics, it is my opinion that a good number of them remain in transitory mode, unable or unwilling to make the complete transition to Catholicism and Catholic doctrine.
- **"The Conference is for Jews only."** While one can hope that a 'clannish' attitude is not widespread among Jewish converts to Catholicism, one single instance can establish a very negative image of the AHC and of any converted Jew . . . . (For example) one of the AHC who was asked by a "gentile" Catholic [they were old friends] for an invitation to the conference in Florida (Jan. 2006), the Hebrew Catholic responded, rather coldly I was told, "It is for Jews only." Can anything be less 'Catholic' than such a response? It was not only rude but can be interpreted as meaning that the Catholic Jew is something special, over and above the non-Jew Catholic.

And then there is the statement by David Moss that makes it appear that, at least in one instance, he is so inordinately attached to a Jewish ritual that he cannot give it up:

> **"(We) accept(ed) an invitation to participate in a Passover Seder on Holy Thursday afternoon. Then, the Holy Thursday Mass that evening so wonderfully fulfilled what we had been prepared for earlier in the day."**

The invitation to *participate* in a Passover Seder would suggest that they joined a Jewish ritual which is prohibited to a Catholic. Whether they were invited by a Jewish family or by a Hebrew Catholic family who performed the rite is not clear. At any rate, while simple *attendance* at Jewish rituals may be permitted to Catholics, *participation* in such rituals is forbidden by the Council of Florence. There is at least one diocese in the U.S.—the Diocese of Brownsville—which forbids Hebrew Catholics to have the Seder Meal ritual. A careful reading of the Council of Florence reveals that even the *attendance* at Jewish rituals is severely frowned upon.

The Council of Florence (A.D. 1438-1445)

Several times I informed David Moss of the prohibition by the Council of Florence against Jewish rites being performed by Jews who have converted to the Catholic Faith. The very first time was in the Open Letter I sent to the Hebrew Catholic Conference which was held on January 27—29, 2006. The Council, speaking of Jews who had converted to the Catholic Faith, was very clear:

> "(This Council) firmly believes, professes, and teaches . . . that whoever, even after the passion, placed hope in these matters of the (Judaic) law and submitted himself to them as necessary for salvation, as if faith in Christ could not save without them, ***sinned mortally*** . . . .
>
> "All, therefore, who after that time observe circumcision and the Sabbath and the other requirements of the law, it declares alien to the Christian faith and ***not in the least fit to participate in eternal salvation***, unless someday they recover from these errors." (Emphasis added.) (Jewish) Converts should be forbidden, under pain of severe penalties, to bury the dead according to the Jewish custom *or to observe in any way the sabbath and other solemnities and rites of their old sect.* (Emphasis

> added.*)* Rather, they should frequent our churches and sermons, like other Catholics, and conform themselves in everything to christian customs.
>
> "If there have been granted to Jews or infidels, or perhaps shall be granted to them in the future, any indults or privileges by any ecclesiastics or secular persons, of whatever status or dignity, even papal or imperial, which tend in any way to the detriment of the catholic faith, the christian name or anything mentioned above, this holy synod decrees them quashed and annulled; the apostolic and synodal decrees and constitutions enacted about the above remaining in force." (See Denziger 712.)

It is unfortunate that David Moss chose to ignore my efforts to remind him and others of the prohibitions of the Council of Florence. I believe that in several subsequent years on Holy Thursday, he either organized, accepted an invitation to, or participated in, a Seder meal on Holy Thursday. And, as he said, it prepared them "so wonderfully" for the Holy Thursday ceremonies which were to follow.

(Does this demonstrate a superficiality of faith among some convert Jews that the ceremonies of the Catholic Church which have Christ—God—as their founder and foundation, are not enough for them, but they must ***add on*** *the Jewish ritual they were steeped in?)*

Recent information gleaned from a recent edition of *The Hebrew Catholic* (No. 87, Winter 2009-2010) shows some improvement, e.g. offensive materials which formerly adorned the cover of the magazine have been for the most part removed. "Light to the Gentiles" which for years adorned the cover of the magazine is missing from that latest edition. Unfortunately, however, there is a clear transgression in terms of obeying the Magisterium, which on several occasions he has said he would never do, or, if he should find that if in any way he was not in tune with the Magisterium, he would take immediate steps to correct that error. Let me quote from the President's Memo on page 7 of the magazine:

> "Each year in St. Louis, the guest of honor at our Passover Seder has been a member of the clergy from the Archdiocese of our Cathedral Basilica parish. This has helped to let them learn and experience a little of what we are about. In 2007, Archbishop Raymond Burke was our guest. In 2008, our guest was Msgr. Joseph Pins, Rector of the Cathedral Basilica. And this past year, 2009, Bishop Robert Hermann, Auxiliary Bishop of the Archdiocese of St. Louis, joined us."

I reminded him immediately of my email of April 25, 2006 which referred to his practice of introducing the Jewish liturgical rite of the Seder Meal in conjunction with the Holy Thursday liturgy of the Catholic Church. The participation by two bishops and the rector of a Cathedral do not represent a statement by the Magisterium. But a statement by an ecumenical council *does* represent the Magisterium. Accordingly, the Diocese of Brownsville in Texas recently refused to permit the Seder Meal when a group of converted Catholic Jews requested permission to observe it. Therefore, in my previous email to Dave Moss (dated Saturday, March 10, 2010), I reiterated much of that same material which I had sent to him in my letter of April 25, 2006.

In perhaps the most perfidious act, David Moss ***entrapped*** a Prince of the Church—Archbishop Burke, who had been kind enough to allow the AHC into his Archdiocese—to act contrary to these prohibitions of the Council of Florence. According to his *Hebrew Catholic* publication which was issued shortly after Holy Week of 2010, he invited Archbishop Burke to a Seder meal on the previous Holy Thursday. Archbishop Burke accepted, attended, and thus was led into personal contravention of the Ecumenical Council of Florence. Mr. Moss seems to believe that an individual bishop or Cardinal is infallible. But we have just seen the mistake made by Cardinal Keeler of Baltimore; and there is the fact that the Conference of Bishops in this country were forced to correct an error in their new Catechism. If only David Moss had followed my advice and shown this information and many other points to Archbishop Burke instead of trying to deceive him, he might have performed an act of charity and saved the good Archbishop from an error.

Jew or Catholic?

In the course of my twenty years in the active priesthood I had a multitude of responsibilities, many of them simultaneously. Only one of those positions was in itself enough to keep me more than busy—five years as National Director of the Papal Volunteer program, organizing within the United States and developing the program in nineteen countries of Latin America. For the reader who is interested, Part III of these memoirs contains a listing of all the things my bishop gave me to oversee, usually three or four at the same time.

I have not so far mentioned one of the most rewarding of all my activities, which was working with and preparing about twenty people who wanted to convert to Catholicism. They came from all Christian religions: Baptists, Lutherans, Methodists, Anglicans, Presbyterians, Calvinists, even an atheist. The latter had a particularly difficult time. He was filled with doubts, see-sawed back and forth as we worked together. I believe he was besieged in a special way by the devil who was about to lose one of his flock.

Each of the converts I worked with had attitudes instilled since childhood, unique to his or her religious upbringing. Those attitudes, insofar as they were incompatible with Catholic Theology, had to be consciously identified so that they could sincerely accept the Catholic doctrine. Most of these concepts revolved around the seven Sacraments of the Catholic Church (most Christian religions recognize no more than three or four Sacraments except for the Anglican religion). And again, the biggest stumbling block was the doctrine of the Real Presence and the Unbloody Sacrifice of the Mass. In a great many of those cases, after the conversion of the non-Catholic party, his or her spouse told me that the convert spouse was a more devout Catholic than any born-Catholic acquaintance. When, in a few cases, I had further contact with the convert, I fully agreed.

As I continued to communicate with Dave Moss, concern was growing within me that his devotion to Catholicism was not as complete as it needed to be, and that he had a hidden agenda—perhaps hidden also to himself—which was at variance with Catholic dogma. His devotion to Jewish rituals seemed to be as strong as his devotion to Catholicism.

Some of the things which gave rise to these concerns are:

1) He said on EWTN that when he was in some fashion transported to an understanding that Jesus Christ was the Messiah, he then was baptized in the Baptist Church and only months later joined the Catholic Church. Would not Christ Himself have guided him into the one true Church that He Himself founded?
2) He said that both my brother, Msgr. Eugene Kevane, and Father Elias Friedman told him, as they urged him to undertake the development of the Association of Hebrew Catholics and he protested that he had no experience in such matters, that he should proceed and both told him that "God will correct your mistakes." Since the sin of presumption is a monstrous thing, I told him that no priest, and especially my brother, would ever say such a thing. If God were to correct all human mistakes, we would never have had a heresy in the history of the Church, and moreover this would militate against the doctrine of Free Will, which God never takes from us.
3) When he responded that he only meant that he prayed for God's guidance, I found that once again he had changed the subject on me. I pointed out that "God will correct my mistakes" and "I pray for guidance" are statements with two

entirely different meanings. He had used such an 'artful dodger' maneuver with me many times, all of which made me question how devout a Catholic he actually is. In a later letter, he denied that the two phrases had different meanings, using a typical subterfuge.

In an effort to help him deal with what apparently were leftover attitudes from his years as a religious Jew, I asked him the following question (this is important enough to repeat):

> "I will close this letter (April 25, 2006] with a burning question: ***Is it more important for you to retain your Jewish identity, or to be a Catholic?*** You and others give the *impression*—however untrue it may be—that your Jewish heritage is more important and that there needs to be an appropriate *melding* (more than has occurred) of Jewish ritual into the Catholic liturgy. That question needs open and honest meditation."

It seems to have been a question he didn't want to deal with, because I had to press him twice more to answer it. He finally came back with the following:

> "Finally, in response to your question about what is most important to me, the answer is simple: that I am in union with our Lord and Saviour in accord with the teachings and discipline of His Catholic Church." [Dec. 5, 2006.]

It is clear from this that he would not directly answer the question, which, unfortunately, probably means, at least in some subconscious level, that it is more important to him that he retain his Jewish Identity—more important than being Catholic, or at least equally important. Which also, of course, can mean that he is not the entirely devout Catholic which all of us should aspire to be.

After his non-response to my question, I suggested to him that Pope Benedict XVI can be a major role model in this regard. When the Pope, to repeat, was asked by journalists during his visit to Poland how he felt about visiting Auschwitz as a German, ". . . the 79 year-old Benedict said, 'I am above all a Catholic. I must say that this is the most important point.'" (Reported by Victor L. Simpson of the Associated Press, May 26, 2006.) In effect he was saying that while his lineage was German, he was—above and beyond that, and far more importantly—a Catholic. The Pope's response was very likely the most powerful example of pure humility I have ever encountered. Although it probably will arouse a charge of anti-Semitism against me, I would like at this point to raise the thought that the Jews have a history of creating God in their own image and likeness, even denying His existence, such as the episode with the golden calf (See Exodus, ch. 32). At the time of Christ, a certain number of Jews—I doubt if anyone knows how large the group was—were under the persuasion that the Messiah would be a worldly leader who would free them from the bondage of the Roman Empire, much as Moses led them out of Egypt. In my opinion, *because* the Jews knew at that time they were a chosen people, they developed an unwarranted pride in that fact, and did not humbly and open-mindedly seek or accept what was the actual Will of God. In the process they appear to have set aside the thought that God created *them* in *His own* image and likeness. They did not, and do not to this day, properly, humbly and open-mindedly interpret what their own prophets foretold about Jesus Christ, the Messiah.

My Earnest Exhortation to Catholic Converts from Judaism

There is an excellent book in print which I wish had never been written. Its title is *Jewish Identity.* Its author is the Rev. Elias Friedman, OCD, a Carmelite priest who was born into a Jewish family in South Africa, and who served at Stella Maris Monastery on

Mount Calvary in Haifa, Israel. He passed away some years ago. My own brother, Msgr. Eugene Kevane, a friend of his, wrote the Preface for the book. A good friend of my wife and me, Ronda Chervin, also a converted Jew, wrote the Introduction to the book. She is one of the few converted Jews whom I know personally who is unreservedly devoted to her Catholicism. We met her shortly after her conversion, and then, about ten years later, spent a good deal of time with her. We found that her devotion had deepened, that her understanding of her Catholicity was greatly broadened and almost unfailingly she attended daily Mass and is a daily communicant. She is the only convert from Judaism I know personally (I know *of* a few others, and I hope there are many) whose faith is stronger and deeper than most born Catholics.

For the most part, Father Friedman wrote his book with complete honesty, accuracy and truthfulness. There are some points where his Jewish bias shows through, but they are few and relatively unimportant. However, there are two reasons why I wish he had not written the book, consequences I am sure did not occur to him or to my brother: 1) It helps keep alive the determination of some of the members of the Association of Hebrew Catholics to develop and maintain a special liturgy which would have its own Jewish tone, embodying certain selected Jewish rites—such as the Seder Meal in conjunction with the Mass of Holy Thursday. After all, the Jews are (or is it better to say were?) the Chosen People—and there are those who will never let anyone forget it. David Moss once spoke to me about Father Friedman's book with obvious awe in his voice; it was clear that he looked upon it almost as if it were the inspired Word of God, approaching the Scriptures in its importance. And then, reason number 2), Father Friedman's book has a section in which he 'whines' a bit because when Jews are converted to Catholicism, they are not welcomed with real enthusiasm or celebration. And I have heard this same complaint from members of the AHC. Personally, every Catholic I have ever known—layman, priest or bishop—has welcomed converted Jews with open arms; there has never been an exception. This fear of rejection with the Church may well be the figment of the Jewish imagination since they have an 'anti-Semitism' mind-set spawned by the German Holocaust when Hitler and his forces seemed intent on wiping the Jews off the face of the earth. They use the charge of anti-Semitism as a tool to stave off every form of criticism. My personal belief is that there is very little anti-Semitism in the world, whether we are speaking of converted Jews or all the various sects of Judaism, and I suggest to all of them that when Jews of any persuasion make mistakes or commit errors, the rest of us should be able to be anti-mistake and anti-error without charges being leveled against us.

(*Actually, coming from the other direction on the part of the Jews, I perceive a greater incidence* of "*anti-gentile-ism," meaning, of course, opposition to gentiles by the Jews, than there is of anti-semitism.)*

And Jews should consider that there have been evils perpetrated in the world which far surpass the Holocaust. An obvious standout in the history of the world is the Slaughter of the Innocents when Jesus Christ was a child in Herod's effort to erase competition by removing the New Born King. Stalin and Trotsky put to death far more people than were killed in the Holocaust. The same is true of Mao Tse Tung in China, where about sixty million were put to death.

At the same time, all of the combined atrocities of the Holocaust, of Stalin and of Mao Tse Tung, fail to match the unspeakable atrocity and barbarity of those who put Jesus Christ, the Son of God, the Second Person of the Holy Trinity, the most important Person ever to be born onto this earth, to death on the Cross. While the Catholic Church which is the Mystical Body of Christ on earth has absolved modern-day Jews from any complicity in the death of Christ, the Church cannot change the historical fact that the forbears of every Jew since the time of Christ were the ones who did actually condemn Him to death. No Jew, even those converted to Catholicism, can escape that truism. I believe it is that knowledge, conscious or buried deep in the psyche of every Jew, that compels them to thirst to have the Catholic Church accept a special Jewish rite, to add certain Jewish rituals to the Catholic liturgy—all done in an effort to receive absolution from what culturally they have been part of. The converted Jew who has become a Follower of Christ should be able to set their culture aside, much as St. Peter did (see the many citations given above) who, in effect, exclaimed "You Jews . . . ." as if he were no longer one.

If indeed there is some antagonism directed by established Catholics against the newly converted Jew, it is undoubtedly caused by the stiff-necked arrogance with which these newly converted Catholics approach their fellow non-Jewish Catholics. See above where there is a summary of many statements made on a television interview by Dave Moss. And consider the Jewish Catholic telling his gentile Catholic friend who asked to be invited to a Hebrew Catholic conference, "it is for Jews only."

The Clarion Call of Vatican Council II

No matter what interpretation individuals and groups with a biased axe to grind put upon it, the primary focus of Vatican Council II is the necessity for all of us to strive for personal holiness and spiritual perfection. The Great Mission of the Church, as Christ commanded, is to spread the Gospel throughout the world and therefore to help all peoples achieve that level of personal holiness. The Catholic Church, composed as it is of the Pope, Bishops around the world, about four hundred thousand priests in all the dioceses of the world, and the aggregate of laity—about a billion souls, more or less twenty five percent of the earth's population—in all corners of the earth, was reminded once again of that command by means of the pronouncements of Vatican Council II as ratified by Pope Paul VI. With that as its primary focus, the Council gave to all the Church's members a number of tools which we all should use in bringing the changeless doctrine given to us by Christ Himself to all the peoples with whom we come in contact. Unfortunately, there are those who choose to interpret the Council documents according to their own personal biases. All of those who do this are almost certainly either immersed in the Heresy of Modernism, or are tainted by its efforts to make changes in the doctrines and Traditions of the Church.

For example, there are those who focus on ***Ecumenism*** as the primary message of Vatican Council II. I've already described the encounter I had with a ***seminary** professor* in the Archdiocese of Chicago who shouted at me that we must forget about the doctrine of the Real Presence of Christ in the Eucharist if we are to have effective ecumenical dialogue with Protestants. In other words, he was saying (and presumably teaching to young vulnerable seminarians) that Vatican Council II teaches that we must become Protestants in order to have efficacious Ecumenism.

Then there are those truly heretical Modernists, who, as the name implies, look to *modernize* the Church and bring her *up to date*, as it were, according to the 'signs of the times.' (This latter phrase was repeated over and over again by Father Louis Colonnese as he sought either to destroy the PAVLA program or to force me to turn it into something akin to a social worker program.) They endeavor to ***change*** the Dogmas, Doctrines and Traditions of the Roman Catholic Church. Their method, of course, is to ignore the actual documents of the Council and *create* statements which they present as actual documents. They use only those actual documents, which, standing alone, can be twisted and turned in such a way that they appear to support their specific misinterpretation.

For another illustrative incident, see above Chapter 37—a representative of the National Council of Churches congratulated me on being the 'only honest man' at the (USCC.)

At some point, while living at the USCC, I became certain that I was living and working amidst a bishop who was a Modernist and about twenty "Catholic" Priests who were also living heretical lives. I believed then and believe now that there were only about two or three exceptions.

CHAPTER 45

Our Visit to Rome and Italy

The turn-of-the-century—the year 2000—had been designated a Holy Year, and Rome and the Vatican in 1999 was nearing the end of a major clean-up effort, preparing for a major influx of tourists. As an example, St. Peter's Basilica in the Vatican (as we found out later) had several centuries of grime sand-blasted off. All the major basilicas and shrines in Rome had received similar treatment. We thought, therefore, that the fall of 1999, before the major incursion of tourists, was a good time for our trip—one that for years we had hoped to make.

In the summer of 1999, we began to make our plans. We decided on six weeks in Rome and Italy, set the departure and return dates in the Fall of 1999, and began the telephone calls required to make reservations at a number of hotels and with a number of religious houses which made rooms available for tourists. Raised by a strong Catholic mother, my wife Lillian had been dreaming of visiting Rome since she was a girl. To me, who had lived seven years of my life in Rome and Italy, it was like a second home and I seriously wanted to re-visit those many years. Simply making the arrangements was exciting for both of us.

It was a long and tiring flight both going and coming, but, we agreed it was worth every minute of it.

All of Italy, it seemed, opened up to us as we landed, and welcomed us every step of the way for six weeks. We collected our luggage, walked through the Customs area as if through an empty room; no one checked our passports or our luggage. We simply walked through the airport to a taxi and told the driver to take us to the first hotel we had made reservations with, which was near Rome's main train station. We checked in, caught up on our sleep and the next morning walked to ***Santa Maria Maggiore*** (St. Mary Major), one of the major basilicas in Rome, and attended Mass.

My wife and I entered into the trip to Rome and Italy as a personal pilgrimage. Our marriage had been strong from the very beginning, built as it was on mutual respect and shared values. We were conscious both during and after the trip that our relationship was even stronger than before, and that increased respect and closeness is growing stronger as the years go by.

There would be no point in simply recording a travelogue of the sites and the cities we visited during our six weeks in Rome and Italy. Numerous books on Rome and Italy are available—I have two or more of each in my personal library—so the observations I make here will be limited to a few of the principal highlights in my mind after seven years in Rome, Italy and Europe fifty plus years ago, and now re-emphasized after a visit of six weeks in 1999. We had planned to spend the first and last weeks in Rome, and, after the first week, to travel to Assisi, Florence, Venice, and, as a complete change of pace, the smaller towns of Bellagio and Corniglia on the northern west coast of Italy, both of them in the region south of Milan known as *Cinque Terra* (literally "five lands" but actually five smaller towns along the Mediterranean coast), then back to the town of Frascati, in the center of wine country, about a half hour by commuter train from the main train station in Rome. I knew as a student many years ago that every year during a wine festival in Frascati, the drinking fountains in the streets dispensed wine, not water, for a day or two. For the last week, we attended daily Mass at the parish church in Frascati, and then took the commuter train into Rome to re-visit the highlights of the first week and to visit a few new ones.

The principal highlights in Rome, of course, were the major basilicas and the people. St. John Lateran, the Pope's Cathedral Church (St. Peter's has been described as his private chapel), where I spent three years studying toward my doctorate in Canon Law and on whose facade is inscribed *Omnium urbis et orbis Ecclesiarum Mater et Caput*: (Literally: 'The mother and head of all churches in the City of Rome and of the world" or more simply: "Cathedral of Rome and of the World.")

Across the street from the facade of that magnificent basilica stands a striking statuary commemorating a visit by St. Francis of Assisi (1181-1226 A.D.) to Rome when he petitioned Pope Innocent III for permission to found a new religious order, existing to this day as the Franciscans.

Across another street from the basilica is housed the "Holy Stairs" which tradition tells us Christ was forced to climb during his Passion on the Way of the Cross. St. Helena, mother of Constantine the Great, in the early fourth century (c.325 A.D.) had the stairs moved from Jerusalem to Rome and installed where they are now, covered with wood, with a series of small 'windows' over each red stain which again tradition tells us were drops of blood from Christ Himself. The Stairs were closed during our visit in 1999, but years ago on the many occasions when I visited the Stairs, there were always hordes of people, on their knees, climbing from bottom to top.

St. Mary Major, where we attended Mass during our first few days in Rome, is its own marvel. Among many, many other things, tradition tells us that the head of St. Peter, the first Pope, is maintained as a relic over the main altar.

St. Peter's Basilica

St. Peter's basilica, at the other end of the City from the two aforementioned basilicas, is, of course, the highlight among highlights. It is the largest church in the world. Remarkably, it was built on the slant of a hill, over a cemetery, and the tradition over the centuries tells us that the tomb of St. Peter was located directly beneath the main altar.

St. Peter's basilica, in my mind, is one of the wonders of the world. In my seven years of study in Rome, I visited St. Peter's over and over. It is filled with wonders, from incredible art work which proclaims the existence of God and His dominion over everything on earth and in the universe, to the Spirit of God which, to anyone who believes in God, clearly pervades that magnificent church. I spent hours in St. Peter's during seven years in Rome many years ago, now some forty years later, as I once again visited St. Peter's, in some sense everything was as if I had never seen it before, and my perception was much more sensitive and I saw it in a new light. I felt as if I had come home again.

A major part of any visit to St. Peter's must include the Sistine Chapel which can be entered directly from the basilica. The first and many other times I visited the Chapel many years ago as a seminarian, I stood in awe of the incredible paintings by Michelangelo—the Last Judgment on the front wall over the Chapel's main altar, and the Creation of Adam on the ceiling. During my last visit in 1999, I was disappointed in that the rich work of Michelangelo had been 'refurbished' and now looked as if it were done in watercolors. My wife, who had never seen it before, was not greatly impressed, expecting as she did the rich colors of the many celebrated paintings which we saw throughout St. Peter's.

Visit to Northern Italy

After a week in Rome, we went north to Assisi, Florence, Venice, Bellagio and Corniglia, and back to Frascati for a final week in Rome. Each of them, once again, had me feeling as if I was coming home. Bellagio and Corniglia were new to me and were simply a visit to the Mediterranean coastal region to experience the beauty of the area. In Assisi, the basilica of St. Francis and the convent of St. Clare were being repaired after a bad earthquake. While we stayed at the convent of St. Clare, the chapel was under repair and unavailable to us. We could simply see the basilica of St. Francis from the outside. But the visit brought back many memories for me, including a visit to the chapel of St. Clare where she is entombed in a glass coffin under the main altar. At that time, 700 years after her death, I saw with my own eyes that there was still flesh on her lips and that there was still flesh on her entire body.

In Florence the main basilica is still as beautiful and majestic as ever, the studio where the incredible statue of David by Michelangelo is open for public viewing, and, then as now most impressive to me, were the unfinished works of Michelangelo, in each case with the figures he had been working on looking as if they were bursting out of the individual block of stone. There were those who said at the time, and undoubtedly to this day, that Michelangelo was inspired in his works of art, much as the writers of the Scriptures were inspired by and under the direct guidance of God Himself.

St. Mark's basilica in Venice was as awesome as ever, but our visit was marred by two or three days of overcast skies and unending rain.

After visiting Bellagio and Corniglia, we returned to Rome, staying at the Hotel Pinnochio in the nearby city of Frascati. From there we commuted to Rome for the final week of our pilgrimage.

As I discovered more than fifty years ago during my seven years as a student, and as I discovered once again in 1999, it is the ***people*** of Italy who provide an indefinable glow to all the highlights, first of Rome, and then of every other city and region of the nation. While as in every society there are exceptions, Italians have a very deep and child-like Faith in God. They show this faith to each other, and they are always willing to talk openly about it. I saw them fifty years ago attend Mass in droves, and saw this once again in 1999. In every basilica we visited there was a steady stream of Italians going to confession. Their charity toward each other and toward us as foreigners was moving.

Monsignor Richard Burns, the Vice-Rector of the North American College, in a general meeting with the student body when I was a student in the fifties, remarked on the tourism in Rome. Any of us could see what he talked about that day—that tourism in Rome, in terms of sheer numbers, outpaced every other city of Europe. In his opinion, and it is mine also, this was because of the sheer charity and the welcoming attitude of the Italian people. Anyone could visit anywhere in Italy and feel entirely welcome. And this was particularly true of Rome.

The Charity of the Italian People

Many times, as a student in Rome in the 1950's, when I couldn't find a particular site which I wanted to visit, I asked an Italian on the street, man or woman, for directions. When the answer was more complicated than simply pointing it out, ***in every case*** the person I asked stopped what he or she was doing and *walked with me* to the site. Every one of them, of course, knew that I was an American. My wife and I had three similar experiences during our two weeks in Rome, two in Rome itself and one in the Tivoli Gardens, a short commute from Rome. In Rome, the first incident occurred when I was trying to remember where the church of St. Peter in Chains was located, because I knew that the statuary of *Moses,* one of the principal works of Michaelangelo, was enshrined there. An elderly woman whom I asked to give me directions actually led us to the church. (An interesting story, purported to be absolutely true, was that the mayor of Rome visited Michaelangelo as he was putting the finishing touches on the *Moses.* The mayor pronounced to Michaelangelo that in his opinion the nose was too long. Michaelangelo then took a handful of stone dust/shavings, climbed up to the nose, simulated pounding on a chisel while letting the stone dust trickle from his hand. When he climbed down, having done nothing to the nose, the mayor pronounced it to be perfect.)

The third incident was at Tivoli Gardens, filled with hundreds of species of green plants, and abounding in fountains and flowing water. Unfortunately, the day we visited during our last week in Rome, all the fountains and waterfalls had been turned off. After that disappointment, we walked around the town and became so thoroughly lost that we ended up a long way from the train station and had no idea where it was. We finally had to ask a young man for directions. We found out from him that the station was directly opposite to the direction we thought it was. He then walked with us, as I recall more than one half mile until we could see the station and recognize it for ourselves.

In a much earlier time, as I reported previously in this book, a group of Italians took special care of my friends from London. For myself, having extensive experience in fifteen to twenty countries, none of the peoples I have come to know can match the Italians in the way they live their religious beliefs, in the charity they show toward everyone, and in the glowing goodness which they radiate. The people in many of the countries of Latin America demonstrate a similar kind of goodness.

St. Peter astutely chose the site for the New Jerusalem because of the nature of its people, or perhaps they are what they are because they have the Vicar of Christ in their midst. Of course, what I say about the Italians I cannot say about their governments. After all, Mussolini at one time allied himself and Italy with Hitler. But then the Italians got rid of Mussolini in their own way once the war was over.

While our marriage had always been strongly based on mutual love and respect, the pilgrimage to Rome added something even stronger which we can only be aware of and find it impossible to explain. That alone, of course, made the entire trip invaluable. Added to that were a number of other values, such as our personal spiritual lives were strengthened, our Catholic religion became more personal and real to us, and there lingers in our minds the memory of all the beauties of Rome, from buildings to works of art, and the image of the Vicar of Christ on earth—Pope John Paul II—as he passed within ten feet of us on three different occasions, as did the next Pope, Benedict XVI as Cardinal Ratzinger when he ordained a class of Deacons from the North American College.

After that last ceremony, we rode up the hill with a busload of the new Deacons and joined in the celebration in the courtyard of the new North American College where we had a very negative and a very positive experience. The negative experience came about as a priest from a diocese in Wisconsin caught up with us as we moved around the courtyard, and, assuming as a laicized priest that I must be a Modernist priest, began to regale us with the thought that when the present Pope (Pope John Paul II) died, that a new Pope worthy of leading the Church in the 'Modern world' would be elected. Like so many Modernist priests, he seemed to give no allegiance to the Providence of God nor to what I had learned over the years that the Holy Spirit guided each Ecumenical Council so that the traditional doctrine of the Church (i.e. the will of God) would be maintained. After his enthusiasm ebbed somewhat, he noticed our reaction and said, "You don't agree with me at all, do you?" My wife said, "We love this Pope." And he disappeared.

It was a positive experience to meet with Msgr. Timothy Dolan, the Rector of the North American College, who obviously was a good Theologian, doctrinally sound, and impressive in every way. Not long after we returned home, we heard that he had been consecrated a bishop. Then he was appointed Archbishop of Milwaukee, and about ten years after we met him, he was appointed, and is now, the Archbishop of New York. Not long after his appointment to New York, he was elected president of the Conference of U.S. Bishops. Thus ended the on-going reign of Cardinal Bernardin. (A late bulletin: As of January, 2012, Archbishop Dolan has been called to be a Cardinal.)

A visit to Rome and the Vatican contributes mightily to anyone's understanding of what it means to be a true Catholic—which is the subject of the final section of this book.

PART VI

TRIUMPH!
DESPITE THE BISHOPS

CHAPTER 46

A Late Dawning Awareness

I deeply respect the Office of Bishop and bishops themselves as successors to the Apostles. It was my misfortune, for approximately five years, to associate with a group of bishops, priests and laity whose apparent purpose was to destroy the Catholic Church in the countries of Latin America and in the United States. They were steeped in, or at the very least strongly tainted with, the tenets of Modernism and Americanism—heresies whose *raison d'etre* is to ***change*** the existing doctrine of the Catholic Church, *e.g.* downplay the Real Presence of Christ in the Eucharist in order to promote Ecumenism toward non-Catholic religions. As National Director of the Papal Volunteers for Latin America, I was in a position to learn some things that others could not.

The tools for this massive undertaking were basically twofold: 1) Liberation Theology which was Marxist doctrine, thinly veiled with theological terminology, and 2) *Communidades de base* (Christian Base Communities) which were Communist Cells in disguise, which were to take over the structure of parishes and dioceses. The ostensible leader, as mentioned before, was Ivan Ilich, a Catholic priest of the New York Archdiocese, but also a committed member of the Communist party and active in that ideology. The "power behind the scenes" may well have been Bishop Bernardin in conjunction with the "***groups***" to which Father Colonnese deferred so often; information on those *groups* is to be found in Appendix A which is the complete text of my 1969 memorandum to the bishops regarding this problem.

As I worked hard to develop the PAVLA program, the enormity of that takeover effort began to dawn on me. However, my concentration on the Papal Volunteer program was so intense that it took a long time to fully sink in. Many years later, as I worked on this book, I understood why those who were behind the takeover plot were so strongly opposed to a *bona fide* lay apostolate program (PAVLA) from the U.S. to Latin America—they wanted it to be a non-religious social work undertaking if it were to exist at all.

"Because they have the proof."

I had my first inkling of this monstrous takeover plan during one of my early visits to Mexico City, waiting for a mid-morning appointment with the Archbishop to talk about PAVLA affairs.

That morning at breakfast in my hotel, I was reading what I believed was Mexico City's leading newspaper. On its front page I saw the stark headline: ***¡Illich es Communista !*** *(Illich is a Communist!).*

Later that morning I asked the Archbishop, who spoke perfect, unaccented American English, "How can they say such a thing publicly without getting into trouble?" His answer: "Because they have the proof." It occurred to me that he had most likely discussed the matter with the powers that be at the newspaper and they had together come to the conclusion that they had whatever proof they needed: he was a Communist and was devoted to some kind of Communist deception related to the countries of Latin America. Subsequent discoveries on my part added to the evidence that this was true, and I was able to determine more specifically what his target was. Since I had experienced the duplicities of a priest/communist years earlier in Italy, I was very wary about this one.

I found out that Ivan Illich was born behind the Iron Curtain, at some point in his early life immigrated to the United States, became a citizen, studied for the priesthood, was ordained a priest for the Archdiocese of New York. Throughout all this, he retained his allegiance to Communism, and, when his hidden Communist superiors dictated it, spearheaded the massive plan to change and control the structure of the Catholic Church in the countries of Latin America.

I learned much more about Illich in an unplanned direct two-hour conversation with him at the airport in Bogotá, Colombia when our connecting flights were delayed for more than two hours. For an account of the confrontation, see above, Part IV, Chapter 42, *Direct Conversation with the Enemy.*

Because of my experience in Italy with the Jesuit priest who was the 'golden voice of the Catholic Church in Italy' who turned out, from the age of twelve, to be a Communist 'plant', I had no trouble believing that Illich was playing a similar role.

As I continued my work with PAVLA, additional information came to my attention which solidified my certainty that there was a monstrous takeover plan under way.

There were four proofs:

1. The Language Training Centers.

These were founded and managed at Cuernavaca, Mexico and Rio de Janeiro, Brazil by Ivan Illich. They could be typified as *brainwashing centers.* I personally saw the effect on a few volunteers who attended the Cuernavaca center initially: their personalities were visibly modified, they had developed the conviction that they should not be going to Latin America (but went anyhow), and they had lost the initial personal confidence which had been completely visible in them. And then there was Camy (see Camy—Part IV, chap. 28), a field representative in Brazil, recommended by Father Colonnese and trained at Illich's center in Rio de Janeiro. Her ideology was diametrically opposed to what I wanted to see in the PAVLA program. Having seen these negative results, I opened the

Hogar Interamericano in Mexico City which was a language training center exclusively for Papal Volunteers.

2. Liberation Theology

The next concept I encountered which fit into the 'takeover' plans I was now painfully aware of was a newly developed "Theology" called "Liberation Theology." This was the basis for the radical changeover planned for the Catholic Church in the Latin American countries. After a quick examination of it, it appeared to me to be Marxist theory cloaked in theological terminology—and I said so publicly. It can be described as thinly veiled Marxism. There are those who call it Christian Marxism. Much to my satisfaction, about two years later, on a visit to Central America, Pope John Paul II condemned Liberation Theology as an aberration. At least some of the practitioners of this new 'theology' describe it as a means of helping those who live in poverty, determined that money should be taken away from the rich and given to the poor. So it was (is?) at least a kind of hyper-socialism. But Christ Himself said, "The poor you will always have with you" (Matthew 26: 11).

3. *IPLA*—Pastoral Institute for Latin America

To accomplish the takeover, Illich,—as I said—established two language training centers in Cuernavaca, Mexico and in Rio de Janeiro, Brazil. I can legitimately call them *brainwashing* centers. In addition, he was one of the main administrators and perhaps the founder of a training center in Quito, Ecuador called IPLA (*Instituto Pastoral para Latina America*—Pastoral Institute for Latin America). The purpose of IPLA was to train carefully selected recruits from every country of Latin America, educate them in Liberation Theology to replace the Catholicism they had grown up in, and train them in administrative skills. Thus properly prepared, they would return to their respective countries and localities and take the next step in replacing the structure and doctrine of the Catholic Church. I don't know whether they were to create a new entity, or simply to take over the existing parish, much as we saw occur in the parish here in McAllen, Texas, as is described a few paragraphs further on.

4. *Communidades de Base*

At any rate, the new entities designed to replace the parish (and, I assume, in some manner, the diocese) were called *Communidades de base* (Christian Base Communities) which, in my view, were simply Communist Cells disguised under religious trappings. I suppose there were larger entities (Cells) to oversee and control the work and activities of the smaller cells.

I believe I saw one example of a Christian Base Community here in the United States, in the city in which we live, and in the parish within whose boundaries we reside. As stated before, we attended Mass at that parish only once when we arrived in McAllen. Now, after two or more years, in a recent visit to the Church for a Sunday Mass, we found that, while the new pastor has made progress, the parish is not yet healed.

The purpose of the *Communidades de Base* (Christian Base Communities) in the countries, dioceses and parishes of Latin America, as far as I was able to ascertain, was to have those trained at IPLA in Quito, Ecuador, where they studied Liberation Theology and take-over techniques, return to their home localities and turn their parishes into Communist Cells, though not designated as such.

Opposition to PAVLA

Many, many years later I think I finally understood why Father Colonnese and the 'groups' to which he reported (and Bishop Bernardin and Ivan Illich) were so strongly and vocally opposed to the Papal Volunteer program and to the content of the studies presented in the PAVLA National Training Center.

Colonnese said, and according to him his 'groups' agreed, that these people (volunteers) should not go into Latin America under a religious banner, but should simply go as 'social workers.' And I should not be teaching them Theology, nor elements of the Lay Apostolate, nor methods of adapting to the Latin Culture. It finally dawned on me belatedly ***why*** all these people were opposed to the courses I insisted on for these Papal Volunteers: They all ran counter to what the recruits at IPLA were being taught as preparation to ***destroy*** the Church as she stands. The Papal Volunteers were being trained and sent to help ***strengthen*** the existing Church. And yet another belated insight: These Papal Volunteers were being sent directly from a large number of bishops in the United States to provide assistance to bishops in countries of Latin America, an action which by its nature *strengthened* each bishop of Latin America and would greatly weaken the Communist efforts to destroy the structure of the Church in those Latin countries.

It was quite clear at the time, and starkly so in retrospect, that Bishop Bernardin was ideologically opposed to the Papal Volunteer program. I'm quite sure at the time that he would have described it as maintaining a *diplomatic silence,* but as a Bishop and General Secretary of the USCC, he was ***obligated*** to speak out—but did not—when Colonnese publicly said things like "We no longer believe in mortal sin," and when he publicly stated that he was strongly opposed to courses in theology, the lay apostolate, scripture, acculturation, etc.—all of which are called for in the documents of Vatican Council II, repeating the centuries-old tradition in the Church. It was clear that Bishop Bernardin was an intimate member of the larger group which was at least friendly to the Communism of Ivan Illich and of the 'groups' on whose letterheads L.M. Colonnese was listed as a member of those boards—The Coordinating Committee on Latin America; and the National Information Network on Latin America. (For documentation, see Appendix A of this book.)

(In my opinion, Bernardin, Illich, Colonnese and his 'groups' were not as concerned about U.S. religious men and women missionaries

in Latin America because their ties to bishops at both ends were not as strong, and many religious women's groups were weakened by their fealty to radical feminism.)

Ivan Illich, like Father Colonnese and his 'groups', was adamantly opposed to sending lay people on an apostolic or missionary role to the countries of Latin America. When I asked him, at a rare meeting between us, why he was so opposed, he remained silent. When I then asked him why he took them for training, he said, "They're going to be sent anyhow and it's better that they have the advantage of my training." Therefore, the reader will recall, I initiated my own language training program in Mexico City so that the volunteers in training need not be subject to a very negative 'brainwashing' ordeal.

CHAPTER 47

Remembering the Papal Volunteers

The Papal Volunteers were outstanding Catholics in the Church in the United States. They have been characterized in similar terms many times. These volunteers were a shining example of what the Lay Apostolate can do to save the Church. (Pope Benedict XVI has inaugurated a special office in the Vatican called the "***New Evangelization***" whose precise purpose is to re-evangelize the faltering faith in all countries including the U.S. It has been reported that it will depend heavily on the laity.)

I knew the Papal Volunteers to be exceptional, of course, because I had the privilege of being their national director. Knowing this, it continues to be a matter of deep personal sorrow to realize that they have been forgotten. During the last few months, I have routinely asked leading Catholics as I have come in contact with them, "Do you remember the Papal Volunteers for Latin America?" The answers have ranged from a blunt "What's that?" to "I've never heard of them," to a more polite "I don't believe I'm aware of them." There has not been one person who knows about the program. Therefore, when Cardinal Madeiros ate humble pie and confessed to my brother, "Your brother was absolutely right; we should have listened to him," he and some of his fellow bishops chose to deny the existence and importance of the PAVLA program. I'm sure it was Bishop Bernardin and his ideologue successors as General Secretary of the USCC and later President of the USCCB who denigrated the Papal Volunteers in the eyes of their fellow bishops. I hope the bishops of the United States now will take whatever steps are required to reinstate the Papal Volunteer program to its proper position in the history of the lay apostolate where it can stand as an inspiration to the members of the Church to inaugurate increasingly effective acts of the Catholic laity in the modern era.

I can never forget the overpowering sense of hopelessness which I felt before, during, and after I presented my written report to the Bishops' Subcommittee in an effort to save the Papal Volunteers for Latin America (PAVLA) from complete destruction. (See the report in its entirety: Appendix A of this book.) As I already said, a friend of mine (Msgr. Claire O'Dwyer of Boston), after I described the entire ordeal to him, whistled and said "You've pushed at the power tower." He meant, of course, the members of the subcommittee of bishops who oversaw the PAVLA program, the committee of bishops who oversaw the work of the Latin America Bureau of which PAVLA was a part, the entire U.S. Conference of Bishops, and of course Cardinal John Dearden, Archbishop of Detroit, who was the elected president of the Conference and who was instrumental in ensuring that Bishop Joseph Bernardin became General Secretary of the United States Catholic Conference (USCC).

My concentration at the time was to ensure that the Bishops clearly understood the inescapable evidence that there were powerful ostensible 'members' of the Catholic Church who were diametrically opposed to the Papal Volunteer program. These were people like Father Louis Colonnese, later to become head of the Latin America Bureau; Bishop Joseph Bernardin, General Secretary of the USCC who in a quiet and subtle way supported Colonese; Msgr. Ivan Illich, founder and head of two language training schools in Cuernavaca, Mexico and Rio de Janeiro, Brazil and a priest of the Archdiocese of New York; Sydney Lens (I don't know if he was a religious man), who was the chairman of the two "groups" which Father Colonnnese had such strong allegiance to, and all the members of those two groups—all of whom are named in Part IV of this book (see, among others, Chapter 48). Sydney Lens, according to U.S. government sources, mentioned before, was intent on the overthrow of governments. Under one name he was devoted to the violent overthrow of governments; and under another name, he advocated peaceful means of protest.

Was Sidney Lens the power behind the scenes? I was never able to find out. Were the names listed on the letterheads of the two "groups" mentioned so often by Colonnese in effect the "board members" who stood behind and controlled Ivan Illich and Louis Colonnese? Because of the awe with which Colonnese spoke of the "groups", I long suspected that to be true but was never certain. Was Bishop Bernardin the "communist leaning" glue that coordinated all these people and groups and gave full support to Colonnese in his anti-PAVLA and un-Catholic activities and diatribe? While I strongly suspected that but could never be certain, he was certainly a major power within that group.

"We've Lost: You'd Best Go Back to Your Diocese."

After my meeting with the bishops on July 1, 1969, I waited in hope that the bishops' decision would be favorable in support of the Papal Volunteers for Latin America. Cardinal Cody of Chicago was in the process of supporting the idea that PAVLA be taken out from under the Latin America Bureau and be independent as a Lay Apostolate entity.

After about two weeks, it was Cardinal Cody who called, telling me as kindly as he could, "We've lost: You'd best go back to your diocese." So with a heavy heart I submitted the requisite letters of resignation. I struggled, of course to see this as the will of God, but it was difficult since I perceived the PAVLA program as perhaps the outstanding action of the Lay Apostolate in the entire history of the

Church. To my mind, the bishops should have supported it and the Pope who called it into being. I was grateful to Cardinal Cody for notifying me. However, for several weeks after the meeting on July 1, 1969, I lived in something of an eerie vacuum; no bishop nor bishops' representative contacted me—I heard absolutely nothing. I thought at the time that the bishops should have had many questions for me, and yet during my presentation no bishop asked a single question, made not a single remark, nor was I contacted afterward by anyone except Cardinal Cody who was not a member of that committee.

I was so wrapped up in my responsibility for the PAVLA program that my faith in the Providence of God was not as strong as it should have been. The outcome of all this would not be as I wanted it to be, but as God Himself determined it should be. St. Paul said it clearly:

> 11 Among human beings, who knows what pertains to a person except the spirit of the person that is within? Similarly, no one knows what pertains to God except the Spirit of God.
>
> 12 We have not received the spirit of the world but the Spirit that is from God, so that we may understand the things freely given us by God.
>
> 13 And we speak about them not with words taught by human wisdom, but with words taught by the Spirit, describing spiritual realities in spiritual terms.
>
> 14 Now the natural person does not accept what pertains to the Spirit of God, for to him it is foolishness, and he cannot understand it, because it is judged spiritually.
>
> 15 The spiritual person, however, can judge everything but is not subject to judgment by anyone.
>
> 16 "who has known the mind of the Lord, so as to counsel him?" (1 Corinthians 2:1-16)

The mind of God, in other words, cannot be understood by the human mind unless it is revealed to us directly or indirectly. The

Papal Volunteer program, while it was a most important program, served a higher purpose—I was to learn over the years. My own grief over the demise of the Papal Volunteer program and the weakness of my own faith kept me from seeing the larger picture until it all came clear as I was finalizing my work on this book.

It is unfortunate that the bishops' failure to act started a process that I can only call ***denial*** among the bishops that there ever was something called ***Papal Volunteers for Latin America.*** Yet it is true that the program can and should be given credit for bringing about a much greater good which was hammered home to me as I wrote this book and contemplated the evidence which was before me.

There began a five step process when, in the writing of this book, it finally dawned on me what had actually happened:

1. **"Your brother was absolutely right.** We should have listened to him."

   About two years after my return to my diocese, my brother, Msgr. Eugene Kevane met with Cardinal Medeiros and described the Archbishop of Boston as "eating humble pie" and saying, "Your brother was absolutely right. We should have listened to him."

   When I heard that Cardinal Medeiros had made that statement, I thought simplistically he meant that they should have supported the PAVLA program. Perhaps he did. There was, however, a much greater benefit which I was to understand a great many years later. It was nice, of course, to know that the bishops had finally, even though a year or so after the fact, grasped the full import of my memorandum. I had only two regrets: that their understanding did not come soon enough to save the Papal Volunteer program; and that Cardinal Medeiros did not see fit to talk to me directly.
2. **The Papal Volunteer Program was quickly terminated about a year after my resignation.**

From this, I concluded that whoever took charge after my resignation was under orders to bring the program to an end. It took me years to fully understand why this lay apostolate program was such a negative element for Bernardin/Colonnese/Illich *et al*, but it should have been obvious to me from the beginning: The PAVLA program was seriously involved in *strengthening the Church* in Latin America, while Bernardin/Illich/Colonnese/IPLA/Liberation Theology/Communidades de base were dedicated to *weakening and destroying* the Latin American Church structure.

3. **Father Colonnese Disappeared from the Public Scene.**

   This would be a natural sequel from the pronouncement made by Cardinal Medeiros to my brother. Apparently some appropriate personnel changes were made at the Latin America Bureau. At the time as I searched for his name, I found it only in the files of the late Cardinal Dearden, under the title, "Troubles with Father Colonnese." My computer would not give me access to that file, and my health did not and does not permit me to travel to Detroit to inspect the file personally.

   Perhaps the important point is that he no longer had anything to do with the Latin America Bureau. The only information we have about him is that ten years ago (1999) he was assigned to duties outside his home diocese of Davenport, Iowa, living in an apartment in El Salvador. I have been unable to track down any further information.

4. **Msgr. Ivan Illich Retired to Germany.**

   Not long after Cardinal Medeiros told my brother that they should have listened to me, I read that Ivan Illich had left his language training schools and retired somewhere in Germany. He has since passed away. Nothing was said about IPLA in Quito, Ecuador.

5. **For Several Years We Have Heard Nothing About Christian Base Communities.**

   There was a time, many years ago, when the ***'communidades'*** were discussed quite openly as the solution to many problems in the Church. As I said earlier, the only example I ever saw was here in the United States. It obviously was exposed for what it was and the bishop terminated it.

Conclusion:

As I have rehashed those terrible events of forty some years ago and written about them in this book, I realized something which my own weak Faith should have told me when the bishops failed to support me in spite of the overwhelming evidence which I presented to them:

> **Everything happened as God in His Providence intended it to happen. The PAVLA program came into being to bring about a greater good, and then, having achieved its purpose, was allowed to come to an end.**

The Papal Volunteers, by sacrificing three years of their lives in dedicated service to specified projects in what was at my own last count, several hundred volunteers in nineteen countries of Latin America, assigned ultimately to a given requesting bishop in one of those countries, gave us an outstanding example of the lay apostolate which may never have been equaled in the history of the Church.

Their selfless work, I believe, and the sacrifice of 3 years of their lives earned boundless graces which assured that everyone could do what they had to do in order to topple the monstrous takeover plot which was underway.

Following is the dawning awareness which I was given as I was finishing this book:

The Communist Effort to Take Over the Church in Latin America was Defeated!

I don't know whether the U.S. Bishops took action in terminating the positions of specific personnel with duties toward Latin America, or whether Latin American Bishops closed IPLA in Quito, Ecuador and the two Illich training institutions in Mexico and Brazil, or whether it was a joint action—which I would hope it was.

Plea to the U.S. Bishops

If I had the names and addresses of all those who served as Papal Volunteers over the years, I would raise the money to thank them all in a personal contact.

However, I know that action on my part would be relatively meaningless compared to a declaration by the Conference of U.S. Bishops, recognizing the valuable contribution made by the Papal Volunteers for Latin America, the individual sacrifices made by each in giving three years to the cause away from home. If the bishops would restore both the volunteers and the program to public awareness, releasing the Papal Volunteers and the Papal Program from the obscurity in which they have been held since that time when the bishops ". . . should have listened . . . ," but didn't—this would be a great benefit to the Church in the United States and in Latin America.

My Plea to the Reader

As you finish reading this book, I hope and pray with all my heart that you found it to be at least somewhat helpful, and I hope that it can inspire you to become even more of an apostle of Jesus Christ than you have been. The Church, in the U.S. at least, is in grave need of your active involvement.

I beg you also to remember me and my wife and family in your prayers; pray, if you will, for the salvation of each of our souls.

PART VII

THE ROMAN CATHOLIC CHURCH IN THE U.S. TODAY

(A Summary of What is Wrong and What Needs to be Done.)

CHAPTER 48

It's *EASY* to be a (Protestant)

During the five year period when I was national director of the Papal Volunteers for Latin America (PAVLA), I took a number of tours of the sites in which the volunteers had been assigned. At each site we arranged a meeting of the volunteers as a group in that location, mainly to give them news from the home front (their term of service was three years, some got homesick, all wanted to meet with someone from the U.S.), and to get feedback from them as to how the program could be improved. After a couple of years or more in a specific country and diocese in Latin America, their insights were invaluable.

At one of the meetings which I remember vividly, but whose location I cannot recall—I believe it was Peru, but I can't be sure—the group was composed of a number of volunteers and about an equal number of Locals. While my Spanish was not all that strong (I could understand—after years in Italy—but I couldn't speak it well. However, a veteran volunteer was always available to serve as translator.) During the gathering I just referred to, a Latin American woman told of an encounter she had within the month when a Protestant missionary approached her. She could not remember which denomination this man belonged to. He told her in the course of his sales pitch that she should convert to (specific denomination) Protestantism because it was ***easy***. I believe the word she used was ***facíl.*** Among the things this missionary told her was the fact that in his church there was no obligation to go to church every Sunday; there was no need for confession because of *justification by faith alone*; there were only three sacraments; no concern about the Real Presence because the bread and wine used at the ceremonies constituted simply a symbolic remembrance of Jesus at the Last Supper; etc., etc., etc . . . .

It was essential for me to tell her that Catholicism is indeed a religion which requires personal commitment. This is demonstrated by the fact that Jesus Christ, her founder, died on the Cross. And all who want to live spiritually in Christ must suffer: (See 2 Tim. 3:12 and Mt. 10:39.) We must observe the Ten Commandments, the Precepts of the Church, attend Mass on all Sundays and Holydays, receive the Sacraments as required . . . and strive toward spiritual perfection with all our powers. And there are those among the bishops and priests in the U.S. who continually try to make it ***easy***, i.e. more like the Protestant religions. For example, the observance of many of the holy days was moved to Sunday, so a person would not be required to attend Mass on a weekday

Christ Himself, however, made it abundantly clear that life in His Church would always require commitment and dedication. It is clear that, as He died on the Cross, it would be necessary for us to join Him, to take up our own crosses and follow Him. He gave us the following example:

> The young man said to him, 'I have kept all these. What more do I need to do?'
>
> [21] Jesus said, 'If you wish to be perfect, go and sell your possessions and give the money to the poor, and you will have treasure in heaven; then come, follow me.'
>
> [22] But when the young man heard these words he went away sad, for he was a man of great wealth.[23] Then Jesus said to his disciples, 'In truth I tell you, it is hard for someone rich to enter the kingdom of Heaven.[24] Yes, I tell you again, it is easier for a camel to pass through the eye

of a needle than for someone rich to enter the kingdom of Heaven.'[25] When the disciples heard this they were astonished. 'Who can be saved, then?' they said. [26] Jesus gazed at them. 'By human resources', he told them, 'this is impossible; for God everything is possible.' (Matthew 19; 21-26; see Luke 18: 22)

CHAPTER 49

The Church Today is Severely Weakened

The following points, some of which have been mentioned earlier in this book, are of such importance that I feel they need to be re-emphasized.

In my twenty years as an active priest, I experienced and observed many things, as recorded in this book. In the remaining forty plus years as a married laicized Catholic priest, a Theologian and a Canon Lawyer, it has been second nature for me to assess the state of the Church as my wife and I have moved to several different parts of the country.

My considered opinion is the Catholic Church in the United States is in a sorry state. While we have an increasing number of bishops who are spiritually strong as well as good Theologians and able administrators, it remains true that many bishops and a large number of priests as well as religious and laity have been tainted with—and in some cases steeped in—the Heresies of Modernism and Americanism. Many of the aberrations which were caused by the acceptance of these Heresies were covered in some detail in earlier sections of this book.

Throughout this section, I will present a number of the errors which have crept into the Catholic Church in the United States, and how monstrously the Faith has been weakened. In addition, based on my observations, my years of uncommon experience, and on my advanced degrees in Theology and Canon Law, I will propose some ways and means in which the Catholic Faith can be restrengthened and bring back to our society the values we formerly took great pride in. Those ways and means have been available in our Church since the time of Christ and they need only to be brought to the attention of her members so that they can successfully set aside the fallacious tenets of the Heresies of Modernism and Americanism.

In the more than forty years which have passed since I left the active priesthood and was given permission to marry, my faith has grown stronger, and my love for the Catholic Church has developed far beyond what it was when I was young in the active priesthood.

CHAPTER 50

A Pattern of Disbelief

When we look back 2000+ years, we find that the core of the Catholic Faith has been subject to on-again, off-again acceptance for a variety of reasons. The ***core*** of the Religion Christ founded, of course, is the Real Presence of Jesus Christ, at the consecration of bread and wine within the Sacrifice of the Mass. For a fairly in-depth examination of this doctrine, see that heading in Part II, Chapter 18, of this book.

In the modern era, according to numerous reports, Catholics today are ambivalent about the doctrine that tells us that the living, resurrected, divine Christ Himself is present in the consecrated Bread and Wine of the Sacrifice of the Mass, and in our tabernacles. Some studies suggest that as many as 70% of Catholics ages 18 to 44 think of the consecrated Species as merely a ***symbol*** of Christ. Another study suggests that if Catholics from 45 and up are added, then the figure of those who believe in the actual presence of Christ in the Eucharist rises to something around 50%. It has been estimated for years that as many as 60% of ***priests*** have significant doubts about the Real Presence. Since all bishops are promoted from among priests, how many bishops stand in doubt about this doctrine? And of course the reader will recall the seminary professor in Chicago who told me that in the interests of ecumenism, we must forget about the Real Presence. Think of the harm that he and others like him have foisted on seminarians year after year. That kind of thinking—i.e., that the Eucharist is merely a *symbol, a remembrance* of Christ—has Catholics becoming Protestants.

A year or so ago, the pastor of Blessed Sacrament Parish in Sioux City, Iowa—where I was assigned during the summer months after I completed my four years of Theology in Rome and before I returned for my three years of Canon Law—took a count on two consecutive Sundays of the parishioners who attended Mass. To his chagrin, only about half attended Mass, and, if I understand it correctly, the results of that count were a major shock to him. That section of the city had always been considered the most devout of all the Catholics in the area. Perhaps, however, the low count would not have been too surprising if one had realized that the wealthiest Catholics of the city maintained their residences there. (Mt. 19:24: "Again I say to you, it is easier for a camel to pass through the eye of a needle than for one who is rich to enter the kingdom of God.")

In the five years during which I was the director of the international Papal Volunteer program—1964 to 1969—I visited more than half of the dioceses in the United States, probably as many as seventy percent of them, met personally with most of those bishops, and with all the priests who were appointed as Diocesan Directors of the diocesan Papal Volunteer program. My impressions, as I said or implied before, were sadly negative, of bishops, of our clergy, and to some degree, of our laity. The truly positive part of that work was the deep faith and devout Catholicity of the Papal Volunteers themselves. I have said or implied this earlier. However, our experience where my wife and I live now—South Texas near our border with Mexico—is very positive. The faith is very strong here, much like I experienced during all my travels through nineteen countries in Latin America.

Starting with my arrival in Chicago as Director of the PAVLA program, I have seen a weakened Catholic Church. I refer you once again to Part IV which presents the various attitudes and heresies which have disrupted the practice of the Faith in the U.S.:

Ugly Americanism, the Heresies of Modernism and Americanism, etc. After I was laicized and my wife and I were married, we have experienced the same kind of weakness and loss of Faith as we lived in Portland, Oregon, moved to Seattle, Washington, and then much later in Las Cruces, New Mexico, and Horizon, Texas. While the Catholic Church in what is called "the Valley" (*viz.* of the Rio Grande river—extending from El Paso, Texas, through many cities and towns including McAllen where we live, all the way to Brownsville, Texas, where the Rio Grande empties into the Gulf of Mexico) has some problems with Modernism, the Faith here is deep and devout, enhanced by a population which is largely Hispanic/Mexican. For that reason, the Rio Grande Valley is one of the most comfortable places for a true Catholic to live in the United States. Even here, however, there are examples of the weaknesses in the American Church. For example, a parish close to us (the one within whose boundaries we live) was a perfect example of the Christian Base Communities (*Communidades de base*) which I encountered in Latin America. We attended one Sunday Mass there. It was beyond disgusting to see how the pastor had allowed the parishioners to take over and modify the liturgy of the Mass. When the bishop knew what was going on in that parish, he courageously removed the pastor and appointed one who would eventually correct the situation; but the people of the parish took the bishop and the new pastor to court in a very public effort to retain control. They lost.

In other instances, we saw pastors who tried to form a 'social' community within their parishes by having coffee and rolls get-togethers after each Mass, forgetting or perhaps not knowing that as members of the Mystical Body of Christ each Catholic is a member of the most perfect community which has ever been formed. We don't even have to work at it. It is simply there and a part of our lives, analogous to the presence of sanctifying grace in our souls. In all the years since being laicized, I have never heard a sermon preached on the subject of the Mystical Body of Christ and what it means to be a member of that ineffable Society.

The number of times at Mass in which the Sign of Peace appeared to be the principal part of the ceremony perhaps lends credibility to the terrible statistic given below that a high number of Catholics don't believe in the Real Presence but look on the consecration of bread and wine as something of a symbolic action. We saw entire congregations spend several minutes moving to many parts of the church shaking hands, it seemed, with everybody else. In every instance, the result was somewhat chaotic. This milling about never seemed at all in keeping with the majesty of the Sacrifice of the Mass and the Real Presence of Jesus Christ at the consecration.

In November 2006, the Catholic Radio Association reported a devastating series of statistics about how Catholics in the U.S. practice their religion. I reported those figures in Part V. I will repeat those statistics in the next section and add my own experiences which corroborate the study.

CHAPTER 51

Creating God in Our Own Image

The human mind, because it is created and therefore limited, can never—even in all eternity—completely comprehend the mind and essence of God. Even in the next life, our minds are finite and God is infinite; we will spend eternity contemplating and learning about His essence. Because of human pride, however, it has been part of human nature to think that mankind—at least those who believe in God—can know what the mind of God really is.

In their natural human pride, Adam and Eve wanted to "be like God" and therefore ate an apple taken from the Tree of the Knowledge of Good and Evil, which God had forbidden to them. Thus, they plunged the entire human race into a dreadful state in which we no longer had a supernatural goal of an eternal life in the presence of God. Since the disobedient act against the Infinite God was infinitely evil, that goal could be restored only by an infinite act of reparation, performed by God Himself. Hence the prophecies in the Old Testament foretold the coming of the Messiah who, as God and man, would restore the human race to its eternal supernatural goal in the presence of God Himself.

What we know about God is restricted for the most part to what He revealed to us. Because of our human pride, we like to ***think*** that we know more than that. And therefore we frequently commit the egregious sin of what we can call "Creating God in our own image and likeness." The following is a well-known example of this very human tendency.

The Jews at the Time of Christ

Although the prophecies of the Old Testament quite clearly described who the Messiah would be and what He would come into the world to accomplish, there were many Jews who determined that He would be a military leader who would release them from the bondage of the Roman Empire. Christ Himself dispelled this notion when He declared to Pilate: "My kingdom is not of this world." (John 18:36)

In a similar fashion, Christ clearly described what His Church would be, and yet there are those who ignore what He proclaimed and create their own image of what He intended or allows.

He said, for example, "Thou art Peter and upon this rock I will build my Church, and the gates of hell shall not prevail against it." St. Peter and all his successors became the ***Vicars of Christ,*** the ***Rock*** upon whom His Church continues to stand. He also said to Peter, "I will give you the keys to the kingdom of heaven. Whatever you bind on earth will be bound in heaven, and whatever you loose on earth will be loosed in heaven." (Matthew 16:19) Christ also said, "Behold, I am with you always to the end of the age." (Matthew 28:20)

It is very easy, as a result of our human pride, to assume that God evaluates the actions of our fellow human beings—yes, even our Popes—exactly as we do. In spite of incredible evidence that God looks upon the papacies of Paul VI and John Paul II with great favor, there is a certain number of "Catholics" who judge that those two popes were each a ***disaster*** to the Church. At least one book has been published which tries to prove that point. So if we judge that a given pope was a 'disaster' to the Church, so also must God Himself, we think, measure that papacy as a disaster. We can call this, as mentioned above, ***creating God in our own image***.

What is True Faith in God?

If we are to save our souls and enter into the Kingdom of Heaven, Jesus Christ told us very explicitly what our faith in God and our spiritual lives must be: We are to become humble as little children before God:

> 1 At that hour the disciples came to Jesus, saying: Who thinkest thou is the greater in the kingdom of heaven? 2 And Jesus calling unto him a little child, set him in the midst of them, 3 And said: "Amen I say to you, unless you be converted, and become as little children, you shall not enter into the kingdom of heaven. 4 Whosoever therefore shall humble himself as this little child, he is the greater in the kingdom of heaven (Matthew 18: 1-4; see also Luke 18:15-17)

And again He said:

> "Amen, I say to you: Whosoever shall not receive the kingdom of God as a child, shall not enter into it." (Luke 18:17)

A realistic interpretation of Christ's words, I believe, is this: our faith in God must look on Him as a small child will look on his parents. We must recognize that our very existence depends on Him. Beyond that, we must know and believe that God created everything in the universe and exercises complete dominion over all things, visible and invisible.

As Christ so clearly said in the texts cited above, He is the active head of the Church He founded, He maintains it in existence, and He is intimately involved in the choice of his Vicar on earth and guides the election of every Pope, staying with His Church until the end of time.

If any of us are so judgmental as to say that a given Pope was a disaster for the Church, we are saying that God made a mistake. We therefore are not approaching God in the humility of a little child, acknowledging that He has dominion over all His creation. While there is an admonition which should be applied to all our relationships, it is particularly appropriate when we consider the actions of the Popes who directly represent Christ Himself: **"Judge not lest thou be judged."** (Matthew 7: 1)

There are those who suggest that the United States, Christian though it may be in its vast majority, is heavilyAgnostic in its belief system. This is true, it has been said, because a large number of the Founding Fathers looked on God through Agnostic eyes. In other words, while they believed that God created the universe and everything in it, He does not intervene in its day-to-day activities, leaving that to the laws of nature which He implanted as He created all things. And yet the Scriptures have statements by Christ Himself that no one can come to Him unless drawn by the Father; how all depends on the dominion of God; we know that God performs miracles in support of beatification and canonization, attesting to the holiness of the individual.

But if a person acts in an agnostic manner, no matter how innocently—for example judging that some popes were disasters for the Church—this is tantamount to believing that God does not intervene in the selection of His Vicars, then to determining that Jesus Christ does not lead His Church, in spite of what He said. Sooner or later this attitude leads some people into Agnosticism—and sometimes to questioning whether God exists. And finally some are led to a certitude that there is no such thing as God-Atheism. We must pray with all our hearts that our Faith be protected from these aberrations to which our human pride can lead us. The texts cited above—and many others—make it quite clear that the Catholic Church is under the uninterrupted protection and guidance of Christ Himself, working through His Vicar as His representative on earth. I have heard a number of things that clearly state that the human race is up to its old tricks of "thinking for God," determining how He should evaluate a given set of circumstances—in other words we are back to ***creating God in our own image and likeness***.

We can surmise from the total dominion which God exercises over all of His creation that every occurrence happens either because He directly wills it to be, or, if it is some evil perpetrated by one of His creatures, He ***allows*** it to be because in his ***limitless*** wisdom, knowledge and power He can bring a good out of it which otherwise would not be. The most important insight for any of us is to realize that ***we do not know*** how God exercises His dominion over His Church and all of His creation.

It has been a personal belief of mine, first occurring to me during my student years in Rome, that Christ Himself communicates to his Vicars in Rome what he wants them to do, and how He wants them to do it, because he said "Behold I am with you all days . . ." While there can be widespread doubt that He *does* communicate directly with His popes, there can be no doubt that He ***Can.***

St. Paul makes it clear that we cannot know the mind of God: "For who has known the mind of the Lord so as to counsel him? But we have the mind of Christ." (1 Corinthians 2:16) Aside from being able to reason to the existence of God, we can know next to nothing about Him except what He has chosen to reveal to us.

When the Jesuits fell into disfavor, Pope John Paul I initiated the actions required to suppress them; he died (some say was killed) after about a month. Pope John Paul II completed the suppression of the Jesuits. The Opus Dei, as an equally sophisticated religious organization, was waiting in the wings to perform specialized activities for the Pope.

It wasn't long before the Opus Dei became controversial—it is praised by some, vilified by others. It would be nice to know what it is in the mind of God. Has it become an evil institution as implied by some? Or is it a good institution with individual members performing actions which are contrary to the organization's purposes and goals?

The founder of the Opus Dei—St. Josemaria Escriva,—in the course of time was perceived to be a holy man and he was entered into the processes of, first, ***Beatification***, and after that was accomplished, ***Canonization.*** The canonization was performed by Pope John Paul II in 2002. Looking at the organization of Opus Dei, there are those who say, citing specific questionable ways, that the canonization should be reversed. However, even if those who revile the Opus Dei are correct in their criticisms, God has attested to the holiness of the man himself.

Part of the process of canonization requires two incontrovertible miracles attributable to the intervention of the person to be canonized, one before his/her beatification and another miracle occurring ***after*** the first one, pointing toward canonization. By stringent rules, the prayers asking for the miracle are directed ***only*** to the person to be beatified/canonized, and a relic of the person is applied to the target (perhaps a person to be cured). Extremely exacting requirements are applied to the certification of the miracle. In every case of canonization, we ***know*** that God has attested to the sanctity of the given individual because He performed a miracle in his/her behalf.

Another way to put it is that canonization is one of the elements of papal infallibility. So no matter what one's opinion of a given pope may be, "what he binds on earth is also bound in heaven."

The ideas that both Pope Paul VI and of Pope John Paul II were disasters for the Church. must originate with enemies of the Church. Our faith should tell us that they became popes because Christ wanted them to be. There are Theologians who say that Pope Paul VI, because of the remarkable things that he accomplished in, *e.g.*, putting the finishing touches on Vatican Council II and finally bringing it to a close thus giving its documents their infallibility, is one of the great Popes of all time. As Christ chose twelve relatively nondescript individuals to be His Apostles, so He chooses the Popes He wants in order to accomplish what He wants to have done in His Church.

Let me say, first of all, that both Popes were duly designated Vicars of Christ who would never have achieved such prominence unless Christ Himself wanted them to have it (see above "Behold I am with you all days . . . ."). More than anyone else they deserve to be given the benefit of the doubt.

Pope Paul VI

This Pope, according to many, was prophesied in the Book of Revelation as the first pope to travel on an extensive basis. As national director of the Papal Volunteer program (brought into being by decree of Pope Paul VI), I was in Bogotá, Colombia on August 22, 1968 when he visited there on the occasion of a Eucharistic Congress. (This was one of a long list of the travels he undertook during his papacy.) When he deplaned, he knelt and kissed the ground, which became his 'trademark' on all of his journeys. The response from the huge crowd at the airport was overwhelming. For two days, as I recall, perhaps three, I attended his public Mass, followed him as he moved about the city. Wherever I went, I heard him talking on the radio and receiving a truly enthusiastic response from the crowds wherever he went. It was obvious that nothing was on his mind other than to communicate with the members of the Mystical Body in Columbia. The Latin American Catholics, in my experience, for the most part possess that childlike faith which Christ told us is required to enter the kingdom of heaven.

Pope Paul VI has been erroneously described as a Modernist Pope who had more Freemasons in the Vatican than ever before. I don't believe this is true. Because he was perceived as something of a liberal minded pope, he may have *attracted* a few more liberals and modernists. But I doubt that the difference was even noticeable except for those who wanted to discredit the Pope. When I was in Rome as a seminarian, it was a matter of common knowledge that where the greatest power for good was located—the Vatican—at that same place were congregated the greatest forces for evil. And I was to learn that all the Popes simply acted in accord with the admonition of Christ: Let the weeds grow with the wheat. If you try to pull the weeds now, you may damage the wheat. At the harvest, bundle the weeds and burn them, gather the wheat into the barn. (See Matthew 13:30)

This was the Pope who, like all the others, was there as Vicar of Christ because ***Christ wanted him to be.*** It was he who, with great courage, wrote the Encyclical ***Humanae Vitae*** which authoritatively, among other things, restated the long-standing doctrine of the Church condemning abortion and artificial contraception. It also preceded the actions of Pope John Paul II in extolling the human body as the Temple of the Holy Spirit. Some of his other encyclicals (e.g. ***Populorum Progressio***) have been badly misinterpreted by what I believe to be enemies of the Church.

It was about this encyclical—*Humanae Vitae*—that Bishop Joseph Bernardin said, "That ***damn*** encyclical." Since Bishop Bernardin, I suspect, was a direct unspoken representative of Satan, nothing could more fully substantiate the importance and validity of that encyclical. In addition, it is important to realize that as a pope publishes an encyclical on any subject that he presents that subject as pertaining to the Magisterium of the Church and therefore it participates in his infallibility. As Christ Himself said: Whatever he binds on earth, it is bound in heaven. (See texts cited above.)

Pope Paul VI energetically worked to bring Vatican Council II to an end, and, in the process corrected a number of errors, including a statement which the Jews wanted to have which he modified so as to be in tune with Church doctrine.

Pope John Paul II

This future pope was simply "one of us" when I was a seminarian in Rome, *i.e.* he himself was a young seminarian at that time. At some point he became the 'talk of the seminaries,' because he had visited Padre Pio who foretold what would happen to him. Padre Pio was a priest, a Franciscan, a holy man, a prophet, and a stigmatic, *i.e.* he carried the wounds which Christ had inflicted on Him as He was crucified: the wounds of the nails in both hands and on both feet, and presumably the marks of the crown of thorns on his head. When this young Polish seminarian visited Padre Pio, he was told that he would someday become Pope and that he would be assassinated. I'm sure thereafter he looked forward to his future with completely mixed emotions.

He was elected Pope on October 16, 1978 and began a pontificate which was one of the longest in the history of the Church—nearly 27 years. He died on April 2, 2005. True to the prophecy by Padre Pio, he was shot by an assassin in 1981. He was not only close to death, but an Italian doctor who ministered to him at the time declared that he was actually dead, but, in the providence of God, was brought back to life to spend another twenty plus years as Pope.

Apparently, God had a different view of the value of Pope John Paul II than do those who describe him, with Pope Paul VI, as a "disaster for the Church." Jesus Christ allowed Pope John Paul II to serve as His Vicar for nearly twenty seven years—and He could have removed him at any time. Then, when the Pope was almost certainly dead, God returned him to serve for another twenty plus years as Pope.

After the Pope (John Paul II) had finally and irrevocably died, his funeral was held in the square in front of St. Peter's Basilica. At the end the pall bearers were in the process of taking the pope's body in its casket into the front of the Basilica, taking him to his burial place with the bodies of other Popes under the Basilica. Before they entered the church, they paused and turned the casket around to face the crowd of people one last time. The sky was totally overcast, leading to a remarkable incident. The clouds parted, allowing a single ray of sunlight to shine down on the casket and on nothing else. The crowd of thousands took this as an act of God, as a sign of God's approval of this (former) pope and reacted with an overwhelming burst of shouting and applause. The crowd was shouting "Santo Subito!" ("Sainthood Now!") He has already been beatified.

How strong is the faith of those who do not trust in God (Jesus Christ) to watch over His Church in a way that only He can do? And as He told us that He would? The Grace of God, certainly available in great abundance in the office of the Pope, certainly will ensure that all human failings will be overcome—or even utilized. While I am not at all sure that there were more enemies of the Church in the Vatican during Pope Paul VI's papacy (they have always been there), who can say that he was trying to subvert the Church? Perhaps he was trying to convert them. The Popes should always be given the benefit of the doubt, because they are working as the closest representatives of God Himself.

CHAPTER 52

The Impact of Heresies on the Roman Catholic Church in the U.S.

Two forces have been wreaking havoc with the Catholic Faith in the United States: Modernism and Americanism. Both have already been presented in this book: See Part IV, Chapters 37, 47, 50 and Part V, Chapter 57; Appendices 2 and 3 are reprints of the two Papal Encyclicals which warned the Church about the presence of the two heresies.

The Heresy of Modernism, true to its name, wants to "*modernize*" the Church, or, in other words, ***change*** it, even though Christ left **His *eternal truth*** with the Apostles who were intent on protecting the Deposit of Faith and maintaining it as Christ gave it to us. The Heresy of Americanism, in the simplest way I can put it, seeks to have an ***American*** Catholic Church with little or no allegiance to the Pope and the Vatican, but seems to want to align itself with the political powers of the United States. In some circles, it is referred to as the "***Amchurch.***" (For more on the subject, I refer the reader to the book "*Amchurch Comes Out*" by Paul Likoudis, publ. The Roman Catholic Faithful, 2002.)

The two heresies are having a dreadful impact on the Catholic Church in the United States—more in this country, in my experience, than in any other part of the world. Perhaps the most urgent goal of the Catholic Lay Apostolate should be to realize the negative impact of these heresies and to put its energies to counteracting the damage being done to Catholic souls.

A few years ago, the Catholic Radio Association issued a report which is devastating: The next chapter presents that report.

CHAPTER 53

Statistics from The Catholic Radio Association

The following figures are horrifying. While there is no real evidence that they have improved somewhat since they were first published a few years ago, they illustrate a major crisis within the Roman Catholic Church in the United States. The Heresy of Americanism is pulling us away from the authority of the pope. (See above, Chapters 37 & 48):

-Only 10% of lay religious teachers accept Church teaching on contraception.

Actually, I strongly suspect that this statistic is not at all restricted to lay religious teachers but extends to a very large percentage of married Catholics. Priests I have talked to report that they very rarely hear the sin of contraception reported in the confessional—and this has been true for years. As a demonstration of how widespread this thinking must be, a few years ago there was an episode on TV's *Hannity and Colmes* on Fox News. Sean Hannity, a Catholic, during a program in 2007 went into near hysterics when a guest told him that artificial contraception was forbidden and was seriously sinful. Hannity denied this vehemently and actually cited as proof that he had been in the seminary for a couple of years where he learned that contraception was completely acceptable. If this is true, think of all the priests who were ordained from that seminary who, as a result, are 'soft' on artificial contraception.

The case can be easily made that artificial contraception is a more heinous sin than abortion. Before an abortion, God has exercised His Will and created a soul and a human being who either 1) remains unbaptised but has an eternal and happy life in Limbo, not in the presence of God, or 2) as the baby dies, he or she is given the full use of reason and the opportunity to receive baptism of desire. Many theologians believe that God in His mercy brings this latter to be.

In the case of artificial contraception, the Will of God is ***completely*** thwarted and He cannot create a new human person—at least not in the way He has always done so except in the case of Adam and Eve. Very few Catholics realize these things because they are not taught these truths; and it is very likely that a large percentage of priests don't think about them. Very few Catholics understand the difference between *artificial* contraception and *natural* contraception—commonly referred to as the Rhythm Method—which is more than merely acceptable because God so designed a woman that she can conceive during only a few days each month. When a couple as an act of love avoid the marital act on those fertile days, out of respect for each other, they enhance and strengthen the marriage bond.

-53% of the laity believe a Catholic can have an abortion and remain a good Catholic; and there are priests (and Bishops) who agree.

While I believe that 53% of Catholics responded to the question in this way, a number of qualifications need to be added. A woman with an unwanted pregnancy may procure an abortion and afterwards, repenting and sincerely sorrowful about what she has done, having gone to confession, remains (or once again becomes) a good Catholic.

Since I was the chaplain for a number of years in a Home for Unwed Mothers, I am perhaps in a special way aware of the pressures that young pregnant women must endure. A number of outside forces acting on a vulnerable young woman reduce the culpability for her, especially of young women who are oftentimes naïve regarding sexual matters.

The ones who are truly culpable in matters of abortion are those who *encourage* pregnant women to terminate the lives of their babies. No amount of civil legislation can erase the moral evil which takes an innocent life. Truly guilty of the sin of abortion are those who are complicit in it, encourage pregnant women to undergo the procedure, parents who promote it for their daughter, surgeons who perform the operation, politicians who publicly favor 'freedom of choice,' and thereby through scandal provide their public support and make it easier for a pregnant woman to decide to have an abortion. People in the latter category who easily come to mind are John Kerry, Nancy Pelosi, Joe Biden, various members of the Kennedy clan. Ted Kennedy was publicly pro-abortion during his political career, but he may have repented before he died. And there are, of course, many other so called 'Catholic' politicians who support abortion. Such people should be denied the reception of Communion, and some courageous bishops have taken that stand.

The former bishop of a Texas diocese, said about a Texas Catholic politician who was publicly pro-abortion, that in his private life he was opposed to abortion, but in his public life had to support abortion because of his constituents. Surely any bishop should be well aware of the concept of the lay apostolate and the idea that as members of the Catholic Church we are to give witness to our Faith as we live and work in the world. If the pressures of politics 'force' a Catholic to give up the tenets of his religion, then he should resign from his position and seek another career, or publicly state his Catholicism and openly state his opposition to un-Catholic practices and see if he can be elected in spite of his Catholic stand. He or she might be surprised at how such honesty will be supported.

-65% believe that Catholics may divorce and remarry.

On the contrary, a marriage between a baptized man and a baptized woman is a Sacrament, instituted by Christ, and is therefore indissoluble: Christ Himself said "What God has joined together, let no man put asunder." (Mark 10:9; Matt. 19:16*)* A civil court has no jurisdiction over a sacramental marriage bond, and certainly cannot declare it null and void; it does, of course, have jurisdiction over the *civil effects* of a marriage. After a divorce granted by a civil court, no Catholic may validly marry again until or unless a Tribunal of the Catholic Church grants a decree of nullity. If a Catholic does obtain a civil divorce and remarries without a declaration of nullity by the Church, that person lives in a state of adultery.

Unfortunately, it has become the custom in at least some dioceses in the U.S. that a person must seek a civil divorce, and, once it is granted, can then proceed toward a decree of annulment from a Church tribunal. Neither the Canon Law of the Catholic Church nor Catholic Theology provides for this, because only the Catholic Church has jurisdiction over the Sacramental bond of two married Catholics. In the days, years ago, when I was responsible for Church Tribunal activities, it was understood that once a decree of nullity was obtained from the Catholic Church, this weighed heavily in a civil court in the granting of a civil divorce. Earlier in this book, in Part IV, there is an examination of how much the Catholic Church in America (Americanism as a heresy?) has allowed itself to be intertwined with the political and legal forces in the United States. This practice of requiring a civil divorce before proceeding with an annulment prolongs the length of time that a couple must wait for a declaration of nullity and puts additional pressure on them to make arrangements for a civil (invalid) marriage. If the U.S. bishops decided that it should be handled in this way, this is yet another example of the effects of the Heresy of Americanism on the U.S. Church.

It is high time that the Catholics in the U.S. return to their pristine understanding of the basic doctrine of their faith and answer correctly the question: Which is more important to you: Being an American or being a Catholic? My own answer is that it is much more important to be a Catholic, but beyond that I say that being a good Catholic allows me to be even more patriotic, because I insist, to whatever extent I can, that my values as a Catholic must be upheld in our American society.

-77% believe one can be a good Catholic without going to Mass on Sundays.

If this is true, then it means that less than a quarter of all the Catholic Faithful believe that a good Catholic, without a justifying reason, ***must*** attend Mass on Sundays and Holydays. But it is a doctrine and a commandment of the Catholic Church that her members, under pain of mortal sin, ***must*** attend Mass on Sundays and Holy Days of Obligation. Apparently fewer attend Mass on Holydays, but perhaps they have a more legitimate reason—*i.e.* work. After many years of observing peoples' attitudes, I believe that every Catholic, among their friends, acquaintances, relatives and in-laws, have at least a couple or more who blithely miss Mass on a routine basis, and will say, when questioned, "I pray a lot," or "I pray—especially on Sundays."

The challenge facing the Church today is how to help our own people realize how important the Sacrifice of the Mass is in their lives, and to realize that participation in the Mass is the most powerful prayer at their disposal. During His Agony in the Garden, Christ paused to speak to his Apostles and found them all sleeping; He asked them, "Could you not watch one hour with me?" (Matt. 26:40) We have been directed by His Church to watch about one hour per week with Him, which, considering the sublime nature of the Mass, is not a burden or an inconvenience. It is rather a sublime privilege, an ineffable benefit and a participation in His redemptive act.

It was to these horrifying statistics that I referred when I asked of certain converted Jews if it would not be better that they apply themselves to helping the Church strengthen these neglectful members than to spend so much energy in trying to bring Jewish rituals into the Church. Again the question: "Is it more important for these converted Jews to be Jews or to be Catholics?" And for any and all of us: Is it more important for us to be Catholics than for whatever other way we perceive ourselves? I believe it is important for all Catholics to study and act upon the section of Vatican Council II which deals with the concept of the Lay Apostolate, whose basic message is to call upon Catholics to ***live*** their religion in their personal lives and in their interactions in the work world.

-A New York Times poll found that 70% of all Catholics (age group 18-44) believe the Eucharist is merely a "symbolic reminder" of Jesus.

I don't necessarily trust the New York Times stories because the paper tends at times to be anti-Catholic in its leanings, but if one were to cut the figure in half—say 30% to 50%—those "Catholics" who believe the Eucharist is merely a 'symbolic reminder' of Jesus, to put it quite bluntly, are simply *not* Catholics; they are Protestants. The bedrock core of the Catholic Church is the doctrine that Christ Himself, body and blood, soul and divinity becomes present on our altars at the consecration of the Mass. I urge the reader to turn to Part II of this book, Chapter 18, to the section entitled "The Core of the Catholic Church" in order to determine how weakened the Catholic Church has become in these times because we have been infiltrated with a number of heresies, the worst of them being, perhaps equally, the Heresies of Modernism and Americanism.

If the figures I have quoted above are only half right, it's all very ominous. The Roman Catholic Church, at least in the United

States, has been badly weakened. It is now incumbent on all devout Catholics and all bona fide Catholic lay organizations to undertake the re-education of their fellow Catholics. Vatican Council II focuses primarily on the development by each individual of his or her own personal spiritual perfection and on striving toward personal holiness. If we each do that, the impact on the world, both fellow Catholics and non-Catholics, will be magnificent.

The First Precept of the Church, tied in with the Commandment to keep Holy the Sabbath, requires that we attend Mass on Sundays and Holy Days of Obligation. Can a person who misses Mass regularly legitimately call himself or herself a Catholic? Do they also fail in their belief in the Real Presence of Christ, at the Consecration of the Eucharist? It seems to me that if we ***really believe*** that Christ, who as the Word of God brought all things into existence and maintains them, comes down upon the altar at every Mass, ***nothing*** except the most pressing reason could keep us away.

As Catholics lose their faith in the Real Presence of God in our tabernacles and on our altars, it is not at all surprising that they would lose their belief in other extremely important doctrines of the Church.

CHAPTER 54

Indissolubility of Marriage

Another firm doctrine of the Church which has been suffering badly as a result of the false interpretations of Vatican Council II is the ***Indissolubility of Marriage.*** According to the sources just cited (Pew Research and Catholic Radio Association), 65% believe that Catholics may divorce and remarry. This is directly contrary to the words of Christ:

> 6 " . . . from the beginning of creation, 'God made them male and female. 7 For this reason a man shall leave his father and mother (and be joined to his wife), 8 and the two shall become one flesh.' So they are no longer two but one flesh. 9 Therefore what God has joined together, no human being must separate." (Mark 10:6-9)

This declaration by Christ Himself clearly rules out homosexual unions.

I've known some Catholics who obtained a civil divorce and remarried. I don't know what kind of ceremony was used for their "remarriage." However it was done, of course, it was invalid. They may have gone through a civil ceremony; they may have made arrangements with a protestant minister. With what I have experienced with Catholic priests, perhaps I should assume that there are those (or have been those) who would perform a marriage ceremony for a Catholic who presented proof of a civil divorce. After all, I have met and had discussions with priests who 'overlooked' the Real Presence in order to promote ecumenism, with priests who supported abortion and artificial birth control as morally acceptable, with bishops who supported the latter priests, with homosexual/pedophile/pederast bishops and priests who routinely violated the Sixth Commandment among themselves and with children and who therefore also lived in violation of their vow of celibacy. It is relatively easy to conclude that bishops and priests who are willing to ignore Church tradition and teaching in such important matters, might also be ready to create their own law, which would ignore the sanctity and indissolubility of marriage. They would therefore perform an illicit marriage ceremony for such people. The second marriage will always be invalid unless a Tribunal of the Church intervenes and declares the first marriage to be null and void for one of the canonically recognized reasons.

To repeat: I have never encountered a priest (or bishop, for that matter) who questioned the indissolubility of marriage. However, as there seems to be a sizeable number who in their desire to promote ecumenism as the major message of the Council, they are ready to ***modify*** the doctrines of the Church so as to make dialogue with Protestants more productive and to hasten the time when unification can take place. Those same priests may be ready to perform marriage ceremonies for divorced Catholics. Their actions might leave these remarried Catholics with an erroneous but quiet conscience.

I have personally encountered a growing number of Catholics who have left the Church who said that, on reflection, they came to realize that the Catholic Church is the only one "that goes back that far" and it therefore must be the only true religion. If we hold to the truth as Christ Himself gave it to us, the Providence of God will be done ". . . on earth as it is in heaven." St. Paul enunciated the posture of the Church for all time when he exhorted: "O Timothy, guard the deposit" of Faith (1 Timothy 6:20).

CHAPTER 55

Importance of the Mass

Attendance at Mass is not uniform throughout the United States. We've seen it at its worst in Seattle, Washington, where the late Archbishop Hunthausen left an unorthodox aftermath in the Archdiocese of Seattle and, as far as I could see, a great reduction in Mass attendance. In Las Cruces, New Mexico and now in McAllen, Texas—south Texas in general—Mass attendance is as strong as I used to see it in Northwest Iowa where I grew up. It is strong here because of cultural differences. The churches are filled every Sunday. The Hispanic culture carries with it a very strong faith, a deep faith in the Real Presence and a personal display of religious belief. Not long ago, the priest celebrant at Sunday Mass called for a round of applause for a lay group which had been very successful in its apostolic work. After the applause died down, he called for a round of applause for Jesus Christ who was with us in the tabernacle. The applause that followed was a standing ovation and was louder and more prolonged. We also see more rosaries hanging from the rear-view mirrors of cars than anywhere else in the country.

In this part of the country—south Texas—where the cultural background is largely Hispanic, people openly talk with each other about their religious beliefs. I found the same to be true in Italy during my years there. In the non-Hispanic sections of the U.S., there has always been a reluctance to discuss such matters. People in the

U.S. will discuss with great passion their political persuasions, but regarding our faith which is far more important, we remain silent.

That we are the world's sole superpower appears to be more important to us than our God-given religious beliefs, when the far greater importance of the latter should be uppermost in our minds.

What is the solution to this backsliding which has taken place in the Roman Catholic Church in the United States? One solution we have already discussed: The Universal Call to Holiness in the Church—see above. If each of us—bishops, priests, religious and laity—strives toward holiness and growth in our spiritual lives (i.e. Living in the Presence of God) this will have its effect not only within each of us, but on all those with whom we come in contact as well. The second major solution has been there since the time of Christ, has been promoted by the Church down through the ages, and has recently been re-emphasized by the Second Vatican Council: The Apostolate of the Laity. (Pope Benedict XVI recently established an office of the New Evangelization which emphasizes the need for the lay apostolate around the world.)

CHAPTER 56

The Signs of the Times

The Council, in at least two places (cited below) mentioned "the signs of the times" and Pope John XXIII, who initiated the Second Vatican Council used the phrase as he announced the beginning of the Council.

Among the Modernist priests among whom I found myself surrounded in Washington, D.C., I occasionally heard the "signs of our times," quoted from the Council, being misused to justify such things as abortion, artificial contraception, denial of the Real Presence. The mistake they made was to assign to themselves the authority to interpret the 'signs of the times.' The Council clearly states that it is ***the Church*** which must interpret the *Signs of the Times:*

> ***Among the signs of our times***, the irresistibly increasing sense of the solidarity of all peoples is especially noteworthy. It is a function of the lay apostolate sedulously to promote this awareness and to transform it into a sincere and genuine love of brotherhood. Furthermore, the laity should be aware of the international field and of the questions and solutions, doctrinal as well as practical, which arise in this field, with special reference to developing nations." (emphasis added) (Decree on the Apostolate of the Laity, Chapter III)

And in *Gaudium et Spes,* the Pastoral Constitution on the Church in the Modern World, we read the following:

> "... . the Church seeks but a solitary goal: to carry forward the work of Christ under the lead of the befriending Spirit. And Christ entered this world to give witness to the truth, to rescue and not to sit in judgment, to serve and not to be served.
>
> "To carry out such a task, the Church has always had the duty of ***scrutinizing the signs of the times and of interpreting them in the light of the Gospel*** (emphasis added). Thus, in language intelligible to each generation, she can respond to the perennial questions which men ask about this present life and the life to come, and about the relationship of the one to the other. We must therefore recognize and understand the world in which we live, its expectations, its longings, and its often dramatic characteristics. Some of the main features of the modern world can be sketched as follows."

The Council goes on to identify the current 'Signs of the Times' and to present ways in which the Church in general and the laity in particular can cope with them. These quotations make it clear that it is the ***Church*** which always has identified and will continue to identify and interpret the Signs of the Times, no one else. Since the laity directly live and work in the world, they can be particularly effective in combating the negative effects of all those forces which increasingly inflict themselves on mankind.

It is the awesome figure of the Pope at one end of the spectrum, and the broad base of the faithful laity at the other, which, guided by the Holy Spirit, have rescued the Church from the many heresies that have plagued her over the centuries.

CHAPTER 57

The True Doctrines of the Catholic Church

The errors which are described in the previous chapters in this current Part VII are unfortunately widespread in the Catholic Church in the United States. It is with great sorrow that I say I have experienced these errors (which in many cases are true heresies) in some bishops, in a lamentable number of priests, quite a few religious order men and women, and in far too many laity. All of this apparently is culminating in a new organization which some are calling ***'AmChurch,'*** which I have mentioned before. In my own mind and in my own conversations, I have simply called it the ***American Church.*** Its equivalent is the 'Church of England' in the United Kingdom which was founded by Henry the Eighth, who, in his quest for a male heir, asked the Pope to allow him to marry again. When the Pope refused, the king simply withdrew the church from the authority of the Pope and declared himself its head. 'AmChurch', as it is being called, seems intent on withdrawing from the authority of the Pope and is no longer the ***Roman*** *Catholic Church.*

We must return to the true Doctrines of the Catholic Church, all of which were left with us by Christ Himself. Foreseeing the coming problem, St. Paul exhorted his colleague, "O Timothy, guard the deposit entrusted to you." (I Tim. 6:20) It is incumbent on the successors of the Apostles, and all Catholics to 'guard the deposit' in order to help as many people as possible to save their souls. I will end these memoirs by presenting the 'doctrinal truths' of the Roman Catholic Church which we need consciously to know, understand, and live by.

It is to these elements of the **"Deposit of the Faith"** which Christ left with His Church that we must return in full fidelity, ridding ourselves of all the contaminations of Modernism, Americanism, and Secularism.

The Existence of God

Theology is the 'study of God,' based upon the Incarnation and the figure of Christ in history who told us He is God and proved what He said by performing almost numberless miracles; and by the statement of St. Paul that if we simply look at ourselves and the rest of created nature, we know that God exists.

It is the discipline of Philosophy (see Part I, Chapter 5) which demonstrates the proofs for the existence of God. St. Thomas Aquinas, who in the eyes of many was the ultimate philosopher, presented five proofs for the existence of God, each of which in its own way is entirely persuasive, some of them, perhaps depending on the nature of the person, more so than the others.

For myself the most persuasive proofs are a combination of St. Paul's which I believe relates to the ***design*** which is much more than simply visible in the universe and created nature in general, and one proof from St. Thomas which is based on ***efficient causality***.

Behind the magnificent organization of all creation, from the expanse of the universe with its unknown billions of stars and planets, to the microscopic atomic and subatomic structures which make up the living and non-living world, there must be a ***designer*** whose intelligence far surpasses our own. If a powerful earthquake were to tear apart and release all the paint in an art store, the chances that an incredible work of art could result by accident would be far greater than that our entire universe with all its living creatures could result from the 'Big Bang' of pre-existing materials. And even granting that such a thing could happen, and that there indeed was a 'Big Bang,'where did the pre-existing materials come from?

The argument from ***efficient causality,*** especially when combined with the argument from ***design*** is particularly persuasive. Everything we see around us did not bring itself into existence but was ***caused by*** another source. If we go back far enough, we eventually come to something caused by a source which (who?) had no cause: in effect an ***uncaused cause;*** we call that God. Those who argue for a 'Big Bang' which resulted from highly compressed pre-existing material simply cannot argue that the pre-existing material was there by accident, but it had to be *created* by an ***uncaused Cause.*** (A complete understanding of this concept, we must realize, is beyond the human intellect.)

Original Sin

Adam and Eve were created by God as our proto-parents. The doctrine of Original Sin as committed by Adam and Eve in the Garden of Eden carries with it incredible ramifications for the human race down through the centuries and millennia. The life that Adam and Eve lived from the moment they were created is for the most part incomprehensible and unimaginable for all of us who are their descendants: God walked and talked with them; they were immortal; they lived, in effect, a supernatural—or supernaturalized—life of perfect happiness. They did not enjoy the Beatific Vision or they could not have done what they did. As far as we know, only one thing was forbidden to them as they lived their idyllic life in the Garden of Eden: to eat of the fruit of the Tree of the Knowledge of Good and Evil.

Satan, of course, in the form of the serpent knew precisely how to tempt Adam and Eve so that they would disobey God—he tapped into the very human pride that is part of all of us and which is behind every sin that we commit. He told them that in eating the fruit of that tree that they would become 'like gods' and they would know what is good and what is evil. They wanted to be 'like god.' Eve ate the apple first and then prevailed on Adam to eat it also. As a result, they were ejected from Paradise—the Garden of Eden—lost their elevated state of life, and passed that lesser state on to the entire human race.

(There is a good deal of speculation as to whether the "forbidden fruit" was precisely that, or whether it symbolized some other activity, such as sexual relations. The professor I had, if my memory serves, was of the opinion that there was an actual tree with actual fruit which they were forbidden to eat. His position, I believe, was that if there is no evidence that the "forbidden fruit" was meant as a symbol, then it is best to interpret it literally.)

With the sin of Adam and Eve, an act of personal pride and disobedience, the entire human race was plunged into the State of Fallen Nature, not yet Redeemed, so that the gates of Heaven were closed for everyone until the death of Christ on the Cross. Since the death of Christ, we have all been in the State of Fallen Nature, now Redeemed, so that entry into heaven became once again possible if we lived the kind of life that God wants us to.

Perhaps Satan was experienced in what would be the vulnerability of Adam and Eve. Lucifer (later Satan) was the most elevated being in God's creation, but, like everyone (angels and humans), he was required to undergo a test before being allowed into the presence of God. St. Thomas Aquinas speculated that the test for Lucifer was the image of Christ on the Cross whom he would be required to bow down and worship. But Christ in his human nature was so far beneath the nature of this angel, that he immediately said, "I will not serve." A faint analogy might be that we be told that a worm would be our superior whom we would be required to obey. As Christ said, He was there when Lucifer in a flash of lightning was consigned to Hell as a result of his pride.

The infinite enormity of the sin of Adam and Eve was such because it was committed against our Creator, an Infinite Being. Since the sin was performed by two human beings, it would have to be a human being who would make reparation for it. But since it was an offense against the infinite God, it would require more than a human being to make reparation. For many centuries or millennia, the animal sacrifices in the Jewish rites prophetically looked forward to the time when God Himself, in the Person of Jesus Christ (the "Lamb of God"), the God/Man would make complete reparation and redemption for the sin of Adam and Eve. Ultimately, then the solution was for the Son of God, the Second Person of the Trinity, to become man and die on the Cross: a human and divine person whose power of redemption was infinite.

The liturgy of Holy Saturday sings of Original Sin as a happy fault which merited to give us such a great and magnificent Redeemer. The plans of God are almost totally incomprehensible to the human mind. Even those that have been revealed to us cannot be fully comprehended by human intelligence. We can understand that it is ***possible*** that there be three Persons in the One God simply by examining the human mind which, after all, is created in the image and likeness of God. We'll look at this in the next section. Human reason can understand that such a concept is possible, but we cannot comprehend it.

The Trinity

The story is told that one day St. Thomas Aquinas was walking on the beach, meditating on the Holy Trinity, when he encountered a young boy with a small bucket, into which he was scooping sand. When St. Thomas asked the young boy what he was doing, he said he was going to put all the sand on the beach into the bucket. When St. Thomas told the boy that it would be impossible, the boy retorted that it would be easier for him to do that than it would be for St. Thomas to understand the Trinity. Then, as the story is told, the boy disappeared.

The Trinity is one of the greatest mysteries among the revelations we have received from God.

While there are some implications in the Old Testament that there are three persons in one God, this was never directly revealed to anyone until Christ Himself spoke about the Father, the Son and the Holy Spirit. Therefore, throughout the history of the Jews, they correctly worshiped the one God, but they had no inkling of the three co-equal Persons in the one God until the Second Person became man in the person of Jesus Christ.

The remarkable understanding which occurred to me during the study of the Holy Trinity connected my mind to the study of Philosophy many years earlier in my last year in college. The human mind, we learned at that time, has the capacity to abstract the essence of something we know and then we 'create'—in effect give birth to—an image of that thing in our mind, *e.g.* a tree, so that when we see a tree we have never seen before, we instantly recognize it as a tree. Since we are created in the image and likeness of God, we can understand with our limited minds that when the eternal, infinite being that is God knew Himself from all eternity, the image of Himself to which He gave birth, was infinite, eternal and—again from all eternity—an existing Person, Son of the Father. When Father and Son perceived their infinite goodness, an eternal, infinite Love sprang up between them which was so powerful as to be a Divine Person—whom we call the Holy Spirit. Thus there are three co-equal Persons in one Divine Being. This has been revealed to us, and we can never fully comprehend it—not even in the next life. But we will be able to learn about the Trinity, and we will more completely understand it. Perhaps one of the great pleasures of life in heaven will be to eternally study the Divine Essence, growing in never ending knowledge as we contemplate the Beatific Vision.

The Blessed Virgin Mary

The tradition of the Church, dating back to the time of the Apostles has told us for centuries that the Blessed Virgin did not die, *i.e.* her soul never left her body, but she was taken up to heaven body and soul intact. Since she was conceived without Original Sin, one of whose consequences was death, and since she was chosen to be the Mother of the Son, it has appeared entirely fitting to all the faithful over the centuries that she be assumed into heaven without undergoing death. In 1955 or 1956, when I traveled to the Holy Land, I visited the site of what has been called for 2000 years the Dormition of the Mother of God, with a full size statue of her lying on a bed. I believe it is generally understood that her assumption occurred while the Apostles were still alive—therefore in the first century.

Four Principal Dogmas Regarding the Blessed Virgin

Over the centuries, many doctrines regarding the Blessed Virgin have been proclaimed by the infallible pronunciations of a succession of Popes. The four principal dogmas relating to the Blessed Virgin Mary are:

Her title as Mother of God
Her Immaculate Conception
Her Perpetual Virginity
Her Assumption into Heaven

Most solemn definitions of Catholic Dogma have taken place because some group attacked its validity. Centuries ago, people gathered in the streets of Greece shouting one of two slogans: *Theotokos* (Mother of God) or *Kristokos* (Mother of Christ). The latter group insisted that Mary simply produced the *body* of Christ and had nothing to do with His Divinity. The other group contended that Mary gave birth to the ***Person*** of Jesus Christ and she therefore deserved the title of 'Mother of God.' The Church decided the matter with a solemn declaration that she is indeed the 'Mother of God.'

These are four of the defined dogmas of the Roman Catholic Church relating to the Blessed Virgin. There are other definable traditions for which there has been no need for a solemn definition.

For example, while hanging on the cross, Jesus Christ said to His mother: "Behold your son," and to John the Apostle, he said "Behold your mother," (John 19:26) thereby designating her as the mother of all mankind, and calling on all of us to recognize her as our mother.

Closely associated with our recognition of her as our mother is another definable tradition relating to the Mother of God: She is the ***Mediatrix of all Graces***. It has been the deep belief and tradition of the Church since her foundation that every grace given to the human race comes through the Blessed Virgin. First of all, she is the chosen vessel through whom the Second Person of the Holy Trinity came into the world—therefore she was conceived without Original Sin in order to be a fitting vessel for Him—and died on the cross for all our sins—the greatest grace ever to come to the human race came through her.

At the wedding feast at Cana, she saw that the host had run out of wine—which would become a major social embarrassment for him. She told her Son: "They have no wine." He was reluctant to take care of the matter, because, as He told her, "My time has not yet come." But He did it at her behest, performing His very first miracle: He turned water into wine. It is for these and many other reasons that the Church has held to the tradition that every grace coming to mankind originates with God, but comes to us through the Mother of God. (See John 2:1-11)

She is our Mother in a very special way, because the sanctifying grace of Baptism comes to us through her. In other words she is the Mother of our Supernatural Life. It is under her watchful motherly eye that we grow in sanctifying grace and perfect our spiritual lives.

The Incarnation

Our principal studies on the Incarnation were presented by Professor Flick, S.J. in the course of my second or third year in Theology. That entire course is still very clear in my mind, but one point of doctrine to me was and continues to be particularly prominent. He presented the following thesis (my translation from the Latin): ***"Only in the hypothesis that God demanded condign justice in atonement for the sin of Adam and Eve was the Incarnation necessary." Condign*** justice or atonement simply means that reparation or punishment for the crime or sin committed must be precisely equal to the enormity of that crime. In the case of Adam and Eve, they were *created* human beings and they disobeyed their infinite *Uncreated* God—the sin committed was infinitely evil. Since it was humans who committed the crime, it had to be a human, i.e. one of the descendants of Adam and Eve, who must make reparation. But no *human* action can make infinite reparation. Therefore, if God wanted there to be *condign* atonement, (and we must remember that God is infinitely Just) of necessity it had to be done by a descendent of Adam and Eve who was also *infinite* and Divine. In the mind of God, it had to be the *Son* of God who was born of the Virgin Mary who was a descendent of the first parents. Then, as God and man He could make complete reparation for Original Sin, redeem us all and make it possible for each of us to work out our eternal salvation.

Thus, as I said before, the Catholic Church in her Holy Saturday liturgy can see a major benefit in the terrible sin of Adam and Eve: "O happy fault which merited such a great and incomprehensible Redeemer." (Translation from my memory of the Latin text.)

The Eucharist and Real Presence—The Core of the Catholic Faith

The Catholic Church is the only religion on earth which professes the Real Presence of Jesus Christ on her altars, during the celebration of the Mass, and Who lives in her tabernacles—and Who lives in each of her members. The only person who can bring this about is a duly ordained priest/bishop who can trace his ordination in an unbroken line back to Christ and His Apostles at the Last Supper.

What I call the ***Judas Syndrome*** is the growing ***lack*** of awareness in the Catholic Church that all its members have at the very center of their lives the actual presence of their God in the appearance of bread and wine in all the Catholic Church tabernacles around the world, and that their God becomes present in the appearance of bread and wine in every Catholic Church around the world each and every time that Mass is celebrated. If we as Catholics truly knew and believed this, every other part of our lives would retreat into relative insignificance, except as those parts of our lives—our marriages, our lives as priests and religious, our prayer lives—permit us to become closer to Him.

My opinion is if a person ***really believes*** in the Real Presence at every Mass celebrated by a duly ordained Catholic priest, nothing could keep that person away from Mass—at least once a week as the law of the Church requires. The realization that the Creator of the Universe, the Lord of the Universe, the One who died on the Cross to make salvation possible for each of us—if we truly believed that—we could not fail to attend Mass as often as possible. How could anyone with that sincere belief ignore that truth and justify not attending Mass by saying "We're good people; we pray a lot; God is love and He won't hold it against us; just so we're comfortable with what we do . . . ." Someone my wife and I are close to said something like that to us recently. But it was Christ Himself who said to His Apostles in the Garden of Gestheseme, "Could you not watch one hour with me?" And it was to St. Peter that Christ said, "Whatever you bind on earth, it will be bound in heaven; and whatever you loose on earth, it will be loosed in heaven." (See Mt. 16:19 & Mt. 18:18.)

In the early Church, the Followers of Christ participated in the daily Breaking of Bread, and in the first century it was established that the Followers of Christ should attend Mass on Sunday, and receive Communion at least once during the Easter season. That rule has stood for more than 2000 years.

The Heresies of Modernism and of Americanism have had a profound negative impact on the Church. And, in terms of my own spiritual life, I am able to say now, more than forty years later, that all those negatives, while at first and for several years they caused me to feel ostracized from the comfortable fraternity I felt with the Catholic priests of the Catholic Church, have become in my later years to be a solid positive factor in my own life. My primary purpose in writing these lines is to help those whose devotion to Christ and His Church have been marred by contact with those Heresies, to regain the purity of their understanding of the Deposit of Faith which Christ left behind with His Church.

It is important that we know our enemy. For a full description of the Heresy of Modernism see the recently published book, "*The Deposit of Faith: What the Catholic Church **Really** Believes*", by Eugene Kevane. And the full texts of the encyclicals of Pope Pius X on Modernism, *Pascendi Dominici Gregis* (Feeding the Lord's Flock) and of Leo XIII on Americanism, *Testem Benevolentiae Nostrae* (Witness to Our Goodwill), is given in the final Appendix of this book.

The Judas Syndrome

What is the phenomenon I referred to earlier as the 'Judas Syndrome?' Let's look at some of the theology which is the underpinning of the Church's doctrine of the Real Presence of Christ, body and blood, soul and divinity, in the Sacrament of the Eucharist. Therefore the ***Judas Syndrome*** (rejection of belief in the Real Presence) began with one of the Apostles, continued occasionally in the Early Church, and flourished in the 1500's when so many different religions sprang up and expanded. None of those had the priesthood and therefore could not have the Sacrament of the Eucharist.

In this connection, we can ask the question, "What is a true Catholic?" The answer to this question will come up in much greater detail later on, but the following is the core issue which a Catholic must understand and live by.

One of the highlights of my study of Theology was the examination of the Sacrament of the Eucharist, the Real Presence of the living Christ, Body and Blood, Soul and Divinity in the Unbloody Sacrifice of the Mass. We studied it from the words and actions of Christ Himself, from the practice in the early Church, the Tradition of the Church down through the ages, and as it was declared in various Ecumenical Councils of the Church. The following is a synopsis of that doctrine.

The Promise of the Eucharist

When Jesus Christ made His ***promise of the Eucharist*** (see John 6, 35-71), He presented what was to become the core of the seven sacraments and the profound distinguishing characteristic of His Catholic Church. The following is taken from **John 6, 35 ff**

> 35 Jesus said to them, 'I am the bread of life. Whoever comes to me will never be hungry, and whoever believes in me will never be thirsty. 36 But I said to you that you have seen me and yet do not believe. 37 Everything that the Father gives me will come to me, and anyone who comes to me I will never drive away; 38 for I have come down from heaven, not to do my own will, but the will of him who sent me. 39 And this is the will of him who sent me, that I should lose nothing of all that he has given me, but raise it up on the last day. 40 This is indeed the will of my Father, that all who see the Son and believe in him may have eternal life; and I will raise them up on the last day.'

Beginning to understand what He was saying, His disciples began to argue among themselves:

> 41 Then the Jews began to complain about him because he said, 'I am the bread that came down from heaven.' 42 They were saying, 'Is not this Jesus, the son of Joseph, whose father and mother we know? How can he now say, "I have

> come down from heaven"?' 43 Jesus answered them, 'Do not complain among yourselves. 44 No one can come to me unless drawn by the Father who sent me; and I will raise that person up on the last day. 45 It is written in the prophets, "And they shall all be taught by God." Everyone who has heard and learned from the Father comes to me. 46 Not that anyone has seen the Father except the one who is from God; he has seen the Father. 47 Very truly, I tell you, whoever believes has eternal life.

Jesus repeats Himself:

> 48 I am the bread of life. 49 Your ancestors ate the manna in the wilderness, and they died. 50 This is the bread that comes down from heaven, so that one may eat of it and not die. 51 I am the living bread that came down from heaven. Whoever eats of this bread will live forever; and the bread that I will give for the life of the world is my flesh.'

The Jews (disciples) then argued among themselves, illustrating how clear Christ was:

> 52 The Jews then disputed among themselves, saying, 'How can this man give us his flesh to eat?'

Christ once again re-emphasized, repeating six times what He has been saying:

> 53 So Jesus said to them, 'Very truly, I tell you, unless you eat the flesh of the Son of Man and drink his blood, you have no life in you. 54 Those who eat my flesh and drink my blood have eternal life, and I will raise them up on the last day; 55 for my flesh is true food and my blood is true drink. 56 Those who eat my flesh and drink my blood

> abide in me, and I in them. 57 Just as the living Father sent me, and I live because of the Father, so whoever eats me will live because of me. 58 This is the bread that came down from heaven, not like that which your ancestors ate, and they died. But the one who eats this bread will live for ever.' 59 He said these things while he was teaching in the synagogue at Capernaum.

Christ emphasized the Words of Eternal Life:

> 60 When many of his disciples heard it, they said, 'This teaching is difficult; who can accept it?' 61 But Jesus, being aware that his disciples were complaining about it, said to them, 'Does this offend you? 62 Then what if you were to see the Son of Man ascending to where he was before? 63 It is the spirit that gives life; the flesh is useless. The words that I have spoken to you are spirit and life. 64 But among you there are some who do not believe.' For Jesus knew from the first who were the ones that did not believe, and who was the one that would betray him. 65 And he said, 'For this reason I have told you that no one can come to me unless it is granted by the Father.' 66 Because of this many of his disciples turned back and no longer went about with him.

To emphasize the importance of this doctrine, Jesus is willing to have the Apostles leave.

> 67 So Jesus asked the twelve, 'Do you also wish to go away?' 68 Simon Peter answered him, 'Lord, to whom can we go? You have the words of eternal life. 69 We have come to believe and know that you are the Holy One of God, the Christ, the Son of the living God;' 70 Jesus answered them, 'Did I not choose you, the twelve? Yet one of you is a devil.'

But Judas, an Apostle, did not believe:

> 71 He was speaking of Judas Iscariot son of Simon for he, though one of the twelve, was going to betray him.

The Institution of the Eucharist

Christ ***fulfilled*** that promise in a way no one could have foreseen and in a way that was perfectly in tune with human sensitivities. At the Last Supper, the night before He was crucified and died, He took bread and said "This is my body . . ." and, when supper was completed, took wine and said "This is the chalice of my blood which will be shed for you . . . . do this in memory of me." His Divine Power accomplished what He said and gave to the Apostles the power to do the same.

Following are four of the pertinent Scriptural texts:

> **Matthew 26: 26-30:**
>
> 26 Now as they were eating, Jesus took bread, and after blessing it broke it and gave it to the disciples, and said, "Take, eat; this is my body." 27 And he took a chalice, and when he had given thanks he gave it to them, saying, "Drink of it, all of you, 28 for this is my blood of the covenant, which is poured out for many for the forgiveness of sins. 29 I tell you I will not drink again of this fruit of the vine until that day when I drink it new with you in my Father's kingdom."
>
> See also: **Mark 14: 22-26; Luke 22: 19-21; St. Paul, 1 Cor 11, v. 23ff**

Using His Infinite Power, Christ accomplished what He said: He changed the substance of bread and wine into the substance of His

Body and Blood, Soul and Divinity while retaining the ***appearance*** of bread and wine. For centuries the Catholic Church has called this ***Transubstantiation***. In effect He said, "As I stand before you now, I am truly present in what appears to be bread and wine. Do as I have just done." In one plain spoken statement, He changed bread and wine into His own body and blood, soul and divinity, gave the Apostles (and their successors) the power to do the same thing, and told them to do it to perpetuate—as an unbloody sacrifice—the bloody sacrifice He made for us on the cross.

In a flash-back to my studies of Philosophy in college, I could see the connection between what we know of all created things and the action that Christ performed. Every created thing, as the discipline of Philosophy teaches us, has in common with all others what is called *existence, e.g.*, a tree, which we can see. Again all created things have *essence*, an element which distinguishes each from all others. For example, a tree and a rock each have *existence*, but it is the essence of each which distinguishes one from the other. We can also say, in philosophical terms, that every created thing has *substance, e.g.*, a rock and a tree, but each also has *accidents* which distinguish one from the other. Christ, in His total dominion over the universe simply used His Divine Power to retain the essence or accidents (appearance) of bread and wine, and replace the existence or substance of bread and wine with His own Body and Blood, Soul and Divinity, and give to His vicar, Peter, and to all legitimate successors of the Apostles—bishops and priests—the power to do the same. As we said, every bishop can trace his ordination back in an unbroken succession to one of the Apostles, and every priest can point to the bishop who ordained him. It is sad to think that at the Reformation, as the various Protestant churches came into existence, they one way or the other lost that succession, no longer had a valid Mass, and therefore finally had to acknowledge that the bread and wine they used in their liturgies were simply symbols of Christ and were not and have not been the Real Presence of the Living Christ.

The Practice of the Eucharist in the Early Church

In the early Church, the Practice of the ***"Breaking of the Bread"*** is recorded many times over in the Acts of the Apostles and in many other locations. A simple reading of the Acts of the Apostles will reveal to the reader the nearly innumerable references to the "breaking of the bread" among the members of the Early Church.

And St. Paul, as recorded above, presents the truism that if one receives the consecrated bread and wine while in the state of mortal sin, he or she commits a sacrilege, because one is consuming the living body and blood, soul and divinity of Jesus Christ (I Cor 11: 23-33).

In the Acts of the Apostles

The apostles celebrated the Sacrament of Holy Eucharist. **(Acts 2:46)** "Day by day, attending the Temple together and breaking bread in their homes . . ."

The Apostles were visibly religious Jews. They wore the *kippah* (prayer hat), the *tallit* (prayer shawl with fringes) and the *tephillin* (phylacteries). Long after Jesus ascended to the Father, Peter protested that he had never in his life eaten anything unkosher.

Acts 10:14—When these Jewish Apostles remembered Christ's command, **Lk 22:19** "Do this in remembrance of Me," they added it to their synagogue worship. They began with synagogue prayer and Scripture readings, and then went to their homes to celebrate the Sacrament of Christ's Body and Blood. To this very day, the Introductory Rite and Liturgy of the Word come directly from Jewish synagogue worship. The Liturgy of the Eucharist comes directly from the Apostles' breaking bread in their homes.

Acts 20:7 At Troas, Paul spoke all night, but he made sure to receive the Holy Eucharist. "On the first day of the week, when we were gathered together to break bread, Paul talked with them, intending to depart on the morrow; and he prolonged his speech until midnight." **Acts 20:11** "And when Paul had gone up and had broken bread and eaten, he conversed with them a long while, until daybreak, and so departed."

On the Adriatic Sea, at dawn, Paul celebrated Mass for 276 people. **Acts 27:35** ". . . he took bread, and giving thanks to God in the presence of all he broke it and began to eat. Then they all were encouraged and ate some food themselves."

Acts 20:11 "When Paul had gone up and had broken bread and eaten . . ." St. Paul explained clearly what "breaking bread" meant.

In The Epistles

1 Cor 10:16 "The cup of blessing which we bless, is it not a participation in the Blood of Christ? The bread which we break, is it not a participation in the Body of Christ?" St. Paul continued, **1 Cor 11:27** "Whoever, therefore, eats the bread *or* drinks the cup of the Lord in an unworthy manner will be guilty of profaning the Body *and* Blood of the Lord." St. Paul in these words confirmed Catholic teaching that the "bread . . . of the Lord" is truly Christ's Body, Blood, Soul and Divinity, and that the "cup of the Lord" is the same substance: "Whoever . . . eats the bread *or* drinks the cup . . . will be guilty of profaning the Body *and* Blood of the Lord."

St. Paul added, **1 Cor 11:29** "For any one who eats and drinks without discerning the Body eats and drinks judgment upon himself."

The Eucharist During 2000 Years in the Catholic Church

With these four sets of circumstances—1) the Promise of the Eucharist by Christ Himself, 2) the Fulfillment of the Eucharist by Christ at the Last Supper, 3) the Eucharistic practice in the early Church, and 4) the unfailing tradition in the Catholic Church for 2000 years—we have the core of the Catholic Church which is the Real Presence of the Living Christ, in the Mass as the source of all the graces which we receive and the source of the grace available in all the other six sacraments. For 2000 years, history attests to the fact that literally thousands of bishops and priests celebrated the Sacrifice of the Mass, each of them almost daily, around the world. In each of those Masses they pronounced the words of the consecration, bringing Christ down upon the altar in His Body and Blood, Soul and Divinity, and then, every week, thousands of the Catholic Faithful received and continue to receive the consecrated host and wine, fulfilling what Christ called for when He admonished everyone to 'eat His flesh and drink His blood' in order to have life everlasting.

The Fathers of the Church carried on the tradition of the Eucharist.

The Council of Trent, (1545-1565) among many other earlier councils, dealt explicitly with the concept of the Real Presence in great detail. For approximately one thousand five hundred years the Catholic Church maintained the unfailing tradition of the Eucharist. Then, in about the year 1500, the **Judas Syndrome** came into the world as a major heresy and spawned a variety of religious groups. It reached its zenith in the time of Martin Luther who started the modern phenomenon of the founding of religions which split off from the Catholic Church. Martin Luther, an ordained Catholic priest, is said to have hated the Sacrifice of the Mass; from that we can conclude that he did not believe in the Real Presence of God in the Eucharist.

The Eucharist in the Church of the 21st Century

The ***Judas Syndrome*** infects the Church today. It infected the Church in lesser ways throughout her entire history, beginning, of course, with Judas. To all other religions which were founded during and after the Martin Luther era, the bread and wine of their liturgy were (and continue to be) no more than symbols. In general terms—with individual differences—they interpret Christ's words, "Do this in memory of me" as simply meaning "eat bread and drink wine to remember me by." But when He said, over the bread, "This is my body" and over the chalice of wine, "This is the chalice of my blood", His words must be taken literally in terms of His Divine Power, particularly when He was so clear in the Promise of the Eucharist: "He who eats my flesh and drinks my blood will have eternal life." Anyone who denies His meaning has fallen victim to the Judas Syndrome, because Christ said nothing about symbolism. And there is no religion in the world except in the Catholic Church where one can encounter the Real Presence and "eat His flesh and drink His blood." See again the **Promise of the Eucharist** above.

From this it seems clear that Judas did not accept Christ's teaching on what was to be the Eucharist—the Unbloody Sacrifice of Christ on the Cross, the Eternal and Infinite Victim, offered once and for all for our sins, and reenacted for all time at the Mass by the presence of that Victim, body and blood, soul and divinity as the source of all the supernatural graces we need to gain eternal life.

Unfortunately, the **Judas Syndrome** is widespread today, even among Catholics (if indeed they are Catholics), because the misinterpretation of Vatican Council II, according to some, emphasizes Ecumenism and it is the opinion of some that the non-Catholic world will never accept the emphasis of the Catholic Church on the Real Presence, so it must be ignored. But such a position is heretical.

The Eucharist and the valid celebration of the Sacrifice of the Mass has been retained intact only in the Catholic Church and in some Eastern Rite churches which are not in communion with Rome and the Pope. Any bishop in the Catholic Church and in certain Eastern rite churches, using records which are available, can trace his episcopacy back to one of the Apostles, having had passed on to him the authority to consecrate other bishops, and each bishop has the power and authority to ordain priests; every priest knows the bishop who ordained him. There is, therefore, an unbroken line of priests and bishops back to the time of Christ and to the Apostles whom He had chosen. No other churches can claim a valid priesthood except in those cases in which a validly consecrated bishop disavowed his allegiance to the Pope, consecrated his own bishops who then ordained their own priests—such as the Russian Orthodox Church.

The Seven Sacraments

For those of us who truly believe in God, it is easy to accept the perception that if God for one instant would withhold His attention from His creation, it would all vanish—the vast array of galaxies, stars, planets and all the living creatures on earth including ourselves would disappear. He therefore holds it all in existence. Beyond that, He provides each of us with the help each of us needs to live a good life and save our souls. The help He provides is grace. He provides two kinds of grace: 1) Actual grace and 2) Sanctifying grace. ***Actual graces*** are daily occurrences given to us by God, such as special people who providentially come into our lives, the moments of awe when we are struck, for example, by a remarkable view of mountains, of the stars, and meditate upon the magnificence and omnipotence of our Creator. ***Sanctifying grace*** is that which is created by God and infused into our souls by means of the Sacraments so that we can have the Indwelling of the Holy Spirit, the Trinity residing within us, our sins forgiven, and live our supernaturalized lives as Children of God.

The Sacraments were instituted by Christ Himself first of all to elevate each of us into a supernaturalized life as Children of God, then to maintain or regain that supernatural life, and to enable it to grow within us in the course of our lives.

What is a Sacrament? Sacraments are outward signs of inward grace, instituted by Christ for our sanctification. They are perceptible, visible signs which efficaciously instill in the soul the grace that they signify. Every Sacrament consists in *Matter* and *Form*. An easy example, of course, is baptism whose *matte*r is water poured on a person in the sign of the cross (signifying cleansing from all sins in the person) and whose *form* consists in the words, "I baptize you in the name of the Father and of the Son and of the Holy Spirit." The effect is to introduce sanctifying grace into the soul for the special purpose of that Sacrament—in the example of baptism, to erase Original Sin and forgive any actual sin on the soul.

Baptism

All of us are born with Original Sin on our souls. Christ Himself initiated the Sacrament of Baptism so that we could be cleansed of that sin, receiving Sanctifying Grace for the first time, and thus become 'children of God', elevated into a supernatural way of life. The baptized person can legitimately say with St. Paul, "I live now, not I, but Christ lives in me." (Gal. 2, 20).

It was so important to Christ that all His people be enabled to live this exalted, supernaturalized life in Him, that before his Ascension he gave His Apostles and His entire Church a monumental command:

> 18 Then Jesus approached and said to them, "All power in heaven and on earth has been given to me. 19 Go, therefore, and make disciples of all nations, baptizing them in the name of the Father, and of the Son, and of the Holy Spirit, 20 teaching them to observe all that I have commanded you. And behold, I am with you always, until the end of the age." (Mt. 28, 18-20)

As Christ ascended into Heaven, this final command was probably not ringing in the ears of His Apostles. They simply saw their Leader apparently moving away from them. Therefore they were given a final reminder of the task ahead of them:

> 8 "But you will receive power when the holy Spirit comes upon you, and you will be my witnesses in Jerusalem, throughout Judea and Samaria, and to the ends of the earth."
>
> 9 When he had said this, as they were looking on, he was lifted up, and a cloud took him from their sight. 10 While they were looking intently at the sky as he was going, suddenly two men dressed in white garments stood beside them. 11 They said, "Men of Galilee, why are you standing there looking at the sky? This Jesus who has been taken up from you into heaven will return in the same way as you have seen him going into heaven" (Acts 1, 8-11).

The Eucharist—First Communion

For extensive treatment of The Sacrament of the Eucharist, see what has been written above about it as the core of the Catholic Faith.

Because Jesus said "I am the living bread that came down from heaven. Whoever eats of this bread will live forever; and the bread that I will give for the life of the world is my flesh" (Jn 6:51), we should begin receiving communion at the youngest possible age. It is the major means of increasing the Sanctifying Grace we have in our souls after Baptism. It is not at all surprising in the light of what Christ said about children, that the tradition of the Church has been that children should receive their first communion at a young age: Then children were brought to him that he might lay his hands on them and pray.

> The disciples rebuked them, 14 but Jesus said, "Let the children come to me, and do not prevent them; for the kingdom of heaven belongs to such as these." (Matthew 18:16 See also Luke 16: 18)

The Code of Canon Law therefore proposes the following requirement:

> For holy communion to be administered to children, it is required that they have sufficient knowledge and be accurately prepared, so that according to their capacity they understand what the mystery of Christ means, and are able to receive the Body of the Lord with faith and devotion. (Can. 913 § 1)

The tradition of the Church has been that a child reaches the age of reason at seven, and can at that point understand the difference between an ordinary piece of bread and a consecrated host.

The Mystical Body of Christ

As I recall, we spent an entire year on the Church as the Mystical Body of Christ. It is a subject which continues to be particularly significant to me in my understanding of and dedication to the Roman Catholic Church.

That the Roman Catholic Church constitutes the mystical presence of Jesus Christ on earth has been the tradition of the Church since the time of Christ. In fact, Christ Himself refers to His Church in that way—"Abide in me, and I in you. As the branch cannot bear fruit of itself unless it remain on the vine, so neither can you unless you abide in me" (Jn 15:4). And implicitly at the Last Supper when He says, "This is my body . . . This is the cup of my blood . . . ."

The Apostles, principally St. Paul, refer to this concept. Paul the Apostle spoke of this unity of Christians with Christ, spoken of in the New Testament also in images such as that of the vine and the branches in terms of a single body that has Christ as its head in Romans 12:5, 1 Corinthians 12:12-27, Ephesians 3:6 and 5:23, Colossians 1:18 and 1:24. The Fathers of the Church unanimously deal with the subject. The following Ecumenical Councils declared this doctrine: The Council of Trent, Vatican Council I, Vatican Council II. And considered to be among the most important encyclicals of his pontificate, Pope Pius XII promulgated the encyclical *Mystici Corporis Christi* (*The Mystical Body of Christ*—June 29, 1943). In it, the Pope cites the many sources in which the tradition of the Mystical Body of Christ is founded. Among many other things, he wrote the following passage:

> Actually only those are to be included as members of the Church who have been baptized and profess the true faith, and who have not been so unfortunate as to separate themselves from the unity of the Body, or been excluded by legitimate authority for grave faults committed . . . . For not every sin, however great it may be, is such as of its own nature to sever a man from the Body of the Church, as does schism or heresy or apostasy.

There is no more important event in our lives than to belong to the Church—the Mystical Body of Christ—the way Christ Himself wants us to be.

The documents of Vatican Council II, produced under the guidance of the Holy Spirit, with the final approval of Pope Paul VI, became another landmark in the history of the Church in which God Himself has told us what He wants us to know. Those who think it was simply the work of learned and dedicated men (the Fathers of the Council) are in error. We must always keep in mind the things that Christ said about His Church: 1) "Thou art Peter, and on this rock I will build my church" (Mt. 16:18); 2) "Behold I am with you all days, even to the end of days" (Mt. 28:20); 3) "Whatever you bind on earth, it will be bound in heaven, and whatever you loose on earth, it will be loosed in heaven." (Mt. 16:19; see also Mt. 18:18).

As soon as the council documents were available in 1965 or early 1966, with my two degrees in Theology and Canon Law fresh in my mind (I received my Canon Law degree in 1957) I undertook my own personal in-depth study of Vatican II, from its very beginning to its close. When I finished, I stood in awe of what I found: ***All*** of the doctrines, dogmas and traditions of the Catholic Church were retained without exception, and they were presented in phraseology as yet unused in the history of councils and church documents. To put it in merely human terms: The Holy Spirit was never in better form as He guided the Fathers of Vatican Council II.

One unusual phrase in the documents of the Council, although it was an old, old concept in the history of God's interaction with His creation, was ***"The People of God."*** Adam and Eve, of course, were created directly, body and soul, by God Himself. Since our first parents, in an interaction between man and woman and God Himself Who created and infused each soul, everyone taken as a group, has constituted the "The People of God." The Second Vatican Council took the concept and embellished it, identifying various groups according to their closeness to God Himself. The initial obvious one is between those who do not believe in God—atheists—and those who do. (According to St. Paul, there is no such a thing as an atheist, but simply those who convince themselves that there is no God (Rom 1:18-23). If this perception were to be put into graphic form, it might be a series of concentric circles, with the outer ring being Atheists, those who are farthest from union with God. A second ring might well be those who believe in a higher power, but do not see Him as One God—such as Pantheism, Polytheism, etc. Thirdly, Agnostics and Deists—i.e. those who believe in God, but He does not intervene in the universe or the world. The fourth ring are those who believe in One God, such as Jews and Muslims, but who do not believe in the Divinity of Jesus Christ. Perhaps the Jews and the Muslims should be each in their own ring. The Muslims believe that Jesus Christ was a great prophet and they revere the Blessed Virgin, while the Jews do not give Jesus an important role, nor do they revere His mother. Each of these levels (rings), depending on their beliefs, either are held at a greater distance from God, or are brought closer to Him. The fifth ring is comprised of those who believe in the Divinity of Christ, three persons in the Divine Trinity, and that the Second Person of the Trinity became Man and died on the Cross to Redeem the human race from the original sin of Adam and Eve, but do not belong to the One True Church which was founded by Christ Himself, and therefore do not have the benefit of all the sacraments nor all the supernatural graces which could be theirs. The final level, the sixth ring, contains all those who are full members of the True Church which Christ Himself founded—the Holy Roman Catholic Church. This is the Mystical Body of Christ—a supernatural community who are living a supernatural life. The person who receives Catholic baptism is cleansed of original sin (and any actual sins), receives the infusion of Sanctifying Grace, and joins that Mystical Body (as St. Paul said, "I live now not I, but Christ lives in me" (Gal. 2:20).) With the reception of Holy Communion, and every time he or she receives Communion, that member increases in Sanctifying Grace and is each time more closely in union with Christ and the Holy Trinity. At the reception of the Sacrament of Confirmation, there is yet another increment in Sanctifying Grace. We therefore, through the Sacraments, can and do grow in our union with God until the end of our lives.

The Sacrifice of the Mass

I spent an entire school year in Rome studying the Mass as the crowning ceremony of the Catholic liturgy. I studied it as the Unbloody Sacrifice of Christ on the Cross. It is a sacrifice because Christ, the perfect, infinite Victim, once having died on the cross in final expiation for the sin of Adam and Eve, and for the sins of all mankind, in each Mass once again is offered up as an eternal Victim.

The very first Mass of the newly forming Catholic Church was celebrated by Christ Himself when, at the Last Supper, the night before He knew He was to die, He took bread in His hands, blessed it, broke it and gave it to his Apostles, saying "Take and eat, all of you: This is my body which will be offered up for you." and again taking the chalice of wine He said, "Take this all of you and drink from it. This is the chalice of my blood which will be shed for you . . . . Do this in commemoration of me."

Christ, in His infinite power, retained the ***appearances*** of bread and wine, and changed the **substance** of bread and wine into Himself as He stood before them: the living incarnate Second Person of the Trinity, not yet having died upon the Cross and before He was betrayed by Judas. Our professor told us of his firm persuasion that if the Apostles had celebrated Mass after Christ died and before His resurrection (and he said that there is no evidence that they did so), that Christ would have become present, body and blood, soul separated from His body but present, together with His full Divinity. In the Masses celebrated now and for two thousand years since his death and resurrection, He becomes present as He is in heaven, the perfect Victim for all eternity, present in His Church and in all of its members. Christ established the Sacrifice of the Mass as the source of all the graces which He left behind for the members of His Mystical Body, which also made possible the fulfillment of His declaration that unless you eat my flesh and drink my blood, you cannot have life everlasting.

As it must have been difficult for anyone to envision eating the flesh and drinking the blood of this Man standing before them at that time, now when Christ gave us such an acceptable way of doing so, we now, particularly since the Middle Ages, have people finding it difficult to believe that what appears to be bread and wine is in reality the living Body and Blood, Soul and Divinity of Christ Himself. We will return to this subject later, but there are estimates that as many as sixty percent of priests no longer believe in the Real Presence, and, since bishops are taken from those who serve as priests, there must be a significant number of bishops who have their doubts about the Real Presence.

During the time I was studying Theology in Rome, Pope Pius XII promulgated a decree which, among many other things, determined that the exact moment of consecration of bread and wine came when the signifying words were pronounced. Therefore, when the priest says "This is my body," the appearance of bread remains but it becomes the Body and Blood, Soul and Divinity of Christ Himself; likewise when the priest says "This is the chalice of my blood," the appearance of wine remains but it becomes the Body and Blood, Soul and Divinity of Christ Himself. The Council of Trent (Session 13, Oct. 11, 1551) was later to define that every portion of the consecrated bread and wine contains the ***entire*** glorified Christ. Over the years, I have had people ask me whether bread and wine consecrated by a priest who no longer believes in the Real Presence, and the Mass itself, is actually valid. The answer is clear: When the words of consecration are pronounced by a validly ordained priest, the results depend upon the power of God, and not at all on the faltering faith of the priest. As long as the Mass has its requisite parts—the Offertory (offering of the gifts), the Consecration, and Communion—it is valid. These days, when one hears in the vernacular the words of Consecration ("This is my Body . . . This is the chalice of my Blood) anyone attending Mass *knows* that the priest is saying what Christ commanded.

The Mass, as it was first celebrated by Christ Himself and continues on around the world every day, is the glory of the Catholic Church.

The intentions of God toward His creatures—the human race—are wonderful to contemplate. When Adam and Eve sinned, it required an infinite act to make reparation for the infinite evil of their action. In an eternal outpouring of love, God sent His only Son to die on the Cross in expiation and to return the human race to a redeemed state so that once again they could live a supernaturalized life and be saved. In a continued outpouring of love, Christ created His Church and established within it the Mass as the source of all the graces which He would for all time pour out upon His flock. The Mass is the source of all the graces as they are made available through the rest of the Sacraments. Every day, as morning dawns around the world, His priests celebrate the Mass thousands of times, bringing

Christ Himself, Body and Blood, Soul and Divinity into the midst of His people, bringing with Him all the graces which His people need to live strong spiritual lives and to bring about their own salvation. "God is Love" says the Apostle (1 John 4:8). And we can only in the vaguest of ways in this life understand what it really means to have the infinite power of the love of God Himself directed upon us.

Christ asked His Apostles during His Agony in the Garden, "Could you not watch one hour with me?" If we actually *knew* what the Mass is, nothing could keep us from watching one hour per week which is all that the precepts of the Church require of us—attend Mass on Sundays and Holy Days of obligation. And, understanding what the Real Presence is, we would all bend every effort to receive communion as often as we can and as the law of the Church permits.

The Sacrament of Penance

The power to forgive sin was instituted by Christ Himself—as all seven Sacraments were—so that anyone who commits sin can be absolved by His priests. Christ entrusted this authority over sin to all the Twelve (Mt. 18:18) after first having given it personally to Peter, the rock, His vicar, when He said: "I will give you the keys to the kingdom of heaven. Whatever you bind on earth shall be bound in heaven; and whatever you loose on earth shall be loosed in heaven." (Mt. 16:19) This was so important in the mind of Christ that during His first contact with the Apostles after His Resurrection He reminded them of their authority over sin. As He appeared among them, He said:

> 'Peace be with you. As the Father sent me, so I send you.' And when he had said this, he breathed on them and said to them, 'Receive the Holy Spirit. Whose sins you forgive are forgiven them, and whose sins you retain are retained.' (Jn. 20:21ff)

Confirmation

Baptism, the Eucharist, and the sacrament of Confirmation together constitute the sacraments of Christian initiation. For by the sacrament of Confirmation, the baptized receive a specialized form of Sanctifying Grace whereby they become, as I learned many, many years ago from the Baltimore Catechism, "soldiers of Christ." Hence they are, as true witnesses of Christ, more strictly obliged to spread and defend the faith by word and deed. Similar to the Apostles at the first Pentecost when the Holy Spirit descended upon them, they receive the grace to help them become stalwart defenders of the Faith and to fearlessly live and promote the Gospel.

It has been sad for me to see in recent years how those who prepare people to receive the Sacrament of Confirmation have turned the Sacrament into something of a "social work" exercise.

I have seen enough of this to believe that the practice is widespread. The trainees are sent out on exercises which provide food and clothing to the poor. If there were to be such an exercise, it would only be appropriate to have the trainees present the truths of the Catholic Faith to non-Catholics. This attitude is undoubtedly the influence of the Heresy of Modernism in the Church which appears to "humanize" every aspect of Catholicism and ignore the internal spiritual life which is the most important part of our lives.

The Sacrament of Matrimony

God created man and woman so that together they could participate in His creative powers. Since Adam and Eve, every man and woman, have been empowered to bring together the created materials which can initiate a new life, into which God Himself implants a soul which He has newly created.

Christ, during His time on earth, initiated Matrimony as one of the seven sacraments, making it a source of special grace. If it is a valid marriage between a baptized man and a baptized woman, it is a

Sacrament, giving the two all the support they need to stay together, increase the strength of their marriage bond, and raise their children as Catholics, and help each other improve their spiritual lives and save their souls.

The Church assigns three purposes to the Sacrament of Matrimony:

1) The ***primary purpose***, as per the Natural Law and the Law of God, is the procreation and nurturing of children. And by extension, we can say that the union of man and woman is so designed as to perpetuate the human race.
2) A **secondary purpose** is to serve as a remedy against sin and concupiscence, to avoid adultery, and ". . . that [believers] might marry and keep themselves undefiled members of Christ's body" (1 Cor 7:9).
3) A **third purpose** of marriage is to provide companionship throughout life, through good and bad, comfort and loss, sickness and health, until death parts the husband and wife.

In view of the primary purpose of marriage and in the light of many Scriptural passages (*e.g.*, the story of Sodom and Gomorrah, references to homosexuality by St. Paul, etc.—all of which will be treated more extensively later on when I narrate my personal experiences with a number of homosexuals.—the position of the Catholic Church on the subject of homosexuality becomes not only understandable but indisputable. For example, marriage is between one man and one woman, both must be baptized for the union to be a Sacrament, homosexuals must observe chastity throughout their lives since they cannot be married, otherwise they fail to observe the Sixth Commandment.

The Sacrament of Sacred Orders—The Priesthood

During the ceremony of the ordination of a priest, the ordaining bishop declares "Thou art a priest forever, according to the order of Melchisedech." As the High Priest of his time, Melchisedech offered his Old Testament sacrifice, using bread and wine. The newly ordained priest thus is empowered to offer the Sacrifice of the Mass and brings down upon the altar the body and blood, soul and divinity of Jesus Christ, the Second Person of the Trinity, under the appearance of bread and wine

When a priest is ordained, the Sacrament generates an indelible, eternal mark upon his soul which remains to his greater glory in heaven, or to his greater degradation in Hell. Two other sacraments leave an indelible mark upon the soul: baptism and confirmation. It is for this reason that the Code of Canon Law makes the following statement:

> Sacred ordination once validly received never becomes invalid. (Can.290)

The Sacrament of Extreme Unction

Now known quite commonly as the Sacrament of the Sick, this Sacrament was instituted by Christ Himself (as is true of all seven) to provide the grace needed as a person passes from this life to the next, and therefore to provide the support the dying person needs as the devil endeavors to inflict the final temptations which would take the soul away from God into Hell. And while this has always been the primary purpose of this sacrament, it has frequently restored good health to a dying person.

I personally wonder if this is an example of the "change" which the Heresy of Modernism has brought into the Church. For 2000 years it has been known as the Sacrament of **Extreme Unction**, i.e. the ***last anointing*** of the sick and dying. I don't know if there has been an authoritative, infallible declaration that the purpose of this sacrament has been extended so as to make it available to anyone who is simply sick and not in danger of dying.

The Universal Call to Holiness

Using all these Sacraments which Christ initiated for us as sources of His saving Grace, observing all the Truisms (Doctrines) which He left with His Apostles, and abiding with all the instructions which His Catholic Church continues to give us ("Whatever you bind on earth, it will be bound in heaven") (Matthew 16:19), we will move toward that holiness.

Earlier, Christ issued this command: "Be Ye Perfect as your heavenly Father is Perfect." (Matthew 5:48) In whatever we do, we are therefore to strive toward personal perfection. This, of course, as mentioned before, is the central theme of Vatican Council II: We are to strive toward personal holiness. As St. Paul put it: "I have been crucified with Christ, and it is no longer I who live, but Christ lives in me . . . ." (Gal. 2:19)

If we, as members of the Mystical Body of Christ, will strive consciously to live in the Presence of God (we do know by Faith that the Holy Spirit dwells within us, that the Divine Trinity, Father, Son and Holy Spirit live in our souls) the holiness that we will thus achieve will have a positive impact on all those with whom we come in contact: Our families, those with whom we work, and upon all our social contacts—and we will also enhance our individual eternal reward.

Hope for the Future

Since the early 1960's everything looked darker for the Catholic Church in the United States when the USCC (United States Catholic Conference) was established, and Bishop Joseph Bernardin became its first General Secretary, chosen in actuality by Archbishop John

Dearden, Archbishop of Detroit. A master politician, Bishop Bernardin outwardly maintained the appearance of an orthodox Catholic bishop, operating secretly as the head of what came to be known as AmChurch which was the direct offshoot of the heresies of Modernism and Americanism. Bishop Bernardin later solidified his position when he was elected president of the USCCB (United States Conference of Catholic Bishops). He initiated what some have called the 'Bernardin Era', so that even after his death as Cardinal Archbishop of Chicago, for years his 'followers' were routinely elected as president of the USCCB.

In 1999, my wife and I met Msgr. Timothy Dolan, Rector of the North American College in Rome, who, when he learned that I was an NAC alumnus, invited us into his office for an extended visit. We were greatly impressed by this obviously truly Catholic Churchman. Not long after our return home, he was appointed Auxiliary Bishop of St. Louis, then bishop of Milwaukee (2002), then Archbishop of New York (2009) and was recently (2012) named a Cardinal.

It was reportedly a surprise to everyone when, on Nov. 16, 2010, he was elected President of the U.S Conference of Catholic Bishops, thus replacing the Bernardin follower who had been favored. There is no doubt in my mind that he is truly loyal to the Vicar of Christ in Rome, that he espouses no taint of Modernism. And he is in the process of proving, in his very strong public opposition to the Obama Administration's promotion of contraception, that he is not afflicted with the heresy of Americanism. All of our prayers should be with him as he bears the burden of the most prominent Catholic prelate in the United States.

APPENDICES

APPENDIX-A

Full Text: Memorandum to Bishops' Committee Regarding PAVLA (Papal Volunteers for Latin America)

MEMORANDUM TO:	Conference of U.S. Catholic Bishops
FROM:	Rev. Raymond A. Kevane, National Director Papal Volunteers for Latin America
DATE:	July 1, 1969
SUBJECT:	Difficulties in the Division for Latin America, United States Catholic Conference

I do not say the following things lightly, nor do I say them for personal reasons. There have been complaints from several sources regarding the position in which the PAVLA program is placed, particularly during the past year. These complaints have come from Papal Volunteers working in Latin America, from PAVLA Diocesan

Directors, and, most recently, from PAVLA's National Planning Committee.

It was in March of this year that the Planning Committee appealed to the bishops through Bishop Hodges. Its members, as well as returned volunteers and Diocesan Directors throughout the country, are waiting for an answer. They have been patient, trusting in my judgment, but the time for an answer is past due. I ask for immediate clarification of the position of the Papal Volunteer program.

A most serious issue lies at the root of the current difficulties in the Division for Latin America. I want no one to mistake the gravity of this issue, and I hope that never again, after this presentation, will it be lightly brushed aside as a "failure in communications" between Father Colonnese and myself. The problems that plagued the PAVLA program and the rest of the Division for Latin America at the time of my memorandum to Father Colonnese of February 20, 1969, remain unresolved at this presentation four months later. I believe that at least an investigation should have begun immediately.

PAVLA is now facing problems, and has been facing them for the past year. The problems are literally destroying the Papal Volunteer program. Immediate action is imperative. If it is not taken, not only will the Papal Volunteer program be destroyed, but all hope of rapport between the Church in the United States and Latin America will soon die. The principles established by a succession of Popes are being undermined. There is likelihood that the Christian heritage of Latin America, mentioned so explicitly by the present Pope and his predecessor (cf. The PAVLA founding document and other sources) will not only be destroyed, but, ironically will be destroyed at the hands of an ostensibly Catholic organization operating under the aegis of the Bishops of the United States.

During the past year in which the programs of the Division for Latin America have for the first time been consolidated in Washington, the Papal Volunteer program has been subjected to a series of administrative failures, to harassment of its personnel and to delays in its programming. Evidence of these things will be submitted as this paper proceeds. This to a program which for several reasons enjoys the special commendation of Vatican Council II. (Decree on the Apostolate of the Laity, ch. IV, nos. 20-22)

Father Colonnese's opposition to the Papal Volunteers is in the order of ideology and is similar to the anti-PAVLA stance of Ivan Illich through the years. This is clear after a cursory reading of Father Colonnese's paper "Imperialism or Servanthood" which was distributed, in English and Spanish, at the Interamerican Bishops' meeting in Caracas, June 3-5 just past. See, for example, pp. 2-6; the criticisms listed (and approved by Father Colonnese: "while I do not negate the general validity of such criticism . . . .") have all been enunciated at one time or another by Ivan Illich, many of them aimed at the Papal Volunteer program. It is remarkable that the Director of the Division for Latin America singles out the PAVLA program for special criticism (p. 7). There are other groups, both lay and non-lay, not LAB programs, which have demonstrably failed or limped and which could have been the subject of his criticism. And he would have it that PAVLA as also other activities was "spawned" by a "sudden burst of enthusiasm." This is a gross misstatement. The Papal Volunteer program was "spawned", to use his term, by action of the Holy See with direct approval of the Pope. Father Colonnese and Ivan Illich share an unwillingness to recognize the role played by the Holy See in personnel-sending programs for Latin America. Father Colonnese's entire paper reflects the Illich ideology, such as is to be found in his (Illich's) letter to me in 1965, and in his two celebrated articles "The Seamy Side of Charity' and "The Vanishing Clergyman", both of which appeared in *America* magazine.

Father Colonnese's views as reported by the National Catholic Reporter a year ago had the familiar Illich ring. Starting in about 1958 or 1959, Father Colonnese acted as editor of *CIF Reports* which emanated from Illich's training center in Cuernavaca. Although Father Colonnese has stated to me that he broke publicly with Illich in the early sixties, I suggest that the break may have been opportunistic and not at all ideological. During the intervening years, I never heard

Illich speak against Father Colonnese, although I personally heard him attack every other LAB official.

It is a matter of record that in 1965 I terminated the training of Papal Volunteers at Cuernavaca, Mexico, under Ivan Illich, and opened a special training program for PAVLA in Mexico City. I did this because I could not countenance the manipulatory nature of Illich training. I personally saw the effects among personnel trained there: people whose minds had been warped, whose confidence was shattered, who had been filled with the "proper" (i.e. conceived in Cuernavaca) solutions for Latin America and who then became rebels on assignment where the local Church's ideas did not coincide with those learned at Cuernavaca. In April of 1965, I found that an entire group of Papal Volunteers in training (the last group to train there) had been filled with doubts about their right to go to Latin America, that they had become anti-Church, anti-institution, and anti-PAVLA. Since I had known some of those people earlier, their apparent personality change appalled me.

When I asked Illich why, in view of his outspoken opposition to PAVLA, he continued to accept Papal Volunteer candidates for training, he answered that since they would go anyhow, they should have the advantage of his training program.

Father Colonnese's paper presents a similar viewpoint. All of Illich's criticisms, he says, are valid, but if personnel receive the proper training, only then will the sending of U.S. personnel to Latin America be relevant. The clear implication is that the proper training is that outlined in his paper and administered by himself.

Make no mistake about it: The person (or group) who controls the nature of training controls the kind of personnel who are sent to Latin America. Manipulation of people is always a danger in any training program. But the danger of manipulation is far greater when we are dealing with dedicated groups going overseas to a strange culture. This is because of the peculiar psychology involved. There is ignorance, there is fear of the unknown, there is the unusually intense desire to do well, there is the fear of failure and attendant embarrassment—all of these factors make it possible for those in charge of training to reshape the individual to an extraordinary degree. Father Colonnese's reference (pp. 13-14) to the missionary's need for a "re-tooling" according to the "signs of the times," in this context is rather disturbing. One wonders what this 're-tooling" really is, who designs it according to the "signs of the times," and who interprets the "signs of the times". The facile answer to the latter, of course, is "Latin America designs and interprets", but we will see a bit later that things may not really be happening this way. Our major challenge is to find and prepare people, not "re-tool" them. We need to find people (leaving aside for a moment the question of professional qualifications) whose spiritual lives are of such dimension that they love both God and His People enough to adjust to the latter wherever they are in the world and in whatever condition. Such people, once found, need preparation for culture change, and need to be provided with various tools, such as language. Far more important than a "re-tooling process" (if it is indeed acceptable in concept) is an adequate selection and preparation process designed to protect both the candidate and the project in Latin America.

In 1965, PAVLA opened its National Training Center in Washington. At a PAVLA Board of Directors meeting prior to the opening, Father Colonnese strongly pushed for an investigation of the training program. An investigating committee was appointed whose members (Father Colonnese and James Lamb—Virginia Leary withdrew) appeared at the site of training during that summer.

In January of 1966, at a meeting of the LAB Advisory Committee, Father Colonnese spoke out strongly against the "thrust" of the PAVLA National Training center. Its greatest error seemed to be that it was teaching theology and spiritual life, that it was not attuned to the "signs of the times," etc.

During the preparation of the first (1965) session of the training center, while administration officials at the Catholic University were most helpful, it was vigorously opposed by Dr. Manoel Cardozo, Head of the Department of History. (Dr. Cardozo also opposed Dr.

José Baquero and his work in International Education.) At CICOP in Boston in 1967, when Father Colonnese for the first time had full charge of CICOP, a panel on foreign lay apostolic action in Latin America was scheduled into the program. Dr. Cardozo was one of the panelists. (James Lamb was chairman and Thomas Quigley a principal speaker.) The session was described as an attack on the PAVLA program—as it might well have been expected to be, since three of the five panelists were known to oppose the Papal Volunteer program. The only panelist that day who defended PAVLA was a Mexican bishop.

These and other incidents occurring prior to May, 1968, when the offices were consolidated make it quite clear that Father Colonnese has been less than satisfied with the PAVLA program. The other incidents are cited in my memorandum of February 20, 1969, to Father Colonnese. He has been active in his opposition, and his opposition is at least in part ideological in nature.

At this time I would like to raise again some of the questions posed in that earlier memorandum:

1. Why is Father Colonnese so opposed to Dr. Baquero? Which are the "groups" that do not accept Dr. Baquero? What "stance" of Dr. Baquero's was objectionable to these groups? Who "practically gave orders" to exclude Dr. Baquero? (Memorandum, pp. 8-9)
2. Why does Father Colonnese belittle the abilities of Papal Volunteers? (Memorandum, pp. 5 & 7)
3. Why did Mr. Hegy, trainee during the 1968 PAVLA training session, insist on relating directly to Father Colonnese rather than to Father Eron or myself? Why did the same Mr. Hegy clandestinely circulate a questionnaire to the trainees, and why did many of the trainees feel that he was a "spy" for Father Colonnese? (Memorandum, pp. 7-8 and various reports)
4. Why was it necessary that a layman teach the course on "Role and Spirituality of the Layman? Which are the "groups" that

> would otherwise object? Why was Thomas Quigley proposed by Father Colonnese as the man to teach the course? (Memorandum, p. 9)

It is clear from what has been said that Father Colonnnese's ideology of training differs from that of PAVLA. In order to understand better what his ideology of training is, I would like to direct attention to Father Colonnese's program for training in Mexico City and in the pastoral institutes (the third stage), which are projected to branch from the parent institute (IPLA) in Quito, Ecuador.

At this point (July 1, 1969), I have little knowledge of the content of the Mexico City training program which is scheduled to begin on September 2, 1969. Some basic information is available, but not much else. Father Colonnese did say at one point that the new training program would use a number of Illich's former staff. This was something less than reassuring. I have not been contacted for consultation about the content for lay personnel. Mr. Frank Danczyk, PAVLA's representative in Mexico, reports that although he has offered his services and has asked about content, he has received no answer and virtually no encouragement.

Beginning early in the Fall of 1968, Father Colonnese devoted increasing time to the establishment of the Mexico City Training Center. At the same time, he promoted the idea of a third stage of training by means of the pastoral institutes in Latin America. As I said above, whoever controls training controls the kind of personnel being sent to Latin America. The Mexico Center is, of course, controlled by Father Colonnese who according to the evidence seems to share the Illich ideology.

The nature of the pastoral institutes now being organized in the countries of Latin America certainly does concern the bishops of Latin America and of the United States. In view of these questions regarding Father Colonnese's ideology of training, the developing pastoral institutes must be carefully analyzed. CELAM is being subsidized heavily each year from the U.S. Bishops through LAB. It is doubtless because of such funds or other funds, that IPLA—The International Pastoral Institute—can be maintained in Quito, Ecuador. Father Colonnese administers these funds and therefore is in a position of major influence with reference to training (among other things) in Latin America.

According to a written report I have received, there are priests in Ecuador who describe the new training center as "Cuernavaca transplanted." The same report described positions taken by the IPLA staff. For instance:

1) IPLA has no official position on violence; the staff sees to it, however, that the students are informed on both the "theology of violence" (even guerilla warfare) approach to development, and the "non-violent" approach. According to this report, the staff does not subscribe to the position of Pope Paul VI made public in his visit to Bogotá during which he called for an end of violence.
2) All IPLA staff members reportedly say that the role of the Church in social development (desarrollo) is limited: a. to becoming the mystique of development, and b. to denouncing injustices. There seems to be no sign of the positive role of the Church in training human resources for development, as envisioned by *Populorum Progressio.*
3) According to this same report, the director of IPLA maintains that development (desarrollo) is *non-violent revolution.*

Since last Fall (1968), Father Colonnese has often said that we will send personnel only to those countries which have a pastoral institute operating. As we will see, these will likely be nothing other than offshoots of IPLA headquarters in Quito, Ecuador. To quote again from my memorandum:

> This is a threatening statement to conferences of bishops who depend a great deal on the foreign personnel already in their countries. They can envision the time when, subject to this kind of influence, the U.S. Church will remove its personnel from their countries and dioceses unless they take immediate action in establishing pastoral institutes locally.

It is not surprising, therefore, that at the meeting in Caracas last month, it was proposed that these pastoral institutes be established in every country. An investigating team, as you know, under the auspices both of CELAM and USCC, is to visit countries of Latin America to conduct a feasibility study. It will not be surprising to me if in nearly every country, there will be found alumnae and alumni of IPLA in Quito, to whom it will be entirely natural for the investigating team (and the local conferences of bishops) to turn for assistance in opening a pastoral institute or "updating" an existing one. Assuming the accuracy of the report I received about IPLA and its ideology, it will not be long until that same ideology will be planted in every pastoral institute in Latin America. As a result of that, the leading clergy, religious and laity of each country (as well as in-coming foreign personnel) will have been exposed to the same doctrinaire training. The end result, of course, is clear: local personnel will have been exposed to the doctrines summarized above. The natural outcome, one would suspect, would be that they would be promoted or not according to their degree of conformity with this doctrine. Such personnel could easily become excessively negative and destructive.

On a massive and unprecedented scale, *desarrollo,* development and change was to be brought about in the cultures of Latin America through the preparation of personnel who were trained in non-violence as a tool to be used as part of mass demonstrations.

While I do not oppose the concept of non-violence, I do oppose some of its practical forms, and I do oppose the apparently *wholesale* identification of development with non-violence.

In addition to this wholesale identification of development with non-violence, these carefully trained personnel will reportedly have been taught to form "communidades de base". Those "communidades" are supra-parochial, formed of "like-minded people", and who strive toward their own personal conversion in order to develop the community. The "conversion", in all likelihood, would include (if not comprise) adherence to the concept of "non-violence as development", of denouncing injustices, and of being the mystique of development. It would not be surprising if the group has as a primary purpose the promotion of non-violent movements.

The team organized to study the feasibility of pastoral institutes was originally scheduled to make the trip in September. At Father Colonnese's instance, this has been re-scheduled to July. This urgency to establish the pastoral institutes (and the training in Mexico) has been characteristic of Father Colonnese since last Fall.

I believe it will be clear, after my few remarks on this subject, that the new LAB training program needs a careful review. This will also give some idea why PAVLA's training has been strongly criticized by the advocates of that new program. And surely it is understandable why PAVLA's Planning Committee—and I wholeheartedly with them—want PAVLA to be responsible for training its personnel (religious and laity by no means excluded). We certainly agree that final training should take place in the country of assignment, but it should be clear why we are reluctant to have this carried out by the local pastoral institutes until their validity is demonstrated.

My next point is, I believe, closely related to what I have already said. But if none of those things had been said, it would still demand your very special attention.

I submit, first of all, two documents. The first is a letter from Mr. Glenn Smiley relating the success of his efforts to carry the non-violent movement to Latin America. While I think the U.S.

effort to carry the non-violent movement to Latin America is of highly questionable validity, the body of the letter is not its most pertinent part. The letter itself is written on the letterhead of the "Coordinating committee of Latin America". At the left side, Mr. Smiley is listed as Executive Secretary. There follow the names of the Executive Committee members. The chairman is Sidney Lens. Also listed are J. Hugh Anwyl, L.M. Colonnese, Dana S. Green, George Lakey, Elaine Mikels, Thomas E. Quigley, Esteban Torres, Brady Tyson, Herman Will, Jr., and Carl Zietlow.

Until this letter arrived, I had never heard of the Coordinating Committee on Latin America. Having heard of it, I do not know what it coordinates. The only people on its Executive committee whom I have met are, of course, L.M. Colonnese; Dana S. Green (who has been rather closely associated with CICOP; Thomas E. Quigley (who works at USCC and whom I have mentioned before); and Brady Tyson (who, as having charge of the Interamerican Forum, is a frequent visitor to the office).

I submit to you also another document announcing the establishment of the "National Information Network on Latin America." According to its definition, the "Network" is for all those "concerned about the urgent need for changing present U.S. politico-economic policies (public and private) toward Latin America". Pages one and two give the expected organizational information. The final page lists the organizations and people who are the founding fathers of the network: both those who were present at the initiating meeting and those who are preliminary consultants. Some of the organizations are quite obviously political. Among the people listed as affiliated with the various organizations pertaining to the "Network" are some of those who are listed on the letterhead of the Coordinating Committee on Latin America: Elaine Mikels, Dana Green, Glenn Smiley, Sidney Lens, Thomas Quigley, L.M. Colonnese, Brady Tyson.

One wonders what precisely is coordinated by the "Coordinating Committee". Is it non-violent movements in Latin America? Is it the Information Notwork? Is it both of these and more than these? And the question naturally arises: Are these, perhaps, the groups that thought Dr. Baquero's stance disqualified him for our training program? Are they the ones which insisted on a layman teaching the course on the Role of the Modern Christian?

Now, as a final point relating to these groups, close attention should be given to the background of Mr. Sidney Lens, Chairman of the Coordinating Committee on Latin America. I draw attention to a number of documents. One is an excerpt from the book "Fabian Freeway" by Rose L. Martin, on Lens' alleged connections with the "Fair Play for Cuba Committee", and relating that he took the Fifth Amendment when asked if he has ever belonged to a Trotskyist organization.

A second set of (two) documents are excerpts from reports by the House Committee on un-American Activities. Both deal with the "Fair Play for Cuba Committee" and the name of Sidney Lens appears in both; and in the one dated June 15, 1961, he is reported as member of the group which started the Fair Play for Cuba Committee. In view of recent statements on Cuba made by Father Colonnese, this raises some most important questions which are entirely obvious.

A final document of great interest in this context is a four-page confidential report produced on October 31, 1962 by the American Security Council. The entire issue is devoted to Sidney Lens, and goes into detail about his past life, including his double identity. Under one name, he was associated with the Revolutionary Workers' League which the report indicates stood for the violent overthrow of the U.S. Government. Under the other name, as the report says, he has been connected with the Fair Play for Cuba Committee and characterizes himself as a "Ghanian", favoring non-violent resistance.

It is noteworthy that Sidney Lens is featured on the front page of the May, 1969, issue of "Latin America Calls", publication of the Latin America Bureau.

I am sure the U.S. Bishops do not want PAVLA associated with unknown or questionable groups.

All these considerations make one wonder how many activities of this nature the Latin America program of the U.S. Bishops has been or is being associated with.

Now to my last point. In view of all that I have said, I am sure it will come as no surprise that administrative difficulties have plagued the PAVLA program to a marked degree since the consolidation of the LAB offices in May, 1968, when Father Colonnese assumed the directorship. I shall mention here only those administrative difficulties of a truly substantive nature. There have been many cases of administrative delays, harassment of staff, and lack of consultation which, taken together with the following, constitute a truly formidable obstacle for those who have been trying to work on the PAVLA program.

There has been no PAVLA budget for a year. Although some people point to the figure for PAVLA submitted to the USCC last Fall, accounting services are so poor that it is impossible to know from month to month where PAVLA stands on its budget. I refer you to the financial reports received by PAVLA for the last half of 1968 and through May, 1969. They are incomplete and quite frankly useless for budgeting purposes.

When Father Colonnese left on his tour of Latin America in early February of this year, I was left with unanswered questions on the summer training program at what was then a late date. I was told at that time by Bishop Bernardin that we must wait until Father Colonnese returned.

The financial reports on PAVLA prepared by the LAB business office for the latter part of 1968 show a $14,000 discrepancy. This was demonstrated in February when copies of those financial reports were made available.

At the same time, my earlier memorandum reported failure of LAB to account for the more than $75,000 in PAVA funds brought along from Chicago in May, 1968. These funds have still not been accounted for.

That same memorandum reported failure of LAB to provide sufficient accounting of the PAVLA Support Fund which is accountable to 40 dioceses and seventy volunteers, which brings in $37,000 a quarter, and now has a balance of more than $35,000. (This sum, of course, has no relationship to the $75,000 figure mentioned immediately above).

The memorandum also reported failure on the part of LAB to carry on with a volunteer support funding plan. The previously existing funding program has now been abolished and nothing effective has been done to reinstate it. Forty-two PAVLA applicants were turned away this year because sponsorship funds were not available. Many, probably most, of these could have been accepted had the fund, established for this purpose, been available to support candidates from dioceses unable to provide finances. This is part, but only part, of the reason why our number of candidates is at a record low this year in spite of a record high in number of applications.

The Papal Volunteer program has been in the process of disintegration for the past year, since it became public knowledge that Father Colonnese was the new LAB Director. A number of diocesan PAVLA directors asked me at that time whether PAVLA could long survive with him in that position. I assured them that there was sufficient backing from the bishops for PAVLA, that they need not worry. I regret to say that the four months' delay in taking action or even investigating since my memorandum of February 20 makes it appear that these assurances were not well founded. Members of the PAVLA Planning Committee are wondering what action the bishops will take and when that action will come. A March letter from the Planning Committee to the Bishops' Committee through Bishop Hodges—a letter urgently requesting immediate action—remains unanswered except for Bishop Hodges' letter acknowledging receipt.

For my own part, after five years as National Director of the Papal Volunteer program, I can no longer put up with the difficulties which PAVLA has always faced during that time within the Latin America Bureau—difficulties now grown in the last year to monstrous proportions. These factors, and others not mentioned in this paper, have done far more than make life difficult for me. They have effectively destroyed all efforts at planning. Each obstacle has made its contribution toward killing the program. If this condition continues, even for a short time, I can only project the complete destruction of the Papal Volunteer program. The PAVLA program must be immediately removed from the authority of Father Colonnese. Make the removal temporary if you must, but free PAVLA from the jurisdiction of the Division for Latin America as long as you leave Father Colonnese in his position. I must have immediate authority, within an established and adequate budget, to hire new staff—both to replace those who were summarily dismissed from PAVLA in February, and to replace those who have loyally remained until this time but who can bear it no longer and are leaving, sickened by the harassment they have had to suffer. In order to continue in good conscience, I must have an adequate budget, control of staff, salaries, administration and PAVLA training.

AMDG

APPENDIX-B

Testem Benevolentiae Nostrae

Concerning New Opinions, Virtue, Nature And Grace, With Regard To Americanism

Pope Leo XIII

Encyclical promulgated on January 22, 1899.

To Our Beloved Son, James Cardinal Gibbons, Cardinal Priest of the Title Sancta Maria, Beyond the Tiber, Archbishop of Baltimore:

Beloved Son, Health and Apostolic Blessing:

We send to you by this letter a renewed expression of that good will which we have not failed during the course of our pontificate to manifest frequently to you and to your colleagues in the episcopate and to the whole American people, availing ourselves of every opportunity offered us by the progress of your church or whatever you have done for safeguarding and promoting Catholic interests. Moreover, we have often considered and admired the noble gifts of your nation which enable the American people to be alive to every good work which promotes the good of humanity and the splendor of civilization. Although this letter is not intended, as preceding ones, to repeat the words of praise so often spoken, but rather to call attention to some things to be avoided and corrected; still because it is conceived in that same spirit of apostolic charity which has inspired all our letters, we shall expect that you will take it as another proof of our love; the more so because it is intended to suppress certain contentions which have arisen lately among you to the detriment of the peace of many souls.

It is known to you, beloved son, that the biography of Isaac Thomas Hecker, especially through the action of those who under took to translate or interpret it in a foreign language, has excited not a little controversy, on account of certain opinions brought forward concerning the way of leading Christian life.

We, therefore, on account of our apostolic office, having to guard the integrity of the faith and the security of the faithful, are desirous of writing to you more at length concerning this whole matter.

The underlying principle of these new opinions is that, in order to more easily attract those who differ from her, the Church should shape her teachings more in accord with the spirit of the age and relax some of her ancient severity and make some concessions to new opinions. Many think that these concessions should be made not only in regard to ways of living, but even in regard to doctrines which belong to the deposit of the faith. They contend that it would be opportune, in order to gain those who differ from us, to omit certain points of her teaching which are of lesser importance, and to tone down the meaning which the Church has always attached to them. It does not need many words, beloved son, to prove the falsity of these ideas if the nature and origin of the doctrine which the Church proposes are recalled to mind. The Vatican Council says concerning this point: "For the doctrine of faith which God has revealed has not been proposed, like a philosophical invention to be perfected by human ingenuity, but has been delivered as a divine deposit to the Spouse of Christ to be faithfully kept and infallibly declared. Hence that meaning of the sacred dogmas is perpetually to be retained which our Holy Mother, the Church, has once declared, nor is that meaning ever to be departed from under the pretense or pretext of a deeper comprehension of them."—*Constitutio de Fide Catholica*, Chapter iv.

We cannot consider as altogether blameless the silence which purposely leads to the omission or neglect of some of the principles of Christian doctrine, for all the principles come from the same Author and Master, "the Only Begotten Son, Who is in the bosom of the Father."—John i, 18. They are adapted to all times and all nations, as is clearly seen from the words of our Lord to His apostles: "Going, therefore, teach all nations; teaching them to observe all things whatsoever I have commanded you, and behold, I am with you all days, even to the end of the world."—Matt. xxviii, 19. Concerning this point the Vatican Council says: "All those things are to be believed with divine and catholic faith which are contained in the Word of God, written or handed down, and which the Church, either by a solemn judgment or by her ordinary and universal magisterium, proposes for belief as having been divinely revealed."—*Const. de fide*, Chapter iii.

Let it be far from anyone's mind to suppress for any reason any doctrine that has been handed down. Such a policy would tend rather to separate Catholics from the Church than to bring in those who differ. There is nothing closer to our heart than to have those who are separated from the fold of Christ return to it, but in no other way than the way pointed out by Christ.

The rule of life laid down for Catholics is not of such a nature that it cannot accommodate itself to the exigencies of various times and places. (VOL. XXIV-13.) The Church has, guided by her Divine Master, a kind and merciful spirit, for which reason from the very beginning she has been what St. Paul said of himself: "I became all things to all men that I might save all."

History proves clearly that the Apostolic See, to which has been entrusted the mission not only of teaching but of governing the whole Church, has continued "in one and the same doctrine, one and the same sense, and one and the same judgment,"—*Const. de fide*, Chapter iv.

But in regard to ways of living she has been accustomed to so yield that, the divine principle of morals being kept intact, she has never neglected to accommodate herself to the character and genius of the nations which she embraces.

Who can doubt that she will act in this same spirit again if the salvation of souls requires it? In this matter the Church must be the judge, not private men who are often deceived by the appearance of right. In this, all who wish to escape the blame of our predecessor, Pius the Sixth, must concur. He condemned as injurious to the Church and the spirit of God who guides her the doctrine contained in proposition lxxviii of the Synod of Pistoia, "that the discipline made and approved by the Church should be submitted to examination, as if the Church could frame a code of laws useless or heavier than human liberty can bear."

But, beloved son, in this present matter of which we are speaking, there is even a greater danger and a more manifest opposition to Catholic doctrine and discipline in that opinion of the lovers of novelty, according to which they hold such liberty should be allowed in the Church, that her supervision and watchfulness being in some sense lessened, allowance be granted the faithful, each one to follow out more freely the leading of his own mind and the trend of his own proper activity. They are of opinion that such liberty has its counterpart in the newly given civil freedom which is now the right and the foundation of almost every secular state.

In the apostolic letters concerning the constitution of states, addressed by us to the bishops of the whole Church, we discussed this point at length; and there set forth the difference existing between the Church, which is a divine society, and all other social human organizations which depend simply on free will and choice of men.

It is well, then, to particularly direct attention to the opinion which serves as the argument in behalf of this greater liberty sought for and recommended to Catholics.

It is alleged that now the Vatican decree concerning the infallible teaching authority of the Roman Pontiff having been proclaimed that nothing further on that score can give any solicitude, and accordingly, since that has been safeguarded and put beyond question a wider and freer field both for thought and action lies open to each one. But such reasoning is evidently faulty, since, if we are to come to any conclusion from the infallible teaching authority of the Church, it should rather be that no one should wish to depart from it, and moreover that the minds of all being leavened and directed thereby, greater security from private error would be enjoyed by all. And further, those who avail themselves of such a way of reasoning seem to depart seriously from the over-ruling wisdom of the Most High—which wisdom, since it was pleased to set forth by most solemn decision the authority and supreme teaching rights of this Apostolic See—willed that decision precisely in order to safeguard the minds of the Church's children from the dangers of these present times.

These dangers, viz., the confounding of license with liberty, the passion for discussing and pouring contempt upon any possible subject, the assumed right to hold whatever opinions one pleases upon any subject and to set them forth in print to the world, have so wrapped minds in darkness that there is now a greater need of the Church's teaching office than ever before, lest people become unmindful both of conscience and of duty.

We, indeed, have no thought of rejecting everything that modern industry and study has produced; so far from it that we welcome to the patrimony of truth and to an ever-widening scope of public well-being whatsoever helps toward the progress of learning and virtue. Yet all this, to be of any solid benefit, nay, to have a real existence and growth, can only be on the condition of recognizing the wisdom and authority of the Church.

Coming now to speak of the conclusions which have been deduced from the above opinions, and for them, we readily believe there was no thought of wrong or guile, yet the things themselves certainly merit some degree of suspicion. First, all external guidance is set aside for those souls who are striving after Christian perfection as being superfluous or indeed, not useful in any sense—the contention being that the Holy Spirit pours richer and more abundant graces than formerly upon the souls of the faithful, so that without human intervention He teaches and guides them by some hidden instinct of His own. Yet it is the sign of no small over-confidence to desire to measure and determine the mode of the Divine communication to mankind, since it wholly depends upon His own good pleasure, and He is a most generous dispenser 'of his own gifts. "The Spirit breatheth whereso He listeth."—John iii, 8.

"And to each one of us grace is given according to the measure of the giving of Christ."—Eph. iv, 7.

And shall any one who recalls the history of the apostles, the faith of the nascent church, the trials and deaths of the martyrs—and, above all, those olden times, so fruitful in saints—dare to measure our age with these, or affirm that they received less of the divine outpouring from the Spirit of Holiness? Not to dwell upon this point, there is no one who calls in question the truth that the Holy Spirit does work by a secret descent into the souls of the just and that He stirs them alike by warnings and impulses, since unless this were the case all outward defense and authority would be unavailing. "For if any persuades himself that he can give assent to saving, that is, to gospel truth when proclaimed, without any illumination of the Holy Spirit, who give's unto all sweetness both to assent and to hold, such an one is deceived by a heretical spirit."—From the Second Council of Orange, Canon 7.

Moreover, as experience shows, these monitions and impulses of the Holy Spirit are for the most part felt through the medium of the aid and light of an external teaching authority. To quote St. Augustine. "He (the Holy Spirit) co-operates to the fruit gathered from the good trees, since He externally waters and cultivates them by the outward ministry of men, and yet of Himself bestows the inward increase."—*De Gratia Christi*, Chapter xix. This, indeed, belongs to the ordinary law of God's loving providence that as He has decreed that men for the most part shall be saved by the ministry also of men, so has He wished that those whom He calls to the higher planes of holiness should be led thereto by men; hence St. Chrysostom declares we are taught of God through the instrumentality of men.—Homily I in *Inscrib. Altar*. Of this a striking example is given us in the very first days of the Church.

For though Saul, intent upon blood and slaughter, had heard the voice of our Lord Himself and had asked, "What dost Thou wish me to do?" yet he was bidden to enter Damascus and search for Ananias. Acts ix: "Enter the city and it shall be there told to thee what thou must do."

Nor can we leave out of consideration the truth that those who are striving after perfection, since by that fact they walk in no beaten or well-known path, are the most liable to stray, and hence have greater need than others of a teacher and guide. Such guidance has ever obtained in the Church; it has been the universal teaching of those who throughout the ages have been eminent for wisdom and sanctity—and hence to reject it would be to commit one's self to a belief at once rash and dangerous.

A thorough consideration of this point, in the supposition that no exterior guide is granted such souls, will make us see the difficulty of locating or determining the direction and application of that more abundant influx of the Holy Spirit so greatly extolled by innovators To practice virtue there is absolute need of the assistance of the Holy Spirit, yet we find those who are fond of novelty giving an unwarranted importance to the natural virtues, as though they better responded to the customs and necessities of the times and that having these as his outfit man becomes more ready to act and more strenuous in action. It is not easy to understand how persons possessed of Christian wisdom can either prefer natural to supernatural virtues or attribute to them a greater efficacy and fruitfulness. Can it be that nature conjoined with grace is weaker than when left to herself?

Can it be that those men illustrious for sanctity, whom the Church distinguishes and openly pays homage to, were deficient, came short in the order of nature and its endowments, because they excelled in Christian strength? And although it be allowed at times to wonder at acts worthy of admiration which are the outcome of natural virtue—is there anyone at all endowed simply with an outfit of natural virtue? Is there any one not tried by mental anxiety, and this in no light degree? Yet ever to master such, as also to preserve in its entirety the law of the natural order, requires an assistance from on high These single notable acts to which we have alluded will frequently upon a closer investigation be found to exhibit the appearance rather than the reality of virtue. Grant that it is virtue, unless we would "run in vain" and be unmindful of that eternal bliss which a good God in his mercy has destined for us, of what avail are natural virtues unless seconded by the gift of divine grace? Hence St. Augustine well says: "Wonderful is the strength, and swift the course, but outside the true path." For as the nature of man, owing to the primal fault, is inclined to evil and dishonor, yet by the help of grace is raised up, is borne along with a new greatness and strength, so, too, virtue, which is not the product of nature alone, but of grace also, is made fruitful unto everlasting life and takes on a more strong and abiding character.

This over-esteem of natural virtue finds a method of expression in assuming to divide all virtues in active and passive, and it is alleged that whereas passive virtues found better place in past times, our age is to be characterized by the active. That such a division and distinction cannot be maintained is patent—for there is not, nor can there be, merely passive virtue. "Virtue," says St. Thomas Aquinas, "designates the perfection of some faculty, but end of such faculty is an act, and an act of virtue is naught else than the good use of free will," acting, that is to say, under the grace of God if the act be one of supernatural virtue.

He alone could wish that some Christian virtues be adapted to certain times and different ones for other times who is unmindful of the apostle's words: "That those whom He foreknew, He predestined to be made conformable to the image of His Son."—Romans viii, 29. Christ is the teacher and the exemplar of all sanctity, and to His standard must all those conform who wish for eternal life. Nor does Christ know any change as the ages pass, "for He is yesterday and today and the same forever."—Hebrews xiii, 8. To the men of all ages was the precept given: "Learn of Me, because I am meek and humble of heart."—Matt. xi, 29.

To every age has He been made manifest to us as obedient even unto death; in every age the apostle's dictum has its force: "Those who are Christ's have crucified their flesh with its vices and concupiscences." Would to God that more nowadays practiced these virtues in the degree of the saints of past times, who in humility, obedience and self-restraint were powerful "in word and in deed"—to the great advantage not only of religion, but of the state and the public welfare.

From this disregard of the angelical virtues, erroneously styled passive, the step was a short one to a contempt of the religious life which has in some degree taken hold of minds. That such a value is generally held by the upholders of new views, we infer from certain statements concerning the vows which religious orders take. They say vows are alien to the spirit of our times, in that they limit the bounds of human liberty; that they are more suitable to weak than ›o strong minds; that so far from making for human perfection and the good of human organization, they are hurtful to both; but that this is as false as possible from the practice and the doctrine of the Church is clear, since she has always given the very highest approval to the religious method of life; nor without good cause, for those who under the divine call have freely embraced that state of life did not content themselves with the observance of precepts, but, going forward to the evangelical counsels, showed themselves ready and valiant soldiers of Christ. Shall we judge this to be a characteristic of weak minds, or shall we say that it is useless or hurtful to a more perfect state of life?

Those who so bind themselves by the vows of religion, far from having suffered a loss of liberty, enjoy that fuller and freer kind, that liberty, namely, by which Christ hath made us free. And this further view of theirs, namely, that the religious life is either entirely useless or of little service to the Church, besides being injurious to the religious orders cannot be the opinion of anyone who has read the annals of the Church. Did not your country, the United States, derive the beginnings both of faith and of culture from the children of these religious families? to one of whom but very lately, a thing greatly to your praise, you have decreed that a statue be publicly erected. And even at the present time wherever the religious families are found, how speedy and yet how fruitful a harvest of good works do they not bring forth! How very many leave home and seek strange lands to impart the truth of the gospel and to widen the bounds of civilization; and this they do with the greatest cheerfulness amid manifold dangers! Out of their number not less, indeed, than from the rest of the clergy, the Christian world finds the preachers of God's word, the directors of conscience, the teachers of youth and the Church itself the examples of all sanctity.

Nor should any difference of praise be made between those who follow the active state of life and those others who, charmed with solitude, give themselves to prayer and bodily mortification. And how much, indeed, of good report these have merited, and do merit, is known surely to all who do not forget that the "continual prayer of the just man" avails to placate and to bring down the blessings of heaven when to such prayers bodily mortification is added.

But if there be those who prefer to form one body without the obligation of the vows let them pursue such a course. It is not new in the Church, nor in any wise censurable. Let them be careful, however, not to set forth such a state above that of religious orders. But rather, since mankind are more disposed at the present time to indulge themselves in pleasures, let those be held in greater esteem "who having left all things have followed Christ."

Finally, not to delay too long, it is stated that the way and method hitherto in use among Catholics for bringing back those who have fallen away from the Church should be left aside and another one chosen, in which matter it will suffice to note that it is not the part of prudence to neglect that which antiquity in its long experience has approved and which is also taught by apostolic authority. The scriptures teach us that it is the duty of all to be solicitous for the salvation of one's neighbor, according to the power and position of each. The faithful do this by religiously discharging the duties of their state of life, by the uprightness of their conduct, by their works of Christian charity and by earnest and continuous prayer to God. On the other hand, those who belong to the clergy should do this by an enlightened fulfillment of their preaching ministry, by the pomp and splendor of ceremonies especially by setting forth that sound form of doctrine which Saint Paul inculcated upon Titus and Timothy. But if, among the different ways of preaching the word of God that one sometimes seems to be preferable, which directed to non-Catholics, not in churches, but in some suitable place, in such wise that controversy is not sought, but friendly conference, such a method is certainly without fault. But let those who undertake such ministry be set apart by the authority of the bishops and let them be men whose science and virtue has been previously ascertained. For we think that there are many in your country who are separated from Catholic truth more by ignorance than by ill-will, who might perchance more easily be drawn to the one fold of Christ if this truth be set forth to them in a friendly and familiar way.

From the foregoing it is manifest, beloved son, that we are not able to give approval to those views which, in their collective sense, are called by some "Americanism." But if by this name are to be understood certain endowments of mind which belong to the American people, just as other characteristics belong to various other nations, and if, moreover, by it is designated your political condition and the laws and customs by which you are governed, there is no reason to take exception to the name. But if this is to be so understood that the doctrines which have been adverted to above are not only indicated, but exalted, there can be no manner of doubt that our venerable brethren, the bishops of America, would be the first to repudiate and condemn it as being most injurious to themselves and to their country. For it would give rise to the suspicion that there are among you some who conceive and would have the Church in America to be different from what it is in the rest of the world.

But the true church is one, as by unity of doctrine, so by unity of government, and she is catholic also. Since God has placed the center and foundation of unity in the chair of Blessed Peter, she is rightly called the Roman Church, for "where Peter is, there is the church." Wherefore, if anybody wishes to be considered a real Catholic, he ought to be able to say from his heart the selfsame words which Jerome addressed to Pope Damasus: "I, acknowledging no other leader than Christ, am bound in fellowship with Your Holiness; that is, with the chair of Peter. I know that the church was built upon him as its rock, and that whosoever gathereth not with you, scattereth."

We having thought it fitting, beloved son, in view of your high office, that this letter should be addressed specially to you. It will also be our care to see that copies are sent to the bishops of the United States, testifying again that love by which we embrace your whole country, a country which in past times has done so much for the cause of religion, and which will by the Divine assistance continue to do still greater things. To you, and to all the faithful of America, we grant most lovingly, as a pledge of Divine assistance, our apostolic benediction.

Given at Rome, from St. Peter's, the 22nd day of January, 1899, and the thirty-first of our pontificate.

APPENDIX-C

Pascendi Dominici Gregis

ENCYCLICAL OF POPE PIUS X ON THE DOCTRINES OF THE MODERNISTS

To the Patriarchs, Primates, Archbishops, Bishops and other Local Ordinaries in Peace and Communion with the Apostolic See.

Venerable Brethren, Health and Apostolic Benediction.

The office divinely committed to Us of feeding the Lord's flock has especially this duty assigned to it by Christ, namely, to guard with the greatest vigilance the deposit of the faith delivered to the saints, rejecting the profane novelties of words and oppositions of knowledge falsely so called. There has never been a time when this watchfulness of the supreme pastor was not necessary to the Catholic body; for, owing to the efforts of the enemy of the human race, there have never been lacking "men speaking perverse things" (*Acts* xx. 30), "vain talkers and seducers" (*Tit.* i. 10), "erring and driving into error" (2 *Tim.* iii. 13). Still it must be confessed that the number of the enemies of the cross of Christ has in these last days increased exceedingly, who are striving, by arts, entirely new and full of subtlety, to destroy the vital energy of the Church, and, if they can, to overthrow utterly Christ's kingdom itself. Wherefore We may no longer be silent, lest We should seem to fail in Our most sacred duty, and lest the kindness that, in the hope of wiser counsels, We have hitherto shown them, should be attributed to forgetfulness of Our office.

Gravity of the Situation

2. That We make no delay in this matter is rendered necessary especially by the fact that the partisans of error are to be sought not only among the Church's open enemies; they lie hid, a thing to be deeply deplored and feared, in her very bosom and heart, and are the more mischievous, the less conspicuously they appear. We allude, Venerable Brethren, to many who belong to the Catholic laity, nay, and this is far more lamentable, to the ranks of the priesthood itself, who, feigning a love for the Church, lacking the firm protection of philosophy and theology, nay more, thoroughly imbued with the poisonous doctrines taught by the enemies of the Church, and lost to all sense of modesty, vaunt themselves as reformers of the Church; and, forming more boldly into line of attack, assail all that is most sacred in the work of Christ, not sparing even the person of the Divine Redeemer, whom, with sacrilegious daring, they reduce to a simple, mere man.
3. Though they express astonishment themselves, no one can justly be surprised that We number such men among the enemies of the Church, if, leaving out of consideration the internal disposition of soul, of which God alone is the judge, he is acquainted with their tenets, their manner of speech, their conduct. Nor indeed will he err in accounting them the most pernicious of all the adversaries of the Church. For as We have said, they put their designs for her ruin into operation not from without but from within; hence, the danger is present almost in

the very veins and heart of the Church, whose injury is the more certain, the more intimate is their knowledge of her. Moreover they lay the axe not to the branches and shoots, but to the very root, that is, to the faith and its deepest fires. And having struck at this root of immortality, they proceed to disseminate poison through the whole tree, so that there is no part of Catholic truth from which they hold their hand, none that they do not strive to corrupt. Further, none is more skilful, none more astute than they, in the employment of a thousand noxious arts; for they double the parts of rationalist and Catholic, and this so craftily that they easily lead the unwary into error; and since audacity is their chief characteristic, there is no conclusion of any kind from which they shrink or which they do not thrust forward with pertinacity and assurance. To this must be added the fact, which indeed is well calculated to deceive souls, that they lead a life of the greatest activity, of assiduous and ardent application to every branch of learning, and that they possess, as a rule, a reputation for the strictest morality. Finally, and this almost destroys all hope of cure, their very doctrines have given such a bent to their minds, that they disdain all authority and brook no restraint; and relying upon a false conscience, they attempt to ascribe to a love of truth that which is in reality the result of pride and obstinacy.

Once indeed We had hopes of recalling them to a better sense, and to this end we first of all showed them kindness as Our children, then we treated them with severity, and at last We have had recourse, though with great reluctance, to public reproof. But you know, Venerable Brethren, how fruitless has been Our action. They bowed their head for a moment, but it was soon uplifted more arrogantly than ever. If it were a matter which concerned them alone, We might perhaps have overlooked it: but the security of the Catholic name is at stake. Wherefore, as to maintain it longer would be a crime, We must now break silence, in order to expose before the whole Church in their true colours those men who have assumed this bad disguise.

Division of the Encyclical

4. But since the Modernists (as they are commonly and rightly called) employ a very clever artifice, namely, to present their doctrines without order and systematic arrangement into one whole, scattered and disjointed one from another, so as to appear to be in doubt and uncertainty, while they are in reality firm and steadfast, it will be of advantage, Venerable Brethren, to bring their teachings together here into one group, and to point out the connexion between them, and thus to pass to an examination of the sources of the errors, and to prescribe remedies for averting the evil.

ANALYSIS OF MODERNIST TEACHING

5. To proceed in an orderly manner in this recondite subject, it must first of all be noted that every Modernist sustains and comprises within himself many personalities; he is a philosopher, a believer, a theologian, an historian, a critic, an apologist, a reformer. These roles must be clearly distinguished from one another by all who would accurately know their system and thoroughly comprehend the principles and the consequences of their doctrines.

Agnosticism its Philosophical Foundation

6. We begin, then, with the philosopher. Modernists place the foundation of religious philosophy in that doctrine which is usually called *Agnosticism*. According to this teaching human reason is confined entirely within the field of *phenomena*, that is to say, to things that are perceptible to the senses, and in the manner in which they are perceptible; it has no right and no

power to transgress these limits. Hence it is incapable of lifting itself up to God, and of recognising His existence, even by means of visible things. From this it is inferred that God can never be the direct object of science, and that, as regards history, He must not be considered as an historical subject. Given these premises, all will readily perceive what becomes of *Natural Theology*, of the *motives of credibility*, of *external revelation*. The Modernists simply make away with them altogether; they include them in *Intellectualism*, which they call a ridiculous and long ago defunct system. Nor does the fact that the Church has formally condemned these portentous errors exercise the slightest restraint upon them. Yet the Vatican Council has defined, "If anyone says that the one true God, our Creator and Lord, cannot be known with certainty by the natural light of human reason by means of the things that are made, let him be anathema" (*De Revel.*, can. I); and also: "If anyone says that it is not possible or not expedient that man be taught, through the medium of divine revelation, about God and the worship to be paid Him, let him be anathema" (*Ibid.*, can. 2); and finally, "If anyone says that divine revelation cannot be made credible by external signs, and that therefore men should be drawn to the faith only by their personal internal experience or by private inspiration, let him be anathema" (*De Fide*, can. 3). But how the Modernists make the transition from *Agnosticism*, which is a state of pure nescience, to scientific and historic *Atheism*, which is a doctrine of positive denial; and consequently, by what legitimate process of reasoning, starting from ignorance as to whether God has in fact intervened in the history of the human race or not, they proceed, in their explanation of this history, to ignore God altogether, as if He really had not intervened, let him answer who can. Yet it is a fixed and established principle among them that both science and history must be atheistic: and within their boundaries there is room for nothing but *phenomena*; God and all that is divine are utterly excluded. We shall soon see clearly what, according to this most absurd teaching, must be held touching the most sacred Person of Christ, what concerning the mysteries of His life and death, and of His Resurrection and Acension into heaven.

Vital Immanence

7. However, this *Agnosticism* is only the negative part of the system of the Modernist: the positive side of it consists in what they call *vital immanence*. This is how they advance from one to the other. Religion, whether natural or supernatural, must, like every other fact, admit of some explanation. But when Natural theology has been destroyed, the road to revelation closed through the rejection of the arguments of credibility, and all external revelation absolutely denied, it is clear that this explanation will be sought in vain outside man himself. It must, therefore, be looked for in man; and since religion is a form of life, the explanation must certainly be found in the life of man. Hence the principle of *religious immanence* is formulated. Moreover, the first actuation, so to say, of every vital phenomenon, and religion, as has been said, belongs to this category, is due to a certain necessity or impulsion; but it has its origin, speaking more particularly of life, in a movement of the heart, which movement is called a *sentiment*. Therefore, since God is the object of religion, we must conclude that faith, which is the basis and the foundation of all religion, consists in a sentiment which originates from a need of the divine. This need of the divine, which is experienced only in special and favourable circumstances, cannot, of itself, appertain to the domain of consciousness; it is at first latent within the consciousness, or, to borrow a term from modern philosophy, in the *subconsciousness*, where also its roots lies hidden and undetected.

Should anyone ask how it is that this need of the divine which man experiences within himself grows up into a religion, the Modernists reply thus: Science and history, they say, are confined within two limits, the one external, namely, the visible world, the other internal, which is consciousness. When one or other of these boundaries has been reached, there can be no further progress, for beyond is the *unknowable*. In presence of this *unknowable*, whether it is outside man and beyond the visible world of nature, or lies hidden within in the subconsciousness, the need of the divine, according to the principles of *Fideism*, excites in a soul with a propensity towards religion a certain special *sentiment*, without any previous advertence of the mind: and this sentiment possesses, implied within itself both as its own object and as its intrinsic cause, the *reality* of the divine, and in a way unites man with God. It is this sentiment to which Modernists give the name of faith, and this it is which they consider the beginning of religion.

8. But we have not yet come to the end of their philosophy, or, to speak more accurately, their folly. For Modernism finds in this *sentiment* not faith only, but with and in faith, as they understand it, *revelation*, they say, abides. For what more can one require for revelation? Is not that religious *sentiment* which is perceptible in the consciousness revelation, or at least the beginning of revelation? Nay, is not God Himself, as He manifests Himself to the soul, indistinctly it is true, in this same religious sense, revelation? And they add: Since God is both the object and the cause of faith, this revelation is at the same time *of* God and *from* God; that is, God is both the revealer and the revealed.

Hence, Venerable Brethren, springs that ridiculous proposition of the Modernists, that every religion, according to the different aspect under which it is viewed, must be considered as both natural and supernatural. Hence it is that they make consciousness and revelation synonymous. Hence the law, according to which *religious consciousness* is given as the universal rule, to be put on an equal footing with revelation, and to which all must submit, even the supreme authority of the

Church, whether in its teaching capacity, or in that of legislator in the province of sacred liturgy or discipline.

Deformation of Religious History the Consequence

9. However, in all this process, from which, according to the Modernists, faith and revelation spring, one point is to be particularly noted, for it is of capital importance on account of the historico-critical corollaries which are deduced from it.—For the *Unknowable* they talk of does not present itself to faith as something solitary and isolated; but rather in close conjunction with some phenomenon, which, though it belongs to the realm of science and history yet to some extent oversteps their bounds. Such a phenomenon may be an act of nature containing within itself something mysterious; or it may be a man, whose character, actions and words cannot, apparently, be reconciled with the ordinary laws of history. Then faith, attracted by the *Unknowable* which is united with the phenomenon, possesses itself of the whole phenomenon, and, as it were, permeates it with its own life. From this two things follow. The first is a sort of *transfiguration* of the phenomenon, by its elevation above its own true conditions, by which it becomes more adapted to that form of the divine which faith will infuse into it. The second is a kind of *disfigurement*, which springs from the fact that faith, which has made the phenomenon independent of the circumstances of place and time, attributes to it qualities which it has not; and this is true particularly of the phenomena of the past, and the older they are, the truer it is. From these two principles the Modernists deduce two laws, which, when united with a third which they have already got from agnosticism, constitute the foundation of historical criticism. We will take an illustration from the Person of Christ. In the person of Christ, they say, science and history encounter nothing that is not human. Therefore, in virtue of the first canon deduced from agnosticism, whatever there is

in His history suggestive of the divine, must be rejected. Then, according to the second canon, the historical Person of Christ was *transfigured* by faith; therefore everything that raises it above historical conditions must be removed. Lately, the third canon, which lays down that the person of Christ has been *disfigured* by faith, requires that everything should be excluded, deeds and words and all else that is not in keeping with His character, circumstances and education, and with the place and time in which He lived. A strange style of reasoning, truly; but it is Modernist criticism.

10. Therefore the *religious sentiment*, which through the agency of *vital immanence* emerges from the lurking places of the subconsciousness, is the germ of all religion, and the explanation of everything that has been or ever will be in any religion. The *sentiment*, which was at first only rudimentary and almost formless, gradually matured, under the influence of that mysterious principle from which it originated, with the progress of human life, of which, as has been said, it is a form. This, then, is the origin of all religion, even supernatural religion; it is only a development of this *religious sentiment*. Nor is the Catholic religion an exception; it is quite on a level with the rest; for it was engendered, by the process of *vital immanence*, in the consciousness of Christ, who was a man of the choicest nature, whose like has never been, nor will be.—Those who hear these audacious, these sacrilegious assertions, are simply shocked! And yet, Venerable Brethren, these are not merely the foolish babblings of infidels. There are many Catholics, yea, and priests too, who say these things openly; and they boast that they are going to reform the Church by these ravings! There is no question now of the old error, by which a sort of right to the supernatural order was claimed for the human nature. We have gone far beyond that: we have reached the point when it is affirmed that our most holy religion, in the man Christ as in us, emanated from nature spontaneously and entirely. Than this there is surely nothing

more destructive of the whole supernatural order. Wherefore the Vatican Council most justly decreed: "If anyone says that man cannot be raised by God to a knowledge and perfection which surpasses nature, but that he can and should, by his own efforts and by a constant development, attain finally to the possession of all truth and good, let him be anathema" (*De Revel.*, can. 3).

The Origin of Dogmas

11. So far, Venerable Brethren, there has been no mention of the intellect. Still it also, according to the teaching of the Modernists, has its part in the act of faith. And it is of importance to see how.—In that *sentiment* of which We have frequently spoken, since sentiment is not knowledge, God indeed presents Himself to man, but in a manner so confused and indistinct that He can hardly be perceived by the believer. It is therefore necessary that a ray of light should be cast upon this sentiment, so that God may be clearly distinguished and set apart from it. This is the task of the intellect, whose office it is to reflect and to analyse, and by means of which man first transforms into mental pictures the vital phenomena which arise within him, and then expresses them in words. Hence the common saying of Modernists: that the religious man must *ponder* his faith.—The intellect, then, encountering this sentiment directs itself upon it, and produces in it a work resembling that of a painter who restores and gives new life to a picture that has perished with age. The simile is that of one of the leaders of Modernism. The operation of the intellect in this work is a double one: first by a natural and spontaneous act it expresses its concept in a simple, ordinary statement; then, on reflection and deeper consideration, or, as they say, *by elaborating its thought*, it expresses the idea in *secondary* propositions, which are derived from the first, but are more perfect and distinct.

These *secondary* propositions, if they finally receive the approval of the supreme *magisterium* of the Church, constitute dogma.

12. Thus, We have reached one of the principal points in the Modernists' system, namely the origin and the nature of dogma. For they place the origin of dogma in those primitive and simple formulae, which, under a certain aspect, are necessary to faith; for revelation, to be truly such, requires the clear manifestation of God in the consciousness. But dogma itself they apparently hold, is contained in the *secondary* formulae.

To ascertain the nature of dogma, we must first find the relation which exists between the *religious formulas* and the *religious sentiment*. This will be readily perceived by him who realises that these formulas have no other purpose than to furnish the believer with a means of giving an account of his faith to himself. These formulas therefore stand midway between the believer and his faith; in their relation to the faith, they are the inadequate expression of its object, and are usually called *symbols*; in their relation to the believer, they are mere *instruments*.

Its Evolution

13. Hence it is quite impossible to maintain that they express absolute truth: for, in so far as they are *symbols*, they are the images of truth, and so must be adapted to the religious sentiment in its relation to man; and as *instruments*, they are the vehicles of truth, and must therefore in their turn be adapted to man in his relation to the religious sentiment. But the object of the *religious sentiment*, since it embraces that *absolute*, possesses an infinite variety of aspects of which now one, now another, may present itself. In like manner, he who believes may pass through different phases. Consequently, the formulae too, which we call dogmas, must be subject to these vicissitudes, and are, therefore, liable to change. Thus the way is open to the intrinsic *evolution* of dogma. An immense collection of sophisms this, that ruins and destroys

all religion. Dogma is not only able, but ought to evolve and to be changed. This is strongly affirmed by the Modernists, and as clearly flows from their principles. For amongst the chief points of their teaching is this which they deduce from the principle of *vital immanence*; that religious formulas, to be really religious and not merely theological speculations, ought to be living and to live the life of the religious sentiment. This is not to be understood in the sense that these formulas, especially if merely imaginative, were to be made for the religious sentiment; it has no more to do with their origin than with number or quality; what is necessary is that the religious sentiment, with some modification when necessary, should vitally assimilate them. In other words, it is necessary that the primitive formula be accepted and sanctioned by the heart; and similarly the subsequent work from which spring the secondary formulas must proceed under the guidance of the heart. Hence it comes that these formulas, to be living, should be, and should remain, adapted to the faith and to him who believes. Wherefore if for any reason this adaptation should cease to exist, they lose their first meaning and accordingly must be changed. And since the character and lot of dogmatic formulas is so precarious, there is no room for surprise that Modernists regard them so lightly and in such open disrespect. And so they audaciously charge the Church both with taking the wrong road from inability to distinguish the religious and moral sense of formulas from their surface meaning, and with clinging tenaciously and vainly to meaningless formulas whilst religion is allowed to go to ruin. *Blind* that they are, and *leaders of the blind*, inflated with a boastful science, they have reached that pitch of folly where they pervert the eternal concept of truth and the true nature of the religious sentiment; with that new system of theirs *they are seen to be under the sway of a blind and unchecked passion for novelty, thinking not at all of finding some solid foundation of truth, but despising the holy and apostolic traditions, they embrace other vain, futile, uncertain doctrines, condemned by the Church, on which, in the height of their vanity, they think they can rest and maintain truth itself.*

The Modernist as Believer: Individual Experience and Religious Certitude

14. Thus far, Venerable Brethren, of the Modernist considered as Philosopher. Now if we proceed to consider him as Believer, seeking to know how the Believer, according to Modernism, is differentiated from the Philosopher, it must be observed that although the Philosopher recognises as the object of faith the *divine reality*, still this reality is not to be found but in the heart of the Believer, as being an object of sentiment and affirmation; and therefore confined within the sphere of phenomena; but as to whether it exists outside that sentiment and affirmation is a matter which in no way concerns this Philosopher. For the Modernist. Believer, on the contrary, it is an established and certain fact that the divine reality does really exist in itself and quite independently of the person who believes in it. If you ask on what foundation this assertion of the Believer rests, they answer: In the *experience of the individual.* On this head the Modernists differ from the Rationalists only to fall into the opinion of the Protestants and pseudo-mystics. This is their manner of putting the question: In the *religious sentiment* one must recognise a kind of intuition of the heart which puts man in immediate contact with the very reality of God, and infuses such a persuasion of God's existence and His action both within and without man as to excel greatly any scientific conviction. They assert, therefore, the existence of a real experience, and one of a kind that surpasses all rational experience. If this experience is denied by some, like the rationalists, it arises from the fact that such persons are unwilling to put themselves in the moral state which is necessary to produce it. It is this *experience* which, when a person acquires it, makes him properly and truly a believer.

How far off we are here from Catholic teaching we have already seen in the decree of the Vatican Council. We shall see later how, with such theories, added to the other errors already mentioned, the way is opened wide for atheism. Here it is well to note at once that, given this doctrine of *experience* united with the other doctrine of *symbolism*, every religion, even that of paganism, must be held to be true. What is to prevent such experiences from being met within every religion? In fact that they are to be found is asserted by not a few. And with what right will Modernists deny the truth of an experience affirmed by a follower of Islam? With what right can they claim true experiences for Catholics alone? Indeed Modernists do not deny but actually admit, some confusedly, others in the most open manner, that all religions are true. That they cannot feel otherwise is clear. For on what ground, according to their theories, could falsity be predicated of any religion whatsoever? It must be certainly on one of these two: either on account of the falsity of the religious sentiment or on account of the falsity of the formula pronounced by the mind. Now the *religious sentiment*, although it may be more perfect or less perfect, is always one and the same; and the intellectual formula, in order to be true, has but to respond to the *religious sentiment* and to the Believer, whatever be the intellectual capacity of the latter. In the conflict between different religions, the most that Modernists can maintain is that the Catholic has more truth because it is more living and that it deserves with more reason the name of Christian because it corresponds more fully with the origins of Christianity. That these consequences flow from the premises will not seem unnatural to anybody. But what is amazing is that there are Catholics and priests who, We would fain believe, abhor such enormities yet act as if they fully approved of them. For they heap such praise and bestow such public honour on the teachers of these errors as to give rise to the belief that their admiration is not meant merely for the persons, who are perhaps not devoid of a certain merit, but rather for the errors which these persons openly profess and which they do all in their power to propagate.

Religious Experience and Tradition

15. But this doctrine of *experience* is also under another aspect entirely contrary to Catholic truth. It is extended and applied to *tradition*, as hitherto understood by the Church, and destroys it. By the Modernists, tradition is understood as a communication to others, through preaching by means of the intellectual formula, of an *original experience*. To this formula, in addition to its representative value, they attribute a species of suggestive efficacy which acts both in the person who believes, to stimulate the religious sentiment should it happen to have grown sluggish and to renew the experience once acquired, and in those who do not yet believe, to awake for the first time the religious *sentiment* in them and to produce the *experience*. In this way is religious experience propagated among the peoples; and not merely among contemporaries by preaching, but among future generations both by books and by oral transmission from one to another. Sometimes this communication of religious experience takes root and thrives, at other times it withers at once and dies. For the Modernists, to live is a proof of truth, since for them life and truth are one and the same thing. Hence again it is given to us to infer that all existing religions are equally true, for otherwise they would not live.

Faith and Science

16. Having reached this point, Venerable Brethren, we have sufficient material in hand to enable us to see the relations which Modernists establish between faith and science, including history also under the name of science. And in the first place it is to be held that the object of the one is quite extraneous to and separate from the

object of the other. For faith occupies itself solely with something which science declares to be *unknowable* for it. Hence each has a separate field assigned to it: science is entirely concerned with the reality of phenomena, into which faith does not enter at all; faith on the contrary concerns itself with the divine reality which is entirely unknown to science. Thus the conclusion is reached that there can never be any dissension between faith and science, for if each keeps on its own ground they can never meet and therefore never be in contradiction. And if it be objected that in the visible world there are some things which appertain to faith, such as the human life of Christ, the Modernists reply by denying this. For though such things come within the category of phenomena, still in as far as they are *lived* by faith and in the way already described have been by faith transfigured and disfigured, they have been removed from the world of sense and translated to become material for the divine. Hence should it be further asked whether Christ has wrought real miracles, and made real prophecies, whether He rose truly from the dead and ascended into heaven, the answer of agnostic science will be in the negative and the answer of faith in the affirmative—yet there will not be, on that account, any conflict between them. For it will be denied by the philosopher as philosopher, speaking to philosophers and considering Christ only in His historical reality; and it will be affirmed by the speaker, speaking to believers and considering the life of Christ as *lived* again by the faith and in the faith.

Faith Subject to Science

17. Yet, it would be a great mistake to suppose that, given these theories, one is authorised to believe that faith and science are independent of one another. On the side of science the independence is indeed complete, but it is quite different with regard to faith, which is subject to science not on one but on three grounds. For in the first place it must be observed that in

every religious fact, when you take away the *divine reality* and the *experience* of it which the believer possesses, everything else, and especially the *religious formulas* of it, belongs to the sphere of phenomena and therefore falls under the control of science. Let the believer leave the world if he will, but so long as he remains in it he must continue, whether he like it or not, to be subject to the laws, the observation, the judgments of science and of history. Further, when it is said that God is the object of faith alone, the statement refers only to the *divine reality* not to the *idea* of God. The latter also is subject to science which while it philosophises in what is called the logical order soars also to the absolute and the ideal. It is therefore the right of philosophy and of science to form conclusions concerning the idea of God, to direct it in its evolution and to purify it of any extraneous elements which may become confused with it. Finally, man does not suffer a dualism to exist in him, and the believer therefore feels within him an impelling need so to harmonise faith with science, that it may never oppose the general conception which science sets forth concerning the universe.

Thus it is evident that science is to be entirely independent of faith, while on the other hand, and notwithstanding that they are supposed to be strangers to each other, faith is made subject to science. All this, Venerable Brothers, is in formal opposition with the teachings of Our Predecessor, Pius IX, where he lays it down that: *In matters of religion it is the duty of philosophy not to command but to serve, but not to prescribe what is to be believed but to embrace what is to be believed with reasonable obedience, not to scrutinise the depths of the mysteries of God but to venerate them devoutly and humbly.*

The Modernists completely invert the parts, and to them may be applied the words of another Predecessor of Ours, Gregory IX., addressed to some theologians of his time: *Some among you, inflated like bladders with the spirit of vanity strive by profane novelties to cross the boundaries fixed by the Fathers, twisting the sense of the heavenly pages . . . to the philosophical teaching of the rationals, not for the profit of their hearer but to make a show of science . . . these, seduced by strange and eccentric doctrines, make the head of the tail and force the queen to serve the servant.*

The Methods of Modernists

18. This becomes still clearer to anybody who studies the conduct of Modernists, which is in perfect harmony with their teachings. In the writings and addresses they seem not unfrequently to advocate now one doctrine now another so that one would be disposed to regard them as vague and doubtful. But there is a reason for this, and it is to be found in their ideas as to the mutual separation of science and faith. Hence in their books you find some things which might well be expressed by a Catholic, but in the next page you find other things which might have been dictated by a rationalist. When they write history they make no mention of the divinity of Christ, but when they are in the pulpit they profess it clearly; again, when they write history they pay no heed to the Fathers and the Councils, but when they catechise the people, they cite them respectfully. In the same way they draw their distinctions between theological and pastoral exegesis and scientific and historical exegesis. So, too, acting on the principle that science in no way depends upon faith, when they treat of philosophy, history, criticism, feeling no horror at treading in the footsteps of Luther, they are wont to display a certain contempt for Catholic doctrines, or the Holy Fathers, for the Ecumenical Councils, for the ecclesiastical magisterium; and should they be rebuked for this, they complain that they are being deprived of their liberty. Lastly, guided by the theory that faith must be subject to science, they continuously and openly criticise the Church because of her sheer obstinacy in refusing to submit and accommodate her dogmas to the opinions of philosophy; while they, on their side, after having blotted out the old theology,

endeavour to introduce a new theology which shall follow the vagaries of their philosophers.

The Modernist as Theologian: His Principles, Immanence and Symbolism

19. And thus, Venerable Brethren, the road is open for us to study the Modernists in the theological arena—a difficult task, yet one that may be disposed of briefly. The end to be attained is the conciliation of faith with science, always, however, saving the primacy of science over faith. In this branch the Modernist theologian avails himself of exactly the same principles which we have seen employed by the Modernist philosopher, and applies them to the believer: the principles of *immanence* and *symbolism*. The process is an extremely simple one. The philosopher has declared: *The principle of faith is immanent*; the believer has added: *This principle is God*; and the theologian draws the conclusion: *God is immanent in man*. Thus we have *theological immanence*. So too, the philosopher regards as certain that *the representations of the object of faith are merely symbolical*; the believer has affirmed that *the object of faith is God in Himself*; and the theologian proceeds to affirm that: *The representations of the divine reality are symbolical*. And thus we have *theological symbolism*. Truly enormous errors both, the pernicious character of which will be seen clearly from an examination of their consequences. For, to begin with *symbolism*, since symbols are but *symbols* in regard to their objects and only instruments in regard to the believer, it is necessary first of all, according to the teachings of the Modernists, that the believer do not lay too much stress on the formula, but avail himself of it only with the scope of uniting himself to the absolute truth which the formula at once reveals and conceals, that is to say, endeavours to express but without succeeding in doing so. They would also have the believer avail himself of the formulas only in as far as they are useful to him,

for they are given to be a help and not a hindrance; with proper regard, however, for the social respect due to formulas which the public magisterium has deemed suitable for expressing the common consciousness until such time as the same magisterium provide otherwise. Concerning *immanence* it is not easy to determine what Modernists mean by it, for their own opinions on the subject vary. Some understand it in the sense that God working in man is more intimately present in him than man is in even himself, and this conception, if properly understood, is free from reproach. Others hold that the divine action is one with the action of nature, as the action of the first cause is one with the action of the secondary cause, and this would destroy the supernatural order. Others, finally, explain it in a way which savours of pantheism and this, in truth, is the sense which tallies best with the rest of their doctrines.

20. With this principle of *immanence* is connected another which may be called the principle of *divine permanence*. It differs from the first in much the same way as the private *experience* differs from the *experience* transmitted by tradition. An example will illustrate what is meant, and this example is offered by the Church and the Sacraments. The Church and the Sacraments, they say, are not to be regarded as having been instituted by Christ Himself. This is forbidden by agnosticism, which sees in Christ nothing more than a man whose religious consciousness has been, like that of all men, formed by degrees; it is also forbidden by the law of immanence which rejects what they call external *application*; it is further forbidden by the law of evolution which requires for the development of the germs a certain time and a certain series of circumstances; it is, finally, forbidden by history, which shows that such in fact has been the course of things. Still it is to be held that both Church and Sacraments have been founded *mediately* by Christ. But how? In this way: All Christian consciences were, they affirm, in a manner virtually included in the conscience of Christ as the plant is included in the seed. But as the shoots live

the life of the seed, so, too, all Christians are to be said to live the life of Christ. But the life of Christ is according to faith, and so, too, is the life of Christians. And since this life produced, in the courses of ages, both the Church and the Sacraments, it is quite right to say that their origin is from Christ and is divine. In the same way they prove that the Scriptures and the dogmas are divine. And thus the Modernistic theology may be said to be complete. No great thing, in truth, but more than enough for the theologian who professes that the conclusions of science must always, and in all things, be respected. The application of these theories to the other points We shall proceed to expound, anybody may easily make for himself.

Dogma and the Sacraments

21. Thus far We have spoken of the origin and nature of faith. But as faith has many shoots, and chief among them the Church, dogma, worship, the Books which we call "Sacred," of these also we must know what is taught by the Modernists. To begin with dogma, we have already indicated its origin and nature. Dogma is born of the species of impulse or necessity by virtue of which the believer is constrained to elaborate his religious thought so as to render it clearer for himself and others. This elaboration consists entirely in the process of penetrating and refining the primitive *formula*, not indeed in itself and according to logical development, but as required by circumstances, or *vitally* as the Modernists more abstrusely put it. Hence it happens that around the *primitive* formula *secondary* formulas gradually continue to be formed, and these subsequently grouped into bodies of doctrine, or into doctrinal constructions as they prefer to call them, and further sanctioned by the public magisterium as responding to the common consciousness, are called dogma. Dogma is to be carefully distinguished from the speculations of theologians which, although not alive with the life of dogma,

are not without their utility as serving to harmonise religion with science and remove opposition between the two, in such a way as to throw light from without on religion, and it may be even to prepare the matter for future dogma. Concerning worship there would not be much to be said, were it not that under this head are comprised the Sacraments, concerning which the Modernists fall into the gravest errors. For them the Sacraments are the resultant of a double need—for, as we have seen, everything in their system is explained by inner impulses or necessities. In the present case, the first need is that of giving some sensible manifestation to religion; the second is that of propagating it, which could not be done without some sensible form and consecrating acts, and these are called sacraments. But for the Modernists the Sacraments are mere symbols or signs, though not devoid of a certain efficacy—an efficacy, they tell us, like that of certain phrases vulgarly described as having "caught on," inasmuch as they have become the vehicle for the diffusion of certain great ideas which strike the public mind. What the phrases are to the ideas, that the Sacraments are to the religious sentiment—that and nothing more. The Modernists would be speaking more clearly were they to affirm that the Sacraments are instituted solely to foster the faith—but this is condemned by the Council of Trent: *If anyone say that these sacraments are instituted solely to foster the faith, let him be anathema.*

The Holy Scriptures

22. We have already touched upon the nature and origin of the Sacred Books. According to the principles of the Modernists they may be rightly described as a collection of *experiences*, not indeed of the kind that may come to anybody, but those extraordinary and striking ones which have happened in any religion. And this is precisely what they teach about our books of the Old and New Testament. But to suit their own theories they note with remarkable

ingenuity that, although experience is something belonging to the present, still it may derive its material from the past and the future alike, inasmuch as the believer by memory *lives* the past over again after the manner of *the present*, and lives the future already by anticipation. This explains how it is that the historical and apocalyptical books are included among the Sacred Writings. God does indeed speak in these books—through the medium of the believer, but only, according to Modernistic theology, by vital *immanence* and *permanence*. Do we inquire concerning inspiration? Inspiration, they reply, is distinguished only by its vehemence from that impulse which stimulates the believer to reveal the faith that is in him by words or writing. It is something like what happens in poetical inspiration, of which it has been said: There is God in us, and when he stirreth he sets us afire. And it is precisely in this sense that God is said to be the origin of the inspiration of the Sacred Books. The Modernists affirm, too, that there is nothing in these books which is not inspired. In this respect some might be disposed to consider them as more orthodox than certain other moderns who somewhat restrict inspiration, as, for instance, in what have been put forward as *tacit citations*. But it is all mere juggling of words. For if we take the Bible, according to the tenets of agnosticism, to be a human work, made by men for men, but allowing the theologian to proclaim that it is divine by immanence, what room is there left in it for inspiration? General inspiration in the Modernist sense it is easy to find, but of inspiration in the Catholic sense there is not a trace.

The Church

23. A wider field for comment is opened when you come to treat of the vagaries devised by the Modernist school concerning the Church. You must start with the supposition that the Church has its birth in a double need, the need of the individual believer,

especially if he has had some original and special experience, to communicate his faith to others, and the need of the mass, when the faith has become common to many, to form itself into a society and to guard, increase, and propagate the common good. What, then, is the Church? It is the product of the *collective conscience*, that is to say of the society of individual consciences which by virtue of the principle of *vital permanence*, all depend on one first believer, who for Catholics is Christ. Now every society needs a directing authority to guide its members towards the common end, to conserve prudently the elements of cohesion which in a religious society are doctrine and worship.

Hence the triple authority in the Catholic Church, *disciplinary, dogmatic, liturgical.* The nature of this authority is to be gathered from its origin, and its rights and duties from its nature. In past times it was a common error that authority came to the Church from without, that is to say directly from God; and it was then rightly held to be *autocratic.* But his conception had now grown obsolete. For in the same way as the Church is a vital emanation of the collectivity of consciences, so too authority emanates vitally from the Church itself. Authority therefore, like the Church, has its origin in the religious conscience, and, that being so, is subject to it. Should it disown this dependence it becomes a tyranny. For we are living in an age when the sense of liberty has reached its fullest development, and when the public conscience has in the civil order introduced popular government. Now there are not two consciences in man, any more than there are two lives. It is for the ecclesiastical authority, therefore, to shape itself to democratic forms, unless it wishes to provoke and foment an intestine conflict in the consciences of mankind. The penalty of refusal is disaster. For it is madness to think that the sentiment of liberty, as it is now spread abroad, can surrender. Were it forcibly confined and held in bonds, terrible would be its outburst, sweeping away at once both Church and religion. Such is the situation for the Modernists, and their one great anxiety is, in consequence, to find a way of conciliation between the authority of the Church and the liberty of believers.

The Relations Between Church and State

24. But it is not with its own members alone that the Church must come to an amicable arrangement—besides its relations with those within, it has others outside. The Church does not occupy the world all by itself; there are other societies in the world, with which it must necessarily have contact and relations. The rights and duties of the Church towards civil societies must, therefore, be determined, and determined, of course, by its own nature as it has been already described. The rules to be applied in this matter are those which have been laid down for science and faith, though in the latter case the question is one of objects while here we have one of ends. In the same way, then, as faith and science are strangers to each other by reason of the diversity of their objects, Church and State are strangers by reason of the diversity of their ends, that of the Church being spiritual while that of the State is temporal. Formerly it was possible to subordinate the temporal to the spiritual and to speak of some questions as mixed, allowing to the Church the position of queen and mistress in all such, because the Church was then regarded as having been instituted immediately by God as the author of the supernatural order. But his doctrine is today repudiated alike by philosophy and history. The State must, therefore, be separated from the Church, and the Catholic from the citizen. Every Catholic, from the fact that he is also a citizen, has the right and the duty to work for the common good in the way he thinks best, without troubling himself about the authority of the Church, without paying any heed to its wishes, its counsels, its orders—nay, even in spite of its reprimands. To trace out and prescribe for the citizen any line of conduct, on any pretext whatsoever, is to be guilty of an abuse of ecclesiastical authority, against which one is bound to act with

all one's might. The principles from which these doctrines spring have been solemnly condemned by our predecessor Pius VI. in his Constitution *Auctorem fidei.*

The Magisterium of the Church

25. But it is not enough for the Modernist school that the State should be separated from the Church. For as faith is to be subordinated to science, as far as *phenomenal elements* are concerned, so too in temporal matters the Church must be subject to the State. They do not say this openly as yet—but they will say it when they wish to be logical on this head. For given the principle that in temporal matters the State possesses absolute mastery, it will follow that when the believer, not fully satisfied with his merely internal acts of religion, proceeds to external acts, such for instance as the administration or reception of the sacraments, these will fall under the control of the State. What will then become of ecclesiastical authority, which can only be exercised by external acts? Obviously it will be completely under the dominion of the State. It is this inevitable consequence which impels many among liberal Protestants to reject all external worship, nay, all external religious community, and makes them advocate what they call, *individual* religion. If the Modernists have not yet reached this point, they do ask the Church in the meanwhile to be good enough to follow spontaneously where they lead her and adapt herself to the civil forms in vogue. Such are their ideas about *disciplinary* authority. But far more advanced and far more pernicious are their teachings on *doctrinal* and *dogmatic* authority. This is their conception of the magisterium of the Church: No religious society, they say, can be a real unit unless the religious conscience of its members be one, and one also the formula which they adopt. But his double unity requires a kind of common mind whose office is to find and determine the formula that corresponds best with the common conscience, and it must have moreover an authority sufficient

to enable it to impose on the community the formula which has been decided upon. From the combination and, as it were fusion of these two elements, the common mind which draws up the formula and the authority which imposes it, arises, according to the Modernists, the notion of the ecclesiastical magisterium. And as this magisterium springs, in its last analysis, from the individual consciences and possesses its mandate of public utility for their benefit, it follows that the ecclesiastical magisterium must be subordinate to them, and should therefore take democratic forms. To prevent individual consciences from revealing freely and openly the impulses they feel, to hinder criticism from impelling dogmas towards their necessary evolutions—this is not a legitimate use but an abuse of a power given for the public utility. So too a due method and measure must be observed in the exercise of authority. To condemn and prescribe a work without the knowledge of the author, without hearing his explanations, without discussion, assuredly savours of tyranny. And thus, here again a way must be found to save the full rights of authority on the one hand and of liberty on the other. In the meanwhile the proper course for the Catholic will be to proclaim publicly his profound respect for authority—and continue to follow his own bent. Their general directions for the Church may be put in this way: Since the end of the Church is entirely spiritual, the religious authority should strip itself of all that external pomp which adorns it in the eyes of the public. And here they forget that while religion is essentially for the soul, it is not exclusively for the soul, and that the honour paid to authority is reflected back on Jesus Christ who instituted it.

The Evolution of Doctrine

26. To finish with this whole question of faith and its shoots, it remains to be seen, Venerable Brethren, what the Modernists have to say about their development. First of all they lay down the general

principle that in a living religion everything is subject to change, and must change, and in this way they pass to what may be said to be, among the chief of their doctrines, that of *Evolution*. To the laws of evolution everything is subject-dogma, Church, worship, the Books we revere as sacred, even faith itself, and the penalty of disobedience is death. The enunciation of this principle will not astonish anybody who bears in mind what the Modernists have had to say about each of these subjects. Having laid down this law of evolution, the Modernists themselves teach us how it works out. And first with regard to faith. The primitive form of faith, they tell us, was rudimentary and common to all men alike, for it had its origin in human nature and human life. Vital evolution brought with it progress, not by the accretion of new and purely adventitious forms from without, but by an increasing penetration of the religious sentiment in the conscience. This progress was of two kinds: negative, by the elimination of all foreign elements, such, for example, as the sentiment of family or nationality; and positive by the intellectual and moral refining of man, by means of which the idea was enlarged and enlightened while the religious sentiment became more elevated and more intense. For the progress of faith no other causes are to be assigned than those which are adduced to explain its origin. But to them must be added those religious geniuses whom we call prophets, and of whom Christ was the greatest; both because in their lives and their words there was something mysterious which faith attributed to the divinity, and because it fell to their lot to have new and original experiences fully in harmony with the needs of their time. The progress of dogma is due chiefly to the obstacles which faith has to surmount, to the enemies it has to vanquish, to the contradictions it has to repel. Add to this a perpetual striving to penetrate ever more profoundly its own mysteries. Thus, to omit other examples, has it happened in the case of Christ: in Him that divine something which faith admitted in Him expanded in such a way that He was at last held to be God. The chief stimulus of evolution in the domain of worship consists in the need of adapting itself to the uses and customs of peoples, as well as the need of availing itself of the value which certain acts have acquired by long usage. Finally, evolution in the Church itself is fed by the need of accommodating itself to historical conditions and of harmonising itself with existing forms of society. Such is religious evolution in detail. And here, before proceeding further, we would have you note well this whole theory of *necessities and needs*, for it is at the root of the entire system of the Modernists, and it is upon it that they will erect that famous method of theirs called the historical.

27. Still continuing the consideration of the evolution of doctrine, it is to be noted that Evolution is due no doubt to those stimulants styled needs, but, if left to their action alone, it would run a great risk of bursting the bounds of tradition, and thus, turned aside from its primitive vital principle, would lead to ruin instead of progress. Hence, studying more closely the ideas of the Modernists, evolution is described as resulting from the conflict of two forces, one of them tending towards progress, the other towards conservation. The conserving force in the Church is tradition, and tradition is represented by religious authority, and this both by right and in fact; for by right it is in the very nature of authority to protect tradition, and, in fact, for authority, raised as it is above the contingencies of life, feels hardly, or not at all, the spurs of progress. The progressive force, on the contrary, which responds to the inner needs lies in the individual consciences and ferments there—especially in such of them as are in most intimate contact with life. Note here, Venerable Brethren, the appearance already of that most pernicious doctrine which would make of the laity a factor of progress in the Church. Now it is by a species of compromise between the forces of conservation and of progress, that is to say between authority and individual consciences, that changes and advances take place. The individual consciences of some of them act on the collective conscience, which brings

pressure to bear on the depositaries of authority, until the latter consent to a compromise, and, the pact being made, authority sees to its maintenance.

With all this in mind, one understands how it is that the Modernists express astonishment when they are reprimanded or punished. What is imputed to them as a fault they regard as a sacred duty. Being in intimate contact with consciences they know better than anybody else, and certainly better than the ecclesiastical authority, what needs exist-nay, they embody them, so to speak, in themselves. Having a voice and a pen they use both publicly, for this is their duty. Let authority rebuke them as much as it pleases—they have their own conscience on their side and an intimate experience which tells them with certainty that what they deserve is not blame but praise. Then they reflect that, after all there is no progress without a battle and no battle without its victim, and victims they are willing to be like the prophets and Christ Himself. They have no bitterness in their hearts against the authority which uses them roughly, for after all it is only doing its duty as authority. Their sole grief is that it remains deaf to their warnings, because delay multiplies the obstacles which impede the progress of souls, but the hour will most surely come when there will be no further chance for tergiversation, for if the laws of evolution may be checked for a while, they cannot be ultimately destroyed. And so they go their way, reprimands and condemnations notwithstanding, masking an incredible audacity under a mock semblance of humility. While they make a show of bowing their heads, their hands and minds are more intent than ever on carrying out their purposes. And this policy they follow willingly and wittingly, both because it is part of their system that authority is to be stimulated but not dethroned, and because it is necessary for them to remain within the ranks of the Church in order that they may gradually transform the collective conscience—thus unconsciously avowing that the common conscience is not with them, and that they have no right to claim to be its interpreters.

28. Thus then, Venerable Brethren, for the Modernists, both as authors and propagandists, there is to be nothing stable, nothing immutable in the Church. Nor indeed are they without precursors in their doctrines, for it was of these that Our Predecessor Pius IX wrote: *These enemies of divine revelation extol human progress to the skies, and with rash and sacrilegious daring would have it introduced into the Catholic religion as if this religion were not the work of God but of man, or some kind of philosophical discovery susceptible of perfection by human efforts.* On the subject of revelation and dogma in particular, the doctrine of the Modernists offers nothing new—we find it condemned in the Syllabus of Pius IX., where it is enunciated in these terms: *Divine revelation is imperfect, and therefore subject to continual and indefinite progress, corresponding with the progress of human reason*; and condemned still more solemnly in the Vatican Council: *The doctrine of the faith which God has revealed has not been proposed to human intelligences to be perfected by them as if it were a philosophical system, but as a divine deposit entrusted to the Spouse of Christ to be faithfully guarded and infallibly interpreted. Hence the sense, too, of the sacred dogmas is that which our Holy Mother the Church has once declared, nor is this sense ever to be abandoned on plea or pretext of a more profound comprehension of the truth.* Nor is the development of our knowledge, even concerning the faith, impeded by this pronouncement—on the contrary it is aided and promoted. For the same Council continues: *Let intelligence and science and wisdom, therefore, increase and progress abundantly and vigorously in individuals and in the mass, in the believer and in the whole Church, throughout the ages and the centuries—but only in its own kind, that is, according to the same dogma, the same sense, the same acceptation.*

The Modernist as Historian and Critic

29. After having studied the Modernist as philosopher, believer and theologian, it now remains for us to consider him as historian, critic, apologist, reformer.

30. Some Modernists, devoted to historical studies, seem to be greatly afraid of being taken for philosophers. About philosophy, they tell you, they know nothing whatever—and in this they display remarkable astuteness, for they are particularly anxious not to be suspected of being prejudiced in favour of philosophical theories which would lay them open to the charge of not being objective, to use the word in vogue. And yet the truth is that their history and their criticism are saturated with their philosophy, and that their historico-critical conclusions are the natural fruit of their philosophical principles. This will be patent to anybody who reflects. Their three first laws are contained in those three principles of their philosophy already dealt with: the principle of *agnosticism*, the principle of the *transfiguration* of things by faith, and the principle which We have called of *disfiguration*. Let us see what consequences flow from each of them. *Agnosticism* tells us that history, like ever other science, deals entirely with phenomena, and the consequence is that God, and every intervention of God in human affairs, is to be relegated to the domain of faith as belonging to it alone. In things where a double element, the divine and the human, mingles, in Christ, for example, or the Church, or the sacraments, or the many other objects of the same kind, a division must be made and the human element assigned to history while the divine will go to faith. Hence we have that distinction, so current among the Modernists, between the Christ of history and the Christ of faith, between the sacraments of history and the sacraments of faith, and so on. Next we find that the human element itself, which the historian has to work on, as it appears in the documents, has been by faith transfigured, that is to say raised above its historical conditions.

It becomes necessary, therefore, to eliminate also the accretions which faith has added, to assign them to faith itself and to the history of faith: thus, when treating of Christ, the historian must set aside all that surpasses man in his natural condition, either according to the psychological conception of him, or according to the place and period of his existence. Finally, by virtue of the third principle, even those things which are not outside the sphere of history they pass through the crucible, excluding from history and relegating to faith everything which, in their judgment, is not in harmony with what they call the logic of facts and in character with the persons of whom they are predicated. Thus, they will not allow that Christ ever uttered those things which do not seem to be within the capacity of the multitudes that listened to Him. Hence they delete from His *real* history and transfer to faith all the allegories found in His discourses. Do you inquire as to the criterion they adopt to enable them to make these divisions? The reply is that they argue from the character of the man, from his condition of life, from his education, from the circumstances under which the facts took place—in short, from criteria which, when one considers them well, are purely *subjective*. Their method is to put themselves into the position and person of Christ, and then to attribute to Him what they would have done under like circumstances. In this way, absolutely *a priori* and acting on philosophical principles which they admit they hold but which they affect to ignore, they proclaim that Christ, according to what they call His *real* history, was not God and never did anything divine, and that as man He did and said only what they, judging from the time in which he lived, can admit Him to have said or done.

Criticism and its Principles

31. And as history receives its conclusions, ready-made, from philosophy, so too criticism takes its own from history. The critic,

on the data furnished him by the historian, makes two parts of all his documents. Those that remain after the triple elimination above described go to form the *real* history; the rest is attributed to the history of the faith or as it is styled, to *internal* history. For the Modernists distinguish very carefully between these two kinds of history, and it is to be noted that they oppose the history of the faith to real history precisely as real. Thus we have a double Christ: a real Christ, and a Christ, the one of faith, who never really existed; a Christ who has lived at a given time and in a given place, and a Christ who has never lived outside the pious meditations of the believer—the Christ, for instance, whom we find in the Gospel of St. John, which is pure contemplation from beginning to end.

32. But the dominion of philosophy over history does not end here. Given that division, of which We have spoken, of the documents into two parts, the philosopher steps in again with his principle of *vital immanence*, and shows how everything in the history of the Church is to be explained by *vital emanation*. And since the cause or condition of every vital emanation whatsoever is to be found in some need, it follows that no fact can ante-date the need which produced it—historically the fact must be posterior to the need. See how the historian works on this principle. He goes over his documents again, whether they be found in the Sacred Books or elsewhere, draws up from them his list of the successive needs of the Church, whether relating to dogma or liturgy or other matters, and then he hands his list over to the critic. The critic takes in hand the documents dealing with the history of faith and distributes them, period by period, so that they correspond exactly with the lists of needs, always guided by the principle that the narration must follow the facts, as the facts follow the needs. It may at times happen that some parts of the Sacred Scriptures, such as the Epistles, themselves constitute the fact created by the need. Even so, the rule holds that the age of any document can only be determined by the age in which each need had manifested

itself in the Church. Further, a distinction must be made between the beginning of a fact and its development, for what is born one day requires time for growth. Hence the critic must once more go over his documents, ranged as they are through the different ages, and divide them again into two parts, and divide them into two lots, separating those that regard the first stage of the facts from those that deal with their development, and these he must again arrange according to their periods.

33. Then the philosopher must come in again to impose on the historian the obligation of following in all his studies the precepts and laws of evolution. It is next for the historian to scrutinise his documents once more, to examine carefully the circumstances and conditions affecting the Church during the different periods, the conserving force she has put forth, the needs both internal and external that have stimulated her to progress, the obstacles she has had to encounter, in a word everything that helps to determine the manner in which the laws of evolution have been fulfilled in her. This done, he finishes his work by drawing up in its broad lines a history of the development of the facts. The critic follows and fits in the rest of the documents with this sketch; he takes up his pen, and soon the history is made complete. Now we ask here: Who is the author of this history? The historian? The critic? Assuredly, neither of these but the philosopher. From beginning to end everything in it is *a priori*, and *a priori* in a way that reeks of heresy. These men are certainly to be pitied, and of them the Apostle might well say: *They became vain in their thoughts . . . professing themselves to be wise they became fools* (*Rom.* i. 21, 22); but, at the same time, they excite just indignation when they accuse the Church of torturing the texts, arranging and confusing them after its own fashion, and for the needs of its cause. In this they are accusing the Church of something for which their own conscience plainly reproaches them.

How the Bible is Dealt With

34. The result of this dismembering of the Sacred Books and this partition of them throughout the centuries is naturally that the Scriptures can no longer be attributed to the authors whose names they bear. The Modernists have no hesitation in affirming commonly that these books, and especially the Pentateuch and the first three Gospels, have been gradually formed by additions to a primitive brief narration—by interpolations of theological or allegorical interpretation, by transitions, by joining different passages together. This means, briefly, that in the Sacred Books we must admit a *vital evolution*, springing from and corresponding with evolution of faith. The traces of this evolution, they tell us, are so visible in the books that one might almost write a history of them. Indeed this history they do actually write, and with such an easy security that one might believe them to have with their own eyes seen the writers at work through the ages amplifying the Sacred Books. To aid them in this they call to their assistance that branch of criticism which they call *textual*, and labour to show that such a fact or such a phrase is not in its right place, and adducing other arguments of the same kind. They seem, in fact, to have constructed for themselves certain types of narration and discourses, upon which they base their decision as to whether a thing is out of place or not. Judge if you can how men with such a system are fitted for practising this kind of criticism. To hear them talk about their works on the Sacred Books, in which they have been able to discover so much that is defective, one would imagine that before them nobody ever even glanced through the pages of Scripture, whereas the truth is that a whole multitude of Doctors, infinitely superior to them in genius, in erudition, in sanctity, have sifted the Sacred Books in every way, and so far from finding imperfections in them, have thanked God more and more the deeper they have gone into them, for His divine bounty in having vouchsafed to speak thus to men.

Unfortunately, these great Doctors did not enjoy the same aids to study that are possessed by the Modernists for their guide and rule,—a philosophy borrowed from the negation of God, and a criterion which consists of themselves.

We believe, then, that We have set forth with sufficient clearness the historical method of the Modernists. The philosopher leads the way, the historian follows, and then in due order come internal and textual criticism. And since it is characteristic of the first cause to communicate its virtue to secondary causes, it is quite clear that the criticism We are concerned with is an *agnostic, immanentist, and evolutionist* criticism. Hence anybody who embraces it and employs it, makes profession thereby of the errors contained in it, and places himself in opposition to Catholic faith. This being so, one cannot but be greatly surprised by the consideration which is attached to it by certain Catholics. Two causes may be assigned for this: first, the close alliance, independent of all differences of nationality or religion, which the historians and critics of this school have formed among themselves; second, the boundless effrontery of these men. Let one of them but open his mouth and the others applaud him in chorus, proclaiming that science has made another step forward; let an outsider but hint at a desire to inspect the new discovery with his own eyes, and they are on him in a body; deny it—and you are an ignoramus; embrace it and defend it—and there is no praise too warm for you. In this way they win over any who, did they but realise what they are doing, would shrink back with horror. The impudence and the domineering of some, and the thoughtlessness and imprudence of others, have combined to generate a pestilence in the air which penetrates everywhere and spreads the contagion. But let us pass to the apologist.

The Modernist as Apologist

35. The Modernist apologist depends in two ways on the philosopher. First, *indirectly*, inasmuch as his theme is history—history dictated, as we have seen, by the philosopher; and, secondly, *directly*, inasmuch as he takes both his laws and his principles from the philosopher. Hence that common precept of the Modernist school that the new apologetics must be fed from psychological and historical sources. The Modernist apologists, then, enter the arena by proclaiming to the rationalists that though they are defending religion, they have no intention of employing the data of the sacred books or the histories in current use in the Church, and composed according to old methods, but *real* history written on modern principles and according to rigorously modern methods. In all this they are not using an *argumentum ad hominem*, but are stating the simple fact that they hold, that the truth is to be found only in this kind of history. They feel that it is not necessary for them to dwell on their own sincerity in their writings—they are already known to and praised by the rationalists as fighting under the same banner, and they not only plume themselves on these encomiums, which are a kind of salary to them but would only provoke nausea in a real Catholic, but use them as an offset to the reprimands of the Church.

But let us see how the Modernist conducts his apologetics. The aim he sets before himself is to make the non-believer attain that *experience* of the Catholic religion which, according to the system, is the basis of faith. There are two ways open to him, the *objective* and the *subjective*. The first of them proceeds from agnosticism. It tends to show that religion, and especially the Catholic religion, is endowed with such vitality as to compel every psychologist and historian of good faith to recognise that its history hides some *unknown* element. To this end it is necessary to prove that this religion, as it exists today, is that which was founded by Jesus Christ; that is to say, that it is the product of the progressive development of the germ which He brought into the world. Hence it is imperative first of all to establish what this germ was, and this the Modernist claims to be able to do by the following formula: Christ announced the coming of the kingdom of God, which was to be realised within a brief lapse of time and of which He was to become the Messiah, the divinely-given agent and ordainer. Then it must be shown how this germ, always *immanent* and *permanent* in the bosom of the Church, has gone on slowly developing in the course of history, adapting itself successively to the different mediums through which it has passed, borrowing from them by *vital* assimiliation all the dogmatic, cultural, ecclesiastical forms that served its purpose; whilst, on the other hand, it surmounted all obstacles, vanquished all enemies, and survived all assaults and all combats. Anybody who well and duly considers this mass of obstacles, adversaries, attacks, combats, and the vitality and fecundity which the Church has shown throughout them all, must admit that if the laws of evolution are visible in her life they fail to explain the whole of her history—the *unknown* rises forth from it and presents itself before us. Thus do they argue, never suspecting that their determination of the primitive germ is an *a priori* of agnostic and evolutionist philosophy, and that the formula of it has been gratuitously invented for the sake of buttressing their position.

36. But while they endeavour by this line of reasoning to secure access for the Catholic religion into souls, these new apologists are quite ready to admit that there are many distasteful things in it. Nay, they admit openly, and with ill-concealed satisfaction, that they have found that even its dogma is not exempt from errors and contradictions. They add also that this is not only excusable but—curiously enough—even right and proper. In the Sacred Books there are many passages referring to science or history where manifest errors are to be found. But the subject of these books is not science or history but religion and

morals. In them history and science serve only as a species of covering to enable the religious and moral experiences wrapped up in them to penetrate more readily among the masses. The masses understood science and history as they are expressed in these books, and it is clear that had science and history been expressed in a more perfect form this would have proved rather a hindrance than a help. Then, again, the Sacred Books being essentially religious, are consequently necessarily living. Now life has its own truth and its own logic, belonging as they do to a different order, viz., truth of adaptation and of proportion both with the medium in which it exists and with the end towards which it tends. Finally the Modernists, losing all sense of control, go so far as to proclaim as true and legitimate everything that is explained by life.

We, Venerable Brethren, for whom there is but one and only truth, and who hold that the Sacred Books, *written under the inspiration of the Holy Ghost, have God for their author* (Conc. Vat., *De Revel.*, c. 2) declare that this is equivalent to attributing to God Himself the lie of utility or officious lie, and We say with St. Augustine: *In an authority so high, admit but one officious lie, and there will not remain a single passage of those apparently difficult to practise or to believe, which on the same most pernicious rule may not be explained as a lie uttered by the author wilfully and to serve a purpose.* (*Epist.* 28). And thus it will come about, the holy Doctor continues, that *everybody will believe and refuse to believe what he likes or dislikes*. But the Modernists pursue their way gaily. They grant also that certain arguments adduced in the Sacred Books, like those, for example, which are based on the prophecies, have no rational foundation to rest on. But they will defend even these as artifices of preaching, which are justified by life. Do they stop here? No, indeed, for they are ready to admit, nay, to proclaim that Christ Himself manifestly erred in determining the time when the coming of the Kingdom of God was to take place, and they tell us that we must not be surprised at this since even Christ was subject to the laws of life! After this what is to become of the dogmas of the Church? The dogmas brim over with flagrant contradictions, but what matter that since, apart from the fact that vital logic accepts them, they are not repugnant to symbolical truth. Are we not dealing with the infinite, and has not the infinite an infinite variety of aspects? In short, to maintain and defend these theories they do not hesitate to declare that the noblest homage that can be paid to the Infinite is to make it the object of contradictory propositions! But when they justify even contradiction, what is it that they will refuse to justify?

Subjective Arguments

37. But it is not solely by objective arguments that the non-believer may be disposed to faith. There are also *subjective* ones at the disposal of the Modernists, and for those they return to their doctrine of *immanence*. They endeavour, in fact, to persuade their non-believer that down in the very deeps of his nature and his life lie the need and the desire for religion, and this not a religion of any kind, but the specific religion known as Catholicism, which, they say, is absolutely *postulated* by the perfect development of life. And here We cannot but deplore once more, and grievously, that there are Catholics who, while rejecting *immanence* as a doctrine, employ it as a method of apologetics, and who do this so imprudently that they seem to admit that there is in human nature a true and rigorous necessity with regard to the supernatural order—and not merely a capacity and a suitability for the supernatural, order—and not merely a capacity and a suitability for the supernatural, such as has at all times been emphasized by Catholic apologists. Truth to tell it is only the moderate Modernists who make this appeal to an exigency for the Catholic religion. As for the others, who might be called *intergralists*, they would show to the non-believer, hidden

away in the very depths of his being, the very germ which Christ Himself bore in His conscience, and which He bequeathed to the world. Such, Venerable Brethren, is a summary description of the apologetic method of the Modernists, in perfect harmony, as you may see, with their doctrines—methods and doctrines brimming over with errors, made not for edification but for destruction, not for the formation of Catholics but for the plunging of Catholics into heresy; methods and doctrines that would be fatal to any religion.

The Modernist as Reformer

38. It remains for Us now to say a few words about the Modernist as reformer. From all that has preceded, some idea may be gained of the reforming mania which possesses them: in all Catholicism there is absolutely nothing on which it does not fasten. Reform of philosophy, especially in the seminaries: the scholastic philosophy is to be relegated to the history of philosophy among obsolete systems, and the young men are to be taught modern philosophy which alone is true and suited to the times in which we live. Reform of theology; rational theology is to have modern philosophy for its foundation, and positive theology is to be founded on the history of dogma. As for history, it must be for the future written and taught only according to their modern methods and principles. Dogmas and their evolution are to be harmonised with science and history. In the Catechism no dogmas are to be inserted except those that have been duly reformed and are within the capacity of the people. Regarding worship, the number of external devotions is to be reduced, or at least steps must be taken to prevent their further increase, though, indeed, some of the admirers of symbolism are disposed to be more indulgent on this head. Ecclesiastical government requires to be reformed in all its branches, but especially in its disciplinary and dogmatic parts. Its spirit with the public conscience, which

is not wholly for democracy; a share in ecclesiastical government should therefore be given to the lower ranks of the clergy, and even to the laity, and authority should be decentralised. The Roman Congregations, and especially the index and the Holy Office, are to be reformed. The ecclesiastical authority must change its line of conduct in the social and political world; while keeping outside political and social organization, it must adapt itself to those which exist in order to penetrate them with its spirit. With regard to morals, they adopt the principle of the Americanists, that the active virtues are more important than the passive, both in the estimation in which they must be held and in the exercise of them. The clergy are asked to return to their ancient lowliness and poverty, and in their ideas and action to be guided by the principles of Modernism; and there are some who, echoing the teaching of their Protestant masters, would like the suppression of ecclesiastical celibacy. What is there left in the Church which is not to be reformed according to their principles?

Modernism and All the Heresies

39. It may be, Venerable Brethren, that some may think We have dwelt too long on this exposition of the doctrines of the Modernists. But it was necessary, both in order to refute their customary charge that We do not understand their ideas, and to show that their system does not consist in scattered and unconnected theories but in a perfectly organised body, all the parts of which are solidly joined so that it is not possible to admit one without admitting all. For this reason, too, We have had to give this exposition a somewhat didactic form and not to shrink from employing certain uncouth terms in use among the Modernists. And now, can anybody who takes a survey of the whole system be surprised that We should define it as the synthesis of all heresies? Were one to attempt the task of collecting together all the errors that have been broached against the faith and to concentrate the sap

and substance of them all into one, he could not better succeed than the Modernists have done. Nay, they have done more than this, for, as we have already intimated, their system means the destruction not of the Catholic religion alone but of all religion. With good reason do the rationalists applaud them, for the most sincere and the frankest among the rationalists warmly welcome the modernists as their most valuable allies.

For let us return for a moment, Venerable Brethren, to that most disastrous doctrine of *agnosticism*. By it every avenue that leads the intellect to God is barred, but the Modernists would seek to open others available for sentiment and action. Vain efforts! For, after all, what is sentiment but the reaction of the soul on the action of the intelligence or the senses. Take away the intelligence, and man, already inclined to follow the senses, becomes their slave. Vain, too, from another point of view, for all these fantasias on the religious sentiment will never be able to destroy common sense, and common sense tells us that emotion and everything that leads the heart captive proves a hindrance instead of a help to the discovery of truth. We speak, of course, of truth in itself—as for that other purely *subjective* truth, the fruit of sentiment and action, if it serves its purpose for the jugglery of words, it is of no use to the man who wants to know above all things whether outside himself there is a God into whose hands he is one day to fall. True, the Modernists do call in *experience* to eke out their system, but what does this *experience* add to sentiment? Absolutely nothing beyond a certain intensity and a proportionate deepening of the conviction of the reality of the object. But these two will never make sentiment into anything but sentiment, nor deprive it of its characteristic which is to cause deception when the intelligence is not there to guide it; on the contrary, they but confirm and aggravate this characteristic, for the more intense sentiment is the more it is sentimental. In matters of religious sentiment and religious experience, you know, Venerable Brethren, how necessary is prudence and how necessary, too, the science which directs prudence. You know it from your own dealings with sounds, and especially with souls in whom sentiment predominates; you know it also from your reading of ascetical books—books for which the Modernists have but little esteem, but which testify to a science and a solidity very different from theirs, and to a refinement and subtlety of observation of which the Modernists give no evidence. Is it not really folly, or at least sovereign imprudence, to trust oneself without control to Modernist experiences? Let us for a moment put the question: if experiences have so much value in their eyes, why do they not attach equal weight to the experience that thousands upon thousands of Catholics have that the Modernists are on the wrong road? It is, perchance, that all experiences except those felt by the Modernists are false and deceptive? The vast majority of mankind holds and always will hold firmly that sentiment and experience alone, when not enlightened and guided by reason, do not lead to the knowledge of God. What remains, then, but the annihilation of all religion,—atheism? Certainly it is not the doctrine of *symbolism*—will save us from this. For if all the intellectual elements, as they call them, of religion are pure symbols, will not the very name of God or of divine personality be also a symbol, and if this be admitted will not the personality of God become a matter of doubt and the way opened to Pantheism? And to Pantheism that other doctrine of the *divine immanence* leads directly. For does it, We ask, leave God distinct from man or not? If yes, in what does it differ from Catholic doctrine, and why reject external revelation? If no, we are at once in Pantheism. Now the doctrine of immanence in the Modernist acceptation holds and professes that every phenomenon of conscience proceeds from man as man. The rigorous conclusion from this is the identity of man with God, which means Pantheism. The same conclusion follows from the distinction Modernists make between science and faith. The object of science they say is the reality of the knowable; the object of faith, on the contrary, is the reality of the unknowable. Now what makes the unknowable unknowable is its disproportion with the intelligible—a disproportion which nothing whatever, even in the doctrine of the Modernist, can suppress. Hence the unknowable remains and will eternally remain unknowable to the believer as well as to the man of science. Therefore if any religion at all is possible it can only be the religion of an unknowable reality. And why this religion might not be that universal soul of the universe, of which a rationalist speaks, is something We do see. Certainly this suffices to show superabundantly by how many roads Modernism leads to the annihilation of all religion. The first step in this direction was taken by Protestantism; the second is made by Modernism; the next will plunge headlong into atheism.

THE CAUSE OF MODERNISM

40. To penetrate still deeper into Modernism and to find a suitable remedy for such a deep sore, it behoves Us, Venerable Brethren, to investigate the causes which have engendered it and which foster its growth. That the proximate and immediate cause consists in a perversion of the mind cannot be open to doubt. The remote causes seem to us to be reduced to two: curiosity and pride. Curiosity by itself, if not prudently regulated, suffices to explain all errors. Such is the opinion of Our Predecessor, Gregory XVI., who wrote: *A lamentable spectacle is that presented by the aberrations of human reason when it yields to the spirit of novelty, when against the warning of the Apostle it seeks to know beyond what it is meant to know, and when relying too much on itself it thinks it can find the fruit outside the Church wherein truth is found without the slightest shadow of error* (Ep. Encycl. *Singulari nos*, 7 Kal. Jul. 1834).

But it is pride which exercises an incomparably greater sway over the soul to blind it and plunge it into error, and pride sits in

Modernism as in its own house, finding sustenance everywhere in its doctrines and an occasion to flaunt itself in all its aspects. It is pride which fills Modernists with that confidence in themselves and leads them to hold themselves up as the rule for all, pride which puffs them up with that vainglory which allows them to regard themselves as the sole possessors of knowledge, and makes them say, inflated with presumption, *We are not as the rest of men*, and which, to make them really not as other men, leads them to embrace all kinds of the most absurd novelties; it is pride which rouses in them the spirit of disobedience and causes them to demand a compromise between authority and liberty; it is pride that makes of them the reformers of others, while they forget to reform themselves, and which begets their absolute want of respect for authority, not excepting the supreme authority. No, truly, there is no road which leads so directly and so quickly to Modernism as pride. When a Catholic laymen or a priest forgets that precept of the Christian life which obliges us to renounce ourselves if we would follow Jesus Christ and neglects to tear pride from his heart, ah! but he is a fully ripe subject for the errors of Modernism. Hence, Venerable Brethren, it will be your first duty to thwart such proud men, to employ them only in the lowest and obscurest offices; the higher they try to rise, the lower let them be placed, so that their lowly position may deprive them of the power of causing damage. Sound your young clerics, too, most carefully, by yourselves and by the directors of your seminaries, and when you find the spirit of pride among any of them reject them without compunction from the priesthood. Would to God that this had always been done with the proper vigilance and constancy.

41. If we pass from the moral to the intellectual causes of Modernism, the first which presents itself, and the chief one, is ignorance. Yes, these very Modernists who pose as Doctors of the Church, who puff out their cheeks when they speak of modern philosophy, and show such contempt for scholasticism, have embraced the one

with all its false glamour because their ignorance of the other has left them without the means of being able to recognise confusion of thought, and to refute sophistry. Their whole system, with all its errors, has been born of the alliance between faith and false philosophy.

Methods of Propagandism

42. If only they had displayed less zeal and energy in propagating it! But such is their activity and such their unwearying capacity for work on behalf of their cause, that one cannot but be pained to see them waste such labour in endeavouring to ruin the Church when they might have been of such service to her had their efforts been better employed. Their articles to delude men's minds are of two kinds, the first to remove obstacles from their path, the second to devise and apply actively and patiently every instrument that can serve their purpose. They recognise that the three chief difficulties for them are scholastic philosophy, the authority of the fathers and tradition, and the magisterium of the Church, and on these they wage unrelenting war. For scholastic philosophy and theology they have only ridicule and contempt. Whether it is ignorance or fear, or both, that inspires this conduct in them, certain it is that the passion for novelty is always united in them with hatred of scholasticism, and there is no surer sign that a man is on the way to Modernism than when he begins to show his dislike for this system. Modernists and their admirers should remember the proposition condemned by Pius IX: *The method and principles which have served the doctors of scholasticism when treating of theology no longer correspond with the exigencies of our time or the progress of science* (Syll. Prop. 13). They exercise all their ingenuity in diminishing the force and falsifying the character of tradition, so as to rob it of all its weight. But for Catholics the second Council of Nicea will always have the force of law, where it condemns those *who dare,*

after the impious fashion of heretics, to deride the ecclesiastical traditions, to invent novelties of some kind . . . or endeavour by malice or craft to overthrow any one of the legitimate traditions of the Catholic Church; and Catholics will hold for law, also, the profession of the fourth Council of Constantinople: *We therefore profess to conserve and guard the rules bequeathed to the Holy Catholic and Apostolic Church by the Holy and most illustrious Apostles, by the orthodox Councils, both general and local, and by every one of those divine interpreters the Fathers and Doctors of the Church.* Wherefore the Roman Pontiffs, Pius IV. and Pius IX., ordered the insertion in the profession of faith of the following declaration: *I most firmly admit and embrace the apostolic and ecclesiastical traditions and other observances and constitutions of the Church.* The Modernists pass the same judgment on the most holy Fathers of the Church as they pass on tradition; decreeing, with amazing effrontery that, while personally most worthy of all veneration, they were entirely ignorant of history and criticism, for which they are only excusable on account of the time in which they lived. Finally, the Modernists try in every way to diminish and weaken the authority of the ecclesiastical magisterium itself by sacrilegiously falsifying its origin, character, and rights, and by freely repeating the calumnies of its adversaries. To all the band of Modernists may be applied those words which Our Predecessor wrote with such pain: *To bring contempt and odium on the mystic Spouse of Christ, who is the true light, the children of darkness have been wont to cast in her face before the world a stupid calumny, and perverting the meaning and force of things and words, to depict her as the friend of darkness and ignorance, and the enemy of light, science, and progress* (Motu-proprio, *Ut mysticum*, 14 March, 1891). This being so, Venerable Brethren, no wonder the Modernists vent all their gall and hatred on Catholics who sturdily fight the battles of the Church. But of all the insults they heap on them those of ignorance and obstinacy are the favourites. When an adversary rises up against them with an erudition and force that render him redoubtable, they try to make a conspiracy of silence around him to nullify the effects of his attack, while in flagrant contrast with this policy towards Catholics, they load with constant praise the writers who range themselves on their side, hailing their works, excluding novelty in every page, with choruses of applause; for them the scholarship of a writer is in direct proportion to the recklessness of his attacks on antiquity, and of his efforts to undermine tradition and the ecclesiastical magisterium; when one of their number falls under the condemnations of the Church the rest of them, to the horror of good Catholics, gather round him, heap public praise upon him, venerate him almost as a martyr to truth. The young, excited and confused by all this glamour of praise and abuse, some of them afraid of being branded as ignorant, others ambitious to be considered learned, and both classes goaded internally by curiosity and pride, often surrender and give themselves up to Modernism.

43. And here we have already some of the artifices employed by Modernists to exploit their wares. What efforts they make to win new recruits! They seize upon chairs in the seminaries and universities, and gradually make of them chairs of pestilence. From these sacred chairs they scatter, though not always openly, the seeds of their doctrines; they proclaim their teachings without disguise in congresses; they introduce them and make them the vogue in social institutions. Under their own names and under pseudonyms they publish numbers of books, newspapers, reviews, and sometimes one and the same writer adopts a variety of pseudonyms to trap the incautious reader into believing in a whole multitude of Modernist writers—in short they leave nothing untried, in action, discourses, writings, as though there were a frenzy of propaganda upon them. And the results of all this? We have to lament at the sight of many young men once full of promise and capable of rendering great services to the Church, now gone astray. And there is another sight that saddens Us too:

that of so many other Catholics, who, while they certainly do not go so far as the former, have yet grown into the habit, as though they had been breathing a poisoned atmosphere, of thinking and speaking and writing with a liberty that ill becomes Catholics. They are to be found among the laity, and in the ranks of the clergy, and they are not wanting even in the last place where one might expect to meet them, in religious institutes. If they treat of biblical questions, it is upon Modernist principles; if they write history, it is to search out with curiosity and to publish openly, on the pretext of telling the whole truth and with a species of ill-concealed satisfaction, everything that looks to them like a stain in the history of the Church. Under the sway of certain a priori rules they destroy as far as they can the pious traditions of the people, and bring ridicule on certain relics highly venerable from their antiquity. They are possessed by the empty desire of being talked about, and they know they would never succeed in this were they to say only what has been always said. It may be that they have persuaded themselves that in all this they are really serving God and the Church—in reality they only offend both, less perhaps by their works themselves than by the spirit in which they write and by the encouragement they are giving to the extravagances of the Modernists.

REMEDIES

44. Against this host of grave errors, and its secret and open advance, Our Predecessor Leo XIII., of happy memory, worked strenuously especially as regards the Bible, both in his words and his acts. But, as we have seen, the Modernists are not easily deterred by such weapons—with an affectation of submission and respect, they proceeded to twist the words of the Pontiff to their own sense, and his acts they described as directed against others than themselves. And the evil has gone on increasing from day to day. We therefore, Venerable Brethren, have determined to adopt at

once the most efficacious measures in Our power, and We beg and conjure you to see to it that in this most grave matter nobody will ever be able to say that you have been in the slightest degree wanting in vigilance, zeal or firmness. And what We ask of you and expect of you, We ask and expect also of all other pastors of souls, of all educators and professors of clerics, and in a very special way of the superiors of religious institutions.

I.—*The Study of Scholastic Philosophy*

45. In the first place, with regard to studies, We will and ordain that scholastic philosophy be made the basis of the sacred sciences. It goes without saying that *if anything is met with among the scholastic doctors which may be regarded as an excess of subtlety, or which is altogether destitute of probability, We have no desire whatever to propose it for the imitation of present generations* (Leo XIII. Enc. *Aeterni Patris*). And let it be clearly understood above all things that the scholastic philosophy We prescribe is that which the Angelic Doctor has bequeathed to us, and We, therefore, declare that all the ordinances of Our Predecessor on this subject continue fully in force, and, as far as may be necessary, We do decree anew, and confirm, and ordain that they be by all strictly observed. In seminaries where they may have been neglected let the Bishops impose them and require their observance, and let this apply also to the Superiors of religious institutions. Further let Professors remember that they cannot set St. Thomas aside, especially in metaphysical questions, without grave detriment.
46. On this philosophical foundation the theological edifice is to be solidly raised. Promote the study of theology, Venerable Brethren, by all means in your power, so that your clerics on leaving the seminaries may admire and love it, and always find their delight in it. *For in the vast and varied abundance of studies opening before the mind desirous of truth, everybody knows how the old maxim describes theology as so far in front of all others that every*

science and art should serve it and be to it as handmaidens (Leo XIII., Lett. ap. *In Magna*, Dec. 10, 1889). We will add that We deem worthy of praise those who with full respect for tradition, the Holy Fathers, and the ecclesiastical magisterium, undertake, with well-balanced judgment and guided by Catholic principles (which is not always the case), seek to illustrate positive theology by throwing the light of true history upon it. Certainly more attention must be paid to positive theology than in the past, but this must be done without detriment to scholastic theology, and those are to be disapproved as of Modernist tendencies who exalt positive theology in such a way as to seem to despise the scholastic.

47. With regard to profane studies suffice it to recall here what Our Predecessor has admirably said: *Apply yourselves energetically to the study of natural sciences: the brilliant discoveries and the bold and useful applications of them made in our times which have won such applause by our contemporaries will be an object of perpetual praise for those that come after us* (Leo XIII. *Alloc.*, March 7, 1880). But this do without interfering with sacred studies, as Our Predecessor in these most grave words prescribed: *If you carefully search for the cause of those errors you will find that it lies in the fact that in these days when the natural sciences absorb so much study, the more severe and lofty studies have been proportionately neglected—some of them have almost passed into oblivion, some of them are pursued in a half-hearted or superficial way, and, sad to say, now that they are fallen from their old estate, they have been dis figured by perverse doctrines and monstrous errors* (loco cit.). We ordain, therefore, that the study of natural science in the seminaries be carried on under this law.

II.—*Practical Application*

48. All these prescriptions and those of Our Predecessor are to be borne in mind whenever there is question of choosing directors

and professors for seminaries and Catholic Universities. Anybody who in any way is found to be imbued with Modernism is to be excluded without compunction from these offices, and those who already occupy them are to be withdrawn. The same policy is to be adopted towards those who favour Modernism either by extolling the Modernists or excusing their culpable conduct, by criticising scholasticism, the Holy Father, or by refusing obedience to ecclesiastical authority in any of its depositaries; and towards those who show a love of novelty in history, archaeology, biblical exegesis, and finally towards those who neglect the sacred sciences or appear to prefer to them the profane. In all this question of studies, Venerable Brethren, you cannot be too watchful or too constant, but most of all in the choice of professors, for as a rule the students are modelled after the pattern of their masters. Strong in the consciousness of your duty, act always prudently but vigorously.

49. Equal diligence and severity are to be used in examining and selecting candidates for Holy Orders. Far, far from the clergy be the love of novelty! God hates the proud and the obstinate. For the future the doctorate of theology and canon law must never be conferred on anybody who has not made the regular course of scholastic philosophy; if conferred it shall be held as null and void. The rules laid down in 1896 by the Sacred Congregation of Bishops and Regulars for the clerics, both secular and regular, of Italy concerning the frequenting of the Universities, We now decree to be extended to all nations. Clerics and priests inscribed in a Catholic Institute or University must not in the future follow in civil Universities those courses for which there are chairs in the Catholic Institutes to which they belong. If this has been permitted anywhere in the past, We ordain that it be not allowed for the future. Let the Bishops who form the Governing Board of such Catholic Institutes or Universities watch with all care that these Our commands be constantly observed.

III.—*Episcopal Vigilance Over Publications*

50. It is also the duty of the bishops to prevent writings infected with Modernism or favourable to it from being read when they have been published, and to hinder their publication when they have not. No book or paper or periodical of this kind must ever be permitted to seminarists or university students. The injury to them would be equal to that caused by immoral reading-nay, it would be greater for such writings poison Christian life at its very fount. The same decision is to be taken concerning the writings of some Catholics, who, though not badly disposed themselves but ill-instructed in theological studies and imbued with modern philosophy, strive to make this harmonize with the faith, and, as they say, to turn it to the account of the faith. The name and reputation of these authors cause them to be read without suspicion, and they are, therefore, all the more dangerous in preparing the way for Modernism.

51. To give you some more general directions, Venerable Brethren, in a matter of such moment, We bid you do everything in your power to drive out of your dioceses, even by solemn interdict, any pernicious books that may be in circulation there. The Holy See neglects no means to put down writings of this kind, but the number of them has now grown to such an extent that it is impossible to censure them all. Hence it happens that the medicine sometimes arrives too late, for the disease has taken root during the delay. We will, therefore, that the Bishops, putting aside all fear and the prudence of the flesh, despising the outcries of the wicked, gently by all means but constantly, do each his own share of this work, remembering the injunctions of Leo XIII. in the Apostolic Constitution *Officiorum: Let the Ordinaries, acting in this also as Delegates of the Apostolic See, exert themselves to prescribe and to put out of reach of the faithful injurious books or other writings printed or circulated in their dioceses.* In this passage the Bishops, it is true, receive a right, but they have also a duty

imposed on them. Let no Bishop think that he fulfils this duty by denouncing to us one or two books, while a great many others of the same kind are being published and circulated. Nor are you to be deterred by the fact that a book has obtained the *Imprimatur* elsewhere, both because this may be merely simulated, and because it may have been granted through carelessness or easiness or excessive confidence in the author as may sometimes happen in religious Orders. Besides, just as the same food does not agree equally with everybody, it may happen that a book harmless in one may, on account of the different circumstances, be hurtful in another. Should a Bishop, therefore, after having taken the advice of prudent persons, deem it right to condemn any of such books in his diocese, We not only give him ample faculty to do so but We impose it upon him as a duty to do so. Of course, it is Our wish that in such action proper regard be used, and sometimes it will suffice to restrict the prohibition to the clergy; but even in such cases it will be obligatory on Catholic booksellers not to put on sale books condemned by the Bishop. And while We are on this subject of booksellers, We wish the Bishops to see to it that they do not, through desire for gain, put on sale unsound books. It is certain that in the catalogues of some of them the books of the Modernists are not unfrequently announced with no small praise. If they refuse obedience let the Bishops have no hesitation in depriving them of the title of Catholic booksellers; so too, and with more reason, if they have the title of Episcopal booksellers, and if they have that of Pontifical, let them be denounced to the Apostolic See. Finally, We remind all of the XXVI. article of the abovementioned Constitution *Officiorum: All those who have obtained an apostolic faculty to read and keep forbidden books, are not thereby authorised to read books and periodicals forbidden by the local Ordinaries, unless the apostolic faculty expressly concedes permission to read and keep books condemned by anybody.*

IV.—*Censorship*

52. But it is not enough to hinder the reading and the sale of bad books—it is also necessary to prevent them from being printed. Hence let the Bishops use the utmost severity in granting permission to print. Under the rules of the Constitution *Officiorum*, many publications require the authorisation of the Ordinary, and in some dioceses it has been made the custom to have a suitable number of official censors for the examination of writings. We have the highest praise for this institution, and We not only exhort, but We order that it be extended to all dioceses. In all episcopal Curias, therefore, let censors be appointed for the revision of works intended for publication, and let the censors be chosen from both ranks of the clergy—secular and regular—men of age, knowledge and prudence who will know how to follow the golden mean in their judgments. It shall be their office to examine everything which requires permission for publication according to Articles XLI. and XLII. of the above-mentioned Constitution. The Censor shall give his verdict in writing. If it be favourable, the Bishop will give the permission for publication by the word *Imprimatur*, which must always be preceded by the *Nihil obstat* and the name of the Censor. In the Curia of Rome official censors shall be appointed just as elsewhere, and the appointment of them shall appertain to the Master of the Sacred Palaces, after they have been proposed to the Cardinal Vicar and accepted by the Sovereign Pontiff. It will also be the office of the Master of the Sacred Palaces to select the censor for each writing. Permission for publication will be granted by him as well as by the Cardinal Vicar or his Vicegerent, and this permission, as above prescribed, must always be preceded by the *Nihil obstat* and the name of the Censor. Only on very rare and exceptional occasions, and on the prudent decision of the bishop, shall it be possible to omit mention of the Censor. The name of the Censor shall never be made known to the authors

until he shall have given a favourable decision, so that he may not have to suffer annoyance either while he is engaged in the examination of a writing or in case he should deny his approval. Censors shall never be chosen from the religious orders until the opinion of the Provincial, or in Rome of the General, has been privately obtained, and the Provincial or the General must give a conscientious account of the character, knowledge and orthodoxy of the candidate. We admonish religious superiors of their solemn duty never to allow anything to be published by any of their subjects without permission from themselves and from the Ordinary. Finally We affirm and declare that the title of Censor has no value and can never be adduced to give credit to the private opinions of the person who holds it.

Priests as Editors

53. Having said this much in general, We now ordain in particular a more careful observance of Article XLII. of the above-mentioned Constitution *Officiorum*. It is *forbidden to secular priests, without the previous consent of the Ordinary, to undertake the direction of papers or periodicals.* This permission shall be withdrawn from any priest who makes a wrong use of it after having been admonished. With regard to priests who are *correspondents* or *collaborators* of periodicals, as it happens not unfrequently that they write matter infected with Modernism for their papers or periodicals, let the Bishops see to it that this is not permitted to happen, and, should they fail in this duty, let the Bishops make due provision with authority delegated by the Supreme Pontiff. Let there be, as far as this is possible, a special Censor for newspapers and periodicals written by Catholics. It shall be his office to read in due time each number after it has been published, and if he find anything dangerous in it let him order that it be corrected. The Bishop shall have the same right even when the Censor has seen nothing objectionable in a publication.

V.—*Congresses*

54. We have already mentioned congresses and public gatherings as among the means used by the Modernists to propagate and defend their opinions. In the future Bishops shall not permit Congresses of priests except on very rare occasions. When they do permit them it shall only be on condition that matters appertaining to the Bishops or the Apostolic See be not treated in them, and that no motions or postulates be allowed that would imply a usurpation of sacred authority, and that no mention be made in them of Modernism, presbyterianism, or laicism. At Congresses of this kind, which can only be held after permission in writing has been obtained in due time and for each case, it shall not be lawful for priests of other dioceses to take part without the written permission of their Ordinary. Further no priest must lose sight of the solemn recommendation of Leo XIII.: *Let priests hold as sacred the authority of their pastors, let them take it for certain that the sacerdotal ministry, if not exercised under the guidance of the Bishops, can never be either holy, or very fruitful or respectable* (Lett. Encyc. *Nobilissima Gallorum*, 10 Feb., 1884).

VI.—*Diocesan Watch Committees*

55. But of what avail, Venerable Brethren, will be all Our commands and prescriptions if they be not dutifully and firmly carried out? And, in order that this may be done, it has seemed expedient to Us to extend to all dioceses the regulations laid down with great wisdom many years ago by the Bishops of Umbria for theirs.

"In order," they say, "to extirpate the errors already propagated and to prevent their further diffusion, and to remove those teachers of impiety through whom the pernicious effects of such dif fusion are being perpetuated, this sacred Assembly, following the example of St. Charles Borromeo, has decided to establish in each of the dioceses a Council consisting of approved members of both branches of the clergy, which shall be charged the task of noting the existence of errors and the devices by which new ones are introduced and propagated, and to inform the Bishop of the whole so that he may take counsel with them as to the best means for nipping the evil in the bud and preventing it spreading for the ruin of souls or, worse still, gaining strength and growth" (Acts of the Congress of the Bishops of Umbria, Nov. 1849, tit 2, art. 6). We decree, therefore, that in every diocese a council of this kind, which We are pleased to name "the Council of Vigilance," be instituted without delay. The priests called to form part in it shall be chosen somewhat after the manner above prescribed for the Censors, and they shall meet every two months on an appointed day under the presidency of the Bishop. They shall be bound to secrecy as to their deliberations and decisions, and their function shall be as follows: They shall watch most carefully for every trace and sign of Modernism both in publications and in teaching, and, to preserve from it the clergy and the young, they shall take all prudent, prompt and efficacious measures. Let them combat novelties of words remembering the admonitions of Leo XIII. (Instruct. S.C. NN. EE. EE., 27 Jan., 1902): *It is impossible to approve in Catholic publications of a style inspired by unsound novelty which seems to deride the piety of the faithful and dwells on the introduction of a new order of Christian life, on new directions of the Church, on new aspirations of the modern soul, on a new vocation of the clergy, on a new Christian civilisation.* Language of this kind is not to be tolerated either in books or from chairs of learning. The Councils must not neglect the books treating of the pious traditions of different places or of sacred relics. Let them not permit such questions to be discussed in periodicals destined to stimulate piety, neither with expressions savouring of mockery or contempt, nor by dogmatic pronouncements, especially when, as is often the case, what is stated as a certainty either does not pass the limits of probability or is merely based on prejudiced opinion. Concerning sacred relics, let this be the rule: When

Bishops, who alone are judges in such matters, know for certain the a relic is not genuine, let them remove it at once from the veneration of the faithful; if the authentications of a relic happen to have been lost through civil disturbances, or in any other way, let it not be exposed for public veneration until the Bishop has verified it. The argument of prescription or well-founded presumption is to have weight only when devotion to a relic is commendable by reason of its antiquity, according to the sense of the Decree issued in 1896 by the Congregation of Indulgences and Sacred Relics: *Ancient relics are to retain the veneration they have always enjoyed except when in individual instances there are clear arguments that they are false or suppositions*. In passing judgment on pious traditions be it always borne in mind that in this matter the Church uses the greatest prudence, and that she does not allow traditions of this kind to be narrated in books except with the utmost caution and with the insertion of the declaration imposed by Urban VIII, and even then she does not guarantee the truth of the fact narrated; she simply does but forbid belief in things for which human arguments are not wanting. On this matter the Sacred Congregation of Rites, thirty years ago, decreed as follows: *These apparitions and revelations have neither been approved nor condemned by the Holy See, which has simply allowed that they be believed on purely human faith, on the tradition which they relate, corroborated by testimonies and documents worthy of credence* (Decree, May 2, 1877). Anybody who follows this rule has no cause for fear. For the devotion based on any apparition, in as far as it regards the fact itself, that is to say in as far as it is *relative*, always implies the hypothesis of the truth of the fact; while in as far as it is absolute, it must always be based on the truth, seeing that its object is the persons of the saints who are honoured. The same is true of relics. Finally, We entrust to the Councils of Vigilance the duty of overlooking assiduously and diligently social institutions as well as writings on social questions so that they may harbour no trace of Modernism, but obey the prescriptions of the Roman Pontiffs.

VII.—*Triennial Returns*

56. Lest what We have laid down thus far should fall into oblivion, We will and ordain that the Bishops of all dioceses, a year after the publication of these letters and every three years thenceforward, furnish the Holy See with a diligent and sworn report on all the prescriptions contained in them, and on the doctrines that find currency among the clergy, and especially in the seminaries and other Catholic institutions, and We impose the like obligation on the Generals of Religious Orders with regard to those under them.
57. This, Venerable Brethren, is what we have thought it our duty to write to you for the salvation of all who believe. The adversaries of the Church will doubtless abuse what we have said to refurbish the old calumny by which we are traduced as the enemy of science and of the progress of humanity. In order to oppose a new answer to such accusations, which the history of the Christian religion refutes by never failing arguments, it is Our intention to establish and develop by every means in our power a special Institute in which, through the co-operation of those Catholics who are most eminent for their learning, the progress of science and other realms of knowledge may be promoted under the guidance and teaching of Catholic truth. God grant that we may happily realise our design with the ready assistance of all those who bear a sincere love for the Church of Christ. But of this we will speak on another occasion.
58. Meanwhile, Venerable Brethren, fully confident in your zeal and work, we beseech for you with our whole heart and soul the abundance of heavenly light, so that in the midst of this great perturbation of men's minds from the insidious invasions of error from every side, you may see clearly what you ought to do

and may perform the task with all your strength and courage. May Jesus Christ, the author and finisher of our faith, be with you by His power; and may the Immaculate Virgin, the destroyer of all heresies, be with you by her prayers and aid. And We, as a pledge of Our affection and of divine assistance in adversity, grant most affectionately and with all Our heart to you, your clergy and people the Apostolic Benediction.

Given at St. Peter's, Rome, on the 8th day of September, 1907, the fifth year of our Pontificate.

/general/privacy_policy.asp
/ewtn/login.asp/ewtn/login.asp

Made in the USA
Lexington, KY
31 May 2013